Pro NuGet

Second Edition

Maarten Balliauw
Xavier Decoster

apress®

Pro NuGet

ISBN-13 (pbk): 978-1-4302-6001-1

ISBN-13 (electronic): 978-1-4302-6002-8

President and Publisher: Paul Manning
Lead Editor: Ewan Buckingham
Technical Reviewer: Jeff Handley, Luan Nguyen
Editorial Board: Steve Anglin, Mark Beckner, Ewan Buckingham, Gary Cornell, Louise Corrigan, Jonathan Gennick, Jonathan Hassell, Robert Hutchinson, Michelle Lowman, James Markham, Matthew Moodie, Jeff Olson, Jeffrey Pepper, Douglas Pundick, Ben Renow-Clarke, Dominic Shakeshaft, Gwenan Spearing, Matt Wade, Steve Weiss, Tom Welsh
Coordinating Editor: Mark Powers
Copy Editor: Sharon Wilkey
Compositor: SPi Global
Indexer: SPi Global
Artist: SPi Global
Cover Designer: Anna Ishchenko

Distributed to the book trade worldwide by Springer Science+Business Media New York, 233 Spring Street, 6th Floor, New York, NY 10013. Phone 1-800-SPRINGER, fax (201) 348-4505, e-mail orders-ny@springer-sbm.com, or visit www.springeronline.com. Apress Media, LLC is a California LLC and the sole member (owner) is Springer Science + Business Media Finance Inc (SSBM Finance Inc). SSBM Finance Inc is a Delaware corporation.

For information on translations, please e-mail rights@apress.com, or visit www.apress.com.

Apress and friends of ED books may be purchased in bulk for academic, corporate, or promotional use. eBook versions and licenses are also available for most titles. For more information, reference our Special Bulk Sales–eBook Licensing web page at www.apress.com/bulk-sales.

Any source code or other supplementary material referenced by the author in this text is available to readers at www.apress.com/9781430260011 as well as www.github.com/myget/pronuget. For detailed information about how to locate your book's source code, go to www.apress.com/source-code/.

To my wife, who is both the love of my life and best friend. Thanks for keeping up with me spending too much time writing and away from home.

—Maarten Balliauw

To my wife, Gaëlle, and our two boys, Jack and Christopher—my inspiration for being the best that I can be.

—Xavier Decoster

Contents at a Glance

Contents

About the Authors

Maarten Balliauw is a technical evangelist at JetBrains. His interests are all web: ASP.NET MVC, PHP, and Windows Azure. He's a Microsoft Most Valuable Professional (MVP) for Windows Azure and an ASPInsider. He has published many articles in both PHP and .NET literature, such as *MSDN Magazine* and *PHP Architect*. Maarten is a frequent speaker at national and international events such as MIX (Las Vegas), TechDays, and DPC. His blog can be found at http://blog.maartenballiauw.be.
E-mail: maarten@maartenballiauw.be
Twitter: http://twitter.com/maartenballiauw

Xavier Decoster is a consultant living in Belgium and cofounder of MyGet, a NuGet-as-a-Service platform on Windows Azure. He's a Most Valuable Professional (MVP) for Visual Studio ALM and has published various articles on MSDN, on CodeProject, and on various other web sites.

He hates development friction, and in order to make other developers aware of how frictionless development can and should be, he tries to share his experiences and insights by contributing to the community as a speaker, author, blogger, and through various open source projects. He blogs at www.xavierdecoster.com, and you can follow him on Twitter (@xavierdecoster).

About the Technical Reviewers

Jeff Handley Jeff Handley is a development lead at Microsoft, working on NuGet. He has also worked on ASP.NET Web Pages, Razor, Windows Azure, and WCF RIA Services. Before joining Microsoft in 2008, Jeff spent over 10 years in the field developing and architecting web applications.

Luan Nguyen Luan Nguyen is senior software development engineer at Microsoft. He has been working on NuGet since its inception in 2010. Since then, he has helped ship all releases of NuGet from version 1.0 to 2.7, implementing numerous features. Luan is also the creator of the popular NuGet Package Explorer (http://npe.codeplex.com), an essential tool for all NuGet package authors and users. He loves interacting with the NuGet community through Twitter, CodePlex, and Stack Overflow, with the common username dotnetjunky.

Foreword

Microsoft can never meet the code needs of every developer. The world is simply too rich and diversified. It wouldn't make sense for Microsoft to invest in libraries to meet every need. Instead, Microsoft focuses on foundational libraries, while its community of developers have taken it upon themselves to write thousands upon thousands of useful libraries and utilities.

Microsoft started the NuGet project to make it easier for developers to discover and distribute one another's libraries. A healthy ecosystem of developers who share code and build libraries is good for Microsoft and good for developers.

But then, an interesting thing happened. Microsoft donated the project and its employees' time to the Outercurve Foundation, a foundation meant to foster open source collaboration with corporations. NuGet is an Apache v2 licensed open source project that accepts contributions from outside Microsoft.

In doing so, Microsoft truly made NuGet a project that belongs to the community. At the same time, Microsoft plans to ship it within its products. It's now available to a huge number of developers as a core component of Visual Studio 2012. NuGet represents a new way for Microsoft to work with the community while delivering a great product.

Although NuGet was designed to be very easy to start working with, NuGet supports more than one workflow, such as checking in packages to source control, or restoring them during compilation. Recent versions of NuGet add support for the Portable Class Library project, the new way forward for writing cross-platform libraries with .NET.

This is why I'm excited about the second edition of *Pro Nuget*. NuGet is simple to get started, but simple tools often have many powerful uses. From very early on, Maarten and Xavier have been involved with NuGet, contributing ideas and building products based on NuGet such as http://MyGet.org, a site for hosting custom (and optionally private) NuGet repositories.

What I hope you get from this book is a sense of all the ways that NuGet can help streamline your day-to-day development and even make it more fun to write code. And for those of you who want to take it further, why not come over and contribute?

—Phil Haack
Project Lead, NuGet

When NuGet was introduced as part of the ASP.NET MVC 3 release in January of 2011, I was intrigued. To be honest, though, the implications of Microsoft shipping a package manager for .NET (let alone an open source one) didn't sink in at first. It wasn't until a few months after publishing my first set of packages (for the WCF RIA Services Toolkit) that it really hit me. Then in August of 2011, I published a blog post entitled "I Get NuGet. You Get NuGet?" that opened with the admission, "Hello, my name is Jeff, and I am addicted to NuGet." Less than a month later, somewhat by chance, I got the opportunity to become the development lead for NuGet and I could barely contain my excitement!

At that time NuGet was still a nascent project. There were fewer than 3,000 unique packages, and there had been 1.7 million package downloads. But more noteworthy than that, NuGet was really being used in only ASP.NET projects, and it wasn't yet shipping as part of Visual Studio. Two years later, NuGet is now included in every edition (free and paid) of Visual Studio—but we had to work hard to make that happen. NuGet supports virtually every project type, including .NET, Silverlight, Windows Store, Windows Phone, Portable Class Library, LightSwitch, F#, C++, WiX, and many more. NuGet also supports a wide range of development environment scenarios, aiming to work for all Visual Studio users. There are over 15,000 unique packages and 100 million package downloads, and these numbers are growing steadily. NuGet is no longer just the package manager for .NET; it's the package manager for the Microsoft development platform.

Whether you're an independent developer working on an open source project, a consultant for small businesses, or an enterprise developer, NuGet is becoming an essential part of your development workflow. Long before this became a reality, though, Maarten Balliauw and Xavier Decoster knew it was inevitable. They became two of the earliest NuGet enthusiasts and started amassing a deep and broad understanding of how to employ NuGet for significant benefits to software development and maintenance. With their writing and their ecosystem contributions including `MyGet.org` (NuGet-as-a-Service), Maarten and Xavier have proven themselves as leading NuGet experts.

Especially considering how much NuGet and its ecosystem have grown over the past couple of years, I am glad Maarten and Xavier have written *Pro NuGet, Second Edition*. This book explains how to consume NuGet packages in your projects, how packages are authored and published, and how you can use several different approaches for hosting your own private or public NuGet feeds. *Pro NuGet* demonstrates how to use valuable NuGet concepts such as package restore so that your builds and build servers can automatically download the right packages. Maarten and Xavier have also illustrated how to extend NuGet to further meet your needs with ecosystem tools or even your own extensions. The book even shows how to use NuGet as an implementation detail for your own extensible systems.

Whether you are just learning what NuGet and package management are, or you are already a daily NuGet user, I promise this book will teach you how to get more value from NuGet. As I was reading through the book, I was really impressed at how thorough Maarten and Xavier have been on so many topics, and I learned several new things myself.

—Jeff Handley
Microsoft Development Lead for NuGet

The NuGet train continues. Have you seen the stats? No? Head on over to `www.nuget.org/stats`. I'll wait here. See that? Literally millions of clients installed, and 7+ million packages downloaded per month. NuGet is the best thing to happen to open source and Microsoft since, well, since the beginning. I enjoy working for Microsoft and I've been doing open source for well over a decade, but getting open source libraries into my projects has always been a hassle. Where is the site? Which file to download? Where do I put it? Which DLL do I get and what framework version? Too many clicks. Now, NuGet.

We in the .NET community have been jealous of RubyGems and Java Maven and all the other package management solutions for developers. It took a while, but Microsoft finally released an open source project that takes commits from non-Microsoft developers and enhances the .NET developer ecosystem. NuGet was a little late in coming, but it's here and I don't know how I wrote software without it.

When this book first came out, there were 3.5 million package downloads in total. With this newly refreshed edition, NuGet surpassed those download numbers every two weeks. Not only that, but NuGet is also officially included in *every* Visual Studio edition, from Express to Ultimate, from Windows Phone to Web. Everyone who uses NuGet suddenly can't live without it.

Why do we need a book on NuGet? Because NuGet is a building block on top of which many other things can be built. Not just NuGet packages and .NET libraries, but innovative services, starter kits, web frameworks, scaffolders, installers, and all sorts of crazy stuff that the NuGet team never imagined.

We've already seen commercial software vendors like JetBrains build NuGet support directly into their TeamCity product, as well as tools and component companies like DevExpress create private NuGet feeds to support the enterprise. NuGet is open source, but it's more than just open source. It's about making building software with new, original and pioneering libraries in *your* application as easy as File ä Add Reference.

I'm happy to be part of this community and, in some small way, to contribute to NuGet and its success. I hope by reading this book that *you* will become part of that success story!

—Scott Hanselman
Principal Community Architect—ASP.NET/IIS/NuGet Microsoft

The Bigger Picture

NuGet is a free, open source, package management tool for the .NET platform, C++, and JavaScript. It is developed by Microsoft and has been contributed to the ASP.NET Gallery on Outercurve Foundation, formerly known as the CodePlex Foundation. NuGet enables .NET developers to easily find packages, including any dependencies, and manage them within Visual Studio projects or from the command line.

A NuGet package can consist of assemblies, configuration files, source code, and more. Software package management is not a new concept, although the tools have been notably missing for years by .NET developers. Some open source tools were available, but as with many things in life, a chicken-and-egg problem existed between having tooling and having a package publishing ecosystem.

In this chapter, you'll learn why you need a package management tool, how NuGet compares to other package management tools, and finally, how you can benefit from using NuGet in your projects.

Leveraging the Community

One thing any .NET developer should be aware of is that the .NET ecosystem is much bigger than and not limited to the .NET Framework itself. There are literally thousands of open source libraries and components available for your perusal.

Those who are aware of this vast ecosystem often ask themselves the same questions:

- How do I know if there already is a suitable solution available?
- Where can I find it?
- How do I install it?
- How do I configure it properly?
- How do I know there is a newer version available?

Usually, this meant searching the web for the best solution, trying to find your way through different blog posts, discussion forums, project sites, and hopefully some documentation as well, and eventually pulling some source code or compiled libraries for reference in your projects. The adventure is just beginning! How do you know what to reference? Do I reference all libraries or only some of them? How do I use these libraries?

By the time you were satisfied with your work and got the thing working, you had usually lost valuable time. Of course, the next time you needed this dependency, you already knew what to do—been there, done that! That is, if the library had not evolved into some new major version full of new features and breaking changes, merged assemblies, and obsolete libraries. If you found out about a new, improved version of the dependency during development, justifying an update of this dependency, then this exact same pain could be waiting already!

Wouldn't it make more sense to leave the hassle of going through all these potential installation and configuration changes up to the people who created it in the first place? Who knows better than the creators of the library about what has changed, or which steps are to be taken to upgrade from an older version to the new one?

If any of this makes sense to you, NuGet will sound like music to your ears. This book will help you leverage NuGet and make sure these situations belong to history.

Get Latest Version

When working on software projects and joining a development team, it's always pleasant to be able to do a Get Latest Version on the source control system being used, press F5 in Visual Studio, and run the application to get accustomed to it.

Unfortunately, this dream scenario of being able to get latest and run is not always reality. Many times developers reference assemblies from the Global Assembly Cache (GAC) that are not present in a default .NET installation. This means every developer needs to be doing some tooling and library installations on their systems in order to get the application to run.

■ **Note** Each computer running the Common Language Runtime (CLR) has a machine-wide code cache called the *Global Assembly Cache (GAC)*. The GAC stores assemblies specifically designated to be shared by several applications on the computer. You can find more info at `http://msdn.microsoft.com/en-us/library/yf1d93sz(v=vs.110).aspx`.

If you are lucky, smart developers add their external libraries to source control as well, so this get-latest scenario just works. However, there's still the pain of keeping everything up-to-date.

Did all of this sound awfully familiar? NuGet is the perfect match to overcome such pains in your development process, and this book will help you with optimizing for the get-latest scenario.

The "Not Invented Here" Syndrome

Many development teams, if not most, suffer from the "not invented here" syndrome. While there are several well-tested open source and even commercial solutions available for many problems, teams still tend to build their own. Consider database accessibility: every developer probably has written their own object-relational mapper (ORM) during their career.

But why do we do this? Because that third-party solution is "not invented here." We tend to build our own solutions and bundle them in a giant, monolithic framework used by the team. Why not package it into smaller components? Why not embrace the third-party ecosystem and have our internal framework depend on it? What happened to the reuse of components?

We've all done this, and yet we still don't seem to be aware of the additional costs associated with reinventing the wheel. Before you know it, you're in a situation called *dependency hell*, where you have to maintain, test, and support many versions of different components you wrote, only to support the code base you really care about: the consuming application. This is the code base that creates real value for you, so that's what you want to focus on.

Escaping from Dependency Hell

To understand the goals of and the reasons behind a package management tool for the .NET platform, it's worth considering how developers have been managing software dependencies so far. If you've ever struggled with updating a referenced assembly to a new version, or searched for documentation on a third-party library to perform a specific task, only to find out such documentation did not exist, you have encountered dependency management issues. If you've ever had a build failing or a runtime exception because of a reference collision, you have entered dependency hell.

Dependency hell is a term for the frustration of software users who have installed software packages which have dependencies on specific versions of other software packages.

—Wikipedia, http://en.wikipedia.org/wiki/Dependency_hell

Note   If you haven't heard of dependency hell, the term *DLL hell* is a similar concept that existed in earlier versions of Microsoft Windows, as software developers were always struggling to find and work with the correct DLL in their software.

An Introduction to Dependency Management

Following industry best practices, a good software architect, technical lead, or developer designs an application with reusability and modularity in mind. There are tons of good books and resources out there that will explain the reasoning behind this, but that would quickly lead us beyond the scope of this book. Creating or consuming reusable components and libraries is generally considered a good thing. In fact, all developers building on top of the .NET Framework already do this implicitly, without paying too much attention to it, as the .NET Framework is the core framework on top of which we all build our solutions.

Over the years, an increasing number of people in the .NET community initiated open source projects or started contributing to such open source initiatives. Some of them gained a huge amount of popularity due to the quality and maturity they had reached, others due to the unique functionality they provided. Many software projects began referencing these third-party libraries and as such became dependent on them.

Both origins of such software dependencies have one thing in common: you don't control them. This is exactly the root cause of the frustration that many developers have experienced when fighting dependency issues: you can't control the third-party reference you rely on.

Table 1. *Example Dependency Matrix for a Modular Application*

Application	Module	Dependencies
Application A	Module X	Library U, Library V
	Module Y	Library S, Library T
	Module Z	

Imagine you're part of a development team working on a single module, module X, for an application, as illustrated in Table 1. Your team's module is depending on two libraries, while one of the other modules has its own dependencies. So far, so good: all teams are working on isolated modules without interdependencies. It seems, however, as shown in Figure 1, that library U, on which module X depends, has a dependency itself to library T from another module. This could be a potential source of headache when one of the two teams requires another version of T, or upgrades T to an incompatible version for library U. You've just encountered a version collision on one of your dependencies.

This very simple example illustrates that you don't need to have a huge dependency graph for an application to encounter dependency issues. Real-life enterprise solutions that can consist of hundreds of modules increase the chance of entering dependency hell exponentially. You can safely conclude that the larger an application's list of dependencies, and its dependencies' interdependencies, the more of a pain point this becomes. Because most business applications are more complex than the preceding simple example, most development teams don't even realize they will hit these issues, until they feel pain and frustration for themselves.

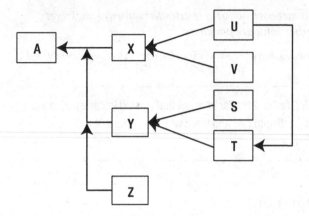

Figure 1. *Example dependency graph for a modular application*

Many development teams have struggled with dependency issues due to incorrect versioning applied to such third-party libraries or components. A typical example would be a library version 1.0 that just released an update using a minor version increment, version 1.1, but nonetheless contains breaking changes. Those companies that hit these issues preferred reinventing the wheel and having control over this dependency. They started creating their own frameworks, trying to solve similar problems. Although this indeed mitigated the risk of dependency issues, it has proven to be a costly workaround due to significantly increased development time, and actually created the illusion of reusability: everyone was applying reusability principles within their own isolated environment. Some smart people realized this, but the reality is that even those people often ended up in an environment where company policies and the economic reality forced them to work this way.

Another approach is to lock down all dependencies at the start of a project. Although you'll never have this kind of dependency issue, your project will never benefit from any new functionality or improvements that a newer version of those dependencies can bring. A variation to this approach is to unlock the dependencies right after a release, when work starts on the next version. At this point, you pick newer versions of your dependencies, and lock them again until after release. The first approach is harsh, and your project doesn't benefit from it in the long term, while the latter has been proven quite successful. If you want to be agile and pick any version of a dependency when you feel fit, you'll be continuously fixing your project instead of driving it toward stable milestones.

You probably have a gut feeling by now that none of these approaches is really satisfying. You're always running behind the fact you'll be dealing with all of this yourself, every single time, over and over again. To understand how NuGet solves these issues, it's important to learn how people came up with answers to these problems over the years, and how they evolved.

A Brief History of Dependency Management

In the early days of the Internet, developers used some sort of repository-based approach, such as the Apache Jakarta Project in Java, where the community surrounded the development platform with lots of open source projects. This helped forge a new approach to dependency management. Around the use of source control, they discouraged checking in binaries and other output of your project. The Apache Ant framework, an XML-based Java build library, helped facilitate this best practice. This tool was the first of its kind because it also allowed you to retrieve files by using HTTP. Typically, an internal site was put in place to be responsible for hosting shared libraries within an organization. At build time, the Ant build files were used to download the libraries locally when not already present. This approach had a shortcoming, however: there was no standard way of setting up these repositories. Also, caching was not uniformly dealt with.

The lessons learned from these experiences were meant to be solved by Java's second-generation build framework, Maven. Maven was an attempt to standardize the dependency management process and to introduce recommendations around repository management and versioning conventions.

As opposed to what the Unix development community was used to, .NET developers found it a convenient practice to put all referenced dependencies into source control, next to their project—convenient, because it was very easy for getting projects set up. Similar to what the Java community experienced, this approach also lacked a standardized strategy for managing different versions of dependencies.

The release of Microsoft MSBuild was a turning point for the .NET community. This free XML-based build platform is bundled with the .NET Framework and is used by Visual Studio as the underlying build engine. Although a port of Ant was available for .NET at the time, MSBuild quickly became the tool of choice. However, MSBuild did not come with any tasks that supported downloading dependencies.

■ **Note** You can read more on MSBuild on MSDN: `http://msdn.microsoft.com/en-us/library/0k6kkbsd.aspx`.

Inmid-2010, the .NET community seemed to be moving in the right direction with the introduction of OpenWrap, immediately followed by an announcement that Microsoft had joined forces with a .NET package management project called Nubular (Nu). Based on RubyGems, a well-known package management system in the Ruby world, it has been rewritten to get rid of the Ruby dependency. The Nu command-line package management system was now to be called NuPack. Shortly thereafter and following one more rebranding, NuGet was born as the result of a collaborative effort by the Nubular team and Microsoft.

■ **Note** You can still visit the Nubular project web site at `http://nu.wikispot.org/Current_Packages`.

■ **Tip** Did you know that Visual Studio project files are actually MSBuild project files? Open the files in Notepad (or any other text editor) to see how they are built out of MSBuild tasks, targets, properties, and items.

What's Wrong with What I've Always Been Doing?

Before the existence of a package management tool such as NuGet, dependency management in .NET was a big problem. There was no uniform way to tackle dependencies; there was no practical guidance that provided a one-solution-fits-all approach to all development environments.

The various approaches to tackle these problems often relied on the development tools being used. For instance, teams using Team Foundation Server's source control system could use shared team projects to manage their internal dependencies. On a smaller scale, you could also have Visual Studio projects shared between multiple solutions. Although in some cases this worked, the main issue was that the code in those shared projects could be easily changed in any of those solutions. Such change in the code often resulted in one solution building correctly, while the other solutions were broken all at once. If some kind of version or change management was applied to those solutions, you'd often experience problems with this as well because every single time a solution built the shared project, the other solutions would get a new version as well.

Some organizations built a huge repository of dependencies on a shared network location. Although it looks like a good idea to centralize your dependencies in one giant catalog, this approach really has some huge flaws. For one, referencing dependencies from a network location slows build time significantly, thus reducing efficiency of all development teams. Second, things get even worse if no proper versioning strategy is being used, allowing builds to be overwritten and immediately impacting all development projects depending on the overwritten component.

Others preferred putting all compiled dependencies in a local folder relative to the Visual Studio solution—often called References, Referenced Assemblies, Libs, or something else, clearly an indication that there was no uniform convention. A positive note in this approach is that a proper release has to be picked for every single dependency, including internal ones, which made some sort of change management possible. Until today, this was the most common approach taken by .NET development teams, independent of which software configuration management tool they use. Nevertheless, for those using Team Foundation Server, upgrading a dependency is often a pain in the behind because of the insufficient tracking of binary differences in source control. When a developer changed a DLL in the folder and wanted it to be checked in, he would often be presented with a dialog box indicating that "Team Foundation Server did not detect any changes. Undoing check-out." As a developer wanting to upgrade an assembly under source control, you had to remember that you needed to explicitly check out the file first, before replacing it and checking it in. This is often used as an argument against Team Foundation Server's source control system, but, although it is indeed a weakness, the argument is actually an indication that the approach itself is maybe not as perfect as one would think it is.

In general, if you think about it, does it make a lot of sense to do the following:

- Store compiled code in a source control system?

- Duplicate those compiled dependencies relative to a solution all over your source control system?

- Store third-party libraries and components, which may be restricted by license and are the intellectual property of others, in your source control system?

We'll provide in-depth answers to these questions , where we will guide you through various scenarios and practices to stay as far away as possible from dependency hell.

An Introduction to Package Management

The idea of a package management system for software libraries and components is actually derived from the concept of operating system package managers that install systemwide software packages or libraries, much like apt-get and similar package management tools do in the non-Microsoft space. Linux-based operating systems and other Unix-like systems typically consist of hundreds of distinct software packages, making a package management system a real necessity. On Microsoft Windows, where the .NET runtime relies on dynamic library linking, the runtime also looks in the GAC for shared libraries to remove the issue of DLL hell. As the central repository for shared DLLs, the GAC is often the place into which applications will find or install common assemblies.

In the area of software development, a package manager is responsible for the automation of the installation, update, configuration, and removal process of software packages in a consistent manner within the scope of the solution. Typically, this tool is also responsible for interpreting package metadata such as version information or package dependencies to prevent conflicts or missing prerequisites.

■ **Note**   When talking about *package manager or package management* throughout this book, we are referring to application-level package management unless otherwise noted.

You might be wondering why we discuss package management instead of dependency management. That is because there is a difference between a package and a dependency. A package typically consists of software libraries that, when installed in a target project, form a dependency the target project relies on. But there's more! A package can also contain source code, configuration files, content such as images, scripts, and other files. Discussing dependencies would limit us to only a part of what a package can contain or what a package manager can contribute to the development process. Package contents and how to create them will be discussed in detail in Chapter 5.

It is also very tempting to confuse a package manager with an installer, often caused by common or very similar terminology and functionality. An installer is usually specific to a given product. In other words, a given product often comes with its own installer. This results in the installer often being tightly coupled to the product being installed, due to product-specific options or installation steps, making it harder or even impossible to reuse the installer. There are also multiple vendors of installers, resulting in different installer formats being used. This is very different from a package manager, which is the one and only installer of packages. Packages need to be of a specific format understood by the package manager. This difference makes a package manager very distinct from an installer.

Because a package manager is aware of package versioning and its dependencies, it is smart enough to detect any potential conflicts. It can add the appropriate binding redirects if needed or warn you upon installation time that a versioning conflict occurred.

■ **Note**   You can redirect an assembly-binding reference to another version of an assembly by using entries in the application or machine configuration files. More info is available at `http://msdn.microsoft.com/en-us/library/2fc472t2.aspx`.

This makes installing packages and dependency conflict management more convenient, especially if it can detect and solve issues with binding redirects, or abort package installation by telling you where the problem occurs. Because the format of packages is restricted by a manifest specification (more on that in Chapter 5) and the package manager is the same for all packages, there is a uniform approach independent of the development environment you are working on.

There are only two things you depend on: the package manager and the package publisher. The package manager is a single point of failure that you can be certain has been well tested and functions as it should. Don't expect major issues from that side. The package publisher, however, is an unknown third-party that is subject to human error. This is not any different from relying on a third-party component without a package manager; you assume that the component or the package contents are well tested and function as expected. Have you seen developers writing unit tests or other kinds of tests on a third-party component before using it? Would it be easy to find the budget to do this? Do you feel this is a natural precaution? The structure of the package content, however, is well-defined according to a manifest that the package manager understands. The only human error the package publisher can make in order to provide you with a dependency issue is an incorrect versioning pattern. Versioning is also a topic of interest in Chapter 5.

Key Benefits of NuGet

NuGet brings you all the benefits of any package manager: it takes care of dependency chains and versioning conflicts at installation time, and it facilitates finding, installing, updating, and uninstalling packages at the application level. Besides these common must-have functionalities, NuGet has much more to offer.

NuGet is more than just a package manager. When changing perspectives, which we will assist you with in Chapter 10, you'll notice that you can leverage NuGet for other means due to its extensibility, its tooling, its integration, and the fact that it is open source.

NuGet Is Open Source

Although NuGet has been developed by Microsoft, it has been made open source and contributed to the ASP.NET Gallery on Outercurve Foundation. Because it is open source, the .NET community has picked it up quite fast and forged an ecosystem around it by providing tools, guidance, and support. Some even came up with innovative solutions for other scenarios based on NuGet, such as scaffolding, hosted private NuGet feeds in the cloud, systemwide package management, and an application plug-in system. Of course, you can also just get the sources and tweak it further to your needs.

Tooling and Integration

NuGet provides a lot of tooling, allowing us to use NuGet in any .NET environment. Whether you use Visual Studio or another IDE, whether you use Team Foundation Server or another source control system, whether you use the public NuGet Gallery or a custom NuGet feed hosted in the cloud or within company firewalls, you'll be able to integrate NuGet into your development environment with a minimum of effort. As NuGet becomes a major citizen in our .NET development stack, we feel certain that this integration will become even smoother in the future, as some third-party development tool vendors already demonstrated recently.

The command-line tool allows you to interact with NuGet from a simple console window. This tool can also be leveraged by continuous integration systems or deployment environments to fetch or publish NuGet packages by using some simple commands.

The Package Manager Console, which is part of the NuGet Visual Studio extension, allows you to interact with NuGet from within Visual Studio by using PowerShell. Providing you with useful cmdlets (*commandlets*) for standard NuGet operations, you'll be able to manage the NuGet packages your projects rely on without leaving the IDE. The ability to register your own cmdlets via this shell provides you with even greater flexibility.

The NuGet Package Manager Visual Studio extension integrates flawlessly with the Visual Studio IDE, which makes installing a package as easy as adding a reference to a project. The Visual Studio extension also comes with configurable settings for caching and package sources.

NuGet Package Explorer is a graphical user interface allowing you to visualize and edit package contents and metadata. It also allows you to create and publish your packages directly into a feed of choice. The NuGet Package Explorer also has a plug-in system, allowing you to extend this application even further to fit your needs.

All these tools will be used in combination, so you'll be able to mix them as you want, as well as stick to a tool and work with it through the book. Chapter 2 of this book will help you find and install these tools.

Extensibility

Because NuGet is an open source project, it is also very easy to extend it or its usage. There are some nice examples out there that leverage NuGet and extend its purpose or functionality:

- *Chocolatey:* A systemwide package manager leveraging NuGet, enabling the quick installation of several useful software packages.

- *Entity Framework Code-First:* Installing this NuGet package extends the Visual Studio IDE with new functionality around working with Entity Framework Code-First. While you're not forced to use this tooling, it does automate a lot of things by leveraging the NuGet Package Manager Console.

- *MyGet:* A "freemium" cloud solution providing you with what we call NuGet-as-a-Service (NaaS). MyGet enables you to avoid the hassle of developing your own NuGet server and to quickly get started leveraging NuGet in your software development environment. They even compile and create packages from your source code.

- *ProGet:* A shrink-wrap NuGet server for use in development teams.

- *Octopus Deploy:* A release management system leveraging NuGet to package and host deployable units.

Competition

The widespread usage of NuGet also has another effect: it creates extra competition for Microsoft products. Microsoft is not the only package provider on the NuGet Gallery, and its packages are listed among other third-party components and frameworks. For instance, the choice of using Entity Framework, NHibernate, Dapper.NET, or a similar product is now a matter of picking a package and installing it. If people query the NuGet feed for the word *database*, they'll find a whole lot more than just Entity Framework.

This means that it will be equally as easy to find and use a non-Microsoft solution for reference in your project, and based on good reviews of those solutions, you might choose the non-Microsoft package. We think this evolution is good and should result in an improved quality of those solutions. The more people who use it, the better the feedback.

A Wild Future

While not there yet, there are a lot of discussions around NuGet going on around the Internet. One we find particularly interesting is the discussion around the future of Visual Studio. Wouldn't it be nice if Visual Studio was just a thin layer containing IDE functionality but not all the functionality you're not using? What if functionality could be installed through NuGet? What if the ASP.NET MVC NuGet package also installed the ASP.NET MVC tooling? We believe there is a bright future for NuGet. And while this book is already in its second edition, we think we're only at the beginning of unlocking NuGet's full potential.

Adoption

NuGet has been adopted by most open source projects out there. Many vendors of third-party components are using NuGet to distribute their assemblies and sample code. Products such as MyGet, ProGet, and Sonatype Nexus prove that there is value in offering "private" NuGet repositories for large development teams.

There's no point in throwing numbers at you in this book, as they would be outdated by the time I finished writing this sentence, but we encourage you to check out some NuGet statistics on the official NuGet Gallery: http://nuget.org/stats. Adoption of NuGet is widely spread!

Who Should Use NuGet

If you feel so familiar with the problems sketched out in this chapter that it scares you, you have definitely been waiting for NuGet to put your mind at ease. If you don't like to go through the manual process of installing third-party frameworks yourself, or experience issues trying to keep up with new releases of those dependencies, then NuGet is your next best friend. Even if you do know your dependencies very well and are very familiar with its installation, configuration, and different versions, you could benefit from using NuGet by gaining precious time you could spend on more-valuable tasks.

In short, the use of a package manager for .NET development is a best practice every developer should consider, and with the proper guidance of this book, you'll wonder one day how you managed to live without it.

CHAPTER 1

▪ ▪ ▪

Getting Started

NuGet, in essence, is a Visual Studio extension that comes bundled with Visual Studio 2012 or newer. A lot of value comes from NuGet's integration with Visual Studio or the Visual Studio Express editions. Taking advantage of this integration offers you a seamless development workflow and enables you to work with NuGet right from within your Visual Studio installation; you'll even have a nice user interface to work with.

Dedicating an entire chapter to installing NuGet is probably overkill since NuGet already comes bundled with recent editions of Visual Studio. In short, all you need to have is Visual Studio 2012 (any edition) or Visual Studio 2013. From Visual Studio, use the Tools ä Extensions and Updates menu to update the NuGet Visual Studio extension to its latest version.

Not everyone is making use of the latest version of Visual Studio, which is why we'll have a look at how to install NuGet into Visual Studio 2010.

Apart from the NuGet Visual Studio extension, there are several other tools you may want to have installed on your system when reading this book and trying out some of the examples. NuGet also comes as a command-line tool, which can be used as a stand-alone feature. A tool like NuGet Package Explorer is not part of Visual Studio, yet it's a great addition to our developer toolbox when working with NuGet. So before we elaborate on working with NuGet from within Visual Studio in Chapter 2, this chapter will help you prepare your workstation and get all the prerequisites to work with NuGet in your development process, including installing Visual Studio, additional components, and NuGet itself.

Preparing Your Workstation

A small set of tools is essential to developing with NuGet. Whether you are a VB.NET or C# developer, whether you develop in Windows Forms, Web Forms, Silverlight, ASP.NET MVC (Model-View-Controller), or for a Windows Phone, you will need Visual Studio or one of the Visual Studio Express editions. You may also need other specific software.

Supported Development Environments

NuGet is supported in the following development environments:

- Visual Studio 2013 (all editions)
- Visual Studio 2012 (all editions)
- Visual Studio 2010 (all editions)
- Visual Web Developer 2010 Express
- WebMatrix 3
- WebMatrix 2
- SharpDevelop

If you do not have access to the Professional, Premium, or Ultimate editions of Visual Studio, you can find some free Visual Studio Express versions at www.microsoft.com/express.

In this book, most examples will use Visual Studio 2012 Ultimate. Keep in mind that the Visual Studio integration is identical across all versions listed in this section, and all versions are equally suited to our purposes. This book will not cover SharpDevelop, but its NuGet integration is similar to that of Visual Studio 2012.

■ **Note** If SharpDevelop is your favorite integrated development environment (IDE), don't throw away this book. SharpDevelop and Visual Studio 2012 share similar ideology and features. SharpDevelop 4.1 includes support for NuGet by default (see http://community.sharpdevelop.net/blogs/mattward/archive/2011/01/23/NuGetSupportInSharpDevelop.aspx).

Installing the Essential Software

Some examples in this book require you to install specific software. For example, some require the ASP.NET MVC 4 framework. Visual Studio 2012 ships with the ASP.NET MVC 4 framework installed, but you may want to upgrade to the latest version. The easiest way to install these components and configure your development environment is through Microsoft's Web Platform Installer, or Web PI, as everyone calls it.

The Web PI allows you to select a set of application components and frameworks, install them all at once, and take care of dependencies. For example, if you install the ASP.NET MVC framework, the Web PI will also install .NET 4.5 on your machine. If you wish to have the default configuration for your local development web server installed, the Web PI will both install and configure this for you.

Installing the Web Platform Installer

The Web PI can be downloaded from http://microsoft.com/web. Click the Downloads menu at the top of the page, and then click the Web Platform Installer link, shown in Figure 1-1.

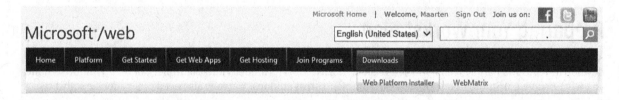

Figure 1-1. *The Downloads link to the Web Platform Installer*

Once you arrive on the download page, click the large Free Download button, shown in Figure 1-2, to download the Web PI to your computer. Note that Internet Explorer will ask you to run or save the installation file. Click the Run button (also shown in Figure 1-2) to run the Web Platform Installer. Other browsers often have similar options hidden under the Open button, for example.

Figure 1-2. *The download page for the Web PI*

Installing Components and Configuring Your Environment by Using the Web PI

Once the Web PI is running, you can select a variety of tools, applications, and frameworks to install on your machine from the Web PI main screen, which looks like Figure 1-3. The Web PI also enables you to configure some of the components that are already on your machine.

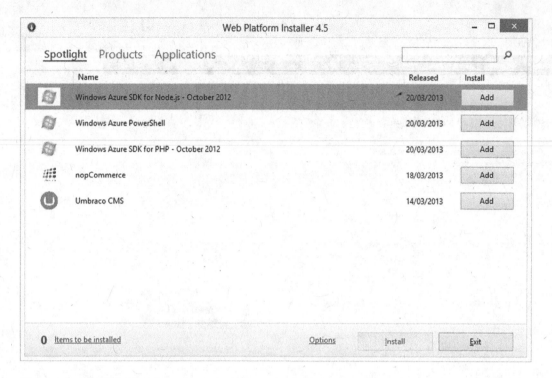

Figure 1-3. *The Web PI main screen*

You'll use the search box at the top-right corner of this screen to find the essential components used in this book. When the Web PI finds a component, simply click the Add button on the right side to add that component to the list of software to install.

Find and add the following components:

- Windows PowerShell

- ASP.NET MVC 4 or higher

- On Windows 7: IIS 7 Recommended Configuration

- On Windows 8: IIS 8 Recommended Configuration

- Microsoft .NET Framework 4 or higher

- Microsoft WebMatrix

After you've added these components, click the Install button near the bottom of the Web PI window. This action will display a confirmation dialog box listing the components you've selected plus their required dependencies, as shown in Figure 1-4. Click the I Accept button to install all these components.

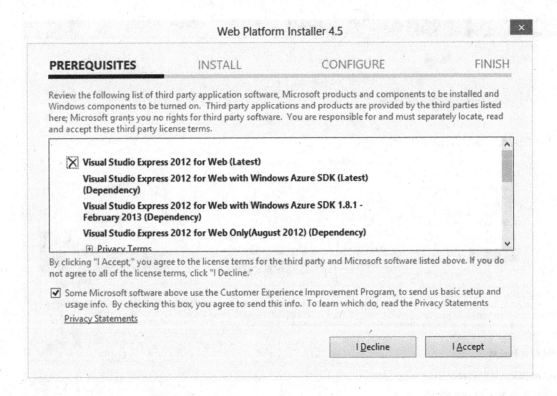

Figure 1-4. *The Web PI confirmation window*

Installing NuGet

Since you are reading a book titled *Pro NuGet*, you can imagine that one of the required components to work your way through this book is NuGet itself. NuGet has a collection of client tools, including the NuGet Visual Studio extension, the NuGet command-line executable, and the NuGet WebMatrix extension. Throughout this book, we'll mostly be using the Visual Studio extension (both the graphical user interface and the PowerShell console). However, some sections will be using the command-line version of NuGet. This section covers finding and installing these two components.

Throughout this book, we will also use the NuGet Package Explorer (NPE) tool. NPE is not an official Microsoft product; it's an open source project hosted on CodePlex. NPE is not required for working with NuGet. However, it's an invaluable tool to have installed for peeking into NuGet packages and seeing how other package authors have done things. It allows you to open, edit, inspect, and validate NuGet packages from an easy-to-use graphical user interface.

Installing the NuGet Visual Studio Extension (Visual Studio 2010)

To get started, navigate to www.nuget.org, the official web site hosting the NuGet tool and a variety of useful NuGet packages to use in your software. Find and click the Install NuGet button. After that, you'll be taken to the Visual Studio Gallery, where the actual download of the latest version of NuGet is located.

The Visual Studio Gallery displays a purple Download link, as shown in Figure 1-5. Click this link to install the NuGet Package Manager into your Visual Studio environment.

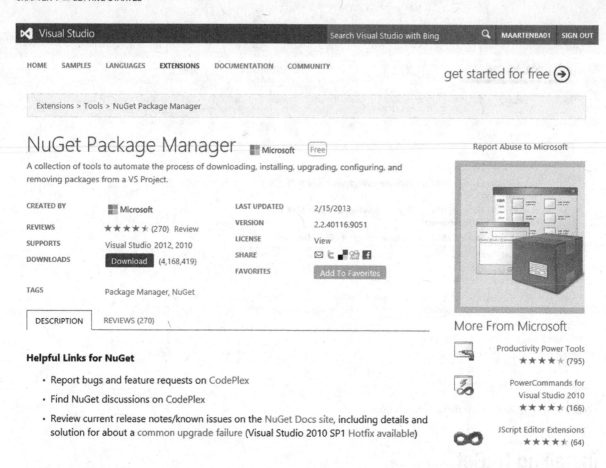

Figure 1-5. *The Visual Studio Gallery, where the NuGet Visual Studio extension can be downloaded*

Installing the NuGet extension into Visual Studio is very straightforward. The Visual Studio Extension Installer (VSIX) will prompt you to install NuGet into one or more versions of Visual Studio available on your system (Maarten happens to have two of those on his machine, as you can see in Figure 1-6). Click the Install button to register NuGet in Visual Studio.

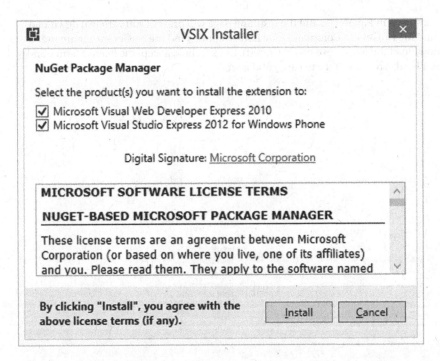

Figure 1-6. *The NuGet installer lists the versions of Visual Studio into which it can be installed*

▪ **Note** NuGet can be installed directly from Visual Studio. In the Tools ä Extension Manager menu, you can search for Visual Studio extensions. Search for *NuGet*, and click the Install button to install NuGet into Visual Studio.

The Visual Studio Extension Manager is also the place where you can install updates to the NuGet Visual Studio extension. NuGet typically is updated every two to three months. The Updates panel on the Visual Studio Extension Manager will allow you to easily update NuGet to its latest version.

Updating the NuGet Visual Studio Extension (Visual Studio 2012)

Every version of Visual Studio 2012 ships with the NuGet Visual Studio extension installed. Because NuGet is updated every two to three months, chances are the bundled extension has an update available.

To install an update of the NuGet Visual Studio extension, we can use the Tools ä Extensions and Updates menu in Visual Studio. Whenever an updated version of the NuGet Visual Studio extension is available, it will be listed in the dialog box that opens.

The NuGet web site also has a list of all installers available, at http://docs.nuget.org/docs/start-here/installing-nuget. This page also lists the latest nightly builds for NuGet, if you want to work with the very latest bits.

Downloading the NuGet Command-Line Tool

The NuGet command-line tool is used in this book as well. You can download its latest version from http://nuget.codeplex.com. (On this page, you can also download the NuGet source code and even contribute if you want to add a feature to NuGet.)

Select the Downloads menu, as shown in Figure 1-7, and the resulting page will present you with two download options: NuGet Package Explorer and the NuGet.exe Command Line Bootstrapper. Find the NuGet.exe command-line download (make sure not to download the NuGet.exe bootstrapper!). Click its link, accept the license terms, and save NuGet.exe to a location on your hard drive that you can easily find later.

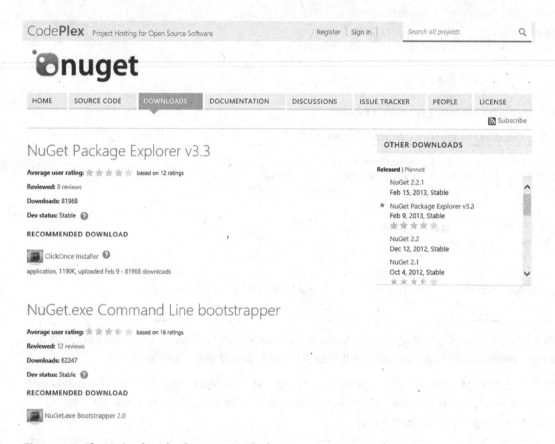

Figure 1-7. *The NuGet downloads page on CodePlex*

Installing NuGet Package Explorer

Although NuGet Package Explorer (or NPE) is not required to work with NuGet, as we mentioned before, it is handy because it allows you to open, edit, inspect, and validate NuGet packages from an easy-to-use graphical user interface.

NPE is a ClickOnce application that can be installed from inside your browser. To add it to your machine, simply navigate to http://npe.codeplex.com and find the latest download that will install the ClickOnce version of NPE.

■ **Note**   ClickOnce is a Microsoft technology that allows you to download and run an application from the Internet. Although that concept is not new or special, ClickOnce adds one feature: applications installed through ClickOnce are automatically updated as needed. This means that your NuGet Package Explorer software will always be kept up-to-date automatically.

After installing NPE, you will be greeted by its welcome screen, as shown in Figure 1-8. You can close NPE for now, because we won't need it again in this chapter. In other chapters, we'll make extensive use of it, though.

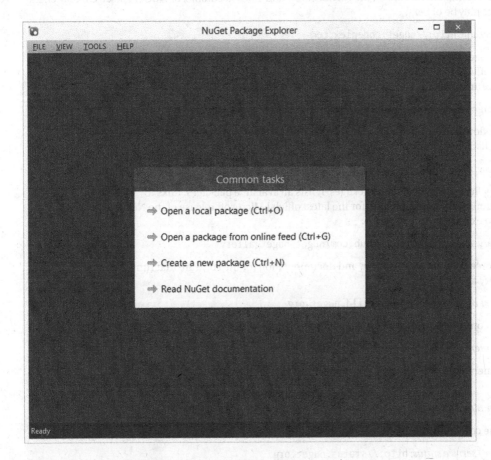

Figure 1-8. *The NuGet Package Explorer welcome screen*

Downloading Development Builds

If you're like us and like to experiment with the latest development builds of the NuGet tooling, then the following pointers will be useful to you. The NuGet team uses a publicly accessible TeamCity build server, allowing you to log in as a Guest user and download the build artifacts you want. Note that there's no guarantee these versions will work as expected, and no support will be given until released. Do not use them in your production environment if you can't accept the risks.

The following permalinks are always pointing to the latest development builds:

- *NuGet Command-Line Executable*: http://build.nuget.org/nuget.exe (The latest stable release can always be found at http://nuget.org/nuget.exe.)

- *NuGet Visual Studio Extension*: http://build.nuget.org/nuget.tools.vsix

Getting Further Information

If you require additional information on NuGet, the NuGet command-line executable, or NuGet Package Explorer, the following list of resources may be of help:

- *NuGet project site*: http://nuget.codeplex.com

  Holds downloads for the NuGet Visual Studio extension and NuGet command-line executable (official releases from Microsoft). It also has source code, an issue tracker, and discussion forums available.

- *NuGet Package Explorer project site*: http://npe.codeplex.com

  Provides the download for NuGet Package Explorer and its source code. It also has an issue tracker and discussion forums available.

- *NuGet Gallery*: www.nuget.org

  The official gallery of public NuGet packages. It lists all available packages, links to documentation, and a download link for the latest official Microsoft release of the NuGet Visual Studio extension.

- *NuGet Gallery sources*: https://github.com/nuget/nugetgallery

  Contains source code, an issue tracker, and documentation for the software that runs the NuGet Gallery at www.nuget.org.

- *NuGet project build server*: http://build.nuget.org

  Contains all continuous integration builds of Outercurve's NuGet project.

- *NuGet documentation*: http://docs.nuget.org

  Holds documentation of features, release notes, and several reference pages for specific scenarios.

- *NuGet Team Blog*: http://blog.nuget.org

  Blog from the core NuGet team.

- *NuGet Gallery service status*: http://status.nuget.org

  Uptime report for www.nuget.org.

NuGet, the NuGet Gallery, and NuGet Package Explorer are open source projects. This means that you can have a look inside to see how a specific feature is implemented, track down bugs, or even add your own contribution to one of these projects. Don't feel shy: if you have a great idea, either file a feature request or build it by yourself and share it with the world. Who knows? Our next version of the *Pro NuGet* book may feature something you contributed to NuGet.

Summary

In this chapter, we covered setting up your workstation and all required tools for developing applications using NuGet. NuGet comes bundled with recent editions of Visual Studio, so apart from updating the NuGet Visual Studio extension, that is all there is to it. You have also seen how to install the NuGet Visual Studio extension with older Visual Studio versions.

There are several other tools you may want to have installed on your system when working with NuGet, such as the command-line tool and NuGet Package Explorer.

We've ended this chapter with a list of resources related to NuGet that offer valuable additional information. This list also contains links to the project sites behind NuGet, where you can contribute to the documentation or the actual code of NuGet; it's all open source!

In the next chapter, we'll show you how to consume your first NuGet package.

■ ■ ■

## CHAPTER 2

Consuming and Managing Packages in a Solution

The introduction of this book introduced you to the bigger picture: the general concept of package management and why it is so extremely powerful. We also introduced NuGet as a solution-wide package management tool and explained its key benefits. Chapter 1 showed you how to get your development environment ready to fully leverage NuGet on your machine. This chapter will build on that knowledge and show you how you can consume your first NuGet package in Visual Studio.

In our first simple scenario, a package will be added to an ASP.NET MVC project. Afterward, we'll explore additional options for installing, updating, and uninstalling NuGet packages in your projects. You will also learn how to adjust NuGet to your needs by configuring custom package sources. There's a nice graphical user interface to do all that, in addition to PowerShell commands and a command-line tool. We'll show you how to use all of those, so you can decide for yourself which method best suits you.

Finally, we'll demonstrate how you can analyze packages installed into a project and how those packages relate to your project and to each other.

Consuming Your First NuGet Package

In this section, we'll show you how you can consume your first NuGet package. Using the tools that are integrated into Visual Studio by installing the NuGet Visual Studio extension, as explained in Chapter 1, we'll search for a NuGet package from the public NuGet repository.

■ **Note**   To most NuGet users, the term *NuGet repository* describes a NuGet package source, but to others, this is a *NuGet feed*. In essence, both names are correct. Since we're talking about a source of NuGet packages, it is a repository. Since those repositories (except the local folder or simple network share) are exposed to the world as an ATOM (XML) feed, the term *feed* is also appropriate.

NuGet packages can be consumed in any type of Visual Studio project, so go ahead and create a new Visual Studio project—for example, an ASP.NET MVC project or a Windows Presentation Foundation (WPF) project. You can also open an existing project and add a NuGet package there.

For this section, we're using a new ASP.NET MVC project, since there's something special about that type of project in relation to NuGet (we'll come to that in a second). Figure 2-1 shows the settings used to create a new ASP.NET MVC project, to demonstrate this NuGet version of "Hello, World." After creating a new ASP.NET MVC project in Visual Studio, you're finished with this section.

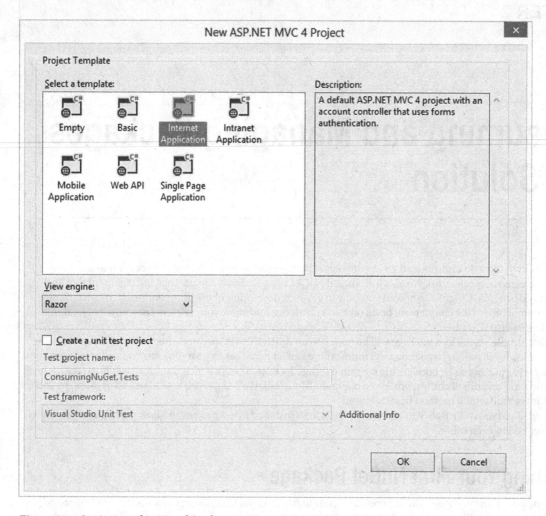

Figure 2-1. *Settings used in Visual Studio to create a new ASP.NET MVC project*

Integrating Visual Studio and NuGet

The NuGet Visual Studio extension adds several menu options to Visual Studio. For example, the Tools menu contains a new entry called Library Package Manager, which features a number of submenus (see Figure 2-2).

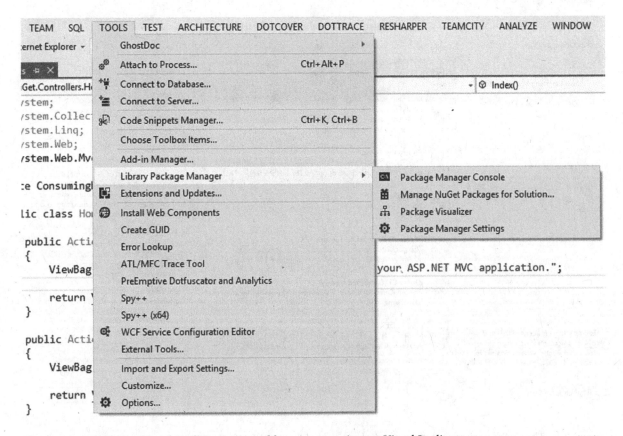

Figure 2-2. The NuGet Visual Studio extension adds a new menu item to Visual Studio

At the solution and project level in the project explorer, a new context menu is available. Find the Manage NuGet Package context menu by right-clicking either the solution or one of the projects in a solution.

■ **Note**   In Figure 2-2, you may notice the Package Visualizer submenu if you have installed Visual Studio 2010 or 2012 Ultimate edition. Although this submenu is not available in all Visual Studio versions, it is a valuable tool when working with NuGet packages, so it will be covered later in this chapter.

Finding the Package You Need

The NuGet Visual Studio extension adds some search functionalities to find a NuGet package. Right-click your project in Visual Studio and click Manage NuGet Packages. This will open a search form with basic filtering options, as shown in Figure 2-3.

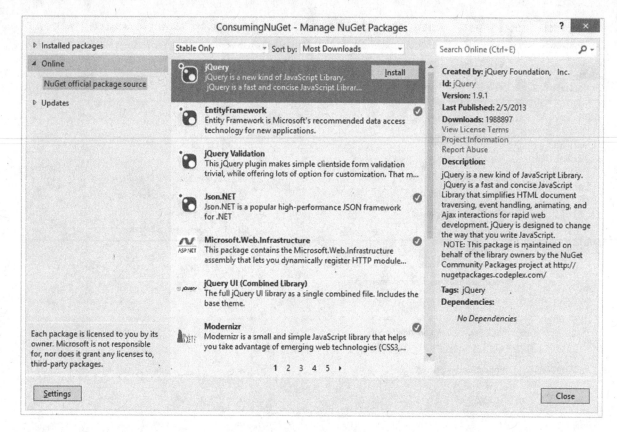

Figure 2-3. *The NuGet package management dialog box enables searching for NuGet packages*

The window presented consists of three panes: one to switch among installed packages, package updates, and a list of packages that you have recently used; another to search packages; and a third to display details of selected packages. Make sure to open the Online pane. From there, you can work with the search functionalities available in the Search Online field.

Note that the Stable Only drop-down can be changed to Include Prerelease, which allows Alpha, Beta, or Release Candidate versions to be included in the results. We'll talk more about these Prerelease versions later. For now, keep the drop-down set to Stable Only.

Searching for packages is a difficult job when you don't know what to search for. The best way to start exploring NuGet is by entering the technology you are working with in the search box in the top-right corner of this window. For example, type **mvc** as a search query when you are working with ASP.NET MVC. If you are looking for something related to Windows Phone 8, enter **wp8**.

The list of NuGet packages will be filtered based on your query but may still yield a large number. Refine your search by adding a second keyword. For example, if you want to work with HTML5, change the search query to **mvc html5** to get a more relevant list of packages to explore. Of course, this method is not ideal, because it is based on filtering titles, descriptions, and tags added to NuGet packages. If the package author forgot to add tags to the published packages, they will probably not be visible when you search for specific keywords. Nevertheless, this way of filtering is the only method of getting a short list of NuGet packages that may provide the functionality you need.

At the time of this writing, over 15,500 NuGet packages are available on nuget.org Some of these packages have multiple versions available, resulting in more than 120,000 unique packages in the public nuget.org repository! By the time you are reading this book, these numbers have probably gone stale, and even more packages are available. Even after you've searched for your technology, how do you find the specific package you need?

Once you filter the list of available NuGet packages based on the technology you are using and an additional keyword that refines that search, the list of packages at your disposal will be easier to process. Note that while you have now searched on technology, a search for things like *Twitter* or *JSON parser* will yield packages that provide a certain functionality.

Since nuget.org contains various packages of a variable quality, it is important to take some other clues into account in choosing packages. It's very similar to all app stores out there, where not every app you install has the same quality baseline.

Luckily, every NuGet package comes with a number of details to inform your choice. If you look back at Figure 2-3, the right-hand pane shows a variety of details about a package:

- The package creator, which may influence whether you deem the NuGet package to be trustworthy.

- The package ID, which will probably not influence your decision but is great to remember if you really like the package and want to reuse it in future projects.

- The package version and last update date, which may give you an idea of how mature and how well-maintained the NuGet package is.

- The number of downloads is a good indication of a package's popularity. But don't judge a package by its number of downloads alone; great-quality packages sometimes have only a handful of downloads.

- The Project Information hyperlink brings you to the NuGet package's project information page, where you can learn a lot about a package.

- The package description, dependencies, and release notes can also give a strong indication about whether the NuGet package will fit your needs.

- The package license. Sometimes a specific open source license cannot be added to the project you are building or a package cannot be used in production because of conflicting license terms. There are packages with many different licenses, and depending on your environment and project, the license can be very important.

Be wise in your decisions, and always try out new packages in a sample application (not on your actual project) if you are not familiar with them!

■ **Note**   As we will see in later chapters, NuGet packages can contain PowerShell code that runs under the same privileges as your Visual Studio application. Package authors can do a lot of interesting things, such as adding PowerShell cmdlets to the Package Manager Console within Visual Studio. However, a malicious PowerShell script could do much damage, as there are no restrictions or validations on the PowerShell code being executed. While we don't want to scare you, always be cautious about the packages you install and report anything you find harmful. You can always extract the package archive or use NuGet Package Explorer to inspect the package contents.

If you do find a nefarious package, use the Report Abuse link on the package page. This will inform the NuGet Gallery administrators and prompt them to investigate the package more closely.

If you know the value of one or more fields displayed in the NuGet package management dialog box or the metadata fields within a package, you can narrow search results further. For example, if you want to search for packages containing the word *Glimpse* in the ID, you can specify a search for id:Glimpse. Similarly, other package metadata fields can be searched as well. Table 2-1 lists some example searches for attributes that can be searched through. Do note that these searches will execute a Contains search, meaning that a search for id:Glimpse will return Glimpse as well as Glimpse.WindowsAzure and so on.

Table 2-1. *Example Searches for Metadata Attributes*

Attribute	Example
id	id:jQuery
title	title:GoogleAnalyticsTracker
description	description:dependency injection (Note that this will search for *dependency or injection*.)
authors	authors:maartenba
owners	owners:xavierdecoster
tags	tags:mvc

Installing a NuGet Package

Let's add a package to our still-blank ASP.NET MVC project. Right-click your project in Visual Studio and click Manage NuGet Packages. Find the package named ELMAH, an error-logging framework for ASP.NET. As shown in Figure 2-4, it is pretty obvious what to do next: click the Install button and watch what happens.

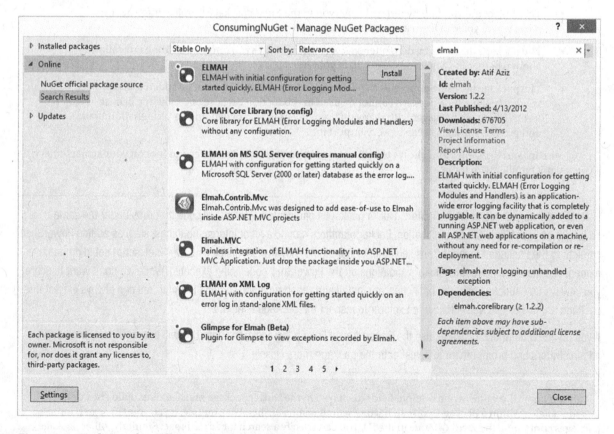

Figure 2-4. *Finding and installing the ELMAH package in a project*

The NuGet Visual Studio extension added a new reference to your project. Also, if you look at the web.config file in the ASP.NET MVC project, some configuration settings have been added as well, as shown in Listing 2-1.

Listing 2-1. The Modified web.config File After Installing the ELMAH NuGet Package

```xml
<?xml version="1.0" encoding="utf-8"?>
<configuration>
  <configSections>
    <sectionGroup name="elmah">
      <section name="security" requirePermission="false"
            type="Elmah.SecuritySectionHandler, Elmah" />
      <section name="errorLog" requirePermission="false"
            type="Elmah.ErrorLogSectionHandler, Elmah" />
      <section name="errorMail" requirePermission="false"
            type="Elmah.ErrorMailSectionHandler, Elmah" />
      <section name="errorFilter" requirePermission="false"
            type="Elmah.ErrorFilterSectionHandler, Elmah" />
    </sectionGroup>
  </configSections>
  <!-- ... -->
  <system.web>
    <!-- ... -->
    <httpModules>
      <add name="ErrorLog" type="Elmah.ErrorLogModule, Elmah" />
      <add name="ErrorMail" type="Elmah.ErrorMailModule, Elmah" />
      <add name="ErrorFilter" type="Elmah.ErrorFilterModule, Elmah" />
    </httpModules>
    <httpHandlers>
      <add verb="POST,GET,HEAD" path="elmah.axd" type="Elmah.ErrorLogPageFactory, Elmah" />
    </httpHandlers>
  </system.web>
  <system.webServer>
    <!-- ... -->
    <modules runAllManagedModulesForAllRequests="true">
      <add name="ErrorLog"
            type="Elmah.ErrorLogModule, Elmah" preCondition="managedHandler" />
      <add name="ErrorMail"
            type="Elmah.ErrorMailModule, Elmah" preCondition="managedHandler" />
      <add name="ErrorFilter"
            type="Elmah.ErrorFilterModule, Elmah" preCondition="managedHandler" />
    </modules>
    <handlers>
      <add name="Elmah" path="elmah.axd" verb="POST,GET,HEAD"
            type="Elmah.ErrorLogPageFactory, Elmah" preCondition="integratedMode" />
    </handlers>
  </system.webServer>
  <!-- ... -->
</configuration>
```

Browse the Solution Explorer tree, and you'll see that ELMAH has been added to the list of references. If you right-click the ELMAH reference and select Properties, the properties pane in Visual Studio will show you where the package has been downloaded and referenced:

`C:\....\YourSolution\packages\elmah.corelibrary.1.2.2\lib\Elmah.dll.`

Looking at the evidence gathered, the following happened automatically just by clicking Install in the Package Manager dialog box:

- The latest version of ELMAH was downloaded from the `NuGet.org` package source.

- The ELMAH package depends on the Elmah.CoreLibrary package, which is also downloaded and referenced.

- The required assemblies and other files have been added to a folder under the solution root.

- The ELMAH assembly has been automatically referenced in the current project.

- The `web.config` file was automatically modified and updated with all required settings for ELMAH.

Impressive, no? Imagine having to search the Internet for the latest version of ELMAH, find the correct download, extract it to your system, read through the documentation to understand what's required to install it into your project, change `web.config`, and so on.

It gets even better. When a package has a dependency on another package, NuGet will download and install the additional required package together with the one you were installing, in one go. This is a first indication of how useful NuGet can be for managing your dependencies: no more time wasted reading through release notes for installation steps and prerequisites. NuGet will figure it out for you!

Uninstalling a Package

When you're refactoring a project, chances are that some dependencies on external libraries may be removed along the way. We've already seen that NuGet offers a clean way of installing NuGet packages; the good news is that uninstalling NuGet packages is equally frictionless.

Open the Manage NuGet Packages dialog box and click the Installed Packages tab. This will list all packages installed in your project, including their dependencies. To uninstall a package, simply click the Uninstall button next to the package. This will uninstall the package from the selected project.

Uninstalling a package goes through the inverse process of installing a NuGet package into your project. For example, when uninstalling ELMAH from the project, the following process will be executed:

1. The NuGet Visual Studio extension will prompt to uninstall dependencies that are no longer used. In this case, you will be asked whether the Elmah.CoreLibrary should be uninstalled as well.

2. The `web.config` file will be automatically modified, and all required settings for ELMAH will be removed. Note that if you have modified these ELMAH-specific settings, the modified version of these settings will be left sitting in your `web.config` and may have to be removed manually. No need to worry about modifications to other parts of the `web.config` file: NuGet is smart enough to detect which modifications happened as part of the ELMAH package installation, and which ones have nothing to do with this event.

3. The ELMAH reference will be removed from your project.

4. The required assemblies and other files that have been extracted from the original package into the solution root will be removed from the file system if no other projects in your solution are dependent on them.

If you try to uninstall a package that is still required by another NuGet package, the NuGet Visual Studio extension will provide you with an error message like the one shown in Figure 2-5.

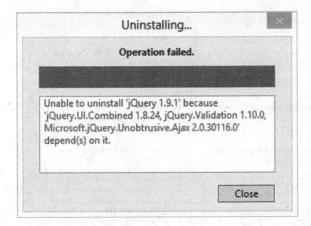

Figure 2-5. *Uninstalling a NuGet package that is still required by other Nuget packages generates an error message*

Uninstalling a package will almost never leave behind any artifacts from the previously installed package. Exceptions to that are framework references and assembly-binding redirects that have been added by a package. NuGet has no way to know if they were added due to the package and used only because of the package, and hence will leave them in the project.

Updating a Package to the Latest Version

What do you do when a dependency you are using in your project publishes a new version? Do you immediately update to the new version? Do you wait? Do you wait because you want to make sure it's stable first, or do you wait because upgrading a dependency again means downloading software, reading manuals, updating configuration, and so on?

If you find yourself waiting to save yourself the work of updating, NuGet offers a clean upgrade path for any NuGet package installed to your project that respects semantic versioning (read more on semantic versioning in Chapter 3).

Just as when installing a new NuGet package into your project, right-click your project in Visual Studio and click Manage NuGet Packages. In the dialog box that opens, select the Updates tab. As shown in Figure 2-6, this tab shows the list of all updates available for NuGet packages installed into your project.

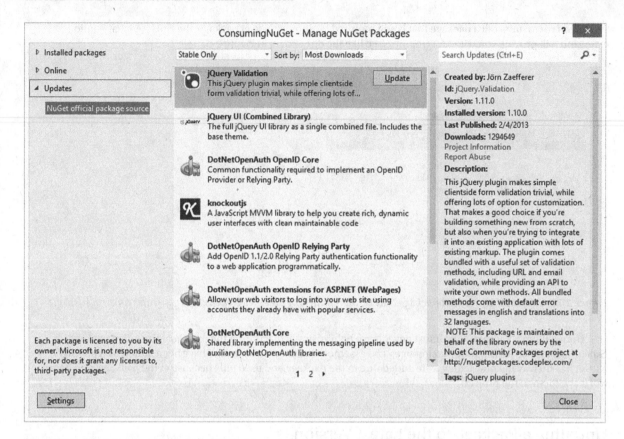

Figure 2-6. Updating a package by using the Manage NuGet Packages dialog box

Since we've installed the ELMAH package earlier in this section and NuGet typically installs the latest version of a NuGet package into your project, the Updates tab will not be showing ELMAH. Nevertheless, you will see some updates available for this fresh, blank project. ASP.NET MVC projects are created with some NuGet package references automatically added, such as Entity Framework, jQuery, jQuery UI, jQuery Validation, and Modernizr. Updates can easily be installed by selecting the reference and clicking the Install button.

■ **Note**   For this section of the book, we've chosen to work with an ASP.NET MVC project because it uses NuGet as part of the project template. The ASP.NET MVC framework features a predefined set of NuGet package dependencies, enabling you to automatically update external dependencies like jQuery with just a few clicks.

Whenever a package update requires additional configuration settings, additional .NET framework dependencies, or dependencies on other NuGet packages, these will also be installed in one go, just as when you are installing a fresh NuGet package into your project.

Be aware that when you change content files that have been installed through NuGet, by default these changes will never be overwritten. This has been done to protect your work from being replaced by a clean, blank state of the NuGet package. This also means that if an update requires changes in these files, you will have to either overwrite your local changes or make the changes required by an updated package yourself. Since NuGet 2.5, a dialog box will be shown in which you can specify whether you want to overwrite one file or all files, or none at all.

For reference, the following happens during a package update. First, the package is uninstalled by applying the following flow:

- Assembly references for the package are removed.

- Framework references are left behind.

- Content files are removed, unless they were edited.

- MSBuild .props/.targets files are removed.

- Configuration transformation files are merged out.

- Configuration XDT transformations named *.uninstall.xdt are processed.

Next, the updated version is installed:

- Assembly references for the package are added.

- Framework references are added.

- Content files are added (or ignored or overwritten, depending on settings).

- MSBuild .props/.targets files are added.

- Configuration transformation files are merged in.

- Configuration XDT transformations named *.install.xdt are processed.

Using the Package Manager Console

You have now learned the basic operations of working with the graphical user interface provided by the NuGet Visual Studio extension. Although working with a graphical user interface is easy, many developers using NuGet prefer working with the Package Manager Console that is also installed as part of the NuGet Visual Studio extension.

The Package Manager Console is an interactive window you can dock in your Visual Studio IDE that allows you to interact with NuGet through commands or, in a broader sense, to automate Visual Studio. This window is special because it's PowerShell enabled, and as such, you can run NuGet commands as well as PowerShell commands. In proper PowerShell terms, we speak about cmdlets (pronounced *commandlets*). The fact that the Package Manager Console enables you to use PowerShell commands inside Visual Studio is probably the main reason that many developers prefer working with the Package Manager Console instead of the NuGet Visual Studio extension: it enables you to work with NuGet and script Visual Studio in a familiar yet powerful manner.

Before we cover a more specific scenario and work with an explicit version of a package, we would like to give you some quick tips on how to make optimal use of the Package Manager Console.

Don't worry if you are not familiar with PowerShell or its syntax. Most operations you will do while working with NuGet packages can be accomplished with one command. You don't have to learn the various commands by heart either, as they are easily discoverable using the built-in autocompletion feature.

As you can see in Figure 2-7, pressing the Tab key in the Package Manager Console at any time opens an IntelliSense-like window showing the commands available. Once you are using a command, pressing the Tab key will display a list of options available for that command, as you can see in Figure 2-8.

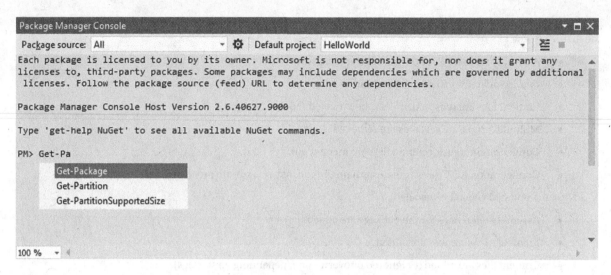

Figure 2-7. *List the available cmdlets in the Package Manager Console, using the Tab key for autocompletion*

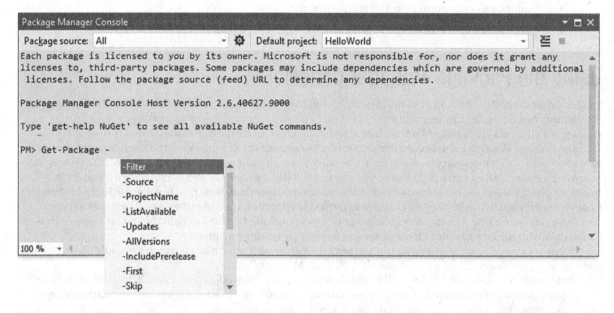

Figure 2-8. *List the available command switches for a given cmdlet, using the Tab key for autocompletion*

Once you are more familiar with the Package Manager Console, you'll see that the naming pattern used for these commands is so intuitive that you'll be able to perform all these actions spontaneously.

■ **Tip** The Package Manager Console also provides you with autocompletion when using the Tab key.

■ **Tip** You can always find out more information about the available commands and how to use them by executing the Get-Help cmdlet. To find out more about a specific command, you can type **Get-Help** followed by the name of the cmdlet—for example, **Get-Help Get-Package**.

Finding a Specific Version of a Package

There are several ways to find a package without using the Manage Packages dialog box. You can browse www.nuget.org for a package, you can use the command line, or you can use the Package Manager Console. Lazy as we are, we don't want to leave our Visual Studio IDE, so we won't use the command line or the NuGet Gallery. We'll cover those later in this book.

To find a package by using the Package Manager Console, you'll need to list the packages available matching your query. This is the purpose of the Get-Package cmdlet. By default, this cmdlet will show you the packages installed in your project. To query the package source, which is by default the NuGet Gallery, you'll have to add the -ListAvailable switch, as illustrated in Figure 2-9. Add a -Filter switch to the command to filter the results.

```
Package Manager Console                                                        ▾ ▢ ✕

Package source: All              ▾  ⚙  Default project: HelloWorld        ▾  ⟰ ▪
PM> Get-Package -ListAvailable -Filter "NewtonSoft.Json"

Id                              Version       Description/Release Notes
--                              -------       -------------------------
Bifrost.JSON                    1.0.0.8       Support for Newtonsoft JSON.net for Bifrost
EventStore.Serialization.Json   3.2.0.28      Additional serialization provider for EventStore...
FsRavenDbTools                  0.5.4         Help using RavenDB from F# (and Newtonsoft.Json)
Newtonsoft.Json.Glimpse         1.0.1         Debug JSON on the server with the Json.NET plugi...
Newtonsoft.Json                 5.0.6         Json.NET is a popular high-performance JSON fram...
Nancy.Serialization.JsonNet     0.18.0        Provides JSON (de)serialization support using Ne...
NanoMessageBus.Json.NET         2.0.39        Additional serialization provider for NanoMessag...
NGon.SST                        1.0.1         Fork of https://github.com/brooklynDev/NGon that...
Simple.Web.JsonNet              0.8.0.51524   Json content-type handling for Simple.Web using ...
SisoDb.JsonNet                  16.2.1        SisoDb is a schemaless document-oriented provide...


PM> |

100 %  ▾
```

Figure 2-9. *Getting a list of packages available on the NuGet Gallery matching a given filter*

By default, only the latest version of a package will be returned. If you want to list all versions of this package available on the package source, you can add the -AllVersions switch, as shown in Figure 2-10. Note that this will not yield prerelease packages.

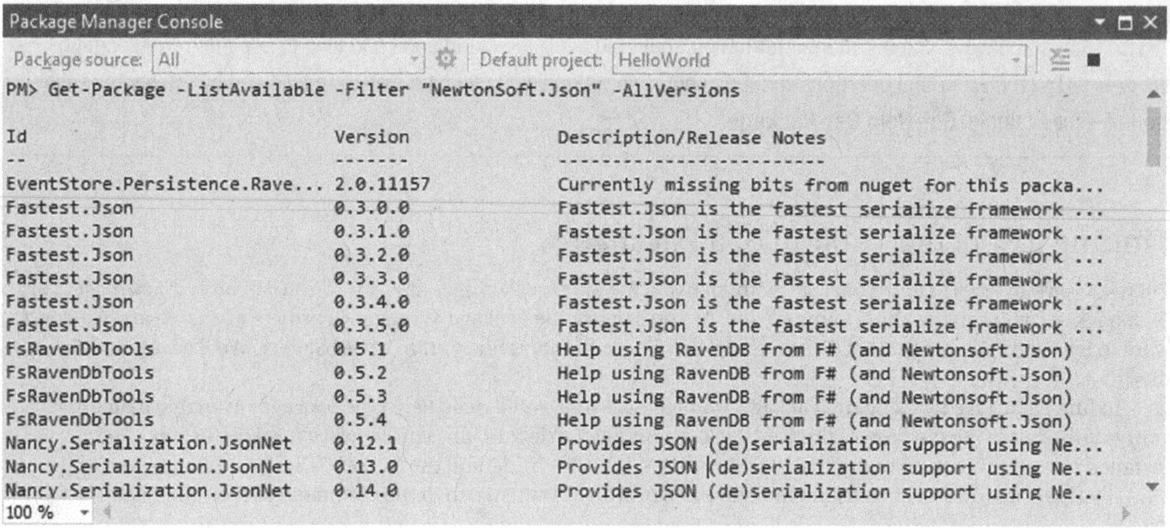

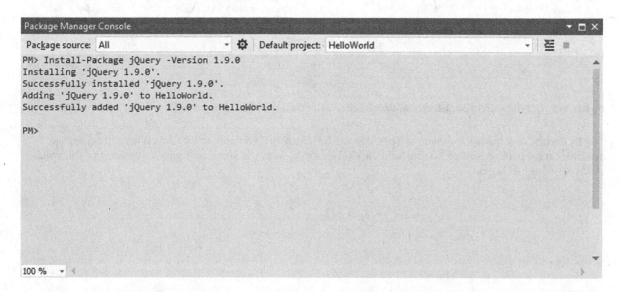

Figure 2-10. Getting a list of all available versions of a package matching a given filter

Installing a Specific Version of a Package

Once you have found the package you need, you'll have to install it. To install a package into a project using the Package Manager Console, you need to use the `Install-Package` cmdlet. To install a specific version of a package, you can simply add the `-Version` switch to the command. If a prerelease package is to be installed, include the `-Prerelease` switch to the `Install-Package` command. Straightforward, isn't it? The only thing left to do is to pick a project in the Default Project drop-down list to make sure the Package Manager Console targets the correct one.

You'll notice that the Package Manager Console will output the progress of the installation procedure. As Figure 2-11 illustrates, any required dependencies that need to be installed or updated will be taken care of.

Figure 2-11. Installing a specific version of a package by using the Package Manager Console

Uninstalling a Package

In the event you need or want to uninstall a package from a project, you can use the `Uninstall-Package` cmdlet. This command's default behavior is to rely on the default project selected in the drop-down list at the top of the Package Manager Console window. To uninstall a package from the default project, simply pass the package ID to the `Uninstall-Package` command, as shown in Figure 2-12. Notice that we did not specify any target project name.

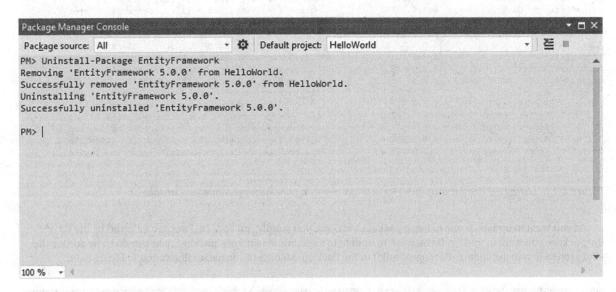

Figure 2-12. *Uninstalling a package from the default project by using the Package Manager Console*

Uninstalling a package can impact the other packages you reference in your project. NuGet will assist you by detecting these dependencies and inform you about any conflicts that might occur. For instance, if another package depends on the package you want to remove, the command will fail. This is a safety precaution and default behavior for this command. However, you can force the removal of a package by using the `-Force` switch, which will instruct NuGet to remove the package, even while another package depends on it.

Another useful switch to this command is the `-RemoveDependencies` option, which will make sure that not only the specified package will be uninstalled but also all unused dependencies of that package. Any dependency depended on by another package will be skipped. Appendix C gives an overview of the available switches.

Updating a Package to a Newer Version

At some point in time, you'll want to update one of your packages to a newer version. The Manage Packages dialog box will, by default, show you the latest available version of any updates that are available. The same can be accomplished by using the Package Manager Console, as shown in Figure 2-13.

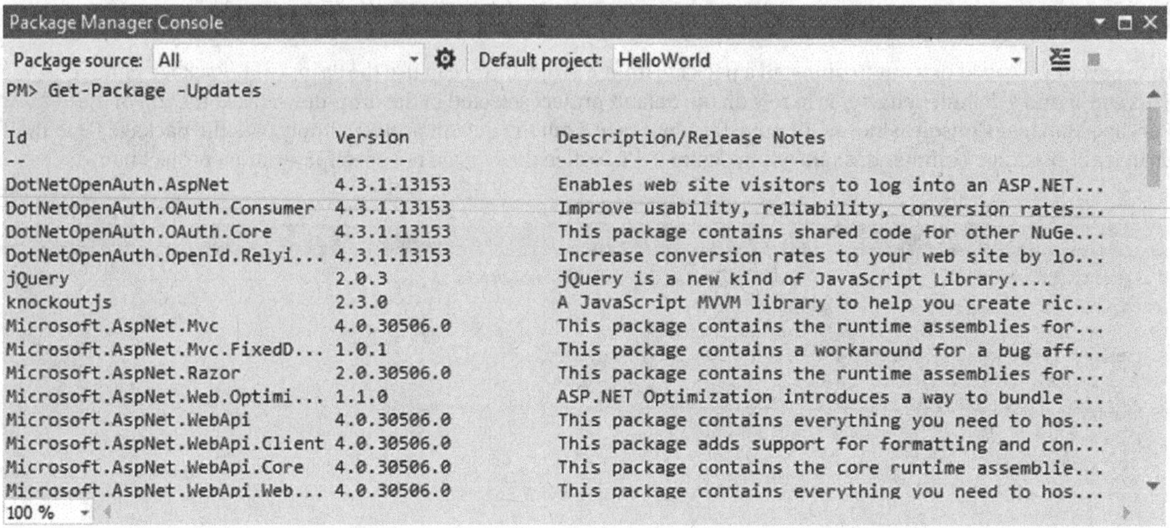

```
Package Manager Console                                                    ▾ □ ✕

Package source:  All              ▾ ⚙  Default project:  HelloWorld          ▾  ᠌  ■

PM> Get-Package -Updates

Id                              Version         Description/Release Notes
--                              -------         -------------------------
DotNetOpenAuth.AspNet           4.3.1.13153     Enables web site visitors to log into an ASP.NET...
DotNetOpenAuth.OAuth.Consumer   4.3.1.13153     Improve usability, reliability, conversion rates...
DotNetOpenAuth.OAuth.Core       4.3.1.13153     This package contains shared code for other NuGe...
DotNetOpenAuth.OpenId.Relyi...  4.3.1.13153     Increase conversion rates to your web site by lo...
jQuery                          2.0.3           jQuery is a new kind of JavaScript Library....
knockoutjs                      2.3.0           A JavaScript MVVM library to help you create ric...
Microsoft.AspNet.Mvc            4.0.30506.0     This package contains the runtime assemblies for...
Microsoft.AspNet.Mvc.FixedD...  1.0.1           This package contains a workaround for a bug aff...
Microsoft.AspNet.Razor          2.0.30506.0     This package contains the runtime assemblies for...
Microsoft.AspNet.Web.Optimi...  1.1.0           ASP.NET Optimization introduces a way to bundle ...
Microsoft.AspNet.WebApi         4.0.30506.0     This package contains everything you need to hos...
Microsoft.AspNet.WebApi.Client  4.0.30506.0     This package adds support for formatting and con...
Microsoft.AspNet.WebApi.Core    4.0.30506.0     This package contains the core runtime assemblie...
Microsoft.AspNet.WebApi.Web...  4.0.30506.0     This package contains everything you need to hos...
100 %  ▾ ◂
```

Figure 2-13. *Listing the available updates for a project by using the Package Manager Console*

If you want to update to one of these package versions, you simply run Update-Package followed by the ID of the package you want to update. If you want to update to a specific version of a package, you can do so by adding the -Version switch to the Update-Package cmdlet in the Package Manager Console, as illustrated in Figure 2-14.

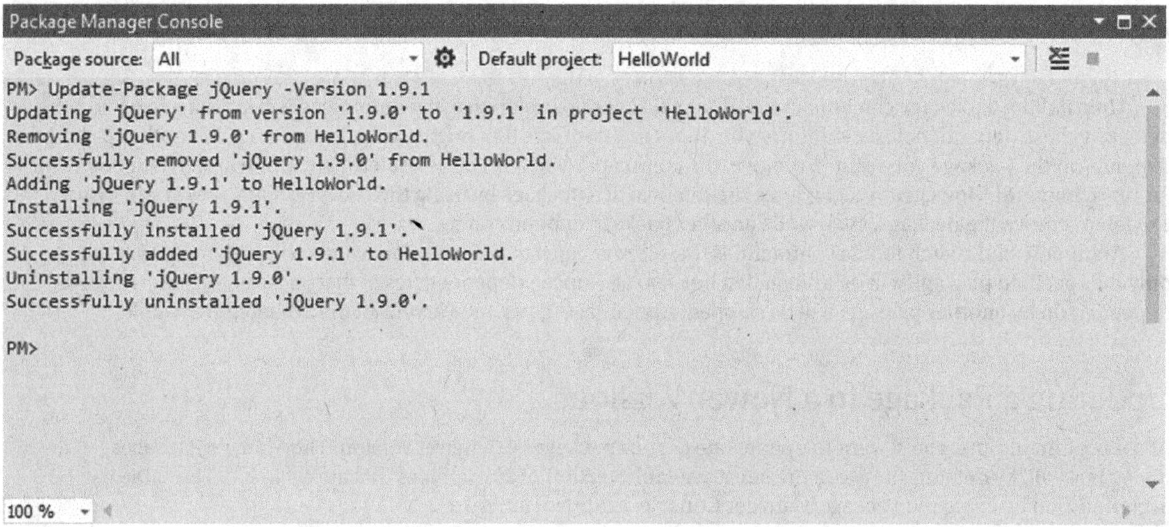

```
Package Manager Console                                                    ▾ □ ✕

Package source:  All              ▾ ⚙  Default project:  HelloWorld          ▾  ᠌  ■

PM> Update-Package jQuery -Version 1.9.1
Updating 'jQuery' from version '1.9.0' to '1.9.1' in project 'HelloWorld'.
Removing 'jQuery 1.9.0' from HelloWorld.
Successfully removed 'jQuery 1.9.0' from HelloWorld.
Adding 'jQuery 1.9.1' to HelloWorld.
Installing 'jQuery 1.9.1'.
Successfully installed 'jQuery 1.9.1'.
Successfully added 'jQuery 1.9.1' to HelloWorld.
Uninstalling 'jQuery 1.9.0'.
Successfully uninstalled 'jQuery 1.9.0'.

PM>




100 %  ▾ ◂
```

Figure 2-14. *Updating a package to a specific version by using the Package Manager Console*

By default, all dependencies that have an update available will be updated as well. By adding the -IgnoreDependencies switch, the update can be limited to just the current package. Also notice that we did not provide any target project for this command. This command targets all projects within the solution, unless you explicitly target a project by using the -ProjectName switch. The Default Project drop-down list at the top of the dialog box does not have any impact on the Update-Package cmdlet. Being aware of these defaults and caveats will allow you to make optimal use of the Package Manager Console. All available switches are explained in Appendix C of this book.

▪ **Tip** Did you know you can update all packages for an entire solution at once, with one simple command? That's exactly what the Update-Package statement will do by default if you don't add anything else to it!

Of course, some human intervention may be required to complete the update process of a NuGet package. Think about updating the references to the new jQuery script files in your HTML or a changed API. These are things that the producer of a package cannot anticipate, so no automation will be available for you to perform these custom steps.

Using the Package Manager Console Default Project

The Package Manager Console toolbar shows a drop-down in which a default project can be specified. It might sometimes seem a bit counterintuitive to have a default project selected when running a cmdlet in the Package Manager Console. We have summarized which cmdlets use the default project in Table 2-2.

Table 2-2. *Using the Default Project in the Package Manager Console*

Cmdlet	Uses the Default Project?
Get-Package	Yes, except when using the -ListAvailable switch
Install-Package	Yes
Update-Package	No
Uninstall-Package	Yes

Reinstalling Packages

The Package Manager Console also allows you to easily reinstall packages. To do so you should make use of the -Reinstall switch that comes with the Update-Package cmdlet. The following command reinstalls the Newtonsoft.Json package:

```
Update-Package Newtonsoft.Json -Reinstall
```

This is a very simple command that makes it super easy to reinstall a certain package. A common use case for this scenario is when you want to retarget your projects to another version of the .NET Framework. Another situation where package reinstallation is useful is during testing of packages as part of a good development workflow, as explained in Chapter 7.

Although this is very straightforward, you have to be very careful and consider the following effects of this command:

- You might be attempting to reinstall a package (or an indirect package dependency) which has no support for the new framework or platform you are targeting.

- Package version constraints only apply on direct package dependencies. This means that when you reinstall a package, one or more of its dependencies can be a newer version than before. To avoid this you can make use of the -IgnoreDependencies switch.

More information about the caveats of reinstalling packages can also be found in the NuGet documentation at http://docs.nuget.org/docs/workflows/reinstalling-packages.

Using the NuGet Command Line

So far, you didn't need to leave the Visual Studio IDE for any operation you wanted to perform using NuGet. Actually, you'll rarely have to do that at all! The NuGet Visual Studio extension provides a great integrated experience, one that many developers will quickly be able to adopt. "Then why is there a need for a command line?" you ask. There are a couple of reasons for using it.

Many people use the NuGet command line for grabbing packages directly from a NuGet feed and creating a local copy of them on their system. The package is not installed into a project but "just downloaded" instead. We personally use it for all kinds of tasks, such as creating packages or fetching a list of available packages from a feed.

There are other scenarios where you will fall back on the NuGet command line, however. One of them is continuous integration. Typically, a build environment contains the bare minimum to be able to build your software. NuGet could be one of those tools that will enable your build servers to consume and produce NuGet packages as part of automated builds. To be able to do so, you'll need a simple tool that allows you to interact with NuGet repositories and packages, preferably a command line. That's exactly what the NuGet command line is for. We'll dive deeper into this topic in Chapter 7.

All of the operations supported by the NuGet cmdlets in the Package Manager Console are also available in the NuGet command line, but note that the NuGet command line can never update your project file. Running a package update by using the command line will fetch the latest version from the NuGet feed and store it on disk, but it will not update the package in a project.

To work with the NuGet command line, you should open a command prompt in Windows. You can do this in many different ways:

- Press the Windows key+R, type cmd, and press Enter. Navigate to the folder where you stored nuget.exe, and interact with it. If you manually downloaded nuget.exe from the Internet, do not forget to unblock it by right-clicking the file and selecting Properties ➤ Security ➤ Unblock.

- On Windows 7 and 8, you can browse to nuget.exe by using Windows Explorer. Shift+right-click the folder containing nuget.exe, and select Open Command Window Here.

The NuGet command-line tool comes with a built-in help function: type **nuget help** to get a list of available commands, as illustrated in Figure 2-15. If you want help about a specific command (for example, the install command), you simply execute nuget help install. Another way to do so is by executing nuget install -help.

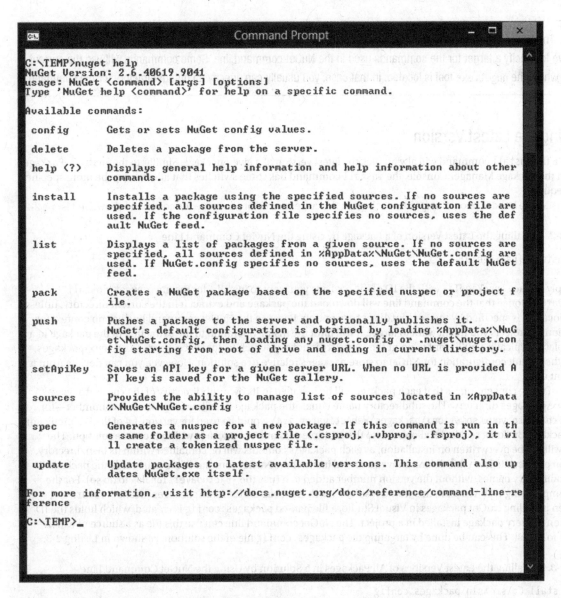

```
C:\TEMP>nuget help
NuGet Version: 2.6.40619.9041
usage: NuGet <command> [args] [options]
Type 'NuGet help <command>' for help on a specific command.

Available commands:

 config      Gets or sets NuGet config values.

 delete      Deletes a package from the server.

 help (?)    Displays general help information and help information about other
             commands.

 install     Installs a package using the specified sources. If no sources are
             specified, all sources defined in the NuGet configuration file are
             used. If the configuration file specifies no sources, uses the def
             ault NuGet feed.

 list        Displays a list of packages from a given source. If no sources are
             specified, all sources defined in %AppData%\NuGet\NuGet.config are
             used. If NuGet.config specifies no sources, uses the default NuGet
             feed.

 pack        Creates a NuGet package based on the specified nuspec or project f
             ile.

 push        Pushes a package to the server and optionally publishes it.
             NuGet's default configuration is obtained by loading %AppData%\NuG
             et\NuGet.config, then loading any nuget.config or .nuget\nuget.con
             fig starting from root of drive and ending in current directory.

 setApiKey   Saves an API key for a given server URL. When no URL is provided A
             PI key is saved for the NuGet gallery.

 sources     Provides the ability to manage list of sources located in %AppData
             %\NuGet\NuGet.config

 spec        Generates a nuspec for a new package. If this command is run in th
             e same folder as a project file (.csproj, .vbproj, .fsproj), it wi
             ll create a tokenized nuspec file.

 update      Update packages to latest available versions. This command also up
             dates NuGet.exe itself.

For more information, visit http://docs.nuget.org/docs/reference/command-line-re
ference

C:\TEMP>_
```

Figure 2-15. Getting help from the NuGet command-line tool

Installing a Package

To install a package by using the NuGet command line, you'll have to run the install command, which can be used in two different ways. You can specify a package source or multiple package sources to be used, or you can specify no package source, in which case the NuGet command line will fall back on using the nuget.config file in your local application data folder. If the configuration doesn't specify any package sources, it will fall back to a hard-coded NuGet feed URL.

> ■ **Note** The NuGet command line is unaware of any context contrary to the NuGet Visual Studio extensions. As such, you'll have to specify a target for the commands used in the NuGet command line. Some commands will use the current directory where the `nuget.exe` tool is located: in that case, you usually can specify an output directory for the command.

Installing the Latest Version

By default, the `install` command will always pick the latest version of a given package. Similar to the `Install-Package` cmdlet in the Package Manager Console, the `install` command has some switches that allow you to be more specific in your request.

To install the latest version of a specific package in the current directory, execute the command shown in Listing 2-2.

Listing 2-2. Installing the Latest Version of a Package by Using the NuGet Command Line

```
nuget install {packageId}
```

Simply replace {packageId} with the ID of the package you want to install—for instance, `nuget install WebActivator`. Notice that the command line will download the package and extract it in the current directory, unless another location is specified by the -outputdirectory option. Because the NuGet command line has no context for the solution or projects you might want to target, it will limit the install operation to the extraction of the package in a specific place. Typically, you'll want to point the -outputdirectory switch to <path to your solution>\packages, which is the default configuration for NuGet to store packages relative to a solution. However, you can deviate from it if you want to.

One of those conventions is that each package will be installed in its own subdirectory of the <path to your solution>\packages directory. The subdirectory name equals the package ID followed by its version number—for instance, <path to your solution>\packages\WebActivator.1.4\ would be used for version 1.4 of the WebActivator NuGet package. By doing so, NuGet allows you to use multiple versions of a package within the same solution. The binaries will not be overwritten on installation, as each package's contents will be contained within its own directory. Again, you can deviate from this default convention and instruct the NuGet command line to use only the package ID for its subdirectory names, without the version number added to it (use the -ExcludeVersion flag to do so). For the given example using WebActivator, this would result in <path to your solution>\packages\WebActivator.

When installing NuGet packages in Visual Studio, a file named `packages.config` is created, which holds the ID and version of every package installed in a project. The NuGet command line can use this file as a source of which packages to install. This can be done by targeting the `packages.config` file of the solution, as shown in Listing 2-3.

Listing 2-3. Installing the Latest Versions of All Packages in a Solution by Using the NuGet Command Line

```
nuget install C:\src\sln\packages.config
```

You need to specify the full absolute path to the `packages.config` file, as shown in Listing 2-3. If the path contains spaces, you'll have to enclose it in quotes—for example, `nuget install "C:\src\sln dir\packages.config"`. Working with `packages.config` from the command line is a technique used by Continuous Integration systems to perform NuGet package restore, explained in Chapter 6.

Installing a Specific Version

You may want to install a specific version of a package. This can be done by adding the `-version` switch and the version number in the command, as shown in Listing 2-4. This allows you to install a specific version of a package from the command line.

Listing 2-4. Installing a Specific Version of a Package by Using the NuGet Command Line

```
nuget install {packageId} -version {packageVersion}
```

For example, `nuget install -version jQuery 2.0.0` will download the jQuery package version 2.0.0 to your system. Of course, all other command options remain valid for this scenario as well. Make sure to include the `-prerelease` switch when installing prerelease packages.

Updating a Package

The NuGet command line allows you to update packages to a newer version. You can do so by using the `update` command (see Listing 2-5 and Listing 2-6).

Listing 2-5. Updating All Packages in a Project to the Latest Versions by Using the NuGet Command Line

```
nuget update packages.config
```

Listing 2-6. Updating All Packages in a Solution to the Latest Versions by Using the NuGet Command Line

```
nuget update solution.sln
```

The `update` command has various options, allowing multiple update scenarios. For example, you can specify a list of package sources to be used by using the `-source` switch, and you can specify a list of package IDs to update by using the `-id` switch.

You can also instruct NuGet to consider only safe packages, by using the `-safe` flag. When you set this flag, NuGet will look for the highest available version of the package within the same major and minor version of the already installed package.

If for some reason you want to deviate from the default `Packages` folder as the package repository path for your solution, you can specify another one by using the `-repositorypath` option.

■ **Tip** The `update` command in the NuGet command line has another option that allows you to update the NuGet command line itself. To update the NuGet command line, execute `nuget update -self`.

Uninstalling a Package

The NuGet command line does not support uninstalling a package from a solution or project, because it doesn't touch the Visual Studio solution or projects at all. Because the `install` command really just downloads and extracts the NuGet package archive, uninstalling a package can be done by just deleting the folder where the package was extracted.

Managing Packages in a Solution

So far, we've shown you how you can add, update, and remove packages at the project level. In a lot of software development projects, multiple projects share the same dependencies. For example, multiple projects in a solution can have a dependency on Microsoft's Entity Framework (which is also on NuGet with package ID EntityFramework).

Both the NuGet Visual Studio extension and the Package Manager Console support managing and updating packages across project boundaries. This enables you to have a consistent set of package dependencies in your solution, all having the same version and assemblies. Imagine having to update references manually in multiple projects!

Using a large Visual Studio solution, this section will show you how to install, update, and uninstall packages in multiple projects at once. As with installing NuGet packages at the project level, you'll find that right-clicking your solution in Visual Studio followed by clicking Manage NuGet Packages for Solution will allow you to perform some magic.

Installing Packages in Multiple Projects

In this section, we will add log4net, a logging framework, to some projects that require logging, and we'll use both the NuGet Visual Studio extension and the Package Manager Console to do so.

Once you select a set of projects and the NuGet package to install, NuGet will download the selected package from its repository and install it into the selected projects. The same package installation steps will happen for each selected project:

1. The latest version of the selected NuGet package is downloaded from the Internet.

2. The required assemblies and other files are added to a folder under the solution root.

3. Assemblies in a NuGet package are referenced in all selected projects.

4. Optionally, configuration files and source files are added or transformed. This depends on the actual package contents.

Using the NuGet Visual Studio Extension

Right-click your solution in Visual Studio and click Manage NuGet Packages. Notice that the exact same Manage NuGet Packages dialog box is displayed as when you wanted to add a package reference to a single project. Figure 2-16 shows you what this screen looks like.

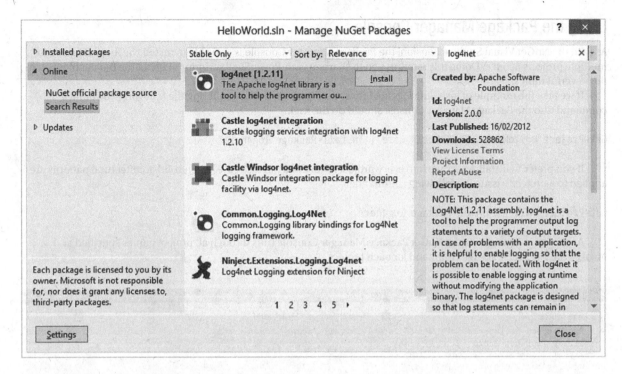

Figure 2-16. *Searching for the log4net NuGet package*

By now, you should be familiar enough with the Manage NuGet Packages dialog box to search for the package log4net. If not, Figure 2-16 shows you what to look for. When you find the package, click the Install button next to it. Notice that, before the package is actually downloaded and installed, the NuGet Visual Studio extension opens a dialog box asking which projects to install the package to (see Figure 2-17). Select the projects to install log4net to and then click the OK button.

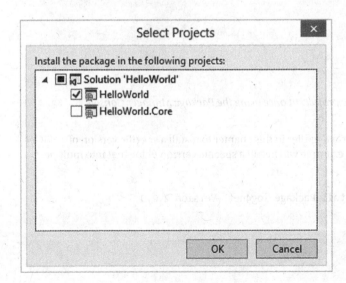

Figure 2-17. *The Select Projects dialog box when installing a NuGet package to multiple projects at once*

Using the Package Manager Console

As with the NuGet Visual Studio extension, the Package Manager Console is also able to install NuGet packages into multiple projects at once. Doing this requires you to sharpen your PowerShell scripting skills a little but enables you to do powerful things.

If we take the example of installing log4net into several projects at once, entering the following PowerShell command into the Package Manager Console should do the trick:

```
Get-Project HelloWorld, HelloWorld.Core | Install-Package log4net
```

If you prefer to install a package into every project (which is a rare use case, when solid architectural patterns are applied to a project!), issue the following command:

```
Get-Project -All | Install-Package log4net
```

As shown in Figure 2-18, the NuGet Package Manager Console runs through all project names specified and invokes the Install-Package command for each project.

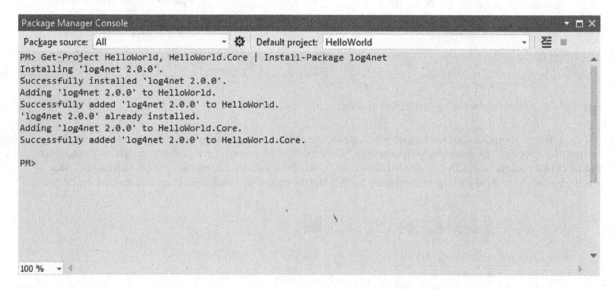

Figure 2-18. *Installing a NuGet package into multiple projects at once using the Package Manager Console*

Of course, you can also apply the commands learned earlier in this chapter to install a specific version of a NuGet package into multiple projects at once. The following example will install a specific version of log4net into multiple projects simultaneously:

```
Get-Project HelloWorld, HelloWorld.Core | Install-Package log4net -Version 2.0.0
```

■ **Note**   The PowerShell command used actually consists of two commands. Get-Project retrieves a reference to one or more Visual Studio projects specified as a parameter. Using the pipe symbol (|) tells PowerShell to loop the selection of projects and invoke the Install-Package command for every project. This very powerful concept enables you to chain multiple commands to do a lot of work, using just a few keystrokes. This power is probably also the reason a lot of developers prefer the Package Manager Console over the NuGet Visual Studio extension.

Uninstalling Packages from Multiple Projects

In the event a package is obsolete, no longer supported by its author, or simply no longer needed in a project, it's perfectly possible to uninstall a package from several or all projects in a solution at once. Again, both the NuGet Visual Studio extension and the Package Manager Console support this. As with single-project package uninstalls, solution-wide package uninstalls will also remove any dependencies that are no longer needed and will try to restore your projects to a state where no, or close to no, traces of the package are left behind.

Using the NuGet Visual Studio Extension

Right-click your solution in Visual Studio and click Manage NuGet Packages for Solution. Here too, the exact same Manage NuGet Packages dialog box is displayed as when uninstalling a package from a single project (see Figure 2-19).

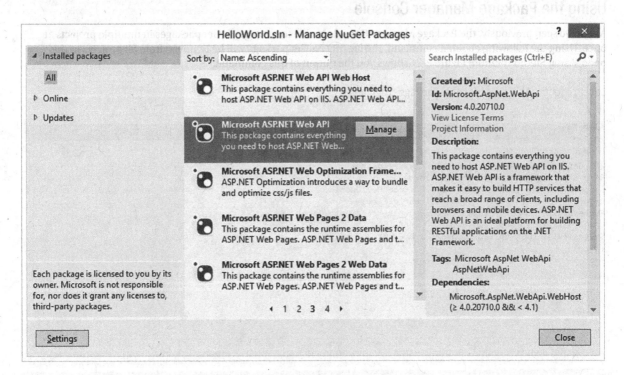

Figure 2-19. *Uninstalling NuGet Packages on a solution level*

Once you select a package, the Manage button becomes visible. After clicking this button, you can deselect the projects from which a NuGet package should be removed, as can be seen in Figure 2-20.

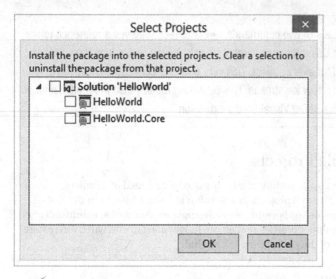

Figure 2-20. *Uninstalling a NuGet package from multiple projects in a solution*

Using the Package Manager Console

As you've seen previously, the Package Manager Console is able to manage NuGet packages in multiple projects at once. Using the following chained command, the log4net NuGet package will be removed from all projects in the open Visual Studio solution; Figure 2-21 shows you the output of this command:

```
Get-Project -All | Uninstall-Package log4net
```

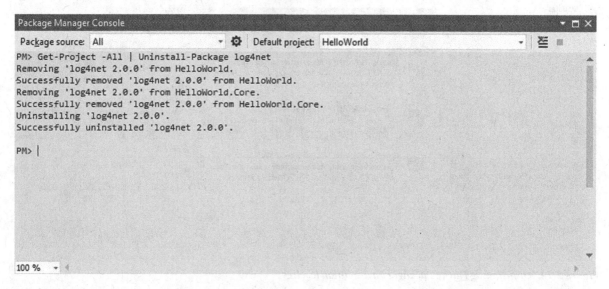

Figure 2-21. *The result of uninstalling a NuGet package from all projects in a solution through the Package Manager Console*

Of course, you can also apply the commands learned earlier in this chapter to remove packages from only a few projects at once instead of removing them from all projects.

Updating Packages in Multiple Projects

Updating packages in a solution to their latest versions can be done using both the NuGet Visual Studio extension and the Package Manager Console. As with single-project updates, solution-wide updates also respect dependencies on other packages and may invoke additional downloads to ensure all package dependencies are met.

Using the NuGet Visual Studio Extension

Right-click your solution in Visual Studio and click Manage NuGet Packages. After clicking the Updates pane, notice the exact same Manage NuGet Packages dialog box that is displayed when you want to update a package reference in a single project. Instead of showing updates for a single project, this dialog box displays a list of all packages used in a solution that have an updated version available. Figure 2-22 shows you what this screen looks like.

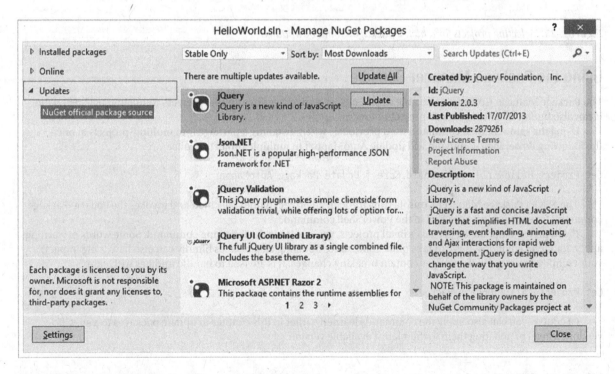

Figure 2-22. *Updating NuGet Packages on a solution level*

An Update All button is available that will update all packages at once. Note that this operation may take a while and potentially can break your solution if a package contains breaking changes and the package author did not version the package correctly.

Once you select a package to update and click its Update button, the Select Projects dialog box is presented (see Figure 2-23). It is important to note that the NuGet Visual Studio extension will preselect all projects that currently have the old version of the selected NuGet package installed. If you wish to selectively update projects, this dialog box allows you to cherry-pick the projects in which the selected NuGet package should be updated.

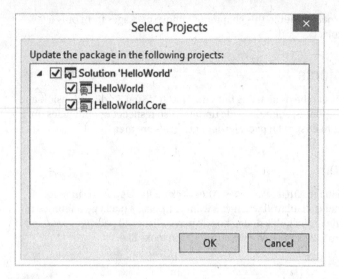

Figure 2-23. *Selecting projects for which a package should be updated*

Using the Package Manager Console

The Package Manager Console is also able to update NuGet packages in multiple projects simultaneously. Then too, it can also update all packages in all projects at once.

Using the same chained command used previously when installing a package into multiple projects at once, the following PowerShell command will update AutoMapper in multiple projects at once:

```
Get-Project HelloWorld, HelloWorld.Core | Update-Package AutoMapper
```

The NuGet Package Manager Console runs through all project names specified and invokes the `Update-Package` command for each project specified in the PowerShell command.

If you prefer to update all packages in all projects, you can issue the following command. Some words of warning apply: for larger solutions, this can take quite some time. Updating all packages blindly can also have a big impact: your compilation may fail if packages contain breaking changes. It is advised to handle updates with care.

```
Get-Project -All | Update-Package
```

Of course, you can also apply the commands learned earlier in this chapter to update packages to a specific version instead of updating them to their latest available version.

Visualizing Package Dependencies by Using the Package Visualizer

In large projects, keeping track of all external package dependencies used in a solution can be difficult. Using the Package Visualizer that ships with the NuGet Visual Studio extension, a graphical diagram of all projects in a solution and their package dependencies can be generated.

The Package Visualizer will be mainly used by technical project leads or architects to analyze which packages are referenced by which project and how a solution is structured.

■ **Note** The Package Visualizer depends on Directed Graph Markup Language (DGML) support in Visual Studio. Anyone with Visual Studio Premium (or higher) can view DGML diagrams. Unfortunately, you'll require someone using Visual Studio Ultimate to create and save this diagram for you.

Open a Visual Studio project that contains references to NuGet packages, and select Tools ➤ Library Package Manager ➤ Package Visualizer, as shown in Figure 2-24. After you click this menu option, a `Packages.dgml` file will be added to your solution.

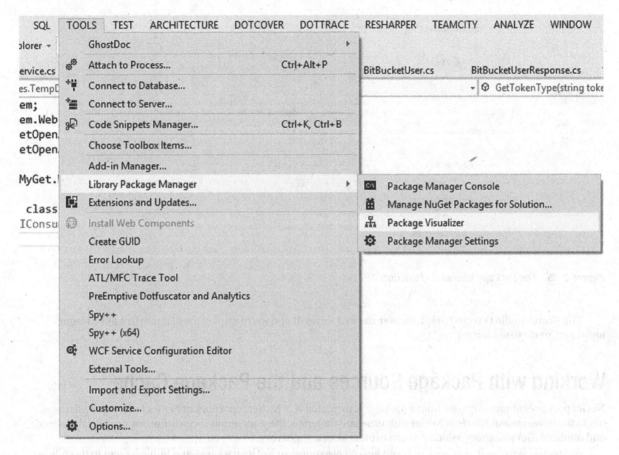

Figure 2-24. *Finding the Package Visualizer menu option in Visual Studio*

The `Packages.dgml` file automatically opens while generating the diagram, and Visual Studio opens a diagram that shows all projects in your solution on the left and maps all package dependencies (and their dependencies). Figure 2-25 shows an example of a project that depends on a large number of NuGet packages.

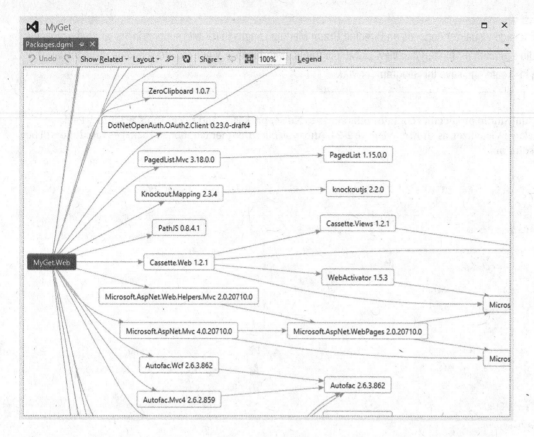

Figure 2-25. *The Package Visualizer in action*

The Visual Studio Directed Graph toolbar shows a series of options to display the diagram in a left-to-right, top-down, or clustered format.

Working with Package Sources and the Package Cache

NuGet packages always originate from a package source, that is, a NuGet repository or NuGet feed. Since Microsoft backs the development efforts of NuGet with time and materials, these materials include hosting an official, default, and public NuGet repository, which you can explore at www.nuget.org.

As you will see later in this book, you can also create your own NuGet packages and publish them to this official repository. What if you want to distribute your private, corporate, in-house developed base framework to just your development team, and not the entire world of .NET developers? We will cover how you can host your own, private NuGet repository later in this book as well.

Managing Package Sources

By default, the NuGet repository at `http://nuget.org/api/v2` will be registered as the NuGet Official Package Source" in the NuGet Visual Studio extension. Open the Visual Studio Tools ➤ Library Package Manager ➤ Package Manager Settings menu, and click the Package Sources item to register additional repositories or to replace the default, public repository with a repository that contains only those packages that you want to use in your projects. Figure 2-26 shows you the dialog box in which you can register additional package sources.

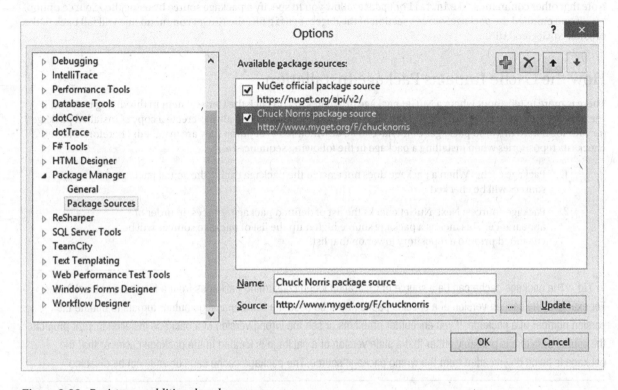

Figure 2-26. *Register an additional package source*

To order the package sources in a specific way, you can select a package source from the list and play with the Move Up and Move Down buttons. When searching for a package, NuGet will respect the order of the package sources as defined here, meaning the first one in the list will be queried first, then the second one, and so on.

■ **Note** While package sources can be added manually, some community members have proposed a Package Source Discovery protocol, described at `https://github.com/myget/PackageSourceDiscovery`. Package Source Discovery, or PSD, provides an easier way for discovering packages related to an individual or organization, by discovering feed information from their web site URL. As an example, you can run the following in the Package Manager Console and install all Xavier's feeds: `Install-Package DiscoverPackageSourcesDiscover-PackageSources -Url "http://www.myget.org/gallery"`.

Package sources are defined in the `nuget.config` file, which can be found in your local application data folder (%AppData%\NuGet\nuget.config). More on the NuGet configuration file(s) can be found in Appendix D. The NuGet Visual Studio extension, the Package Manager Console, and the command line make use of this file to determine where a package can originate from. Some tools, like the NuGet Visual Studio extension, offer a graphical user interface for managing the package sources listed in this file, as we've just seen. The NuGet command line also has a command for managing package sources: the `sources` command. Let's add a MyGet feed as a package source: `nuget sources add -Name GoogleAnalyticsTracker -Source https://www.myget.org/F/googleanalyticstracker`. Note that other commands, like `install` or `update`, allow you to specify a package source by using the `-Source` option.

If you emptied the `packageSources` section of the `nuget.config` file, the NuGet command line will fall back to the original NuGet feed URL.

How the Cache Impacts Package Installation

There is more to tell about where a NuGet package originates. If you click the General item in this dialog box, you'll see an entry named Package Cache. The NuGet Visual Studio extension will always create a copy of installed packages on your local hard drive, so packages don't have to be downloaded every time they are installed. Therefore, NuGet checks its repositories when installing a package in the following sequence:

1. Package cache: When a package does not exist in the package cache, the actual package sources will be checked.

2. Package sources: Next, NuGet checks the list of defined package sources, in order of appearance. This means a package source higher up the list of package sources will be consulted prior to a repository lower on that list.

■ **Tip**   The package cache can be a source of frustration when consuming packages from a file share or local folder. For example, the cached version of a specific package will be used if a NuGet package author forgets to update the version number of a package. If you encounter problems or see the wrong version of a package installed in your projects, the source of failure is probably either that a stale version of a package is located in the package cache or that the package is being downloaded from the wrong package source. The package cache can currently not be disabled.

Authenticating Package Sources

Whichever NuGet client you're using, whether the NuGet command line or from within Visual Studio, some package sources require you to provide some kind of authentication before you can access them.

The `nuget.org` feed doesn't require authentication for any operation that is consuming packages. The feed is by definition public and read-only at this point. Publishing packages will require an API key, but more about that in Chapter 4.

MyGet, which will be discussed in Chapter 9, supports the concept of private feeds, which additionally enforce basic authentication for read operations. Whenever you need to authenticate while running an operation against a feed that has basic authentication enabled, the NuGet command line will prompt you for your username and password.

From within Visual Studio, there is currently no way to store these credentials in the `nuget.config` file. The NuGet command line, on the other hand, does support storing feed credentials in the `nuget.config`, albeit using machine-specific encryption. The code snippet in Listing 2-7 illustrates how you can store your username and password for a secured feed, encrypted in your global `nuget.config` file.

Listing 2-7. Storing Feed and Encrypted Feed Credentials in the Global nuget.config File

```
nuget sources add -name {name} -source {feedUrl}
nuget sources update -Name {name} -User {username} -pass {password}
```

Because the encryption is machine-specific, this means you can't commit this `nuget.config` file containing your encrypted credentials and expect it to work on another machine. For that, you'll have to make use of the cleartext password feature, allowing you to store your password in a nonencrypted (and thus readable!) format. You can target a solution-specific `nuget.config` with the command from Listing 2-8 and add the file to your version control system. Note that by doing so, you are sharing your feed's password with anyone who has access to the sources!

Listing 2-8. Storing Feed Credentials in Cleartext in a Local nuget.config File

```
nuget.exe sources add –Name {name} -User {username} -Password {password} -ConfigFile
nuget.config -StorePasswordInClearText
```

Also, nothing prevents you from creating your own preconfigured PowerShell cmdlets for use in the Package Manager Console, or just from within PowerShell itself.

Choosing Stable vs. Prerelease Versions

In general, when installing NuGet packages, we want the latest *stable* release of those packages. For some scenarios, we want to be able to grab the latest prerelease version of a package. For example, a specific hotfix or much-needed new feature of a library may be in a prerelease package.

The NuGet ecosystem defines stable packages as packages that are considered stable by the package author. Prerelease packages typically are considered bug-prone and should be handled with caution! All NuGet tools support installing, updating, and uninstalling stable and prerelease packages.

Distinguishing between stable and prerelease packages is done based on the Semantic Versioning specification found at `www.semver.org`. In short, *semantic versioning*, or *SemVer*, is a convention for versioning software in which the version number has a meaning attached to it. In short, version numbers will always look like `major.minor.patch-prerelease`—for example, `2.1.0-nightly`. The major version describes breaking API changes; the minor version describes new features while retaining backward compatibility; and the patch number describes internal changes or bug fixes that do not affect the public API at all. By appending a string to the patch number, prefixed with a dash (`-`), we can denote a prerelease version. Table 2-3 contains some versioning examples.

Table 2-3. *Example Version Numbers in Semantic Versioning*

Version	Stability
1.0.0	Stable
1.0.1	Stable, containing bug fixes or internal changes
1.1.0-alpha	Prerelease, alpha version of a new feature
1.1.0-beta	Prerelease, beta version of a new feature
1.1.0	Stable, containing a new feature
2.0.0	Stable, breaking public API changes since previous version

Note that the versions in Table 2=3 are ordered from lowest to highest and that prerelease tags are ordered alphabetically (technically, in lexicographic ASCII sort order). We will cover semantic versioning, and especially prerelease versioning, in more detail in Chapter 3.

Summary

In this chapter, we covered the basics of consuming NuGet packages. We showed you how you can consume NuGet packages in Visual Studio by using different options, like the NuGet Visual Studio extension and the Package Manager Console.

You learned how to perform basic operations by using the NuGet command line and how package sources can be configured. We also explained how you can install a specific version of a package.

We explored additional options for installing, updating, and uninstalling NuGet packages in your projects and how you can manage package references in multiple projects at once.

We have seen where packages originate from. Package sources can be added and multiple NuGet feeds can be consumed by all NuGet clients.

Finally, we demonstrated how you can analyze packages installed into a project and how they relate to your project and to each other, so you can quickly analyze interdependencies in a project.

CHAPTER 3

■ ■ ■

Authoring Packages

In Part 1 of this book, we introduced you to the concept of package management and how NuGet can help you when building software for the .NET Framework. We also discussed how you can take immediate benefit from using NuGet by consuming packages in your projects. This chapter will change perspective and put you on the producer side of the package management flow.

Before we dive into how to create NuGet packages by using the different tools available, we'll introduce you to some conventions and semantics that need to be respected by you, as a NuGet package producer, and as a result also by the packages you will be producing. Once you become familiar with these basic conventions and how a well-designed NuGet package looks, we'll guide you through the process of actually creating those packages by using both the NuGet command line and the Package Manager Console. We will take various approaches to creating a package, starting from a convention-based working directory, and moving on to the NuGet manifest, Visual Studio projects, and compiled assemblies.

Finally, before publishing packages in the next chapter, we will show you how you can easily test your packages locally. Following the motto "eat your own dog food," you will consume your own packages and see if they work as expected.

Understanding Package Definition Strategies

NuGet uses a convention-over-configuration approach. These conventions are rather simple and easy to remember, but deserve special attention before we start creating our first packages. Many of these conventions will be described throughout this book as we dive deeper into more-advanced topics, but you need to be aware of one set of conventions before creating your first NuGet package. These are defined in the NuGet package manifest, also known as a nuspec file.

The NuGet specification (nuspec) file is the one that describes the contents and the metadata of your package. It is included in each NuGet package, or nupkg file, and it is also the file you'll need to create the actual package. In short, before you can create a package, you'll need to describe it.

■ **Note** *Convention over configuration*, also known as *coding by convention*, is a design paradigm that aims to decrease the number of decisions, and as such configurations, a developer needs to make. This results in increased simplicity without loss of flexibility.

Besides this package manifest, there's a second, more implicit package convention you need to take into account: the structure of a NuGet package. A NuGet package can contain different sorts of content, each having a different purpose. To indicate this, the NuGet Package Manager does not force you into providing an exhaustive settings file, or any other type of configuration, for that matter. Instead, you will be describing your content by the way you structure your packages using folders, which are named using a simple set of conventions.

Next to package content/metadata and structure, a third convention should be taken into account: package versioning. Of all package conventions, this is probably the most important one because in package management, everything breaks or stands with proper package versioning. And this, again, is the responsibility of the package producer.

No need to worry; these conventions will feel very natural, and the NuGet Package Explorer will greatly assist you in setting up a correct NuGet package structure until you're ready to take matters into own hands and play with the underlying eXtensible Markup Language (XML).

Creating a Simple Package Manifest

All package meta-information is to be found in a package manifest, the nuspec file. This file provides information about the package's version, dependencies, contents, license, creators, and so on. The NuGet Package Manager uses this kind of information to automate dependency management in a smart way. Without exposing such critical information, automatically fetching any dependencies or informing you about available updates would be impossible.

The manifest contains all metadata of a given NuGet package. It informs NuGet where to find the contents, what it is supposed to do with them, and what extra steps should be triggered during a package's initialization, installation, or uninstall process. A NuGet package specification describes both its content and metadata in a predefined XML format. Because of the importance of these two aspects of package metadata, we'll handle both the pure metadata itself and the package contents as two separate topics.

The easiest way to create a nuspec manifest file is by using the NuGet Package Explorer. When using the NuGet Package Explorer to create the nuspec file, you'll notice that some defaults will be set, even when you didn't explicitly specify their values. The other way to create a nuspec file is simply by creating your own XML file that adheres to the nuspec.xsd format. The default nuspec file that the NuGet Package Explorer produces looks like Listing 3-1.

Listing 3-1. *The Default NuGet Manifest File Created Using NuGet Package Explorer*

```xml
<?xml version="1.0" encoding="utf-8"?>
<package xmlns="http://schemas.microsoft.com/packaging/2010/07/nuspec.xsd">
  <metadata>
    <id>MyPackage</id>
    <version>1.0.0</version>
    <title />
    <authors>Xavier Decoster</authors>
    <owners />
    <requireLicenseAcceptance>false</requireLicenseAcceptance>
    <description>My package description.</description>
  </metadata>
  <files />
</package>
```

To create a nuspec manifest, you could also use the NuGet command-line tool. Simply run the following command to create a default nuspec file in the current directory of the console prompt:

```
nuget spec
```

The default nuspec file created by the NuGet command line is slightly different from the one that NuGet Package Explorer will create, but both just serve as examples and need to be edited to suit your needs anyway. In short, it doesn't matter which one you start from. As you'll find out with NuGet in general, there's a lot of room for personal preferences, so use it the way you like most. In Listing 3-2, you'll find the default nuspec file created by the NuGet command line.

Listing 3-2. *The Default NuGet Manifest File Created Using the NuGet Command Line*

```xml
<?xml version="1.0"?>
<package>
  <metadata>
    <id>Package</id>
    <version>1.0.0</version>
    <authors>Xavier Decoster</authors>
    <owners>Xavier Decoster</owners>
    <licenseUrl>http://LICENSE_URL_HERE_OR_DELETE_THIS_LINE</licenseUrl>
    <projectUrl>http://PROJECT_URL_HERE_OR_DELETE_THIS_LINE</projectUrl>
    <iconUrl>http://ICON_URL_HERE_OR_DELETE_THIS_LINE</iconUrl>
    <requireLicenseAcceptance>false</requireLicenseAcceptance>
    <description>Package description</description>
    <releaseNotes>Summary of changes made in this release of the package.</releaseNotes>
    <copyright>Copyright 2013</copyright>
    <tags>Tag1 Tag2</tags>
    <dependencies>
      <dependency id="SampleDependency" version="1.0" />
    </dependencies>
  </metadata>
</package>
```

The preceding nuspec file could be considered a sample, guiding you in what metadata you preferably should provide with your packages. That's OK, especially for open source projects that will end up on the public NuGet.org gallery. For enterprise use, you'll probably end up with your own default XML template anyway, which might even be better in terms of consistency.

Exposing Package Metadata

NuGet packages are more than a container for delivering files. They also provide metadata information about the package such as the version and id which allow you to uniquely identify a NuGet package. This metadata information is stored in an XML file with a .nuspec extension, also called the NuGet package manifest as seen in the previous section of this chapter.

This might sound complicated at first, but this is really nothing new. The NuGet package format is just a well-defined format following the Open Packaging Conventions (OPC). OPC is a container-file technology initially created by Microsoft to store a combination of XML and non-XML file that together form a single entity. If this entity is a ZIP archive, then you should use the term *package*. Well-known examples of file formats following OPC are .docx (Word document), .xlsx (Excel spreadsheet), .pptx (PowerPoint presentation), and now also .nupkg (NuGet packages).

Required Metadata

Before we jump into the contents of a package and how they should be organized, we need to introduce you to the world of package metadata. The metadata element is a mandatory section within the package manifest. The metadata section itself also has a set of mandatory elements. These required elements must be specified before you can create a package based on the nuspec manifest. Here is the list of all required metadata fields:

- id
- version
- description
- authors

The first pieces of metadata your package exposes are the package ID and the package version. This pair of fields will uniquely identify your package on any NuGet feed. We'll come back to versioning later in this chapter, with more in-depth guidance. Remember that these package IDs will be used in commands run by the Package Manager Console or the NuGet command-line tool, so make sure you give your package a meaningful ID to ease discoverability of your package. In general, a package ID follows the same naming rules as namespaces in the .NET Framework: it can be only 100 characters and cannot contain any spaces or characters that would be invalid in an URL. If you're not sure what to use, usually a dot-separated or dash-separated component or framework name will do (for instance, SilverlightToolkit-Input or Glimpse.Mvc4).

The description field allows you to provide a few words that describe your package. This package description will be used by the Add Package dialog box as well as by some commands in the Package Manager Console (for example, Get-Package). Next to the description field is an optional title field, which is meant to display your package in a more human-friendly way. If not specified, the package ID will be used as a title by default. If your package ID contains dots or dashes, we recommend you provide a title field, where they are replaced with a whitespace character.

The last required metadata field is the authors field. This indicates the author or authors of the package code or contents. You can specify multiple authors by using a comma-separated list. A related field is the owners field, which is optional. This field is intended to indicate the package owners, which are not necessarily the creators of its contents, although often the two are the same.

Optional Metadata

In addition to the required metadata elements and derived defaults, you can specify more fine-grained information about your package. NuGet v2.6 has the following list of allowed, optional metadata elements:

- title
- owners
- releaseNotes
- summary
- language
- projectUrl
- iconUrl
- licenseUrl
- copyright
- requireLicenseAcceptance
- dependencies
- references
- frameworkAssemblies
- tags
- minClientVersion

Copyright and License Information

If your package concerns an open source project or requires some kind of license acceptance by the consumer, you can indicate as much by using the `licenseUrl` and `requireLicenseAcceptance` elements. When the `requireLicenseAcceptance` element is set to `true`, the Add Package dialog box will present you with a License Acceptance dialog box during installation of the package, as illustrated in Figure 3-1. Notice the little link View License Terms, which will direct your browser to the license URL specified in the package.

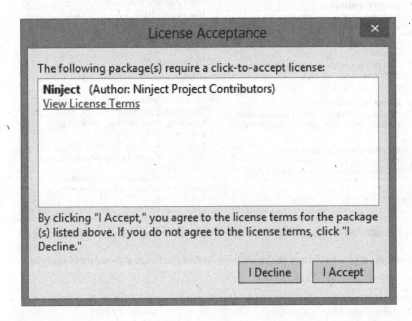

Figure 3-1. *The License Acceptance dialog box appears during installation of a package that requires license acceptance*

Referring back to Listing 3-1, notice that the `title`, `owners`, and `requireLicenseAcceptance` fields in the metadata section have been provided with default values. Disregard the empty `files` section for now, as we will dive deeper into that element when we discuss package contents. As of NuGet v1.5, you can also use the `copyright` element to provide copyright information for the package.

You don't necessarily have to install a package in order to view the license terms, as the Manage NuGet Packages dialog box will show the same View License Terms link for a package when you are browsing the package repository. Clicking the link, shown in Figure 3-2, will open a browser so you can navigate to the `licenseUrl` for that package.

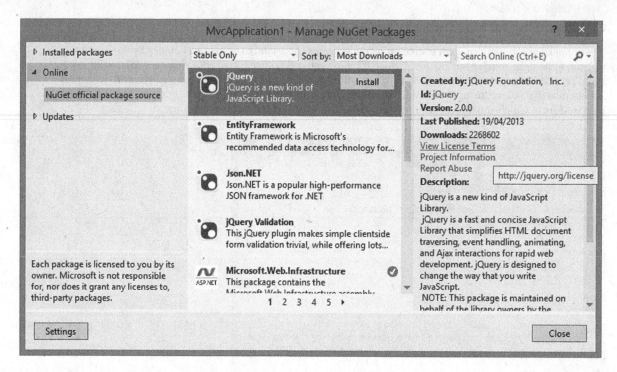

Figure 3-2. *Click the View License Terms link for a given package in the Manage NuGet Packages dialog box to navigate to the license URL of the package*

Release Notes

When shipping a new version of a package, you might want to inform the consumer about the changes you made in this version. A NuGet package can expose this metadata in the form of release notes and a readme file.

The `releaseNotes` element gives you the opportunity to communicate the changes you made directly in the Package Manager dialog box, even before installing the package.

Simple Dependencies

As your package will be a dependency to anyone who consumes it, it is critical to specify your own dependencies in a way that is appropriate to the consuming project. Installing a package that has a whole load of other, unnecessary package dependencies is not the experience you want to provide your package consumers. Your package metadata specifies how your package should be handled during the installation process. It is important to understand the elements that provide extra information about either the dependencies of your package or the dependencies of the target project and as such provide instructions to the installation process.

The first one of these elements is called `dependencies`. It's a straightforward list of package references, using their package ID and version (or version range). Combined, this list of packages indicates your package prerequisites. In other words, these packages must be installed prior to installing your own package and thus are to be considered as your package dependencies. An example of how to indicate your package dependencies in the manifest file is shown in Listing 3-3. Notice that there is no indication whatsoever about the origins or the location of these other packages. This will allow us to set up some more advanced scenarios later on in this book.

Listing 3-3. Indicating Package Dependencies in the metadata Section of a Nuspec Manifest

```xml
<?xml version="1.0"?>
<package xmlns="http://schemas.microsoft.com/packaging/2010/07/nuspec.xsd">
  <metadata>
    ...
    <dependencies>
      <dependency id="Some.Awesome.PackageId" version="1.0.0" />
      <dependency id="Some.Other.Awesome.PackageId" version="1.1.0" />
    </dependencies>
  </metadata>
  <files />
</package>
```

By default, all libraries contained in a package that match the targeted platform will be installed into the target project.

■ **Note**   The version attribute is optional for specifying dependencies. By adding the version attribute, dependencies can be specified more elaborately: it will instruct NuGet to make sure a version constraint is satisfied. For example, you can specify a particular version or a supported version range for your dependencies.

Group Dependencies by Target Framework

If your package is targeting multiple platforms, then it might also be a good idea to group your dependencies. You can make use of group elements and distinguish them from each other by using the targetFramework attribute, as shown in Listing 3-4.

Listing 3-4. Specifying the Minimum Client Version for a Package

```xml
<?xml version="1.0"?>
<package xmlns="http://schemas.microsoft.com/packaging/2010/07/nuspec.xsd">
  <metadata minClientVersion="2.0">
    <dependencies>
      <group>
        <dependency id="Newtonsoft.Json"/>
      </group>
      <group targetFramework="net40">
        <dependency id="jQuery"/>
      </group>
      <group targetFramework="windows8">
      </group>
    </dependencies>
  </metadata>
  <files />
</package>
```

The preceding example will require the Newtonsoft.Json dependency for all target frameworks except for .NET 4.0 or later, and Windows 8. If the target framework is .NET 4.0 or later, only the jQuery dependency will be installed. Likewise, if the target framework matches the windows8 constraint (note that *zero* dependencies are defined for that group), no package dependencies will be installed. There is *no inheritance between groups*, so if a project matches a group's target framework, only the dependencies defined in that group will be installed.

You cannot mix group dependencies and dependencies outside of a group. As an example, Listing-3-5 would result in an invalid nuspec manifest.

Listing 3-5. Invalid Manifest Because of Mixed-Dependency Declaration Formats

```xml
<?xml version="1.0"?>
<package xmlns="http://schemas.microsoft.com/packaging/2010/07/nuspec.xsd">
  <metadata minClientVersion="2.5">
    <dependencies>
      <dependency id="Newtonsoft.Json"/>
      <dependency id="WebActivatorEx"/>

      <group targetFramework="net40">
        <dependency id="jQuery"/>
      </group>
    </dependencies>
  </metadata>
  <files />
</package>
```

Note that this feature was introduced in NuGet v2.0 so you'll need to upgrade if you're still using an older version. Older versions won't be able to deal with these packages, because they are not aware of this change in the nuspec scheme.

Minimum Client Version

Any change to the nuspec file format is a breaking change. Compatibility (both backward and forward) is hard to manage. That is also why the XML Schema Definition (XSD) for the nuspec file format has not been officially made available. The XSD is embedded in the NuGet clients and is used for validation during package creation. The introduction of the dependency groups feature is a good example of this: the scheme changed, and the new feature is supported only as of a given NuGet client version.

As of NuGet v2.5, the `minClientVersion` attribute on the `metadata` element allows you to indicate the minimum NuGet client version required to properly consume the package, as shown in Listing 3-6. This feature was introduced to improve the experience as a consumer of a package that requires a newer version of the NuGet client.

Listing 3-6. Specifying the Minimum Client Version for a Package

```xml
<?xml version="1.0"?>
<package xmlns="http://schemas.microsoft.com/packaging/2010/07/nuspec.xsd">
  <metadata minClientVersion="2.5">
    ...
  </metadata>
  <files />
</package>
```

As of NuGet v2.5, if you attempt to install a package that requires a newer version of the client, or if package installation fails due to an unrecognized schema version, you'll be guided to upgrade your version of NuGet.

Specifying References

You can also use the references element in the metadata section to indicate explicitly which of the binaries in your package you want to be referenced in the target project after installation. Listing 3-7 shows you how you can specify explicit references in the nuspec metadata section. Files that are not explicitly indicated for treatment as references will be installed into the Packages folder of your solution but will not be added as references in the target project.

For example, the xUnit package uses this approach to exclude the test runner executable (.exe) from being referenced in the project in which xUnit is installed.

Listing 3-7. Specifying Explicit References in the nuspec metadata Section

```xml
<?xml version="1.0"?>
<package xmlns="http://schemas.microsoft.com/packaging/2010/07/nuspec.xsd">
  <metadata>
    ...
    <references>
      <reference file="Some.Awesome.Library.dll" />
      <reference file="Some.Other.Awesome.Library.dll" />
    </references>
  </metadata>
  <files />
</package>
```

Notice that there is no need to specify any other information besides the full filename (including the extension). Be careful not to specify any path to the file, as this piece of metadata will be derived based on the target project and platform. NuGet will look into the correct place in your package to retrieve this file. More information on how this package can be structured is given in the next section in this chapter.

Group References by Target Framework

Very similar to how dependencies can be grouped, it is also possible to group references. This functionality was introduced in NuGet v2.5 and makes use of group elements, similar to how you can group dependencies.

Grouping references allows you to granularly define which references should be added to the consuming project based on the target framework. Again, mixing grouped and ungrouped references within a single nuspec file is not allowed and would produce an invalid package being rejected by NuGet.

Listing 3-8 shows an example of grouped references within a nuspec manifest.

Listing 3-8. A Manifest with Grouped References

```xml
<?xml version="1.0"?>
<package xmlns="http://schemas.microsoft.com/packaging/2010/07/nuspec.xsd">
  <metadata>
    ...
    <references>
      <group>
        <reference file="Some.Awesome.Library.dll" />
        <reference file="Some.Other.Awesome.Library.dll" />
      </group>
      <group targetFramework="windows8">
        <reference file="Some.Awesome.WinRT.Library.dll" />
      </group>
```

```
      </references>
    </metadata>
    <files />
</package>
```

Framework References

When it comes to dependencies and references, there's one thing we haven't mentioned yet. All .NET Framework projects depend on the .NET Framework itself. Occasionally, we might want to instruct NuGet to add some references to a .NET Framework assembly during package installation. When distributing a Windows Communication Foundation (WCF) contracts package, for instance, you'd probably want to add a reference to System.Runtime. Serialization. However, we don't want to distribute portions of the .NET Framework in all our NuGet packages every single time, over and over again—definitely not when these things are readily available in the Global Assembly Cache (GAC) on most development machines, as well as on build servers.

This is where the frameworkAssemblies element comes into play. This section instructs NuGet to add all listed framework assemblies as a reference into the target project during package installation, without the binaries being included inside the package. NuGet will pick them up directly from the GAC. Listing 3-9 shows you an example of how to define dependencies to framework assemblies.

Listing 3-9. Defining Required Framework Assembly References for the Target Project

```
<?xml version="1.0"?>
<package xmlns="http://schemas.microsoft.com/packaging/2010/07/nuspec.xsd">
  <metadata>
    ...
    <frameworkAssemblies>
      <frameworkAssembly assemblyName="System.Runtime.Serialization" />
      <frameworkAssembly assemblyName="System.Core" targetFramework="net40"/>
    </frameworkAssemblies>
  </metadata>
  <files />
</package>
```

Notice that this works for different versions and profiles of the .NET Framework and Silverlight. Each frameworkAssembly element within this section can have two attributes. The assemblyName attribute is required and obviously indicates the name of the framework assembly to be referenced. Optionally, you can add a targetFramework attribute, which dictates that this framework assembly will be referenced after installation only if the target project is targeting the specified target framework.

The example in Listing 3-9 used the value net40 to indicate that the .NET Framework 4.0 should be used as the target framework in order to have the System.Core assembly referenced by the target project. If no targetFramework value is specified for the frameworkAssembly, the reference will always be added into the target project. The target framework of the project the package is installed into is irrelevant in this case.

Note that multiple target frameworks can be specified by separating them with commas. For example, net40,net45 will target both .NET 4.0 and 4.5.

Icon and Project Information

After going through all these functional metadata fields, it's time to customize our package and add some branding and aesthetics. One thing you can do to make your package stand out is to use a custom icon. This icon will then be used in the Add Library Package Reference dialog box and on the NuGet Gallery web site. To specify a custom icon, you should use the iconUrl element in the package metadata, pointing to an image. This image should be a 32 × 32–pixel .png file with a transparent background.

A nicely chosen icon is not enough, however. Your package needs to be easily discoverable as well. You can improve the discoverability of your package by tagging it with some relevant descriptive terms. That's why you should use the tags element in the metadata section with a space-delimited list of keywords you foresee will be meaningful. People looking for relevant functionality on NuGet will often search using such keywords. There are tons of hidden gems on the public feed because people don't know the name of those packages ; if yours are properly tagged, people will find them with ease.

Especially when you expose open source packages on the public NuGet Gallery, you might consider adding a projectUrl to your package. This allows consumers to click through to your online project page and provide feedback or report issues, or even better, submit patches!

Specifying the Package Contents

A NuGet package can be compared to an archive (for example, a zip file). It's an archive of package contents and metadata. You can simply open any NuGet package in an archive tool or zip utility to inspect its contents. The first piece of content has already been discussed: it is the nuspec file. This manifest will always be part of any NuGet package. You don't need to do anything for that. When creating a NuGet package, you'll always start out of a nuspec file, and the file itself will be embedded in the root folder of the resulting package.

■ **Tip**   You can simply open any NuGet package and inspect its contents by using an archive tool or zip utility.

A NuGet package can have different kinds of content. The package's content files can be organized into libraries, content, tools, build and sources:

- *Libraries*: Assembly files (.dll files) that will become references in the target project.

- *Content*: Content and source code to be injected into the target project.

- *Tools*: PowerShell scripts and executables.

- *Build* (as of NuGet v2.5): Automatic import of MSBuilt targets and properties. You can place two files with fixed names, {packageid}.targets or {packageid}.props. These two files can be either directly under \build or under framework-specific folders just like the other folders.

- *Sources*: the special \src folder can contain symbols for the assemblies shipped in the package. We'll cover symbols packages later in this chapter.

We'll explain each of these in the next sections. If you want to create your own packages, you should do so starting from a convention-based working directory, containing the nuspec file, and any libraries, content, and tools you want to distribute with your package.

Libraries

The first thing you'll probably want to do when creating your first NuGet package is replace a library with a NuGet package that distributes this library. This is also the most common way of using NuGet: managing real software dependencies, or referenced assemblies, using NuGet packages as a means of distribution.

It is important to understand that a NuGet package can target multiple platforms or project types. As such, it is not necessary, or even desired, to create separate packages for all possible framework versions (for example, Silverlight 4, Silverlight 5, Windows Phone 7, and .NET Framework 4). You can achieve the same level of isolation with a single NuGet package because of the implicit package content conventions that you'll use to structure the package contents.

Framework-Specific Libraries

All binary files that should be installed into a consuming target project should be put inside the \lib folder of your package. The simplest package just puts all .dll files inside this platform-agnostic library folder. This indicates that you are not targeting any specific platform or framework version. However, if your package is built against version 4.0 of the .NET Framework, for instance, you might want to explicitly indicate that your package requires this. Actually, you should! To do so, you need to create a subfolder of \lib with a name that indicates the desired platform, version, and/or profile. Table 3-1 lists the supported conventions for these subfolders.

Table 3-1. *Framework Profile and Version Specifications for NuGet Package Libraries*

Framework Name	Abbreviation	Supported Profiles	Profile Abbreviations
.NET Framework	net	Client Profile, Full Profile, Micro Framework, Compact Framework	client, full, mf, cf, compactframework
Silverlight	sl	Windows Phone	wp, windowsphone

NuGet is very flexible in how you use these conventions and allows you to be very specific in what you target. Targeting the .NET Framework version 4.0 would result in a folder called net40. Because the .NET Framework is the most commonly used target framework, you could even skip the framework name and mention only its version. This means that a folder named 40 would be treated as if it were called net40. NuGet will assume you meant the .NET Framework and use it as a default framework name. Libraries in your package that target the .NET Framework 4.0 should thus be put into the following folder structure: \lib\net40 or \lib\40.

Table 3-2 provides examples of how you could combine the framework names, profiles, and versions based on the conventions from Table 3-1.

Table 3-2. *Examples of Common Package Library Targets*

Target	Library's Path	Supported Alternative
.NET Framework 4.5.1	\lib\net451	
.NET Framework 4.5	\lib\net45	
.NET Framework 4.0	\lib\net40	\lib\40
.NET Framework 4.0 Client Profile	\lib\net40-client	
.NET Compact Framework 3.5	\lib\net35-cf	\lib\net35-compactframework
Windows 8 Store Apps	\lib\netcore45	\lib\windows8
Silverlight 5.0	\lib\sl5	
Silverlight for Windows Phone 7.0	\lib\sl3-wp	\lib\sl3-windowsphone
Silverlight for Windows Phone 7.1 Mango	\lib\sl4-wp71	\lib\sl4-windowsphone71
Windows Phone 8	\lib\wp8	
Portable class libraries	\lib\portable-{frameworks}	
Native libraries	\lib\native	

Knowing all this, you can now very easily create a package that supports different frameworks and profiles. You can accomplish this by organizing your lib folder accordingly. Listing 3-10 shows an example of a package that targets the .NET Framework 4.0, Silverlight 4, and Windows Phone 7. Of course, the binaries inside those folders are built against those frameworks.

Listing 3-10. A Multiplatform Package Library Structure

```
\lib
    \net45
    \sl4
    \sl3-wp
```

NuGet will attempt to parse these folder names to the FrameworkName object behind the scenes. Folder names are case insensitive, and the abbreviations listed in Table 3-1 are allowed. NuGet is open source, so you could dive into the code base and find out how this was implemented. More information on the FrameworkName class can be found on MSDN, http://msdn.microsoft.com/en-us/library/dd414023.aspx.

Content

Besides binaries and libraries, you also can distribute content with your package, such as application configuration settings, images, JavaScript files, Cascading Style Sheets (CSS), or even code files!

Simple Content Injection

By convention, all these files should be put under the \content folder inside your package, or any subfolder of it. Notice that when you create a subfolder in \content, this folder will also be created inside the target project if it doesn't exist yet. All content under a subfolder will as such be placed in the same subfolder structure inside the consuming project. This means you'll have an exact content structure mapping between your package content folder and the consuming project. Think of the \content folder as the root folder of the consuming project. For example, \content\scripts\filename.js would map to project\scripts\filename.js.

Grouping Content Files by Target Framework

It is possible to group content files in a similar fashion as grouping dependencies. The very same folder structure for specifying target frameworks as it is applicable to the \lib folder also applies to the \content folder.

Listing 3-11 provides an example folder structure to illustrate this capability. Obviously, NuGet will identify the subfolders as one of the platform-naming conventions and not attempt to create these folders in the target project.

Listing 3-11. A Multiplatform Package Content Structure

```
\content
    \net45
        \GridControl.cs
    \sl4
        \GridControl.xaml
        \GridControl.xaml.cs
```

So far, we have mentioned only copying files from within the package to the consuming project. You might be wondering now why we're not simply using a zip file or other type of archive containing these files. Let us introduce you to one of the neat features that NuGet supports out of the box: source code and configuration transformations. On some occasions, you might want to just inject some configuration settings or source code into the target project.

If you haven't been using this functionality before, we invite you to explore this cool feature after reading this chapter, because it is straightforward and yet so powerful! It allows you to modify existing files in the target project to fit your requirements or create them if they don't exist already. This gives you tremendous flexibility to make it even easier for the consumer to install your package, without needing to touch a single file manually.

Configuration Transformations

If your package relies on certain configuration settings in the app.config or web.config file of the consuming project, you have a very good reason to modify this file during installation of your package. Before the existence of NuGet, people had to go through documentation, if any, and find out for themselves which settings or sections in the configuration files were required. Once they found that information, they still needed to discover how to use those settings and provide them with proper values for any specific requirements. As a package producer, you can now facilitate this yourself and provide the consuming project with whatever settings you require.

■ **Tip**   You can check the Error Logging Modules and Handlers for ASP.NET (ELMAH) NuGet package for an example of adding an httpModule section to the web.config file.

The convention to be used to provide your package with an application or web configuration file transformation is the .transform suffix. In other words, if you add a file named app.config.transform or web.config.transform to the \content folder of your package, it will be picked up by NuGet during installation, and the transformation will be applied on the app.config or web.config file of the consuming project.

■ **Note**   Between you and us, configuration transformations work for any *.config file (except for e.g. *.Debug.config or *.Release.config). In fact, this works for any file, as long as its contents are XML and you use the filename.ext.transform convention. The only drawback is that you need to know the target filename up front.

The *.transform file, or transformation file, is an XML file that includes only the sections to be merged into the target file that needs to be transformed. As a built-in safety precaution, only additions of sections, elements, or attributes are supported. These transformations are merged into the target file, as NuGet walks the XML tree of the target file and picks up any additions defined in the transformation file. This means you cannot use this feature to remove or modify existing elements or attributes of the target XML files. The reason is quite simple: there's no way NuGet would be able to restore the original state of the file after uninstalling the package. It would have to keep track of all changes it overwrites or removes and keep track of all changes to that file since installation, which is not the responsibility of a package management tool—not to mention the additional amount of complexity that doing so would bring to the tool.

EXAMPLE CONFIGURATION TRANSFORMATION

Let's say you have a Visual Studio web project containing a `web.config` file. This file already contains settings required by your application defined in the `appSettings` section of the configuration file, as shown here:

```
<configuration>
  <appSettings>
    <add key="webpages:Version" value="1.0.0.0"/>
    <add key="ClientValidationEnabled" value="true"/>
    <add key="UnobtrusiveJavaScriptEnabled" value="true"/>
  </appSettings>
</configuration>
```

Using simple configuration transformations, there is no way to change these settings using a transformation file during installation of a NuGet package. Only additions can be merged into the file.

Let's suppose we are installing a module that is configurable through a specifically named element defined in this `appSettings` section. Our example module depends on one application setting named `OutputFormat`. The default value is XML. As a package producer shipping a product that depends on this application setting, it is desirable to inject this setting in the target project's configuration file, as well as setting the default value. In this scenario, our transformation file named `web.config.transform` would have the following contents:

```
<configuration>
  <appSettings>
    <add key="OutputFormat" value="XML"/>
  </appSettings>
</configuration>
```

The existing `web.config` file will be merged with this transformation file after installation of this package. Notice that NuGet has not changed any other elements, attributes, or values in the original configuration file. The resulting `web.config` file follows, with the changes highlighted in bold:

```
<configuration>
  <appSettings>
    <add key="webpages:Version" value="1.0.0.0"/>
    <add key="ClientValidationEnabled" value="true"/>
    <add key="UnobtrusiveJavaScriptEnabled" value="true"/>
    <add key="OutputFormat" value="XML"/>
  </appSettings>
</configuration>
```

Source Code Transformations

In addition to configuration transformations, NuGet also supports source code manipulation, a feature that is very similar to Visual Studio project templating and very useful if you need to add some code to the target project. Typically, this additional code initializes or bootstraps the component or module you installed.

ASP.NET web applications are the most common type of projects that make good use of this feature because of the shared workflow these applications go through in Internet Information Services (IIS). The hook points in the life cycle of an ASP.NET web application are exposed in the `global.asax` code-behind. This is the same for every

ASP.NET web application. As such, during package installation, the producer could instruct NuGet to create this file, if it's not present, and inject custom startup or shutdown logic required by the package libraries. However, there's a better way for this specific scenario: using WebActivator.

■ **Tip**   A component that allows you to make very good use of this feature in ASP.NET web projects is the WebActivator package, which you can find at `http://nuget.org/List/Packages/WebActivator`.

The WebActivator NuGet package allows other packages to easily inject startup and shutdown code into a web application. The convention is that you put your preprocessed code files in the `\content\App_Start` folder in your package. As such, all startup and shutdown logic of a web application can be installed into the project's `App_Start` folder. Don't forget to indicate that your package depends on the WebActivator package if you want to make use of this feature.

A code transformation file has a similar filename convention as for configuration transformation files: you need to append the `.pp` suffix to the filename of the code file you want to transform during installation. For example, `global.asax.cs.pp` will be transformed into `global.asax.cs`.

Source code transformations can be specified by using Visual Studio project properties in the code files you inject in the consuming application. These properties are delimited with dollar signs ($). The most commonly used project property for source code transformations will definitely be $rootnamespace$, which gets replaced by the target project's default namespace.

■ **Tip**   For more information and a full list of project properties, visit the following MDSN page at `http://msdn.microsoft.com/en-us/library/vslangproj.projectproperties_properties(VS.80).aspx`.

EXAMPLE SOURCE CODE TRANSFORMATION

Let's say you want a set of model classes injected in the target project's `Models` folder. It would make sense to have these models in the appropriate namespace. Since you don't know the target namespace up front, you could construct it by using the target project's `$rootnamespace$` property and append `.Models` yourself.

```
namespace $rootnamespace$.Models {
    public class Employee {
        public int Id { get; set; }
        public string Name { get; set; }
        public string ContractId { get; set; }
    }
}
```

If the target project's root namespace equals `CompanyName.ProductName.Web`, you'd get the following code file injected into the target project's `Models` folder:

```
namespace CompanyName.ProductName.Web.Models {
    public class Employee {
        public int Id { get; set; }
        public string Name { get; set; }
        public string ContractId { get; set; }
    }
}
```

XML Document Transformations

XML Document Transformations, introduced in NuGet v2.6, are really a more advanced version of the configuration transformation feature that also works on XML documents, also known as XDT transforms. XDT has a syntax designed to apply very specific XML transformations onto a file. Whereas configuration transformations can inject XML and produce a merged result, XDT allows you to query for specific XML elements, and inject, remove, or alter them without the need to write any scripts. In short, XDT is lifting the limitations imposed by the configuration transformation feature.

The differences between the configuration transformation feature and the XML Document Transformation feature are highlighted in Table 3-3.

Table 3-3. *Differences Between Configuration Transformations and XML Document Transformations*

Support For	Configuration Transformations	XML Document Transformations
Target any XML file	Yes	Yes
Target config files	Yes	Yes
Add XML elements	Yes	Yes
Remove XML elements	No	Yes
Modify/replace XML elements	No	Yes
Package folder	\content	\content
Usage (web.config example)	web.config.transform	web.config.install.xdt web.config.uninstall.xdt It is not required to have both files. *.install.xdt is applied during package installation, whereas *.uninstall.xdt is applied during package uninstallation.

■ **Tip** For more information about the XDT project, please visit https://xdt.codeplex.com/.

XDT support was a much requested feature, and in order to enable the NuGet project to take advantage of XDT, the Microsoft XML Document Transformation project was open sourced as well! Although the project does not accept any contributions, the source code is published under the Apache License 2.0, allowing anyone to use the XDT library in his own applications. In fact, there is a `Microsoft.Web.Xdt` NuGet package available on `NuGet.org`. Open sourcing XDT was a prerequisite for this feature, as it allowed the core NuGet components to remain cross-platform compatible.

You might have used XDT before to transform application configuration files at compile-time, based on a specific build configuration such as `Web.Release.config` and `Web.Debug.config`. Using the `xdt:Locator` and `xdt:Transform` attributes, the XDT syntax describes how XML elements should be changed when transforming the XML file.

In order to use XDT features in your NuGet package, you need to know the target filename up front. You can hook into the installation and uninstallation process for each individual XML file, allowing you to take full control over the transformation process during these events. To do so, simply append the `.install.xdt` or `.uninstall.xdt` suffix to the target filename, define the XDT transformations within the files, and add them to the package's `\content` folder.

The example in Listing 3-12 provides an illustration of a `web.config.transform.xdt` file inserting an application setting into a `web.config` file during installation.

Listing 3-12. Inserting XML Elements by Using XDT Transformations During Package Installation

```xml
<?xml version="1.0"?>
<configuration>
  <appSettings>
    <add key="MyPackageSetting" value="SomeValue" xdt:Transform="Insert" />
  </appSettings>
</configuration>
```

To remove this setting during the package uninstall process, you need to reverse this transformation in the `web.config.uninstall.xdt` file, as shown in Listing 3-13.

Listing 3-13. Removing XML Elements by Using XDT Transformations During Package Uninstallation

```xml
<?xml version="1.0"?>
<configuration>
  <appSettings>
    <add key="MyPackageSetting" xdt:Transform="Remove" xdt:Locator="Match(key)" />
  </appSettings>
</configuration>
```

■ **Tip**   For full details on the XDT syntax, please refer to the MSDN documentation available at `http://msdn.microsoft.com/en-us/library/dd465326.aspx`.

Tools

The `\tools` folder has a special purpose. It allows you to embed tools, binaries, scripts, and other useful files that should be used by the Package Manager but are not necessarily something that the consuming application should use, or even care about.

Hook into Package Installation Events

The most typical use case for having this folder is to hook into the package initialization, installation, and uninstallation processes. By convention, this can be achieved by providing PowerShell scripts with a filename indicating which hook point will execute the script. In other words, NuGet will automatically run these scripts based on their filename. NuGet supports three hook points:

- init.ps1
- install.ps1
- uninstall.ps1

Nothing prevents you, of course, from importing other PowerShell modules or scripts or even calling executables embedded in your package. It is, however, important to know how and when these files are triggered by NuGet.

The init.ps1 script will be triggered the first time a package is installed into a solution. Installing the same package in a second project in the same solution will not trigger init.ps1. In addition, every time the solution opens, the init.ps1 script, for each installed package that has one, will be executed. This is something you should be aware of when designing a package that needs additional initialization steps. This is also exactly what made it possible to extend the NuGet Package Manager Console (PMC) easily, as you will learn in Chapter 9.

The install.ps1 script runs when a package is installed into a project. This means that if you install the same package in multiple projects within the same solution, install.ps1 will be executed during every single installation of that package. If your package also contains an init.ps1 file, the install.ps1 script will be executed after init.ps1. However, the install.ps1 script will run only when there is actual content inside of the \lib or \content folder.

■ **Note**   A package that contains only a \tools folder does not have anything to install into a project. Such a package can, however, provide meaningful functionality and extend the NuGet Package Manager Console by adding custom cmdlets. If the package contains a \tools\install.ps1 file, the script will be executed during installation in a solution.

The uninstall.ps1 script obviously runs every time the package is uninstalled from a project. If you need to perform any kind of cleanup or custom actions during the uninstall process of your package, this is the place where you could hook into the process.

At the top of each of these scripts files, you should add the following statement, which will give you access to some variables you might find useful:

```
param($installPath, $toolsPath, $package, $project)
```

These values are provided automatically by the NuGet Package Manager Console. Each of these parameters is described in Table 3-4.

Table 3-4. PowerShell Script Parameters Provided by the NuGet Package Manager Console

Parameter	Description
$installPath	The path to the folder where the package is installed—by default, $(solutionDir)\packages.
$toolsPath	The path to the \tools directory in the folder where the package is installed—by default, $(solutionDir)\packages\[packageId].[version]\tools.
$package	A reference to the package object.
$project	A reference to the target EnvDTE project object. This type is described on MSDN, at http://msdn.microsoft.com/en-us/library/51h9a6ew(v=VS.80).aspx. The value will be null during init.ps1 because there's not yet a reference to a particular project while you're initializing the package at the solution level.

Group Scripts by Target Framework

It is also possible to group these PowerShell scripts by target framework. Again, you'll have to use the same folder structure for specifying target frameworks as it is applicable to the \lib and \content folders, as shown in Listing 3-14.

Listing 3-14. Grouping Scripts by Target Framework

```
\tools
    init.ps1
    \net40
        \install.ps1
        \uninstall.ps1
    \net45
    \sl4
        \install.ps1
        \uninstall.ps1
```

■ **Warning**   The \tools\init.ps1 file should not be put in any framework-specific folder, as this script is executed at the solution level. This effectively means that the script is not project-specific and thus not dependent on any framework specifics.

If NuGet encounters an init.ps1 file in a subfolder of the \tools folder, the file will be ignored.

The example in Listing 3-14 also shows an empty \tools\net45 folder. This means that no install or uninstall scripts will be run when targeting a .NET Framework 4.5 project.

Sources

The \src folder has a special purpose. It allows you to embed debugger symbols for the assemblies shipped in the NuGet package. We will cover symbols packages later in this chapter.

MSBuild instructions

As of version 2.5, NuGet supports an additional package folder convention that allows you to inject some MSBuild instructions into the consuming project file. The \build folder can contain two files with fixed names: {packageId}.targets or {packageId}.props. The .props file is added at the top of the project file, and the .targets file is added at the bottom of the project file. These files can be listed directly in the \build folder, but similar to the other package folders, you can also put them under framework-specific subfolders.

This feature enables you to define MSBuild properties or add MSBuild instructions to the consuming project file, effectively allowing you to hook into the build process.

Imagine you want to output the latest Git revision details in the build log of a project, for all projects that you currently are working on. Ideally, you would add some build tasks to the project files and be done. What if you could move these additional build tasks into a NuGet package that you could reuse on different projects? Let's create one!

If you are unfamiliar with the Git source control system or the Git command line, getting the latest revision information from the current working directory (if under Git control) can be done with a simple command: git log -1. This command can be run from a command prompt. Hence, you can use an MSBuild <Exec /> task to run this during a build.

You can create a package called GitRevisionBuildLog by using NuGet Package Explorer. In the package itself, new build targets can be added in the folder defined by NuGet conventions: \build\{packageId}.targets, or in the case of this new package, \build\GitRevisionBuildLog.targets.

Source code for the targets file can be seen in Listing 3-15.

Listing 3-15. An MSBuild Targets File Containing a Command That Displays the Current Git Revision Information

```xml
<?xml version="1.0" encoding="utf-8"?>
<Project ToolsVersion="4.0" xmlns="http://schemas.microsoft.com/developer/msbuild/2003">
    <PropertyGroup>
        <SolutionDir Condition="$(SolutionDir) == ''
          Or $(SolutionDir) == '*Undefined*'">$(MSBuildProjectDirectory)\..\</SolutionDir>

        <!-- Git executable path - use git from current PATH by default -->
        <GitExePath Condition=" '$(GitExe)' == '' ">git</GitExePath>
    </PropertyGroup>

    <PropertyGroup>
        <!-- Commands -->
        <LogCommand>$(GitExePath) log -1</LogCommand>

        <!-- Enlist our build targets in the project build -->
        <BuildDependsOn>
            GitRevision;
            $(BuildDependsOn);
        </BuildDependsOn>
    </PropertyGroup>

    <Target Name="GitRevision">
        <Exec Command="$(LogCommand)"
              LogStandardErrorAsError="true"
              WorkingDirectory="$(SolutionDir)"
              Condition="Exists('$(SolutionDir)\.git')" />
    </Target>
</Project>
```

The \build\GitRevisionBuildLog.targets file contains several properties. The first PropertyGroup defines two variables: SolutionDir, which will hold the current solution directory, and GitExePath, which will be the full path to the Git executable. Since on most systems this is available from the PATH environment variable, the value git is sufficient, but users of this package can always change this manually if needed.

The second PropertyGroup defines the LogCommand variable, the full command for retrieving the latest Git revision. It also registers the GitRevision build target as a dependency for the build in which this targets file is included.

All the heavy lifting is done in the GitRevision target itself: it makes use of the Exec task to run the git log -1 command in the solution directory, but only if there is a .git folder in the solution directory.

When installing the package into a project, NuGet will change the project file and include the GitRevisionBuildLog.targets file from your package:

```
<Import Project="..\packages\GitRevisionBuildLog.1.0.0\build\GitRevisionBuildLog.targets"
Condition="Exists('..\packages\GitRevisionBuildLog.1.0.0\build\GitRevisionBuildLog.targets')" />
```

When running the build for a project in which the package has been installed, you can now see the output of the MSBuild targets file you have created. Figure 3-3 displays some sample build output.

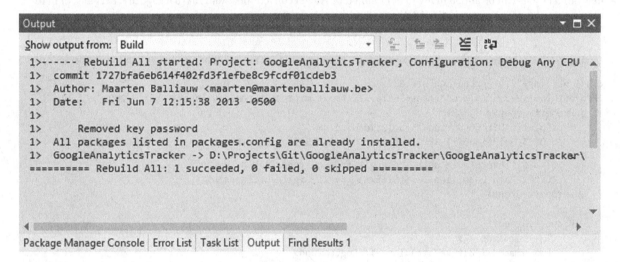

Figure 3-3. *The output of our custom build target that has been included from a NuGet package*

Package Versioning

One of the first things you expose to any consumer of your package is the version number. This happens even before any other part of the package metadata is consumed. The version number is also the first piece of the contract between package producer and consumer. If done properly, a version number provides a lot of meaningful information. Versioning is critical in terms of dependency management, and as such also for package management.

Semantic Versioning

The most simple and pragmatic versioning pattern one could use is called *semantic versioning*. Semantic versioning consists of a set of simple rules and requirements that dictate how a software assembly or package should be versioned and how you should increment this version for future releases.

■ **Tip** Visit `www.semver.org` for more detailed information and guidance on semantic versioning.

An assembly or package version consists of a maximum of four numbers, out of which the first three are the most meaningful. You should read version information as `major.minor.patch`. An explanation of the meaning of these version numbers is given in Table 3-5. Semantic versioning (SemVer for short), allows you to use a fourth version part, the build number, to uniquely identify a given build. SemVer does not enforce the usage of the fourth number, but there might be use cases in favor of it, which is totally fine and not a violation of the SemVer rules.

Table 3-5. *Semantic Versioning*

Version Number	Usage
Major	Indicates a breaking change in the public API
Minor	Indicates a fully backward-compatible release containing public API additions, such as new features or functionality
Patch	Indicates a fully backward-compatible release containing hotfixes or internal changes that do not affect the public API at all

Although NuGet supports SemVer quite well, the optional build number defined in the specification came in too late in the NuGet v1.6 release process. Therefore, NuGet does not support the build number notation as defined in rule 11 of SemVer 2.0.0. The rule says that a build number may be denoted by appending a plus sign (+) and a series of dot-separated identifiers immediately following the patch version or prerelease version (for example,`v1.0.0-rc+2011.12.28`).

Because NuGet does not support the build number notation using the plus sign, you'll have to come up with a different versioning scheme for your continuous integration and nightly builds. These are typical scenarios requiring a more fine-grained identification of the produced package.

SemVer might sound very common sense, and probably you are doing something close to this already. The problem is that close is not good enough! NuGet as a tool will not enforce using this versioning pattern in any way, although it is optimized for it. The message here is that you, as a package producer, should be very clear in terms of the contract you'll expose to a potential consumer. If you tell the consumer you didn't create any breaking changes in your newest version, you'd better make sure you didn't. If you repeatedly break this promise, you'll end up with unhappy consumers of your packages, who then might choose to no longer use any of your packages at all! If you want to be considered a trustworthy package producer, you might consider sticking to semantic versioning. This is especially true for component vendors who want to use NuGet as a distribution channel and expose their component packages on a NuGet feed.

Prerelease Packages

Starting from version 1.6, NuGet also supports the concept of prerelease packages. The intent of a prerelease package is to get early feedback on a pending release. A prerelease as such should not be considered stable. Actually, even the version number of a prerelease package should not be considered correct. (It has not been proven yet that there are no breaking changes, as those breaking changes could still be introduced while stabilizing the release.)

Prerelease packages are indicated by a special tag trailing the patch number, separated with a dash sign (-), for example, `v1.0.0-alpha`. This format still is supported by SemVer, so nothing is preventing you from fully using semantic versioning as your standard.

Except for the build number: if you want to uniquely identify a given build (in a Continuous Integration scenario, for instance), you should, according to the SemVer 2.0.0 specification, use a plus (+) character to indicate a build number. The easiest way is to increment the build number on each successful compilation (for example, v0.9.1-alpha+112 becomes v0.9.1-alpha+113).

NuGet does not support this build notation, so you'll have to come up with something different. The first thing that comes to mind to work around this issue is to add some dot-separated information to the prerelease patch number (for example, v0.9.1-alpha.112). This, again, is fine with the SemVer specifications, but NuGet does not support this either. You'll need another workaround, while making sure that a new build (that incremented the version) is still considered a newer version by NuGet. Sadly enough, there is no nice solution at hand that doesn't mess up the package version ordering.

The order of precedence of prerelease packages is determined by lexicographic ASCII order. This means you have to really pay attention when to use digits or uppercase and lowercase characters; they affect the way your packages will be sorted! If this doesn't mean anything to you, no worries; we'll explain this by example. Consider the following prerelease packages, ordered by precedence (lowest to highest version):

- 0.9.1-alpha+1 (not supported by NuGet)

- 0.9.1-alpha+2 (not supported by NuGet)

- 0.9.1-alpha+10 (not supported by NuGet)

- 0.9.1-alpha

- 0.9.1-alpha2

- 0.9.1-beta

- 0.9.1-rc

- 0.9.1

- 0.10.0

- 1.0.0

■ **Caution** An important side-effect of depending on a prerelease package is that the produced package itself is also required to be a prerelease package. This makes a lot of sense if you consider the fact that a prerelease package is considered unstable. As soon as you introduce unstable code into a stable code base, the whole code base should be considered unstable.

Version Ranges

While discussing how to expose package metadata, and more-specific package dependencies, we briefly mentioned you could denote package dependencies with a package ID and a package version. Although this is correct, there is more to know about this feature, which is very important when dealing with dependencies. After all, we want to keep you out of dependency hell, remember?

It is important to understand that, by simply specifying a version for the dependency, you are actually saying that any version is good, as long as it is equal to or higher than the specified version. A single version number is in fact a short notation for a version range with an inclusive lower boundary, and no upper boundary. Mathematically speaking, version 0.9.1 corresponds to ≥ 0.9.1.

However, you might one day have a need to exclude some versions, or limit the range of allowed versions, or even explicitly set a version number while disallowing any other versions. If all package producers were properly using semantic versioning, version ranges wouldn't even be needed. The reality is different, though, and there's a whole lot of legacy open source packages out there predating the SemVer guidelines. Some are even ignoring any other standards used in other, even non-.NET, communities.

NuGet supports interval notation for specifying version ranges, inspired by but not identical to the Maven Range Specification. Table 3-6 summarizes the various supported version range notations, where x stands for the packages that match the specified dependency.

Table 3-6. *NuGet Version Range Notation*

Version Range	Interpretation
0.9.1	$0.9.1 \leq x$
(,0.9.1]	$x \leq 0.9.1$
(,0.9.1)	$x < 0.9.1$
[0.9.1]	$x == 0.9.1$
(0.9.1)	Invalid
(0.9.1,)	$0.9.1 < x$
(0.9.1, 1.0)	$0.9.1 < x < 1.0$
[0.9.1, 1.0]	$0.9.1 \leq x \leq 1.0$
Empty	Latest version

Constraining Package Dependencies

On the other side of the feed, as a package consumer, you can also lock the versions of the dependencies you installed through the use of NuGet packages. When a NuGet package gets installed into your project, an entry for that package ID and version is added into the project's `packages.config` file.

You might be wondering why one would want to lock down a NuGet package dependency. When calling the `Update-Package` command (or through the dialog box), you update your dependency for that package to the latest version. Because NuGet also supports updating all packages in a solution at once, this could become a very intrusive operation—especially if you know up front that your application is compatible with a newer version 2.*x* of a package, but not with version 3.*x*. This is a good reason to lock down those dependencies with a proper version range before performing any updates. Even when you're not planning any updates, it is a good piece of metadata indicating that your application has known incompatibilities with newer versions of certain dependencies.

Locking down package versions in the `packages.config` file must be done manually, as shown in Listing 3-16.

Listing 3-16. Constraining Package Dependencies in the packages.config File

```xml
<?xml version="1.0" encoding="utf-8"?>
<packages>
    <package id="SomePackage" version="2.1.0" allowedVersions="[2,3)" />
</packages>
```

SemVer and Automatic Versioning

You have learned how to apply semantic versioning, define prereleases, and constrain dependencies using NuGet. When practicing continuous integration (which we really recommend you do), you'll most probably be wondering how you'll deal with automatic versioning. In fact, you'll likely want to produce a NuGet package as part of the automated build, preferably with an incrementing version that would allow for a smooth upgrade path during development. How can one apply semantics when versioning an unstable package? Maybe the scope of the release isn't fixed either, in which case no one really knows what the semantic version of the release will be until someone clicks the release button. Isn't this a contradiction in terms: automatic versioning a yet unknown semantic version?

Conceptually, it's not too hard to come up with a solution to this problem:

- The version of the latest release is known.

- The minimal semantic version increment toward the next release is a patch increment.

- Anything in between two releases is indicated by prerelease tags and/or build numbers (at the time of writing, NuGet 2.6 still supports only prerelease tags).

Given these factors, it's pretty straightforward to come up with an automatic versioning scheme. Given a released package with version 1.2.1, the next stable release should have a minimal version equal to 1.2.2. Anything in between is a prerelease of the next release (for example, 1.2.2-beta).

That's easy, right? However, we still didn't do any automatic versioning so far. We simply defined the base version numbers to work with. The tricky part is to apply an automatic versioning scheme that doesn't break the semantic versioning rules, remains compatible with the NuGet tools, and maintains package precedence to ensure a smooth upgrade path.

Before the release of SemVer 2.0.0, there were two options: append incrementing digits (with leading zeros if required) to the prerelease tag, or append a datetime stamp to the prerelease tag. SemVer 2.0.0 disallows the usage of leading zeros in any numeric part of the version number, so we will also stick to the datetime stamp approach. Anything else is to be considered history. To have an incrementing datetime stamp, you should define the following format: *yyyyMMddHHmmss*. For example,20131004114652 contains the following information: 2013 (year), 10 (month), 04 (day), 11 (hour), 46 (minutes), 52 seconds. It's up to you whether you want to use the 24-hour clock or intersect the date and time parts with the AM or PM notation: both will work just fine, as prerelease tags are sorted in alphabetic order. Just make sure you don't mix both clock modes! Actually, it's not even required to have any alphabetic characters in the prerelease tag (as long as it is a prerelease tag—don't use a third dot to separate the version numbers).

Let's continue building on the previous example, where 1.2.1 is the latest release and we work toward the next release, anticipated to be 1.2.2. The package creation log could show you the following list of packages in order of precedence (lowest to highest):

- 1.2.1 (latest release)

- 1.2.2-20131004AM114652

- 1.2.2-20131004PM062308

- 1.3.0-20131005AM100912 (oops, we realized we had a nonbreaking change in the public API)

- 1.3.0-alpha20131204AM113412

- 1.3.0-rc

- 1.3.0 (next release)

Using this versioning scheme, you can easily highlight the semantic part of a version number that matters to the consumer (*major.minor.patch*). The prerelease tag does have meaning to the consumer as well, but the build stamp (date, time, VCS changeset/commit number, auto-incrementing digit ...) doesn't. That's why we really hope to see full SemVer support in NuGet one day, so we can make use of the build (+) notation, which also has no meaning in terms of package precedence. But for now, the preceding versioning strategy should do the trick.

Nuspec Inheritance

If you're producing a lot of packages in batch, it can be quite cumbersome to maintain the various nuspec files involved. Although it is not recommended to align version numbers or to share too much information between packages, some metadata elements will most likely always be the same for the entire batch (for example, copyright information, license information, or perhaps the icon and project URL).

One approach could be to create a nuspec template to start from every time you create a new package manifest. This is straightforward and easy to accomplish. The downside is that you're still facing quite a bit of manual work if you need to change a certain element across all these packages.

Another approach could be to come up with some kind of nuspec inheritance mechanism: have a central nuspec template and dynamically apply it to all nuspec files involved. You could do this as a prebuild step during the automated build process and parameterize the things you want to make configurable.

■ **Tip** We've briefly touched the surface of XML Document Transformation (XDT). This technology is really helpful for this scenario.

Check the following URL to see an example implementation of how the Cassette project is using XDT in a nuspec inheritance strategy to maintain and create their NuGet packages:
`http://kamranicus.com/Blog/Posts/32/using-nuspec-inheritance-to-reduce-nuget-maintenan`.

Creating Packages by Using the NuGet Command Line

Now that you know what the conventions for creating NuGet packages are and what a good package structure looks like, let's create one by using the command line. This section will guide you through creating NuGet packages by using the NuGet command line; it starts off with the creation of a simple, HelloWorld-type package for NuGet.

After creating a simple package from the command line, we'll guide you through some alternative methods of creating NuGet packages. Why craft everything yourself when nuget.exe provides a whole bunch of automation for you? We'll show you how NuGet creates the package manifest based on an assembly or Visual Studio project file and how you even can skip the process of creating a package manifest.

Creating a Package from a Convention-Based Directory

Creating a NuGet package from the command line is a very easy process that consists of three steps:

1. Create and modify a package manifest (a .nuspec file) containing all metadata for your NuGet package.
2. Create the package folder structure containing source code, assemblies, PowerShell scripts, and so on.
3. Package a combination of the package manifest and the folder structure.

Creating a fresh package manifest is probably the easiest task available in NuGet. Open a command prompt and navigate to an empty folder. Make sure the nuget.exe file can be found, and run the following command:

```
nuget spec HelloWorld
```

After you press the Enter key, NuGet will greet you with a success message in the form of "Created 'HelloWorld. nuspec' successfully." When you check the folder in which you just ran this command, you'll find a file that looks, when opened in an XML editor, roughly the same as the code in Listing 3-17.

Listing 3-17. A Newly Created NuGet Package Manifest Using the NuGet Command Line

```xml
<?xml version="1.0"?>
<package>
  <metadata>
    <id>HelloWorld</id>
    <version>1.0.0</version>
    <authors>Xavier</authors>
    <owners>Xavier</owners>
    <licenseUrl>http://LICENSE_URL_HERE_OR_DELETE_THIS_LINE</licenseUrl>
    <projectUrl>http://PROJECT_URL_HERE_OR_DELETE_THIS_LINE</projectUrl>
    <iconUrl>http://ICON_URL_HERE_OR_DELETE_THIS_LINE</iconUrl>
    <requireLicenseAcceptance>false</requireLicenseAcceptance>
    <description>Package description</description>
    <releaseNotes>Summary of changes made in this release of the package.</releaseNotes>
    <copyright>Copyright 2013</copyright>
    <tags>Tag1 Tag2</tags>
    <dependencies>
      <dependency id="SampleDependency" version="1.0" />
    </dependencies>
  </metadata>
</package>
```

Note that NuGet adds some default values in the package manifest: The id element contains the name issued on the command line. The version by default is version 1.0. Both the authors and owners elements have been populated with your Windows username, if you have one. All elements in this file, like dependencies on other packages and dependencies on framework assemblies, are explained earlier in this chapter.

Modify the package manifest to something useful, like the package manifest in Listing 3-18.

Listing 3-18. The NuGet Package Manifest for the HelloWorld Package We Are Creating

```xml
<?xml version="1.0"?>
<package >
  <metadata>
    <id>HelloWorld</id>
    <version>1.0.0</version>
    <authors>Maarten Balliauw and Xavier Decoster</authors>
    <owners>Maarten Balliauw and Xavier Decoster</owners>
    <requireLicenseAcceptance>false</requireLicenseAcceptance>
    <description>This package provides a HelloWorld class, written in C#.</description>
    <copyright>Copyright Maarten Balliauw & Xavier Decoster 2013</copyright>
    <tags>ProNuGet Apress HelloWorld Chapter Sample</tags>
  </metadata>
</package>
```

As discussed earlier, we have to create and/or add some package contents. To do this, create the folders required for your package:

- The lib folder can contain assemblies that should be added as a reference to a project when consuming the package.

- The content folder can contain configuration files, code, text files, images—any file you want to add as content in the project consuming the package.

- The tools folder can contain PowerShell scripts that are run on installation or uninstallation of the NuGet package.

Create a lib folder under the same folder as the .nuspec file just created.

For the HelloWorld package, find the sample Visual Studio 2012 solution HelloWorld.sln that comes with this book. It consists of a simple class, HelloWorld, which contains a method, Greet, that takes a string and returns a Hello World message. After compiling the project, copy the HelloWorld.dll file into the lib folder created earlier.

The final step in the process is creating the NuGet package: in essence, just copying the package manifest and package contents into a zip archive with a .nupkg extension. To do so, run the following command from the command line or a PowerShell prompt:

```
nuget pack HelloWorld.nuspec
```

nuget.exe should greet you with a message similar to "Successfully created package 'C:\temp\pro nuget\ HelloWorld.1.0.0.nupkg'", as shown in Figure 3-4. Note that when the package folder structure is incorrect or package manifest information is missing, NuGet will provide a detailed list of errors found so you can easily fix those.

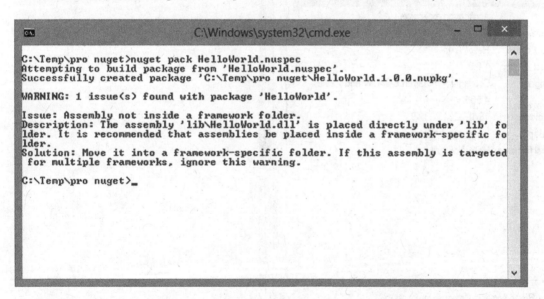

Figure 3-4. *The nuget.exe output after successfully packaging the HelloWorld NuGet package*

The HelloWorld.1.0.0.nupkg file created by the NuGet command line can now be consumed by using the NuGet Visual Studio extension, the NuGet Package Manager Console, or the NuGet command line. This chapter contains a "Testing Packages" section that covers how you can test your package in all of these tools. For now, just to verify that the newly created package works as expected, run the following command:

```
nuget install HelloWorld -Source "c:\temp" -OutputDirectory "test"
```

When running this command, the NuGet command line will download the latest version of the HelloWorld package from the folder specified in the –Source switch, "c:\temp". It will extract the package to a subfolder called test.

Congratulations! You've just created and consumed your first NuGet package.

Creating a Package from an Assembly

In the previous example, we used the nuget spec command, which resulted in a blank package manifest that you could modify and enrich. The NuGet command line offers some extra features with the nuget spec command. One of these features is generating a package manifest from an assembly.

Using the assembly created earlier, HelloWorld.dll, NuGet can look into the assembly details to generate the package manifest. This metadata about an assembly can be revealed by right-clicking the assembly and selecting Properties followed by Details. Windows will give you information similar to what's shown in Figure 3-5.

Figure 3-5. Assembly properties as shown by Windows

From the command line, issue the following command to create a package manifest based on this information:

```
nuget spec -AssemblyPath HelloWorld.dll
```

This command should complete very fast and create a file called HelloWorld.nuspec. The contents of this file are based on the assembly information retrieved from the assembly specified using the –AssemblyPath switch. Listing 3-19 shows you the contents of this file. Note that the id, version, authors, and owners elements contain the information previously consulted through the Windows file property dialog box.

Listing 3-19. The Package Manifest File Generated Using Assembly Information

```xml
<?xml version="1.0"?>
<package >
  <metadata>
    <id>HelloWorld</id>
    <version>1.0.0</version>
    <authors>Maarten Balliauw and Xavier Decoster</authors>
    <owners>Maarten Balliauw and Xavier Decoster</owners>
    <requireLicenseAcceptance>false</requireLicenseAcceptance>
    <description>Package description</description>
    <releaseNotes>Summary of changes made in this release of the package.</releaseNotes>
    <copyright>Copyright 2013</copyright>
    <tags>Tag1 Tag2</tags>
    <dependencies>
      <dependency id="SampleDependency" version="1.0" />
    </dependencies>
  </metadata>
</package>
```

Of course, this package manifest still requires some additional fine-tuning. For example, the copyright, tags, and dependencies elements still contain just sample data. After modifying the package manifest, a NuGet package can be created using the same technique as described previously. Run the following command to package the manifest and assemblies:

```
nuget pack HelloWorld.nuspec
```

The end result will be a NuGet package named HelloWorld.1.0.0.nupkg.

Creating a Package from a Visual Studio Project

In the previous example, we generated a package manifest from the metadata that is stored in an assembly, a great way to create package manifests from already compiled or even third-party assemblies. When you are in control of your own projects, there's an easier way to create a package manifest: create it using the information available in your .csproj, .vbproj, or .fsproj.

Generate a Tokenized Package Manifest

Creating a package manifest from a Visual Studio project is as easy as running the following command in the same folder where your project file resides. It will result in a HelloWorld.nuspec file:

```
nuget spec
```

Using the project file as the source for package manifest generation offers several advantages. First of all, you are not required to build the project first before generating the package metadata. The second advantage is that NuGet will add some so-called *replacement tokens* in your .nuspec file, as you can see in Listing 3-20.

Listing 3-20. The Package Manifest Generated Based on a Visual Studio Project File

```xml
<?xml version="1.0"?>
<package >
  <metadata>
    <id>$id$</id>
    <version>$version$</version>
    <title>$title$</title>
    <authors>$author$</authors>
    <owners>$author$</owners>
    <licenseUrl>http://LICENSE_URL_HERE_OR_DELETE_THIS_LINE</licenseUrl>
    <projectUrl>http://PROJECT_URL_HERE_OR_DELETE_THIS_LINE</projectUrl>
    <iconUrl>http://ICON_URL_HERE_OR_DELETE_THIS_LINE</iconUrl>
    <requireLicenseAcceptance>false</requireLicenseAcceptance>
    <description>$description$</description>
    <releaseNotes>Summary of changes made in this release of the package.</releaseNotes>
    <copyright>Copyright 2013</copyright>
    <tags>Tag1 Tag2</tags>
  </metadata>
</package>
```

Replacement tokens in the package manifest will be populated with project-specific values retrieved from the AssemblyInfo.cs file at the moment the NuGet package is being created. Table 3-7 lists the replacement tokens that can be used in the package manifest as well as their sources.

Table 3-7. *An Overview of the Available Replacement Tokens*

Token	Description
id	The assembly name of the project's output.
$version$	The assembly (informational) version as specified in the project's AssemblyInfo file.
$title$	The assembly title as specified in AssemblyTitleAttribute.
$author$	The company as specified in AssemblyCompanyAttribute.
$company$	The company as specified in AssemblyCompanyAttribute.
$description$	The description as specified in AssemblyDescriptionAttribute.
$references$	This element contains a set of <reference> elements, each of which specifies an assembly that will be referenced by the project. The existence of this element overrides the convention of pulling everything in the lib folder.
$configuration$	The current configuration (for example, Debug or Release).

If you're using replacement tokens, creating NuGet packages suddenly becomes more interesting: you can create a package manifest that contains all required metadata and replace some parts of the manifest with data coming from the Visual Studio project itself. This results in less maintenance of package manifests.

Once the package manifest has been modified with the correct copyright notice, tags, logo URL, and such, it can be packaged. A NuGet package can be created using the same technique as described previously. Run the following command to package the project and the package manifest at once:

```
nuget pack HelloWorld.nuspec
```

If the target project is at version 1.0.0, the end result will be a NuGet package named HelloWorld.1.0.0.nupkg.

The $version$ Token Explained

If you're going to create NuGet packages during automated builds—a topic that we'll cover in greater detail in Chapter 6—the NuGet command line and the $version$ token will allow you to apply automatic versioning. Typically, a project is versioned by using the AssemblyVersionAttribute in a file called AssemblyInfo.cs. Even though there are alternatives for automatic versioning, the $version$ token deserves a little more attention.

A Visual Studio project can make use of three different attributes to provide version information:

- AssemblyVersion
- AssemblyFileVersion
- AssemblyInformationalVersion

This is usually where people get confused: where does the version number come from? How does NuGet replace the $version$ token if there are possibly three different attributes providing version information? For example, consider the version information in Listing 3-21.

Listing 3-21. Detailed Version Information from the AssemblyInfo File

```
[assembly: AssemblyVersion("1.0.0")]
[assembly: AssemblyFileVersion("1.0.0")]
[assembly: AssemblyInformationalVersion("1.0.0-alpha")]
```

To decide which version number is used when creating a NuGet package from a project with this version information and a tokenized nuspec, the following decision flow is used:

1. If the AssemblyInformationalVersion attribute is defined, that one is used. Note how this attribute supports prerelease tags!

2. If the AssemblyInformationalVersion attribute is undefined, the AssemblyVersion attribute is used.

3. If neither the AssemblyInformational attribute nor the AssemblyVersion attribute are defined, your project output will have a version number of 0.0.0.0, as well as the resulting NuGet package.

4. NuGet totally ignores the AssemblyFileVersion attribute.

This behavior is exactly the same when skipping the nuspec at all and building a NuGet package directly from an assembly by using nuget pack SomeAssembly.dll.

Packaging a Visual Studio Project

In the previous example, we generated a package manifest from a Visual Studio project, and you saw that less maintenance of the package manifest is involved. If NuGet can create a manifest of a project, shouldn't it be possible to package a project without the intermediate step of creating a package manifest? The answer is yes.

Open a command prompt in the same folder where your `.csproj` or `.vbproj` file lives, and run the following command to package the project:

```
nuget pack HelloWorld.csproj
```

The end result will be a NuGet package named `HelloWorld.1.0.0.nupkg`. Unfortunately, the package metadata for this project is incomplete and consists only of the package identifier, its version, the authors, and a description—there are no traces of a copyright message, a logo URL, or a list of tags that the consumer of this package can use to search.

The reason for the absence of additional package metadata simply is the absence of that data: NuGet has no means of generating this information if you don't provide it. Therefore, it's always best to create a package manifest, ideally using replacement parameters to get the best of both worlds.

■ **Note** The NuGet `pack` command provides some additional command-line switches. Noteworthy are the `-Build` switch, which will trigger a fresh build of the project when packaging; `-Symbols`, which creates an additional package containing all `.pdb` files for your project; and `-Version`, which overrides the version information listed in the package manifest. More NuGet pack switches are described in the NuGet documentation wiki at `http://docs.nuget.org/docs/reference/command-line-reference#Pack_Command`.

Include Referenced Projects

We are not all building single-project redistributable components, and it is quite likely that the project you want to package is referencing other projects within the same solution. These referenced projects are in fact dependencies that you'll need to ship with your package.

The NuGet command-line `pack` command provides an option you'll need in order to solve this issue: `-IncludeReferencedProjects`. This single option can have two behaviors depending on the presence of nuspec files next to each of your referenced projects.

If a referenced project has a corresponding nuspec file with the same name, that referenced project will be added as a package dependency. If the referenced project is lacking the presence of a corresponding nuspec file, or the name doesn't match the project name, then the referenced project's build output will be added to the contents of the package you're creating.

Imagine the following solution structure:

```
Solution.sln
   - Product.Core.csproj
   - Product.Payments.csproj (depends on Product.Core)
   - Product.ShoppingCart.csproj (depends on Product.Payments and Product.Core)
```

If you want to package `Product.ShoppingCart`, you'll also need to ship the `Product.Payments` and `Product.Core` projects. If none of the referenced projects has a nuspec file, the following command will recursively add all three projects into a single package and produce `Product.ShoppingCart.1.0.0.nupkg`:

```
nuget pack Product.ShoppingCart.csproj -IncludeReferencedProjects
```

If the referenced projects have a corresponding nuspec file, the very same command will produce three NuGet packages with their dependencies:

- `Product.Core.1.0.0.nupkg` (no dependencies)

- `Product.Payments.1.0.0.nupkg`

  - Depends on package ID `Product.Core` and version `>= 1.0.0`

- Product.ShoppingCart.1.0.0.nupkg

  - Depends on package ID Product.Core and version >= 1.0.0

  - Depends on package ID Product.Payments and version >= 1.0.0

Generating the Dependencies Element

So far, all XML generated in the package manifest consisted of the package metadata such as the package identifier, version, and description. What is not generated is the dependencies element, which indicates whether the package requires other NuGet packages to be installed prior to installing it.

If you're creating packages from scratch, we're afraid we can't help you. You'll have to craft your own list of package dependencies and include that list in the package manifest. If you're creating packages by using replacement tokens or when creating packages from a Visual Studio project file, things are different.

Many times, your project will have dependencies on other NuGet packages. These dependencies can be referenced using the Visual Studio NuGet extension or the Package Manager Console. Doing this generates a packages.config file contained in the Visual Studio project. The packages.config file contains a list of all dependencies for a project, including their package identifiers and versions (or a range of supported versions). Listing 3-22 shows the contents of the packages.config file for our HelloWorld project, which is consuming the IFluentInterface package.

Listing 3-22. The packages.config File Containing a Package Dependency on IFluentInterface Version 1.1

```xml
<?xml version="1.0" encoding="utf-8"?>
<packages>
  <package id="IFluentInterface" version="1.1" targetFramework="net45" />
</packages>
```

■ **Note** The IFluentInterface package injects a single interface into the consuming project. Implementing this interface effectively hides all default System.Object members from Visual Studio's IntelliSense. You can find more info at http://bit.ly/ifluentinterface.

Try using the technique described in "Creating a Package from a Visual Studio Project": generate a package manifest using the nuget spec command; update the package manifest; and package the project using either the nuget pack HelloWorld.nuspec command or the nuget pack HelloWorld.csproj command. You might want to remove all unmodified sample values from the generated nuspec file. Their presence will be detected and cause warnings during package creation. The NuGet command line will run this command and provide the output shown in Figure 3-6.

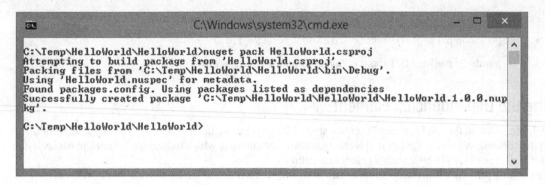

Figure 3-6. *The nuget.exe output when creating a package that consumes packages.config for metadata*

Note the message "Found packages.config. Using packages listed as dependencies." The NuGet command line looks for a packages.config file present in the project directory, and if it finds one, it will use the data as additional metadata and include it in the package manifest. In the case of our HelloWorld project, NuGet lists IFluentInterface version 1.1 as a dependency and will make sure the consumer of our package is also required to install this dependency in his project.

Creating Packages by Using NuGet Package Explorer

Creating NuGet packages is something currently best done by using a package manifest or by packaging your Visual Studio project. The reason for this is that artifacts are created in a reproducible way: the manifest is kept around, the project is kept around, and the same version of all code will always result in the same NuGet package. It can even be automated by creating a batch script that runs several nuget.exe commands at once.

In many situations—for example, when exploring what other people do in their NuGet packages or when creating a test package—a dedicated user interface to work with NuGet packages is preferable. For this purpose, the NuGet Package Explorer (NPE) is a great tool to have in your developer tool belt. It allows you to open, edit, inspect, and validate NuGet packages from an easy-to-use graphical user interface.

As described in Chapter 1, NPE is a ClickOnce application that can be installed from within your browser. Simply navigate to http://npe.codeplex.com and find the Downloads page. You can install and run NPE by clicking the ClickOnce Installer download.

Figure 3-7 shows you the HelloWorld.1.0.0.nupkg created before, opened in NuGet Package Explorer. On the left-hand side, all package manifest metadata is displayed. The right-hand side shows the package's contents. Since we've packaged only some project output, the package consists of only a lib folder containing the HelloWorld.dll assembly.

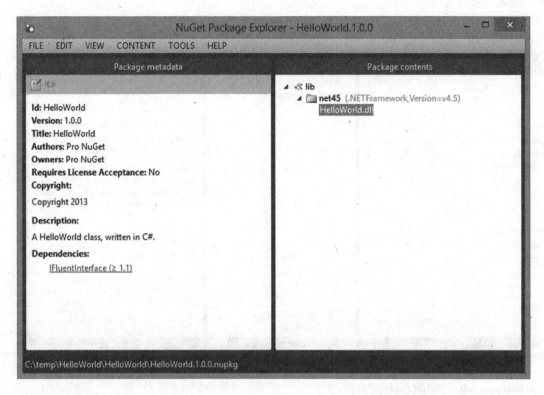

Figure 3-7. NuGet Package Explorer's main windows after opening a NuGet package

Browsing through the menus, you'll find a number of interesting options:

- Selecting File ➤ Export allows you to extract a package to disk.

- Clicking Edit ➤ Edit Package Metadata makes the left-hand screen editable, enabling you to modify the package manifest, add dependencies, and so on.

- By clicking Content ➤ Add, you open an interesting menu to add contents to the package. It enables you to add assemblies, framework folders, files in the tools folder, and so on.

- Finally, selecting Tools ➤ Analyze Package offers probably one of the most interesting menus. After clicking this option, NuGet Package Explorer will scan the complete NuGet package for convention violations and provide warnings and errors when some rule has not been respected. An example is shown in Figure 3-8.

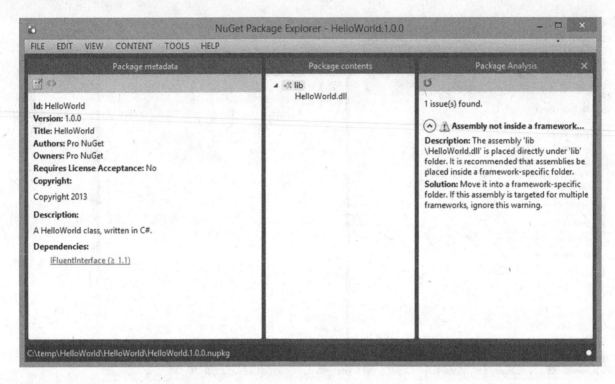

Figure 3-8. *Package analysis in NuGet Package Explorer*

We often use NuGet Package Explorer to open up existing NuGet packages from the official NuGet package source, as many packages contain interesting hidden NuGet gems. For example, if you are wondering about how a `web.config` transform has been created, simply find a package that applies this technique.

An interesting one, for example, is jQuery. Click the File ➤ Open from Feed menu, and search for jQuery. When you find it, double-click the package version you wish to load. Figure 3-9 shows the search we've done while writing this book.

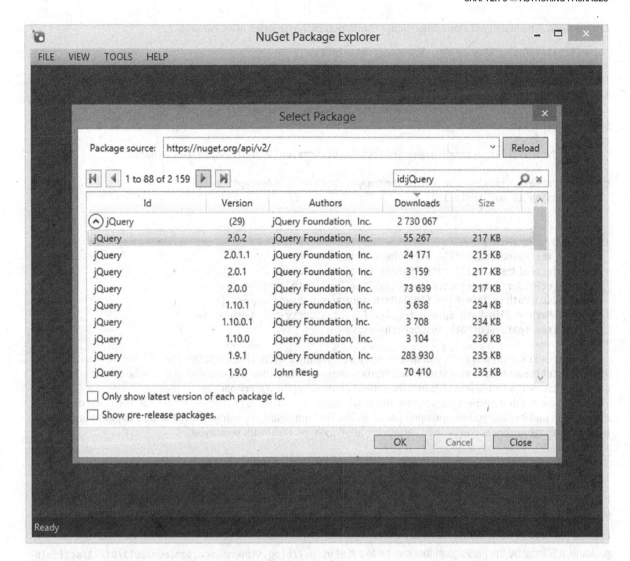

Figure 3-9. *Searching for jQuery by using NuGet Package Explorer*

After opening the latest jQuery package, have a look at the package's contents. Of course, a `content` folder exists, containing all JavaScript files related to jQuery. What is surprising, however, is that there is also a `tools` folder containing both the `install.ps1` and `uninstall.ps1` PowerShell scripts. The contents of `install.ps1` are shown in Listing 3-23.

Listing 3-23. The install.ps1 PowerShell Script Contained in the jQuery NuGet Package

```
param($installPath, $toolsPath, $package, $project)

$extId = "JScriptIntelliSenseParaExtension.Microsoft.039ee76c-3c7f-4281-ad23-f6528ab18623"
$extManager = [Microsoft.VisualStudio.Shell.Package]::GetGlobalService(↪
    [Microsoft.VisualStudio.ExtensionManager.SVsExtensionManager])
$copyOverParaFile = $false
try {
    $copyOverParaFile = $extManager.GetInstalledExtension($extId).State -eq "Enabled"
}
catch [Microsoft.VisualStudio.ExtensionManager.NotInstalledException] {
    #Extension is not installed
}

if ($copyOverParaFile) {
    #Copy the -vsdoc-para file over the -vsdoc file
    #$projectFolder = Split-Path -Parent $project.FileName
    $projectFolder = $project.Properties.Item("FullPath").Value
    $paraVsDocPath = Join-Path $toolsPath jquery-1.6.4-vsdoc-para.js
    $vsDocPath = Join-Path $projectFolder Scripts\jquery-1.6.4-vsdoc.js
    Copy-Item $paraVsDocPath $vsDocPath -Force
}
```

If you read through this code, you may notice that it's being used to check whether the JScriptIntelliSenseParaExtension Visual Studio extension is installed and enabled. If that's the case, it copies an additional JavaScript IntelliSense file into the project consuming the jQuery package.

Of course, we don't expect you to grasp this entire script, nor do we expect you to write one. The point that we are trying to make is that you should open packages you find interesting by using NuGet Package Explorer and look at how the package author accomplished certain installation steps. Steal with your eyes!

■ **Note** The *craziest* NuGet package we've found so far is Steve Sanderson's MvcScaffolding package. It is a NuGet package that contains a bunch of T4 templates (which are a means of code generation in Visual Studio). It also adds PowerShell commands to the NuGet Package Manager Console and enables you to do code generation in ASP.NET MVC. Find the package by using NuGet Package Explorer, and see for yourself. And if you're interested in working with this package, a tutorial by the package author can be found at http://blog.stevensanderson.com/2011/01/13/scaffold-your-aspnet-mvc-3-project-with-the-mvcscaffolding-package/.

Creating Localized Packages

If the component you want to package makes use of resource files, you might want to provide a localized experience to your package consumers. If you have only a handful of cultures to support, you could ship everything within the same single package. This has always been supported and is very straightforward to accomplish.

Resource files tend to be quite large, and this has a negative impact on package size. As a package producer, you have no idea of the localization preferences of your package consumer. If you picked a good default culture, then it doesn't make any sense to force all available languages to everyone all the time. To avoid cluttering your package with many languages the consumer doesn't want or need, it might be a good idea to ship them in separate localized satellite packages.

NuGet supports both scenarios, and it is important to consider the differences between these two approaches.

Setting the Default Language

A NuGet package can optionally expose a metadata element called language. If you intend to support localization, you should really define the package's default language by setting the locale ID, as shown in Listing 3-24.

Listing 3-24. Setting the Package's Default Language

```xml
<?xml version="1.0"?>
<package >
  <metadata>
    <id>$id$</id>
    <version>$version$</version>
    <authors>$author$</authors>
    <description>$description$</description>
    ...
    <language>en-US</language>
  </metadata>
</package>
```

Using a Single-Package Approach

Usually, the simplest approach for localization is to include all of the localized satellite assemblies and XML IntelliSense files in the same package as your runtime. Listing 3-25 shows how the package's \lib folder layout could look.

Listing 3-25. Sample lib Folder Layout of a Single Localized Package

```
\lib
    \net40
        \Component.dll
        \Component.xml
        \nl-BE
            \Component.resources.dll
            \Component.xml
        \fr
            \Component.resources.dll
            \Component.xml
```

The preceding package contains a single component library, Component.dll, located in \lib\net40 that contains the English resources as part of the runtime assembly.

The package also contains two additional culture-specific resource folders, \lib\net40\nl-BE and \lib\net40\fr-FR. Each of them contains localized satellite assemblies and XML IntelliSense files, for Dutch, Belgium, and French respectively.

■ **Tip** Take a look at the Microsoft.Data.OData package for another great example of this scenario (starting from v5.4.0). You'll find it in the NuGet Gallery using the following URL:
http://nuget.org/packages/Microsoft.Data.OData/5.4.0

Using a Satellite-Package Approach

The .NET Framework itself has the concept of satellite assemblies, DLL files containing only localizable resources such as strings, bitmaps, and so on. They typically do not contain any compiled code, except for some autogenerated utility classes. For every culture our application or library has to support, we can create a separate satellite assembly. You can take the same approach with NuGet packages: have one NuGet package containing all application logic, and several secondary packages containing just the localizable resources.

Imagine you have a library called SampleLib and you want to create localized versions of it for nl-BE (Dutch, Belgium) and fr (French). Using the satellite-package approach, you would create three packages:

- SampleLib, containing all binaries for the library

- SampleLib.nl-BE, containing the localizable resources for Dutch, Belgium

- SampleLib.fr, containing the localizable resources for French

Listing 3-26 shows a sample \lib folder for each of these three packages and how you would structure the resource assemblies in them.

Listing 3-26. Lib Folder Layouts for the SampleLib, SampleLib.nl-BE, and SampleLib.fr Packages Using the Satellite Package Approach

SampleLib
```
\lib
    \net40
        \Component.dll
        \Component.xml
```

SampleLib.nl-BE
```
\lib
    \net40
        \nl-BE
            \Component.resources.dll
            \Component.xml
```

SampleLib.fr
```
\lib
    \net40
        \fr
            \Component.resources.dll
            \Component.xml
```

As you can see from the sample package structures, there is one "main" package, which contains a single component library, Component.dll, located in \lib\net40 that contains the English resources as part of the runtime assembly. Next, we have two satellite packages, which contain a culture-specific subfolder under \lib (for example, \lib\net40\nl-BE for Dutch, Belgium). Each of these satellite packages contains localized satellite assemblies and XML IntelliSense files.

For each localized package, the <language /> element should be set in the package metadata. Listing 3-27 shows the package metadata for the French satellite package of SampleLib.

Listing 3-27. Setting the Satellite Package's Culture

```
<?xml version="1.0"?>
<package >
  <metadata>
```

```
    <id>$id$</id>
    <version>$version$</version>
    <authors>$author$</authors>
    <description>$description$</description>
    ...
    <language>fr</language>
    <dependencies>
        <dependency id="SampleLib" version="[1.1.0]" />
    </dependencies>
    </metadata>
</package>
```

There are some conventions to be respected when working with satellite packages. In order for a package to be treated as a satellite package, all of the following conventions must be respected:

- The ID of the satellite package must match that of the library package, followed by a dot (.) and then the target culture. For example, the SampleLib package can have a satellite package named SampleLib.fr for French.

- In the package metadata, a <language /> element should be specified that matches the target language, as shown in Listing 3-27. Unless specific subcultures are being provided, the higher-level culture is recommended. For example, use ja instead of ja-JP for Japanese packages. The language element's value must exactly match the language suffix on the package ID.

- The satellite package must have an exact dependency on the library package. This means the SampleLib.fr package must have a dependency on the SampleLib package. This dependency should have a specific version defined by using square brackets—for example, [1.1.0].

- NuGet will install only culture-specific files within the lib folder. For example, localizable resources for Japanese should be under the \lib\ja or \lib\ja-JP folder to be installed. This folder name should also be an exact match with the culture specified in the package metadata and the package name.

By following these conventions, NuGet will recognize that the package is a satellite during installation and copy the localized files from the \lib folder into the \lib folder of the main package under the project's packages folder. Upon compilation, Visual Studio will copy these contents into the output folder.

When uninstalling a satellite package, only the localized files from that package are uninstalled, and the library package or other satellite packages will remain untouched.

Comparing Approaches

There are some benefits and drawbacks for both approaches of creating localized packages. The single-package approach has the following benefits:

- A single-package installation contains all supported localizable resources.

- Easy to maintain and package, as there is just one package to create from a compiled library.

- Versioning is easy: each version of the package is self-contained, and there are no situations where the library itself and its resources can have a different version being used.

When using the single-package approach, there are some drawbacks as well:

- Package size can be massive, depending on the number of supported cultures and size of resources. Every installation of this package will pull down all localizable resources.

- Shipping support for new cultures is difficult, as that would encompass shipping a new single package.

These drawbacks can be solved by working with satellite packages:

- The actual library package is kept small, and package consumers can opt into installing additional localized bits, culture by culture.

- If after a release you want to ship support for a previously unsupported culture or want to ship an update for specific cultures, you would ship just those satellite packages.

- Package metadata can be localized. Each satellite assembly can have a localized description and tags, making discoverability in the official NuGet Gallery easier.

But guess what: there are some drawbacks to the satellite-package approach as well:

- For a single library supporting 50 cultures, there would be 51 packages to ship and maintain. This means clutter in search results and projects, for the package producer as well as for package consumers.

- Versioning: satellite packages must have an exact version dependency on the associated package in which the library itself resides. Whenever a new version of the library is shipped, all satellite packages have to be shipped as well, even if the localizable resources did not change.

As you can see from this comparison, there are benefits and drawbacks to both approaches. Depending on the situation and scenario you are working with, an approach should be chosen. Generally, if you have just a few cultures to support, the single-package approach may be easy to work with. If you have multiple or want to be able to ship updates to resources out-of-band, the satellite package approach will be the way to go. And remember, since NuGet packages are versioned according to SemVer, all it takes is a major version number increase to change the approach taken.

Adding the Finishing Touches

Most packages will simply inject some content or add dependencies to the consuming project, but sometimes it is really useful or even desired to perform some configuration in the target project, automate a few things, or even provide automation capabilities to the package consumer. When you start creating your first NuGet packages, you might immediately hit such a requirement and find yourself in an uncomfortable situation because you might have no idea how to tackle this challenge. Well, you already did a great job in buying this book and doing some research, and while we highly recommend you read this chapter in full detail, we'd like to pay a little extra attention to the details that make your package stand out.

Provide a Smooth User Experience

The user in this case is the package consumer. NuGet already provides quite a few options to provide a smooth installation experience. A smooth user experience, however, goes beyond installation of your package.

Let's take the example of another HTTP handler being shipped through NuGet: the Glimpse web debugging and diagnostics tool. Strictly speaking, it would be enough to add a reference to the Glimpse HTTP handler during installation. That would make the handler available to the package consumer, but that consumer would need to go through the project's documentation in order to properly configure the component and only then, if no mistakes were made, the component would be ready to use. This is where the parallel with open source projects can be drawn: what distinguishes great open source projects from good ones? Documentation. Taking this to another level: what distinguishes great NuGet packages from the good ones? A reduced need for documentation! We believe the Glimpse project is doing a great job in setting the standard for open source projects as well as for package creators.

■ **Tip** You can read up on the Glimpse project at `http://getglimpse.com`.

Learn from Others by Inspecting Their Packages

The best way to learn how to create that awesome package you want to build is to learn from others. Find a package that is providing the installation experience you're after and download it for inspection. Extract it, read its scripts, and walk the dependency chain.

We'll continue using Glimpse as an example, but there are quite a few others out there that deserve your attention. The Glimpse package serves as a good example in this chapter because the package content is not too crowded; it's making use of quite a few features such as multiplatform targeting, configuration file transformations, and PowerShell hooks; and it has a nice dependency chain. For example, installing the Glimpse.Mvc4 package will also install the Glimpse.AspNet and Glimpse.Core packages, each serving a very specific purpose.

To inspect a package (for instance, the Glimpse.AspNet package), we recommend you use the NuGet Package Explorer tool, which is available at http://npe.codeplex.com. Start the application, select Open a Package from Online Feed (or press Ctrl+G) and enter the Glimpse.AspNet query into the search box to fetch it from the official NuGet Gallery feed, as shown in Figure 3-10 and Figure 3-11.

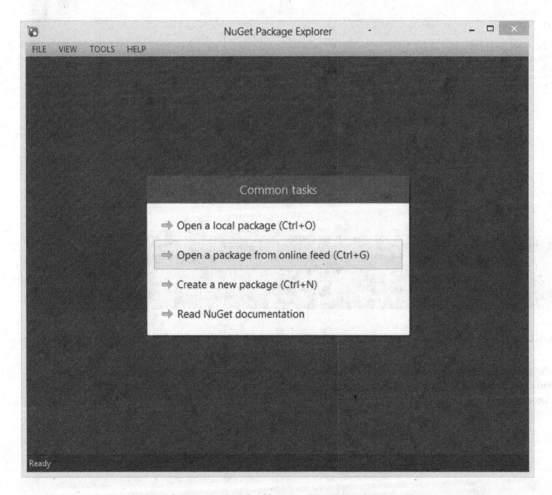

Figure 3-10. *Open a package from an online feed by using NuGet Package Explorer*

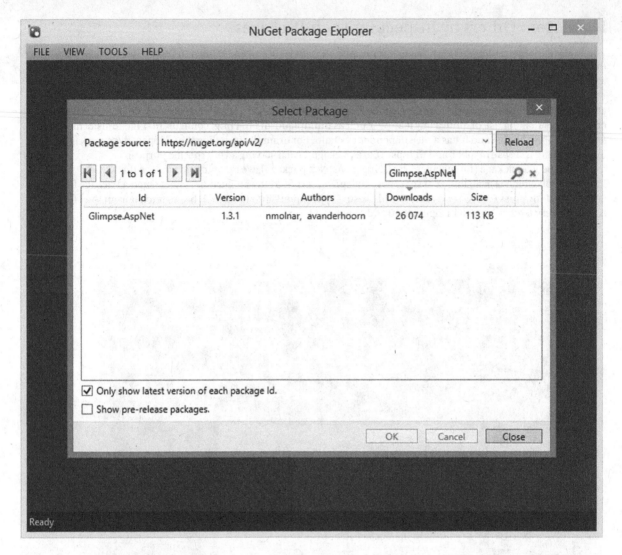

Figure 3-11. *Using NuGet Package Explorer to query the NuGet Gallery feed for the latest Glimpse.AspNet package*

Select the package and click the OK button to download and open the package for inspection. Once you have done this, you can take a look at the package's content. To open a file (for example, the `web.config.transform` file), simply double-click it. You should see something similar to Figure 3-12.

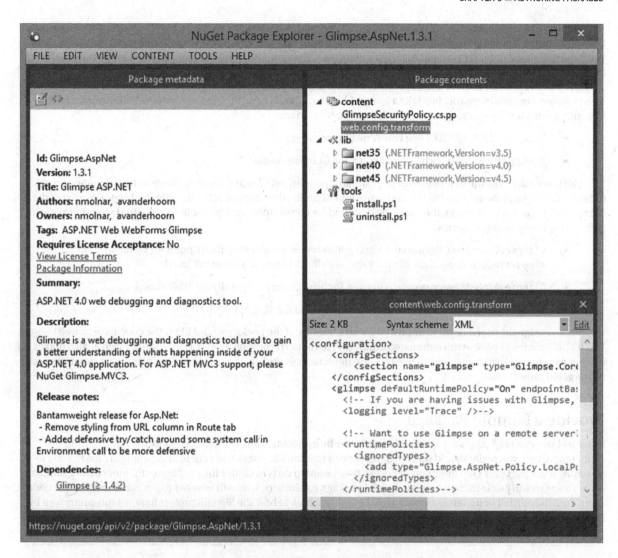

Figure 3-12. A closer look at the Glimpse.AspNet package's web.config.transform file

Design from a Consumer's Perspective

In order for your package to be consumed, it must fulfill the needs of a consumer. That should also be a reason for you to create the package in the first place. This perspective is what you need to hold on to when authoring NuGet packages. In fact, that's likely true as well for the package's contents.

This seems so obvious at first, but quite often people run into issues using NuGet because this basic principle is not applied in their software design. Typical symptoms of this issue are as follows:

- The need to auto-update packages depending on a newly shipped version of a package

- Excessive build time or chained automated builds producing a large graph of dependent NuGet packages

- Excessive list of NuGet dependencies for a single NuGet package

We'll go into detail about how to deal with automated builds starting in Chapter 6, but the concept of designing from a consumer's point of view is critical for package authors. The preceding symptoms are often an indication that you have a reversed order for your package dependencies. Often this also indicates that you need to split your software into smaller distributable components by applying separation of concerns and the single-responsibility principle.

It is a better practice to have a few specialized packages, optionally depending on a shared generic component. This is quite a common scenario; just take a look at `Glimpse.Core`. When you want to consume Glimpse, you have a few entry points forcing you to question which one you want to use:

- Using ASP.NET MVC4? Then consume `Glimpse.Mvc4`.

- Using ASP.NET Web Forms? Then consume `Glimpse.AspNet`.

Did you notice how the `Glimpse.Mvc4` package is depending on `Glimpse.AspNet`, which in turn depends on `Glimpse.Core`? All of them are using the same core functionality: the Glimpse HTTP handler is shipped as part of the `Glimpse.Core` package. However, the packages designed for consumption are providing specialized support for each of their respective target platforms.

- `Glimpse.Core`: The Glimpse core library; also serves as the extensibility point for Glimpse *plug-ins* (which depend on this package as well, for example, `Glimpse.Elmah`)

- `Glimpse.AspNet`: Entry-point to Glimpse for projects targeting ASP.NET Web Forms

- `Glimpse.Mvc4`: Entry point to Glimpse for projects targeting ASP.NET MVC 4

These design decisions result in improved maintainability of the packages (and likely the code base as well). You'll also have fewer issues with automated builds due to reduced complexity of the dependency tree. It also makes it super easy for package consumers to just pick the right package and get the best installation and user experience for the targeted project platform.

Provide a Sample Package

If you feel you can help your package consumers better by providing some sample code demonstrating how to use your component, you really should do that! Sometimes a readme file just doesn't cut it, and people are asking you to just show them the code. One thing you definitely don't want to do is to clutter the package with unnecessary sample code. Doing so will cause friction for your faithful package consumers, who will now need to remove this sample code every time they install or update your packages. Let's take a look at how the SignalR project handles this pretty well by creating a sample package.

■ **Note** The SignalR project is designed to make it incredibly simple to add real-time web functionality to your applications, such as real-time server-side content publication to the connected clients.

You can read more about the SignalR project at `http://signalr.net`.

If you search the NuGet Gallery for packages matching the term *SignalR*, you'll notice the existence of the `Microsoft.AspNet.SignalR.Sample` package. The existence of a sample package makes it incredibly easy to get started with SignalR and learn how to add real-time functionality to a web application. Just create an empty web application project and run `Install-Package Microsoft.AspNet.SignalR.Sample`.

You'll see that the sample code is grouped into a `SignalR.Sample` folder (except for the `Scripts` and `App_Start` folders, which are common conventions for a web project). If you followed the preceding steps, you should see the SignalR Stock Ticker Sample, as shown in Figure 3-13.

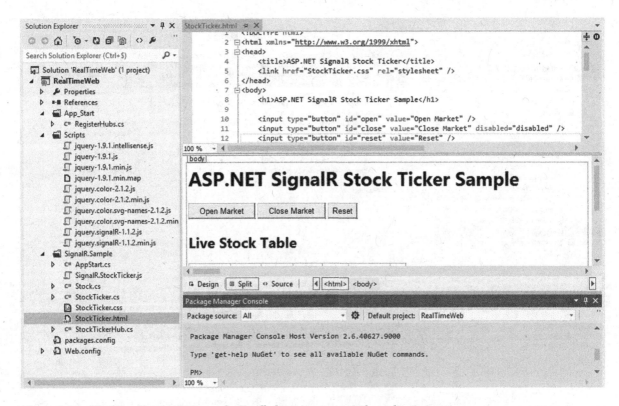

Figure 3-13. *The SignalR ASP.NET sample installed into an empty web application project*

The key take-away here is that the sample code is not forced upon your package consumers. Those who want to consume the sample explicitly need to install the sample package. But what is really neat is that the sample package is depending on the package you're providing the sample code for, in this case `Microsoft.AspNet.SignalR`. This means that when the consumer of a sample package wants to get rid of the sample code while leaving the actual SignalR dependency intact, he can do so with a single command:

```
Uninstall-Package Microsoft.AspNet.SignalR.Sample
```

Figure 3-14 clearly highlights that all other packages, including the `Microsoft.AspNet.SignalR` package and its dependencies, are left untouched and only the sample code got removed.

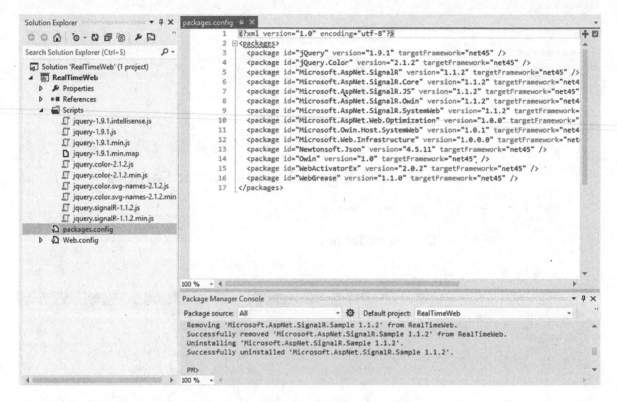

Figure 3-14. Removing the sample package should leave the actual package dependencies intact

Testing Packages

So far, we've created a series of NuGet packages. One of the methods to test and consume those packages is to push these packages to the official NuGet package source. Chances are you don't want to do that; maybe the package you are creating is just a test package or isn't stable enough to be on the public package source. Maybe it even contains intellectual property that you don't want landing on the streets of the Internet, for everyone to use!

A solution is to set up your own NuGet package source, which we will explain in Chapter 6. However, there's no need to set up a full-blown package repository when all you want to do is consume your freshly created NuGet package.

The easiest way to set up a test NuGet package source is by simply copying all your .nupkg files in a folder. For example, I have a folder on my drive where I copy packages that I want to test: C:\Sources\NuGet Repository. This folder can be specified as a package source for the NuGet command line, the NuGet Visual Studio extension, or the Package Manager Console. In Chapter 3, you learned how to configure each of these clients.

The NuGet command line does not have any toolbars to select out of a list of package sources. By default, the NuGet command line will use all package sources defined in the nuget.config file, which can be found in %AppData%\NuGet\nuget.config. You can change this file and add a permanent reference to the folder on your disk containing NuGet packages. Most commands (for example, the install command) support a command-line switch, -Source, which uses the specified package source only for one action.

To configure package sources for the NuGet Visual Studio extension or the Package Manager Console, open Visual Studio and find the Tools ➤ Library Package Manager ➤ Package Manager Settings menu. To add a package source, provide a name and a path to the package source, and click the Add button. Figure 3-15 shows you a sample configuration of package sources.

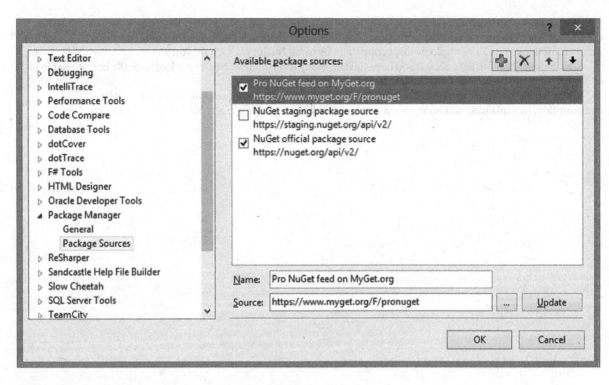

Figure 3-15. *Configuring package sources in Visual Studio*

From the moment a local package source has been configured, all that's left to do to test your packages is issue some commands on the command line or open a new Visual Studio project and add a package reference to it, making sure to select the package source containing your test packages.

Summary

In this chapter, you have learned that NuGet embraces the conventions-over-configuration principle, using a set of simple rules. You have been introduced to the NuGet package manifest, which contains all metadata and describes the package contents. This manifest and these rules deserve special attention by package producers, because both the package management tool and consumers are relying on them. This also explains why shipping a component or framework is more than just combining a set of library files in a zip archive.

We also explained to you how a good NuGet package should be structured—separating libraries from contents and tools. As such, a NuGet package can do more than add a reference to some assemblies by injecting content and code into the consuming Visual Studio project, or through the execution of custom scripts or executables during specific steps of the package management flow. This also opened the door to extensibility and automation of Visual Studio, the Package Manager Console, or NuGet itself. This extensibility is something we will come back to in Chapter 9.

In addition, we illustrated how you can easily create manifest files and NuGet packages using either the NuGet command line or NuGet Package Explorer. Creating your own manifest files gives you a lot of flexibility as a package producer and helps you to support various scenarios of package creation, both manual and automated, starting from an assembly, a Visual Studio project, or a convention-based working folder containing a NuGet manifest file.

We've stated that a great package is designed from a consumer's perspective and should provide a smooth user experience and perhaps even a sample package. The Glimpse and SignalR packages are a great resource to learn from. This is something you can easily do by inspecting them by using NuGet Package Explorer.

Last but not least, we have shown you how you can easily test your own NuGet packages locally before pushing and publishing the package to a NuGet feed for consumption.

In the next chapter, we will continue with the next step in the process of shipping your own packages for consumption, by explaining you how you can push and publish a package to any NuGet feed or repository.

CHAPTER 4

Publishing Packages

In Chapter 3, we demonstrated how you can create your own NuGet packages. It would be a shame if those packages weren't available to others, right?

This chapter will bridge the gap between package creation and package consumption. We'll show you how you can publish those precious packages to a NuGet feed—whether to nuget.org which is available to everyone, or to your own private package feed. You'll learn that all this relies on three simple things: your NuGet package, a feed, and an API key.

We'll also explore how you can publish source code and debug symbols along with your binary NuGet package. This will enable consumers of your NuGet package to debug and step through your source code automatically from inside Visual Studio.

Creating a Sample Package

Let's start this chapter with creating a simple package that we'll deploy to nuget.org. Feel free to create your own Visual Studio project containing code you wish to ship through the nuget.org Gallery, or use the project we'll create in this section. This section briefly covers creating a NuGet package. Refer to Chapter 3 for in-depth knowledge about creating NuGet packages.

Open Visual Studio and create a new Class Library project titled **ProNuGetStringExtensions**, as shown in Figure 4-1.

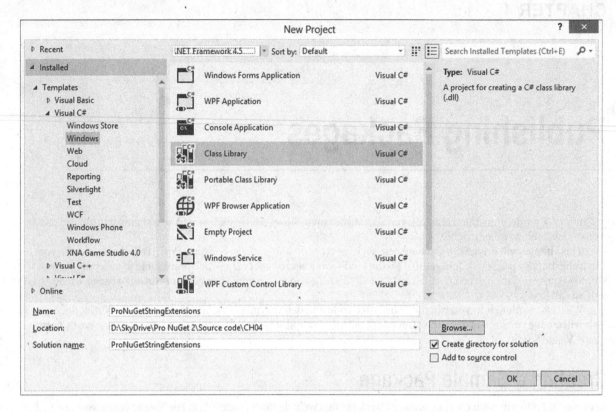

Figure 4-1. *Creating a sample class library project that will be published to* nuget.org

By default, this new project will contain a file named Class1.cs. Since it's more fun to publish a useful NuGet package rather than a simple Hello World–style package, we'll provide some useful code. Remove this file and add a new class called StringExtensions. The code for this class can be found in Listing 4-1.

Listing 4-1. The StringExtensions Class

```
namespace System
{
    public static class StringExtensions
    {
        public static string Truncate(this string input, int length)
        {
            return Truncate(input, length, "...");
        }

        public static string Truncate(this string input, int length, string suffix)
        {
            if (input == null)
            {
                return null;
            }
```

```
        if (input.Length <= length)
        {
            return input;
        }

        if (suffix == null)
        {
            suffix = "...";
        }

        return input.Substring(0, length - suffix.Length) + suffix;
    }
}
}
```

The class that you have just added to this project will provide people with a useful extension method for strings: Truncate. For example, if you have a long string, you can use the Truncate extension method to truncate the string and add an ellipsis at the end. If we run Truncate(9, "...") on the current paragraph, the result would be "The class...".

■ **Note** An *extension method* is a language feature of C# and Visual Basic.NET that enables you to add behavior to existing types without creating a new derived type, recompiling, or modifying the original type. This makes it possible to extend existing types such as System.String, even if the original source code is out of your control.

Try compiling the project (press Ctrl+Shift+B, or choose Build ➤ Build Solution). If the project compiles correctly, it's time to create a NuGet package for this project. Open the folder where the ProNuGetStringExtensions.csproj file is located, and create a NuGet package manifest by running the nuget spec command from the command line. A file named ProNuGetStringExtensions.nuspec should be created; modify its contents to something similar to the package manifest shown in Listing 4-2.

Listing 4-2. The Sample Package Manifest That Will Be Used Throughout This Chapter

```
<?xml version="1.0"?>
<package >
  <metadata>
    <id>$id$</id>
    <version>$version$</version>
    <title>$title$</title>
    <authors>Maarten Balliauw, Xavier Decoster</authors>
    <owners>Maarten Balliauw, Xavier Decoster</owners>
    <requireLicenseAcceptance>false</requireLicenseAcceptance>
    <description>Some useful string extensions for everyday use.</description>
    <copyright>Copyright 2013 Maarten Balliauw and Xavier Decoster</copyright>
    <tags>string extensions extension methods truncate</tags>
  </metadata>
</package>
```

As you learned in Chapter 3, the various tokens in the package manifest (id, $version$ and $title$) will be acquired from the project's AssemblyInfo attributes. Packaging this project is now very straightforward: run the command nuget pack ProNuGetStringExtensions.csproj -Version 1.0.0, and witness the NuGet package file ProNuGetStringExtensions.1.0.0.nupkg being created. We now have created the NuGet package that will be used throughout this chapter.

■ **Note**   To ensure that the installation process of the package is what you'd expect, feel free to test the `ProNuGetStringExtensions.1.0.0.nupkg` NuGet package by using the approach described in the "Testing Packages" section of Chapter 3.

Contributing to `nuget.org`

Whenever you create a NuGet package, chances are that you will want to publish this package on a NuGet feed. For example, you can publish your company's NuGet packages to a private NuGet feed, something we'll continue to describe in the next chapter. Another option is to publish a NuGet package to the public NuGet Gallery found at `www.nuget.org`.

The NuGet Gallery is an online collection of NuGet packages available out of the box in Visual Studio after you install the NuGet Package Manager extension. As Figure 4-2 shows, the Packages tab allows you to search for packages, inspect package information, consult package ratings, and find out the author of a NuGet package. It contains NuGet packages contributed by a variety of authors, including Microsoft, which is interesting: your NuGet package will be equally visible in these listings as, say, Microsoft's Entity Framework.

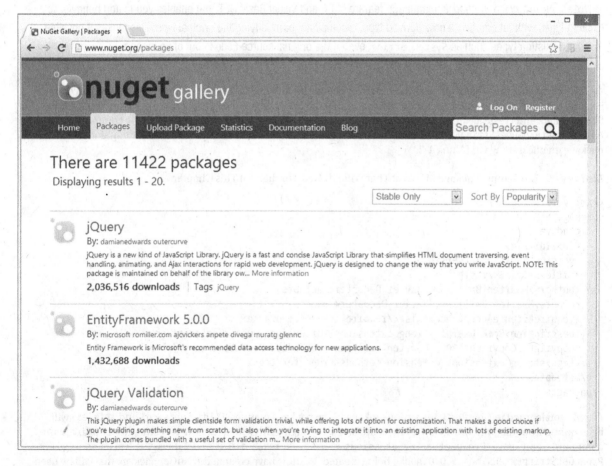

Figure 4-2. *The NuGet Gallery found at* `www.nuget.org`

Creating an Account

Before being able to publish a NuGet package on www.nuget.org, an account is required. Obtaining an account is a simple and short process in which you select a username and a password and provide your e-mail address. The account registration page for www.nuget.org can be found at www.nuget.org/Account/Register.

After creating an account (and confirming it by using the link sent to the e-mail address you provided), you can log on at www.nuget.org/Users/Account/LogOn and click your username in the top-right corner of the screen. This will bring you to an overview page of your account on www.nuget.org, as can be seen in Figure 4-3.

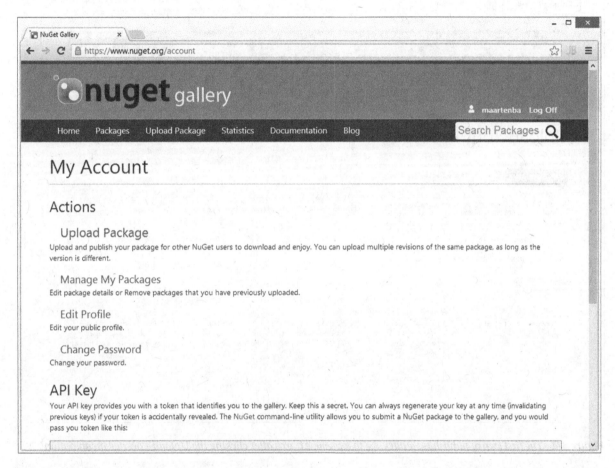

Figure 4-3. *The My Account page on www.nuget.org, displaying a summary of all management options for a NuGet account*

The My Account page offers some management options related to your account on www.nuget.org. It allows you to upload packages, manage your packages, edit your profile, change your password, and manage your API key.

The first option allows you to upload a new package. The second option, Manage My Packages, allows you to manage your packages. These first two options are the topic of the next section of this chapter. Edit Profile allows you to edit your public profile as it will be seen by other users of www.myget.org. Change Password speaks for itself: you can use this option to change your password. Finally, we can manage our API key, an option we'll discuss in the "Obtaining an API Key" section of this chapter.

Publishing a NuGet Package

The only way to let the world know about your package is to publish it to a NuGet feed. Publishing a package to nuget.org can be done by anyone who has an account on www.nuget.org, as you now have since you are following the steps in this chapter. After signing in to www.nuget.org, click the Upload Package link in the top menu. This should navigate you to the page shown in Figure 4-4.

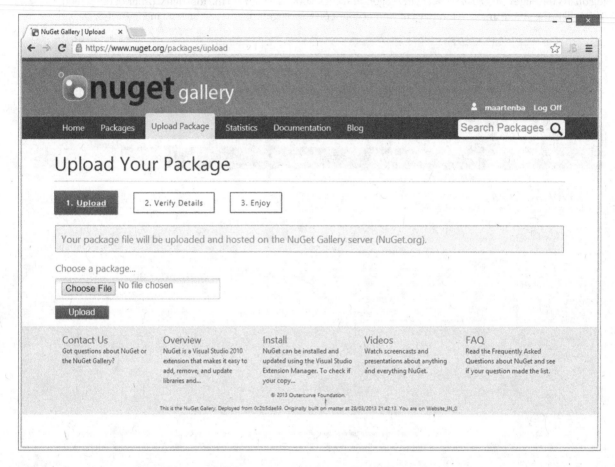

Figure 4-4. *The first step of publishing a package to* www.nuget.org *after clicking the Upload Package menu option*

Using the file upload, you can upload the package you created from your local computer. Browse for the ProNuGetStringExtensions.1.0.0.nupkg file located on your computer. Next, click the Upload button, and wait until the NuGet package has been uploaded to www.nuget.org. After uploading the NuGet package, you will be presented with the screen shown in Figure 4-5.

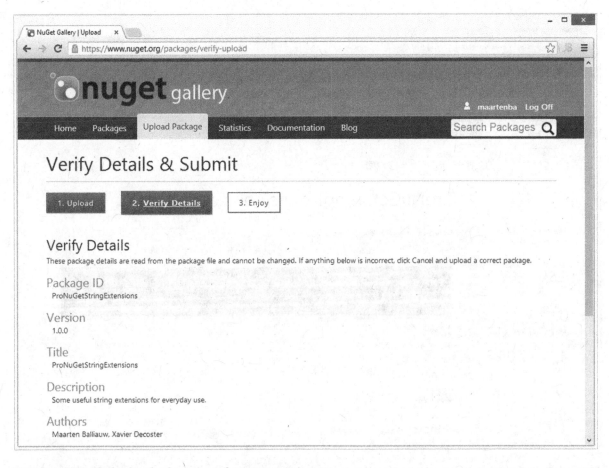

Figure 4-5. *Verify the details of your contribution to* nuget.org

On this page, you can verify the details of your NuGet package. All data shown comes directly from the package manifest, which was embedded in the NuGet package file. You cannot change these values, but if something looks wrong, you can cancel the upload, correct the values in the NuGet package manifest, and upload a corrected version of the package. The List This Package in Search Results check box at the bottom of the page can be left untouched, as otherwise your package will not be shown in the NuGet Gallery.

■ **Note** An unlisted package can be downloaded from the NuGet feed when there are other packages depending on it, but will never show up in search results.

When the information about the package to be published is correct, click the Submit button at the bottom of this page. This will present you with a package details page, as shown in Figure 4-6. After a short time, usually less than a minute, you should be able to find your freshly submitted NuGet package in the NuGet Gallery.

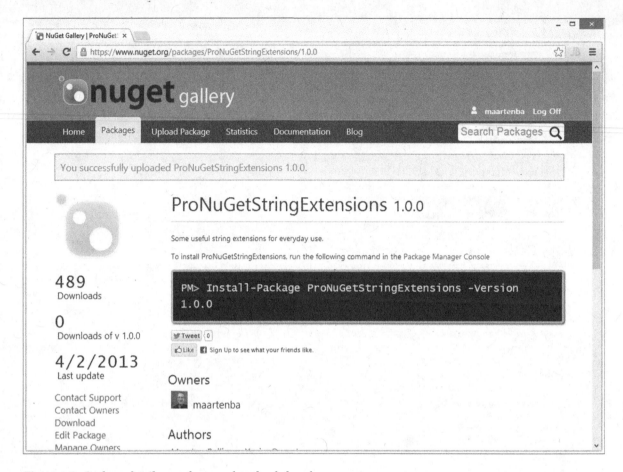

Figure 4-6. *Package details page for a newly uploaded package*

■ **Note** This section demonstrated the happy path of submitting a NuGet package. It is important to know that from the moment you upload a package on `www.nuget.org`, it will be available under the Manage My Packages page, under the Unpublished Packages listing. From there, you can either delete a pending package submission or finalize and publish the submission to the NuGet Gallery.

Managing Published Packages

After a few submissions of a package on `nuget.org`, chances are you want to manage all of your submitted packages. Also, if you've previously started submitting a package to `www.nuget.org` but weren't able to complete the publishing process, you may want to either finalize or abandon the unpublished package.

Log in at `www.nuget.org` using your account and find the Manage My Packages page. It can be found by clicking your username when logged in and navigating directly to `www.nuget.org/Account/Packages`. This page will show an Unpublished Packages list, if any exist, as well as a list of submissions that have been published to the NuGet Gallery. Figure 4-7 shows you what this page may look like (we admit, we're addicted to publishing NuGet packages).

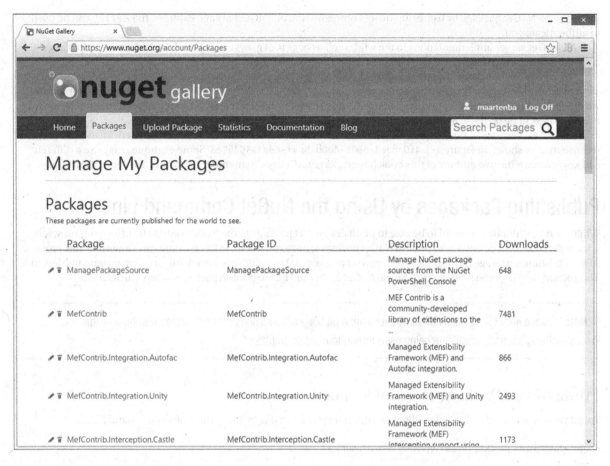

Figure 4-7. *Overview of your packages on* nuget.org

In addition to being able to finalize a package submission from the Unpublished Packages list (at the bottom of this page), you can also list or unlist packages on nuget.org.

■ **Caution**   Nuget.org does not allow package authors to remove nor overwrite their package on www.nuget.org, and that's a good thing! People may depend on your NuGet package and may even depend on a specific version you've published. This puts you in a powerful position: you have the ability to break people's development process by suddenly removing one of their dependencies. You are responsible for software builds worldwide! This is why nuget.org forces you to be nice and keep every package version you publish on the NuGet Gallery, even if it is buggy or outdated.

Obtaining an API Key

Since you created an account on www.nuget.org earlier in this chapter, the My Account page (refer to Figure 4-3) showed the existence of something known as an API key. This API key provides you with a token that identifies you to a NuGet feed. An API key is not required to work with the NuGet Gallery through www.nuget.org in a web browser, as you will always have to log in using your account's username and password combination. However, when you're publishing a NuGet package by using the NuGet command line or NuGet Package Explorer, the API key will be used to authenticate you.

All NuGet server implementations in the wild, such as nuget.org, myget.org, and the NuGet.Server package have the notion of an API key.

On the My Account page, you can easily find your API key to publish packages to nuget.org. It also features a Generate New Key button, which you can use to generate a new API key and invalidate your current one, something we did after writing this chapter to ensure that you, dear reader, cannot publish NuGet packages under our NuGet.org account—just to be on the safe side.

In the next sections of this chapter, the API key listed under the My Account page will be used. Most examples will use the key shown in Figure 4-3, 4f0ebaea-d608-4e0b-bd4f-eda3a59865e8. Some examples may use a different API key, because the two authors of this book have different API keys. Remember that yours is listed on NuGet.org.

Publishing Packages by Using the NuGet Command Line

While there's no doubt it is useful to be able to publish a NuGet package to the NuGet Gallery by using your browser, it is not the most convenient way to publish NuGet packages, not to mention the fact that you can't automate this process. Also, publishing a package through your web browser probably takes more time than doing so using a command-line tool. This section will show you how you can use the NuGet command line to publish packages to any NuGet feed.

■ **Note** Since nuget.org does not allow overwriting packages, you'll see different version numbers of the ProNuGetStringExtensions package being used throughout the examples.

Publishing a Package to a NuGet Feed

To get you started quickly, issue the following command on a console by using the NuGet command line:

```
nuget push ProNuGetStringExtensions.1.0.0.nupkg
```

As you can see in Figure 4-8, this command fails, because no API key was specified to authenticate you to the NuGet Gallery and to identify you as the package owner.

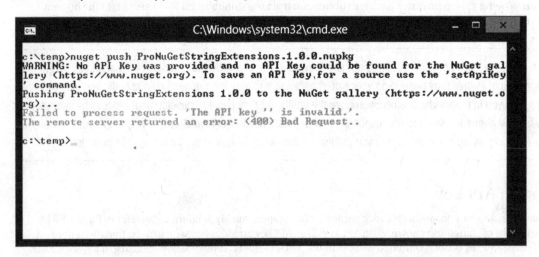

Figure 4-8. Pushing a NuGet package to nuget.org fails because no API key was specified

To overcome this failure, specify the API key retrieved earlier in this chapter in the command. Let's retry using the following command:

```
nuget push ProNuGetStringExtensions.1.0.0.nupkg 4f0ebaea-d608-4e0b-bd4f-eda3a59865e8
```

Figure 4-9 shows you the result of specifying the API key when publishing our NuGet package—a successful publication. After approximately a minute, the ProNuGetStringExtensions package should be visible in the NuGet Gallery at www.nuget.org.

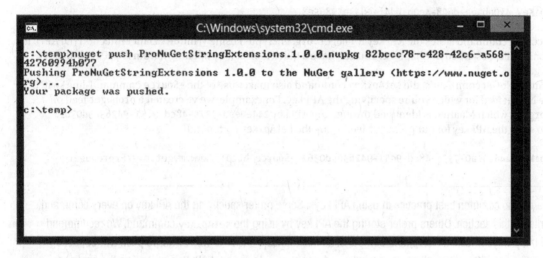

Figure 4-9. *The result of a NuGet push command publishing a package to nuget.org*

Most NuGet commands, including the nuget push command, support the -Source switch and support pushing packages to feeds other than nuget.org. The following command pushes our package to the pronuget feed on www.myget.org:

```
nuget push ProNuGetStringExtensions.1.0.0.nupkg 8572d509-9860-4236-9016-d15dfa7e264b
    -Source http://www.myget.org/F/pronuget
```

■ **Note** You may notice that the API key used in this command is different from the API key used earlier in this section. The reason for this is that, since we are pushing to a NuGet feed other nuget.org, the API key for that other repository will be different.

Managing API Keys

As you've seen in the previous section, all NuGet server implementations out there, such as nuget.org, myget.org, and the NuGet.Server package, have a notion of an API key. This API key is used to authenticate you and to identify you as the rightful owner of a package published on a NuGet feed.

The NuGet command line features a setApiKey command, which is used to store API keys in a central location in an encrypted manner. Doing so makes publishing packages easy, because you have to specify the API key only once. Open a console, and use the NuGet command line to store the API key for nuget.org:

```
nuget setApiKey 4f0ebaea-d608-4e0b-bd4f-eda3a59865e8
```

The preceding command stores the API key for nuget.org, encrypted using Windows Data Protection (DPAPI), in the nuget.config file, described in Chapter 2. You can have a quick look at it by opening it from %AppData%\NuGet\ NuGet.config.

As with most NuGet commands, the setApiKey command also makes use of the –Source command-line switch to specify the NuGet feed for which you're specifying the API key. For example, we've created a pronuget feed on www.myget.org, on which Maarten is identified through the API key 244e9ea0-737e-48cd-9c51-9426365d0362. Here's how to store the API key for our pronuget feed using the setApiKey command:

```
nuget setApiKey 244e9ea0-737e-48cd-9c51-9426365d0362 –Source http://www.myget.org/F/pronuget
```

■ **Note** There is no common best practice in using API keys. Some prefer specifying the API key on every command, as shown earlier in this section. Others prefer storing the API key by using the setApiKey command. We recommend storing the API key on your local development computer, as this makes it easier to work with. To push NuGet packages from a build server or a different machine, it's probably safer to specify the correct API key, as well as the package source to be used, on every command.

Publishing Packages by Using NuGet Package Explorer

In the previous chapter of this book, we showed you that you can use both the command line and a GUI-based tool called NuGet Package Explorer (NPE) to create NuGet packages. The same is true for publishing NuGet packages: NPE contains all tools to publish NuGet packages directly from its user interface.

As explained in Chapter 1, NuGet Package Explorer is a ClickOnce application that can be installed from inside your browser. Simply navigate to http://nuget.codeplex.com and find the Downloads page. You can install and run NPE by clicking the ClickOnce Installer download.

Open NuGet Package Explorer on your system, and open the package we created in this chapter, ProNugetStringExtensions.1.0.0.nupkg. Figure 4-10 shows you what this should look like.

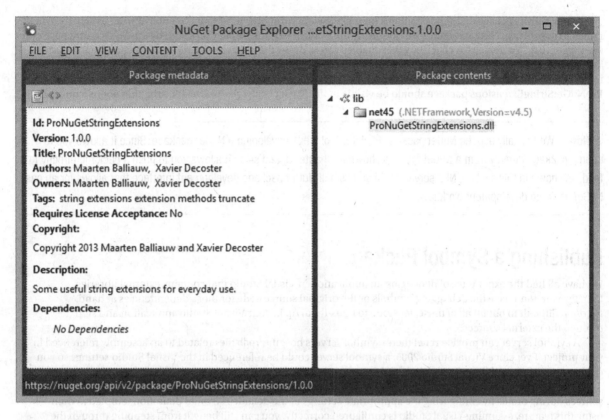

Figure 4-10. *The ProNuGetStringExtensions package opened using NuGet Package Explorer (NPE)*

Using the Edit Metadata button, you can modify the package version number to, for example, 1.1.0. From the File menu, the Publish menu item will do what you would expect: publish the package that is currently open to a NuGet feed. Figure 4-11 shows you the Publish Package dialog box.

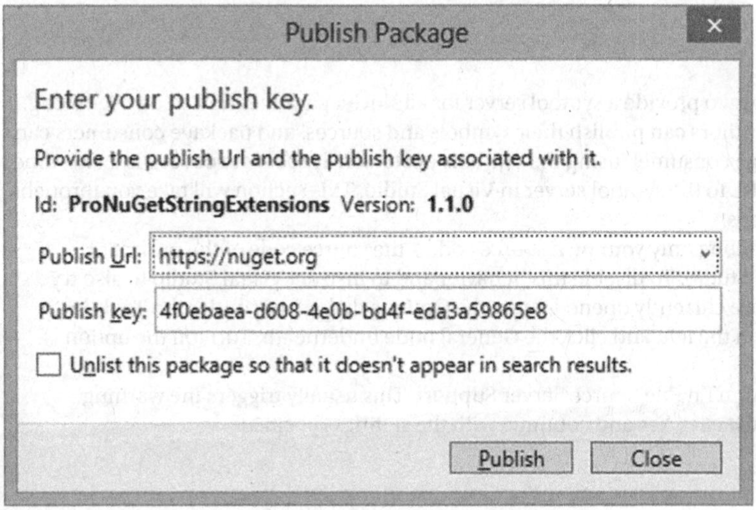

Figure 4-11. *The Publish Package dialog box in NuGet Package Explorer*

The Publish Package dialog box contains no rocket-science options: it asks for the Publish URL, which, by default, points to nuget.org. Next, it requires you to specify the Publish key, the API key provided by the My Account page on www.nuget.org. There's also a check box that enables you to unlist the package so it doesn't appear in search results.

As with the nuget push command you saw earlier, the Publish button will perform the actual work and make sure your NuGet package is pushed directly to the destination feed from the graphical user interface. The ProNuGetStringExtensions package should be visible in the NuGet Gallery at www.nuget.org after about a minute.

■ **Note**   We typically use the NuGet package Explorer tool while developing a NuGet package. Since it allows you to open a package directly from a NuGet feed, as shown in Chapter 3, and since it allows you to push a package directly to a feed, as shown in this section, NPE serves as a handy small NuGet package development interface that allows for an easy NuGet package development workflow.

Publishing a Symbol Package

We have all had the experience of debugging an application in Visual Studio that contains external libraries. Usually, you don't have the debugging symbols or the original source code for those dependencies at hand. It's often difficult to obtain all of those, let alone to hook them up in your Visual Studio application and step through the external sources.

A symbol server can provide relief there: symbol servers host the .pdb files related to an assembly referenced in your project. Ever since Visual Studio 2005, a symbol server could be referenced in the Visual Studio settings so you could retrieve from it debugging symbols and source code for external assemblies.

Users of Microsoft Team Foundation Server (TFS) can make use of the built-in symbol server and index their sources during builds by configuring the appropriate settings in the default TFS build definition template. When using this feature, assuming Visual Studio is configured correctly, you can still benefit from stepping through the source code directly from TFS Source Control while inheriting all built-in security and permission checks on these sources. However, not everyone is using TFS, and NuGet is meant to be version control system (VCS)–agnostic. That's where SymbolSource.org comes in. This section will show you how to configure Visual Studio to consume the symbol server for nuget.org hosted on SymbolSource.org and how you can provide debugging symbols and source code to consumers of your NuGet packages.

Configuring Visual Studio

NuGet has teamed up with SymbolSource.org to provide a symbol server for all NuGet packages hosted on nuget.org. With almost no additional effort, package authors can publish their symbols and sources, and package consumers can debug them from Visual Studio. As a package consumer, using the symbols hosted on SymbolSource.org is a one-time action that consists of adding the correct URL to the symbol server in Visual Studio. This section will take you through the required Visual Studio configuration steps.

First of all, Visual Studio typically will debug only your own source code—the source code of the project or projects that are currently opened in Visual Studio. To disable this behavior and to instruct Visual Studio to also try to debug code other than the projects that are currently opened, open the Options dialog box (under the Tools ➤ Options menu). Find the Debugging node on the left, and click the General node underneath. Turn off the option Enable Just My Code.

In the same dialog box, turn on the option Enable Source Server Support. This usually triggers the warning message shown in Figure 4-12. It is safe to just click Yes and continue with the settings specified.

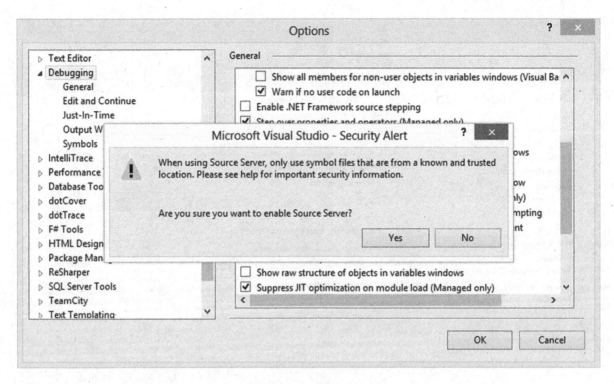

Figure 4-12. *When enabling the use of a source server, a warning is displayed*

Keep the Options box dialog open, and find the Symbols node under the Debugging node on the left. In the dialog box shown in Figure 4-13, add the symbol server URL for nuget.org: http://srv.symbolsource.org/pdb/Public. After that, click OK to confirm configuration changes and consume symbols for NuGet packages.

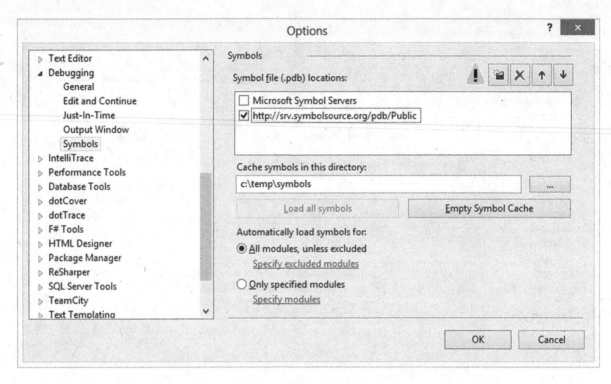

Figure 4-13. The NuGet symbol server added to the list of symbol servers configured in Visual Studio

---

■ **Tip** Did you know that most assemblies of the Microsoft .NET Framework also provide their debugging symbols from a symbol server? For example, you can debug your ASP.NET MVC application and step into Microsoft's code to see what happens inside those System.* assemblies. To do so, open the Options dialog box, and then open the Debugging node and click Symbols. Add the Microsoft symbol server, located at `http://msdl.microsoft.com/download/symbols`. Some Visual Studio installations will already have the Microsoft symbol server listed. In those versions, just enabling it through the dialog box mentioned earlier in this note is enough to step into any core .NET assembly.

Consuming Symbols for NuGet Packages

While technically not in the scope of this book, we do want to demonstrate how you can consume symbols for NuGet packages from Visual Studio. Create a new project in Visual Studio, a console application, and install the ProNuGetStringExtensions package into it by using either the NuGet Visual Studio extension or the Package Manager Console (`Install-Package ProNuGetStringExtensions` will do the trick). In the `Program.cs` file, add the code from Listing 4-3.

Listing 4-3. A Simple Console Application Consuming the Truncate() Method from the ProNuGetStringExtensions Package

```
using System;

namespace ConsoleApplication1
{
    class Program
    {
        static void Main(string[] args)
        {
            string longString = "This is a long string that I'll truncate later.";
            string shortString = longString.Truncate(5, "...");

            Console.WriteLine(shortString);
            Console.ReadLine();
        }
    }
}
```

The code fragment shown creates a long string and then uses the Truncate method from the ProNuGetExtensions package created earlier in this chapter. Add a breakpoint on line 10 (string shortString = longString.Truncate(5, "...");). Run the application by pressing F5 and step through the source code.

As you can see in Figure 4-14, Visual Studio downloads the symbols from the symbol server we've added to the Visual Studio configuration. You are now able to step through this code and debug it as if it were your own source code.

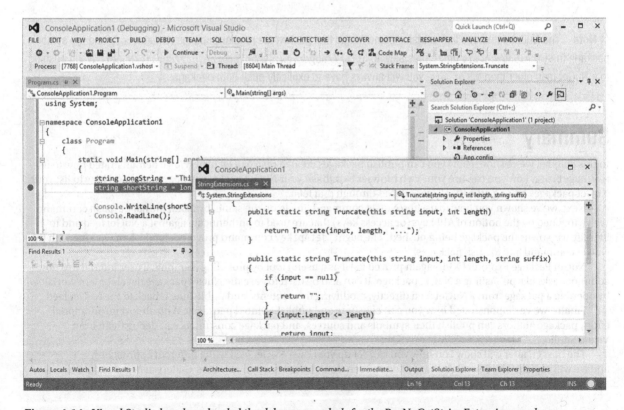

Figure 4-14. Visual Studio has downloaded the debugger symbols for the ProNuGetStringExtensions package

Publishing Symbols for Your Own NuGet Packages

Before you can publish a symbols package for a NuGet package, the symbols package has to be created. As you learned in Chapter 3, creating a symbols package can be done by using the nuget pack command and specifying the -Symbols switch. Run the following command to create a symbols package for ProNuGetStringExtensions:

```
nuget pack ProNuGetStringExtensions.csproj -Symbols -Version 1.0.0
```

On your file system, two NuGet packages should now be created:

- ProNuGetStringExtensions.1.0.0.nupkg: The NuGet package that will be published to nuget.org

- ProNuGetStringExtensions.1.0.0.symbols.nupkg: The NuGet package containing debugging symbols (.pdb files), which will be published to the symbol server at SymbolSource.org

Assuming the API key for publishing to nuget.org is 4f0ebaea-d608-4e0b-bd4f-eda3a59865e8, the following command will publish these two packages in one go:

```
nuget push ProNuGetStringExtensions.1.0.0.nupkg 4f0ebaea-d608-4e0b-bd4f-eda3a59865e8
```

If you wish to just push the symbols package, the following command can be used to achieve that goal:

```
nuget push ProNuGetStringExtensions.1.0.0.symbols.nupkg 4f0ebaea-d608-4e0b-bd4f-eda3a59865e8
```

■ **Note** The NuGet command line contains some magic that pushes the regular package to NuGet.org and the symbols package to SymbolSource.org (more precisely, to http://nuget.gw.symbolsource.org/Public/NuGet). When pushing to a NuGet feed other than NuGet.org, you will always have to explicitly push both packages.

Summary

In this chapter, we've shown how you can publish packages created on a NuGet feed. We've demonstrated how to use www.nuget.org, how you can use your web browser to publish your NuGet package to nuget.org, and how to list your NuGet packages among other packages offered through that feed.

Next, we've shown you how to use the NuGet command line to do the same, by using the nuget push command. We've touched on the notion of API keys (or access keys) that are used to authenticate against a NuGet feed and to identify who owns the package being pushed. The nuget setApiKey command proved helpful when working with the NuGet command line to push packages.

NuGet Package Explorer (NPE) again proved itself as a useful tool by providing a graphical user interface to do common tasks like publishing a NuGet package. It can also be used to ease the NuGet package development workflow by opening a package from a NuGet feed directly, modifying the contents, and publishing it back to the NuGet feed.

Finally, we've demonstrated how you can consume and publish symbol packages. With almost no additional effort, package authors can publish their symbols and sources, and package consumers can debug them from Visual Studio.

The next chapter will show you how you can set up your own NuGet feed using different approaches, and we will explain why you might want to do so even though there's a public NuGet Gallery at nuget.org.

CHAPTER 5

■ ■ ■

Hosting Your Own NuGet Server

In Parts 1 and 2 of this book, we introduced you to package management with NuGet. By now, you know everything you need to know to get started with NuGet and consume or produce packages. In Chapter 4, we demonstrated how you can easily publish those packages onto any NuGet server.

Based on this knowledge, we will now start with the fun part! So far, we have mainly been targeting the official NuGet Gallery. The public NuGet feed is aimed at the distribution of open source libraries and components. We really want to encourage you to share your cool projects and contribute to those projects and libraries you really enjoy! Contributing is a wonderful learning experience, and before you know it, you will be able to call yourself an active member of the community.

While the NuGet model is very interesting, the team behind NuGet realized that not everyone is developing open source software for a living and wants to contribute their valuable in-house software packages to this official NuGet package source. Many companies eventually might want to set up their own package repositories, preferably using NuGet, to escape from dependency hell and overcome common package management issues.

This chapter will dive a bit deeper into why you may want to host your own NuGet feed and what it takes to set up your own NuGet repositories. We'll start with the labor-intensive option of creating our own NuGet server, after which we'll have a look at some of the alternatives out there. And after reading this chapter, you will be able to set up your own NuGet repositories!

Why Host Your Own NuGet Feed?

A good place to start this chapter is with one of the *W* questions: why host your own NuGet feed? To be honest, there are many valuable reasons to do this, reasons that we'll touch on briefly in this chapter and that will become more clear in the next chapters, for example, when we explain continuous package integration.

The first and obvious reason to host your own NuGet feed is simple. By default, your NuGet world consists of only the official NuGet package source. Anyone can post packages to this, and all packages are public. A big consequence of this is that to distribute your company's internal application framework using NuGet, your only option would be to publish it to the official NuGet package source. Are you sure you want to submit all your in-house–developed intellectual property and make it public? Probably not. Your own, private NuGet feed would come in handy in such a situation.

Maybe you do want to push packages to either the official NuGet package source or to your own feed. And maybe you want to do that from your build server. Why not first push those packages to your personal NuGet feed before doing the actual push to the target feed? This workflow ensures that you can safely validate submitted packages before publishing them officially.

Another reason for setting up a personal NuGet feed may be that you want to provide your developers access to only *approved* packages, that is, packages that have been tested and validated for use in your company's software projects. The easiest way to do this is to set up your own NuGet feed and "mirror" specific packages from NuGet.org. As a result, your feed will be limited to only packages that you as a team lead approve.

Hold on; there are more reasons for setting up your own NuGet feed. Good reason number four is simply that the official NuGet package source is growing every hour. What if you are interested only in packages related to ASP.NET MVC? Or only packages meant to be used with Windows Phone 8 development? This problem can easily be solved by creating a feed that contains just packages of interest, with no packages related to technologies you're not even using in your projects.

Packages on the official NuGet package source are maintained by their respective package authors. This means that whenever a package author updates a NuGet package or removes a package from the official NuGet package source, your developers may have difficulties consuming existing NuGet package references. It may be a good idea to mirror these packages and host your own NuGet feed simply to make sure packages that are being used are always available, regardless of what the package author decides to do with it.

Yet another reason to set up a personal NuGet feed is security: NuGet feeds can prompt users to authenticate to consume packages listed on the feed. Combine that fact with your corporate Active Directory or Lightweight Directory Access Protocol (LDAP) account, and you'll notice that it becomes very easy to authenticate users to a private feed by using their corporate credentials. What if you want some users to just consume packages while others are permitted to publish them? You can do all of this on your private NuGet feed!

Another reason for hosting your own NuGet feed may be your network connection. Maybe the official NuGet package source has a high latency where you are located, or a corporate firewall prevents you from connecting there. A solution can be to host your own NuGet feed within your firewall and keep both speed and security high.

■ **Note**   The reasons we've listed here are based on our own experience with customers and our employers. There are probably a number of other reasons to host your own NuGet feed.

Setting Up a Simple NuGet Package Repository

The easiest and fastest way of setting up your own NuGet package repository is by setting up a simple network share to act as the physical repository. A folder containing a bunch of NuGet packages (.nupkg) will be treated as a NuGet package source. This is a very cheap way of getting started with NuGet today with almost no effort! No matter what type of NuGet repository you will end up with later, they all have one thing in common: under the hood, simple binary large object (BLOB) storage is used. A network share is a good starting point, as we will show you later in this chapter, because you can easily extend it with more-advanced NuGet server functionality. It all builds on top of a simple package repository. Before spending much effort in a full-fledged NuGet server, we strongly suggest you get started with this minimal setup and get familiar with the concepts while taking immediate benefit from NuGet's package management.

Figure 5-1 illustrates a network share acting as a NuGet package repository in Windows Explorer. You can simply host your packages in a central folder on any network-attached storage (NAS) device or server.

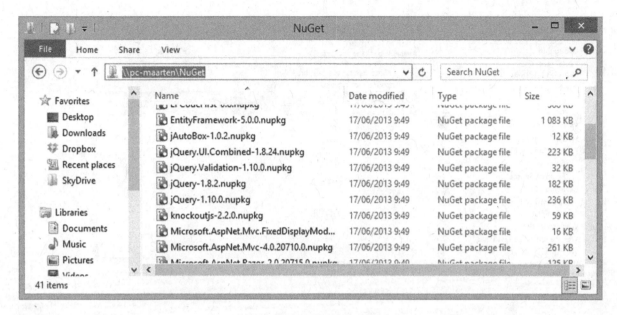

Figure 5-1. *A Windows Explorer view on a network share acting as a NuGet package repository*

■ **Tip** If you are the only person who will be using a simple package repository, you can achieve the same results by using a local folder instead, as we showed while testing your packages in Chapter 3.

To start using this network share as a NuGet package source, you'll need to configure the NuGet Visual Studio extension to use it. To do so, click Tools ➤ Options, and navigate to the Package Manager ➤ Package Sources tab (see Figure 5-2). For network shares, you can provide the path to the shared folder using the Univeral Naming Convention (UNC) format: \\server\share\filepath. The only thing left to do is to communicate this package source setting to your fellow team members. Congratulations! You have just created your own private NuGet package repository!

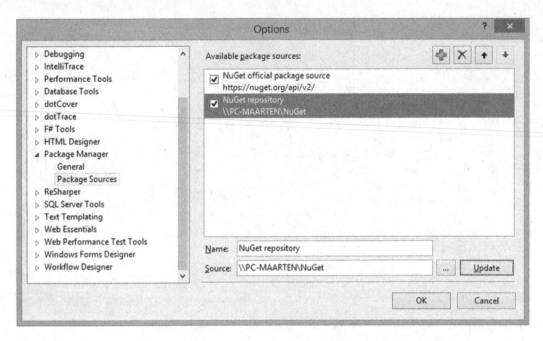

Figure 5-2. Configuring a network share as a NuGet package source in Visual Studio

---

■ **Note**   While a network share is a great way of sharing some NuGet packages across a team, it comes with a serious disadvantage: NuGet will always open and parse all NuGet packages on this file share when querying from Visual Studio or the Package Manager Console. Since there is no indexing of metadata going on behind the scenes, the more packages stored in this network share, the slower searching and installing will become.

Creating a Basic NuGet Server

The NuGet team realized that people would need to set up a NuGet server with support for API keys, an OData feed on top of the physical package repository, and maybe a web interface as well. We've also explained that NuGet itself is fully open source, so you can grab the bits and pieces and tweak it to your needs. However, you might want to make sure your NuGet server implementation can evolve together with the public one and consider building on top of the released versions instead of extending the sources directly.

NuGet is really well designed in terms of extensibility. There are two main components that make a NuGet server: NuGet.Core and NuGet.Server. Of course, using the open source mantra that "it doesn't exist unless it's on NuGet," these two components are available as NuGet packages.

Since we want to host a NuGet feed, we will need a simple web application that can serve as a basic NuGet server. We will choose an ASP.NET MVC web application, but know that it would work as well for the more classical ASP.NET Web Forms approach. Let's get started and create an empty ASP.NET MVC web application in Visual Studio. From the well-known File ➤ New Project dialog box, you select ASP.NET MVC 4 Application in the Web category, as shown in Figure 5-3.

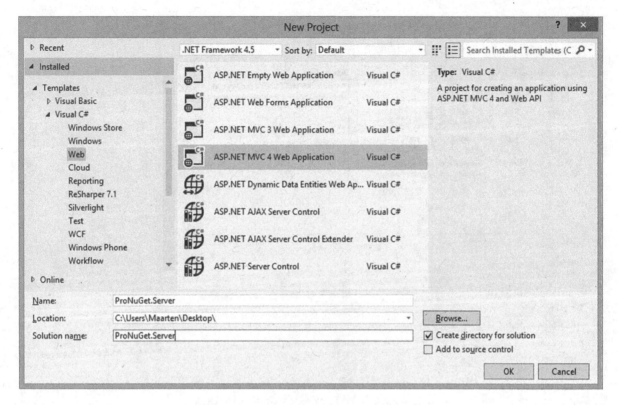

Figure 5-3. Creating a new ASP.NET MVC web application project in Visual Studio 2012

■ **Tip**   If you are unfamiliar with ASP.NET MVC, we recommend reading *Pro ASP.NET MVC 4 Framework* by Adam Freeman (Apress, 2013).

Choose a location for your project and give it a meaningful name. We have chosen `ProNuGet.Server` for this example. After clicking the OK button, you'll be prompted by a dialog box to choose the desired recipe for your ASP.NET MVC web application. You can choose an empty project, an Internet application, or an intranet application. If you feel like building everything from scratch, you should pick the Empty option. If you want to get a template for an Internet application, preconfigured with Forms Authentication, the Internet Application recipe will be most suitable for you. For the purpose of this book, we want to build a NuGet server hosted on the corporate intranet, which is likely to be the most realistic scenario for a custom NuGet server implementation. Hence we will continue our sample using the Intranet Application recipe, as illustrated in Figure 5-4.

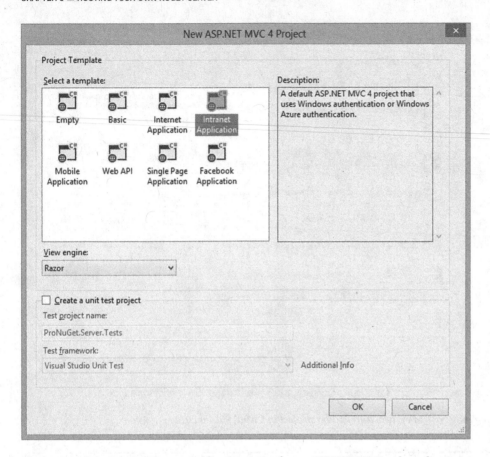

Figure 5-4. *Selecting the Intranet Application recipe for an ASP.NET MVC web application*

CONFIGURING INTRANET AUTHENTICATION

The Intranet Application recipe comes preconfigured for Windows Authentication, and the readme file will be opened by default, providing you with detailed instructions on how to configure authentication on Internet Information Services (IIS) or IIS Express.

To use the Intranet Application template, you'll need to enable Windows Authentication and disable Anonymous Authentication. For detailed instructions (including instructions for IIS 6.0), please visit `http://go.microsoft.com/fwlink/?LinkID=213745`. To guide you through this process, we provide the following instructions for IIS 7, 7.5, 8, and IIS Express.

IIS 7, 7.5, and 8

1. Open IIS Manager and navigate to your web site.

2. In Features view, double-click Authentication.

3. On the Authentication page, select Windows Authentication. If Windows Authentication is not an option, you'll need to make sure Windows Authentication is installed on the server. To enable Windows Authentication, follow these steps:

   a. In Control Panel, open Programs and Features.

   b. Select the option Turn Windows Features On or Off.

   c. Navigate to Internet Information Services ➤ World Wide Web Services ➤ Security, and make sure the Windows Authentication node is selected.

4. In the Actions pane, click Enable to use Windows Authentication.

5. On the Authentication page, select Anonymous Authentication.

6. In the Actions pane, click Disable to disable anonymous authentication.

IIS Express

1. Right-click the project in Visual Studio and select Use IIS Express.

2. Click your project in the Solution Explorer to select it.

3. If the properties pane is not open, make sure to open it (press F4).

4. In the properties pane for your project, complete the following:

   a. Set Anonymous Authentication to Disabled.

   b. Set Windows Authentication to Enabled.

You can install IIS Express by using the Microsoft Web Platform Installer.

For Visual Studio, visit `http://go.microsoft.com/fwlink/?LinkID=214802`.

For Visual Web Developer, visit `http://go.microsoft.com/fwlink/?LinkID=214800`.

If all went well, you should now have a standard ASP.NET MVC intranet web application, fully running with Windows Authentication. Pressing F5 (or selecting Debug ➤ Start Debugging) in Visual Studio should give you the result shown in Figure 5-5.

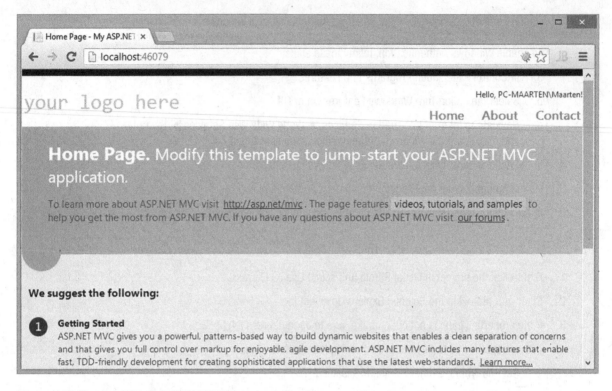

Figure 5-5. First run of the ASP.NET MVC intranet application

With minimal effort, you managed to create a nice-looking, fully functional intranet application. If you look closely at what's included in this Intranet Application recipe, you'll notice something very cool: this project template already is consuming NuGet packages!

■ **Tip**   Creating an ASP.NET MVC recipe of your own is a very interesting approach in an enterprise scenario. It's an easy way to quickly start new projects or solutions, preconfigured, for instance, to consume specific NuGet packages, such as a default company design theme, corporate frameworks, and so on.

Although this is not an ASP.NET MVC book, we highly value the importance of its early adoption of NuGet and the way it opens up possibilities to quickly set up a fully functional web application by selecting the building blocks you want.

If we want to turn this web application into a NuGet server, we need to install some additional building blocks. As you, by now, are getting familiar with the NuGet Package Manager, you might have guessed those building blocks could be found on NuGet.org. You would have guessed right! The very building blocks of NuGet itself are available on NuGet.org. We mentioned earlier you'd need the NuGet.Core and NuGet.Server packages, so let's go ahead and install those into our web application project. Run the following command from within the NuGet Package Manager Console, targeting the web project:

```
Install-Package NuGet.Server
```

Installing the NuGet.Server package will add a set of packages to your project, including the NuGet.Core package because NuGet.Server depends on it. After installation, you'll notice that Default.aspx and some other files were installed into your project. Because the NuGet.Server package is targeting an ASP.NET Web Forms application, we'll manually adjust the Home view to contain the contents from Default.aspx. To do so, open the Views\Home\Index.cshtml file, and paste the markup code of Default.aspx. After adjusting the Home view, your file should look similar to Listing 5-1.

Listing 5-1. Default Home Page for NuGet.Server in an MVC Web Application

```
@using System.Configuration
@{
    ViewBag.Title = "Home Page";
}
<h2>@ViewBag.Message</h2>
<div>
    <h2>
        You are running NuGet.Server
            v@(typeof(NuGet.Server.DataServices.Package)
                .Assembly.GetName().Version)</h2>
    <p>
        Click <a href="@VirtualPathUtility.ToAbsolute("~/nuget/Packages")">here</a> to view
        your packages.
    </p>
    <fieldset style="width: 800px">
        <legend><strong>Repository URLs</strong></legend>In the package manager settings,
        add the following URL to the list of Package Sources:
        <blockquote>
            <strong>@Helpers.GetRepositoryUrl(Request.Url, Request.ApplicationPath)</strong>
        </blockquote>
        @if (String.IsNullOrEmpty(ConfigurationManager.AppSettings["apiKey"]))
        {
            <text>To enable pushing packages to this feed using the nuget command line tool
            (nuget.exe). Set the api key appSetting in web.config.</text>
        }
        else {
            <text>Use the command below to push packages to this feed using the nuget↪
command line tool (nuget.exe).</text>
        }
        <blockquote>
            <strong>nuget push {package file} -s @Helpers.GetPushUrl(Request.Url,↪
Request.ApplicationPath) {apikey}</strong>
        </blockquote>
    </fieldset>
    @if (Request.IsLocal) {
    <p style="font-size: 1.1em">
        To add packages to the feed put package files (.nupkg files) in
        the folder "@NuGet.Server.Infrastructure.PackageUtility.PackagePhysicalPath".
    </p>
    }
</div>
```

■ **Note** If you are familiar with ASP.NET MVC, you obviously could plug in these changes anywhere in your application that you want. This sample page contains both the physical and virtual paths to the NuGet package source. It also contains instructions on how to configure Visual Studio to use your brand new NuGet repository.

Configuring the Packages' Location

You now have set up a basic NuGet server, preconfigured with a NuGet OData feed and a default package location. Any .nupkg file that you put in the packages' location will be immediately picked up by the OData feed the moment you query it for packages.

Go ahead and copy a few packages into the {applicationPath}\packages folder. You should see your packages listed when using a browser such as Internet Explorer to navigate to the OData feed located on {applicationUrl}/nuget/packages.

■ **Tip** You could change the location of the packages—by default, located under {applicationPath}\packages—by configuring a virtual directory in IIS to point to any path you want. The package location doesn't even have to be on the same machine. Just make sure you configure security permissions accordingly.

Starting from NuGet.Server version 1.5, you can also point the application to a specific location for packages by setting the packagesPath application setting in web.config, as shown in Listing 5-2.

Listing 5-2. Setting the packagesPath Configuration Setting for NuGet.Server v1.5

```
<appSettings>
    <!-- Set the value here to specify your custom packages folder. -->
    <add key="packagesPath" value="C:\MyPackages" />
</appSettings>
```

If you start the application now, you should see something similar to the page shown in Figure 5-6.

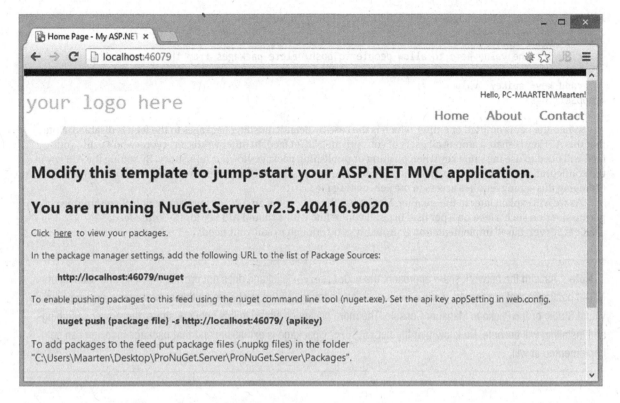

Figure 5-6. First run of the NuGet server implementation

In order for your team members to start using this NuGet feed, they need to add the package source to the NuGet configuration in Visual Studio. The NuGet.Server package has configured the routing of your application for you and located the NuGet repository URL under {applicationUrl}/nuget. This is the package source URL you'll need to configure in Visual Studio.

You now have everything in place to start building a fully fledged NuGet server in ASP.NET MVC. Instead of manually placing packages into the packages' folder, you could build a complete package management user interface, where you could upload packages, for instance. We'll leave it up to you to build it, because these needs will most likely be different for each organization. If your organization wants to use multiple package repositories and feeds, you'll need to deploy and configure this web site multiple times as well, because the NuGet.Server package supports only a single feed per web application.

In short, the NuGet.Server package is very useful if you have only basic requirements or if you want to build the web application hosting the NuGet feed completely from scratch. If you want something more feature-rich and don't want to develop everything yourself, you might consider the NuGet Gallery implementation, which is also used at NuGet.org. We'll discuss it in the next section.

Setting the API Key

You can still use the nuget.exe command-line tool to push and publish packages to your own feed. To enable this functionality, you'll need to configure your server with an API key. This is done through another application setting in your server's web.config file, as shown in Listing 5-3.

Listing 5-3. Setting the Packages' Path Configuration Setting for NuGet.Server v1.5.

```
<appSettings>
    <!-- Set the value here to allow people to push/delete packages from the server.
        NOTE: This is a shared key (password) for all users. -->
    <add key="apiKey" value="" />
</appSettings>
```

When the key is omitted or empty, which is the case by default, pushing packages to the feed is disabled. Note that this API key is shared among all users of your private NuGet feed. In other words, everyone who's using your feed will need to use the same key when pushing or publishing packages to your repository. By setting the API key in the configuration file, this also means that you can't change this as easily as a registered user on NuGet.org could do. Changing this setting requires access to the web.config file.

As we will explain later in this chapter, MyGet has the concept of an API key per user, which allows unique permissions on such a feed on a per user basis. If you're fine with a shared API key for the entire feed, a NuGet.Server-based implementation is probably good enough to suit your needs.

■ **Note**   As with the network share approach, the NuGet.Server package does not provide indexing and caching of NuGet packages that are hosted. It will always open and parse all NuGet packages on this server when querying from Visual Studio or the Package Manager Console. The more packages stored in this network share, the slower searching and installing will become. Do know that the NuGet.Server package is extensible and that package indexing can be implemented at will.

Using the NuGet Gallery

If you like the look and feel of the official NuGet Gallery at www.nuget.org, you might be very pleased to learn that you can actually host the exact same web application yourself. The NuGet Gallery is built using ASP.NET MVC and can be installed on your own web server as well as on Microsoft's cloud computing platform, Windows Azure.

This section will show you how you can download, compile, and deploy the NuGet Gallery source code to your own web server.

Downloading the Source Code

The NuGet Gallery has to be compiled and installed from its source code. There are two options to obtain the source code for the NuGet Gallery:

- If you are familiar with the Git version control system, you can easily clone the NuGet Gallery Git repository by using the git clone https://github.com/NuGet/NuGetGallery command. This will download the latest source code version from GitHub to your local disk.

- A zip file containing the exact same source code can be downloaded by browsing to https://github.com/NuGet/NuGetGallery/zipball/master. This URL will trigger a download of the latest version of the NuGet Gallery source code. You can save and extract the zip file to your local disk.

Make sure the source code is extracted on your local disk. We'll use these extracted sources to compile and deploy the NuGet Gallery.

Creating a SQL Server Database

Many applications, including NuGet Gallery, require a SQL Server database to store their data. NuGet Gallery can make use of SQL Server and SQL Server Express, a free version of which can be downloaded from www.microsoft.com/sqlserver/en/us/editions/express.aspx.

The NuGet Gallery database has to be created on a SQL Server instance. Once you are connected to the SQL Server instance of your choice—we use our local SQL Server instance represented by the dot (.) notation—you can right-click Databases in the Object Explorer window, and select New Database from the contextual menu, as shown in Figure 5-7.

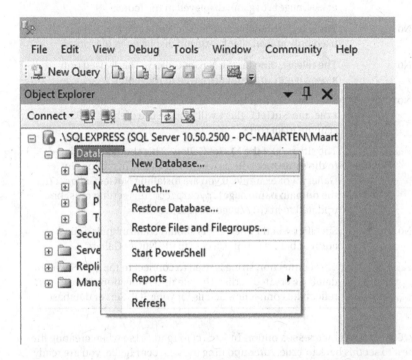

Figure 5-7. *Creating a new SQL Server database using SQL Server Management Studio*

We will call our database NuGetGallery, but this name can be anything you find meaningful.

Configuring NuGet Gallery

The folder where you initially extracted the NuGet Gallery source code will contain a folder named Website. This folder contains a web.config file, which you should edit and update according to your situation. Open this file in Visual Studio (or your XML editor of choice), and update the appSettings and connectionString section accordingly. Table 5-1 lists the available configuration keys and their descriptions.

Table 5-1. *Overview of Possible NuGet Galery Configuration Settings*

Setting Name	Required?	Description
GalleryOwner	Yes	The name and e-mail address of the NuGet Gallery owner. Update this to your own name and e-mail address.
Gallery:ReleaseName	No	The release name for the NuGet Gallery. This is used only at www.nuget.org and displayed in the footer.
Gallery:ReleaseSha	No	The release hash for the NuGet Gallery. This is used only at www.nuget.org and displayed in the footer.
Gallery:ReleaseBranch	No	The release branch name for the NuGet Gallery. This is used only at www.nuget.org and displayed in the footer.
Gallery:ReleaseTime	No	The release time for the NuGet Gallery. This is used only at www.nuget.org and displayed in the footer.
Gallery:RequireSSL	No	Specifies whether the use of SSL is required. When set to true, the NuGet Gallery will enforce use of the HTTPS scheme in all URLs.
Gallery:SiteRoot	Yes	The site root of the NuGet Gallery. This should be updated to the same root URL as where you will be installing NuGet Gallery. For example, if you are installing NuGet Gallery on the domain name nuget.mycorp.com, this setting must be updated to http://nuget.mycorp.com/.
Gallery:ConfirmEmailAddresses	No	Specifies whether new users should confirm their e-mail address before gaining access to the NuGet Gallery.
NuGetGallery connection string	Yes	This connection string is used to connect to the SQL Server database created earlier. Update the connection string to reflect the connection details for your SQL Server database.

We recommend setting the Gallery.ConfirmEmailAddresses option in web.config to false when creating the first user. Once that user is created, it is best to set this back to true. After updating the web.config file, you are ready to compile NuGet Gallery.

Compiling NuGet Gallery

Before being able to deploy and use the NuGet Gallery server, you will have to compile it. In the source code folder for the NuGet Gallery, there is a PowerShell script called Build-Solution.ps1. This script can be run from a PowerShell console and will download all dependencies required to compile the NuGet Gallery (using NuGet, of course). It will also run all unit tests and compile the NuGet Gallery source code to a web application, which you can deploy on your web server.

To compile NuGet Gallery, open a PowerShell console (by choosing Start ➤ All Programs ➤ Accessories ➤ Windows PowerShell ➤ Windows PowerShell), navigate to the folder on your local disk where the NuGet Gallery sources have been extracted, and run the command .\Build-Solution.ps1. Figure 5-8 shows you a part of the output of this compilation process.

Figure 5-8. The build script output for NuGet Gallery's Build-Solution.ps1 script

After this script has been run, the folder where you initially extracted the NuGet Gallery source code will contain a folder named Website. This is the actual application you'll have to deploy to your server in order to run your own NuGet feed.

Our next action is initializing the database schema. The NuGet Gallery uses Entity Framework Code-First and can create its database schema by running all database migrations from the Package Manager Console. Open the NuGetGallery.sln file in Visual Studio, and from the Package Manager Console run Update-Database to ensure that the database schema and initial data are created. Example output is shown in Figure 5-9.

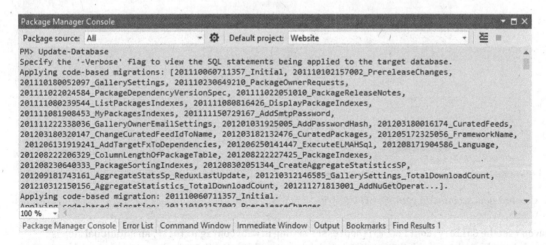

Figure 5-9. Output of the Update-Database cmdlet in the Package Manager Console

Finalizing Your NuGet Gallery Installation

After you have deployed the NuGet Gallery to your web server, navigate to the URL where the NuGet Gallery web site can be found. We have installed NuGet Gallery on a local IIS server available at `http://localhost: 46613/`. You will be greeted by a similar web site to `www.nuget.org` (in fact, `www.nuget.org` runs on the same code you have just deployed).

Since you are installing NuGet Gallery, chances are you will be the administrator for the installation as well. To enable the administration user interface, you will have to register on your NuGet Gallery first. Click the Register link in the top-right corner of NuGet Gallery, and specify the username and password you would like to use. Figure 5-10 shows you this registration page in action.

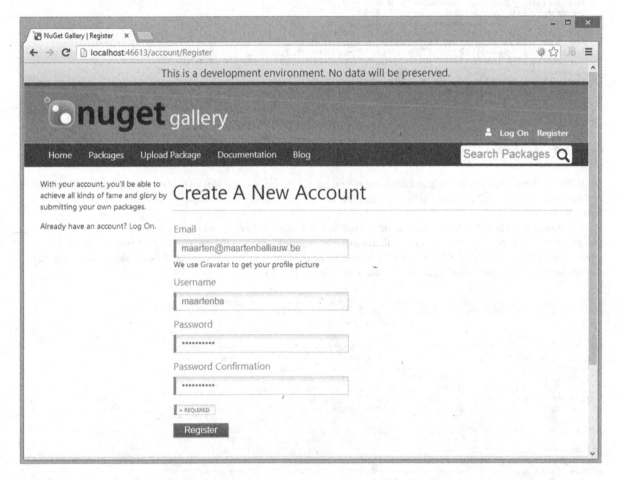

Figure 5-10. *Create a new account on your NuGet Gallery*

If you haven't set the `Gallery.ConfirmEmailAddresses` setting in `web.config` to `false`, an additional step is involved before being able to log in with the newly created user. Since this is the first user being created, and settings (for example, the mail server to use) have not yet been updated, NuGet Gallery creates a registration e-mail in the `Website\App_Data\Mail` folder. Open this folder, and double-click the e-mail message generated after registering your username. This confirmation e-mail contains an URL that is used to validate the registration. Navigate to this link and validate your registration.

After confirming your registration, you are a regular user of your NuGet Gallery. This means you can create and upload NuGet packages just as anyone else would.

To become the administrator of your NuGet Gallery, you will have to upgrade your account to an administrator account. To do so, connect to the NuGetGallery database you've created on SQL Server and run the following query:

```
INSERT INTO [dbo].[Roles] ([Name])
    VALUES ( 'Admins' )

INSERT INTO [dbo].[UserRoles] ([UserKey],[RoleKey])
    VALUES ( (SELECT TOP 1 [Key] FROM [dbo].[Users]), 1)
```

This query adds the first user in your NuGet Gallery (which should be your newly created account, as you are the only user at this time) and assigns it the Admins role. From now on, you'll be able to manage the application, indexes, and database directly from the URL http://localhost:46613/Admin/.

Congratulations, you are now running your own version of www.nuget.org! Publishing and consuming packages is now identical to the gallery described in Chapter 4. It is, after all, the same software you are running now.

■ **Note** The NuGet team created an additional project on GitHub, https://github.com/NuGet/NuGetOperations, providing a set of operations tools designed for the official NuGet.org site. While these tools were created for running and maintaining that web site, some might be useful for running your own NuGet Gallery. The project features a PowerShell console for managing the NuGet Gallery, tools for backup, and so on.

Using NuGet as a Service: MyGet

So far, you've learned how to set up a NuGet server based on a local directory or a file share, as well as using an open source NuGet server implementation. But why do everything yourself if someone else can do it for you? At least, that's what we thought when creating MyGet.

MyGet is our attempt to create a hosted private NuGet feed. It offers everyone the possibility to create their own, private, filtered NuGet feeds for use in the Visual Studio Package Manager. It can contain packages from NuGet.org as well as private packages. In short, it supports all usage scenarios we mentioned at the start of this chapter (in the "Why Host Your Own NuGet Feed?" section). And it's easy to set up. Plus, it comes with a free plan.

This section will take you through some characteristics of MyGet and show you some features that you would have to develop yourself when using one of the solutions mentioned earlier in this chapter. But let's start at the beginning: where do you find MyGet, and how can you create a NuGet feed?

Creating a NuGet Feed on MyGet

Before being able to create a NuGet feed, you have to sign in to MyGet. The MyGet web site can be found at www.myget.org. If you navigate to this web site using your browser of choice, you'll be greeted with the MyGet front page shown in Figure 5-11. Because we envisioned MyGet to be easy to use, we have chosen not to provide a user registration page. Locate the Sign In link in the top-right corner, or find the big green Get Started for Free button to log in to MyGet.

Figure 5-11. *The MyGet front page after navigating to www.myget.org*

The sign-in page does not require you to have a login for MyGet. Instead, it cleverly uses one of many external identity providers, such as Microsoft Account, Google Accounts, Facebook, Yahoo!, GitHub, StackExchange, and OpenID. Simply click the logo of your identity provider of choice, and you will immediately be signed in to MyGet.

At your very first login, you will be prompted for some additional information, as shown in Figure 5-12. MyGet will ask you for your name, e-mail address, and a username/password combination. We advise you to immediately choose a username and password on this page, as that combination will be used to authenticate against your private NuGet feeds when working with the NuGet Visual Studio extension or the Package Manager Console.

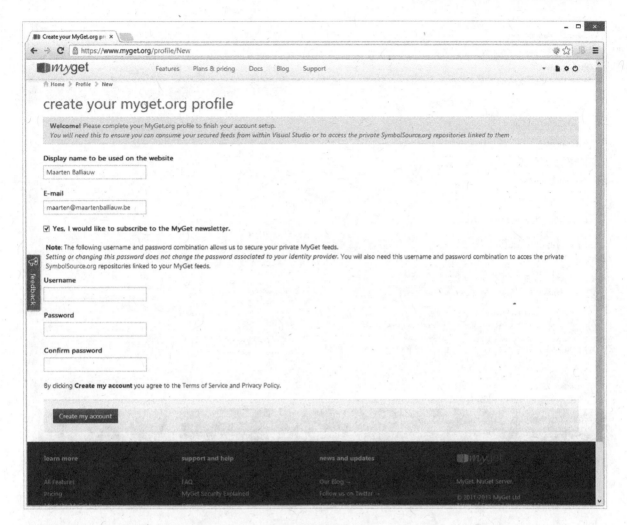

Figure 5-12. *Some additional profile information is requested the first time you sign in to MyGet*

After updating and saving your profile, you're ready to go. Creating a NuGet feed by using MyGet can be done through the Create New Feed icon, which can be found in the top navigation bar, right next to your username. This will take you to the page shown in Figure 5-13. A feed, of course, requires a name, which has to be unique across MyGet. Popular feed names such as myget, nuget, and pronuget (the name of our book) may be taken by someone else, just as is the case with domain names on the Internet. Name your feed carefully: you cannot change the feed name later. The second piece of information asked for is a short description for the feed. This can be anything you want to identify the feed in your list of feeds.

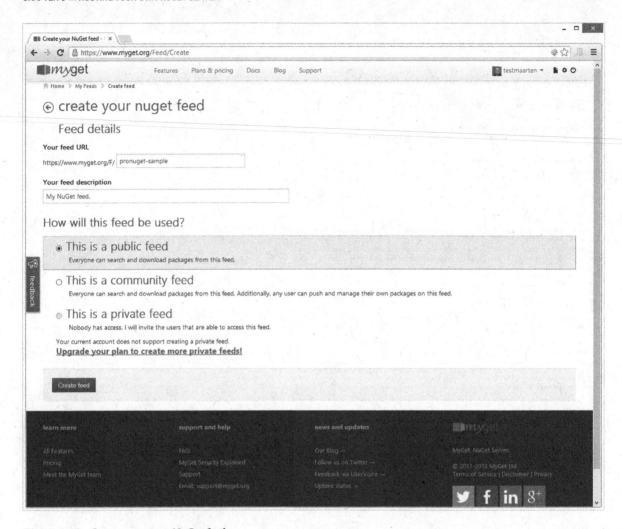

Figure 5-13. *Create your own NuGet feed*

After clicking the Continue button, you'll be taken to the list of packages hosted in this feed. As Figure 5-14 shows, this page contains a number of tabs on the left (Packages, Feed Details, Feed Activity, Feed Security, and so on). The list of packages hosted on your new feed will still be empty.

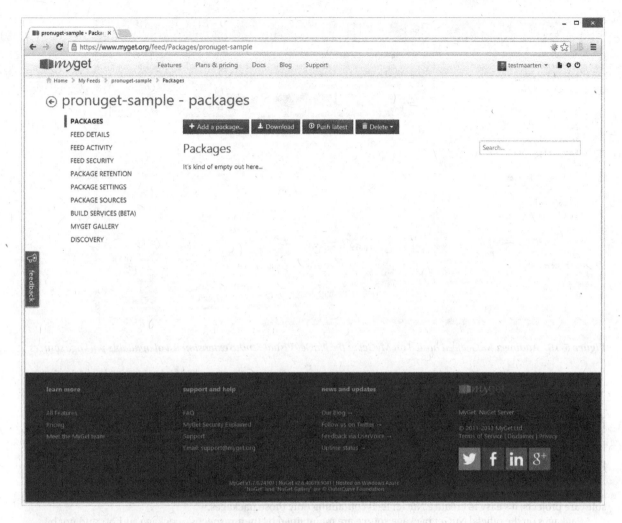

Figure 5-14. *The overview page of your newly created NuGet feed*

The Packages tab contains the list of packages you are hosting on this feed. Obviously, this list is empty when you've just created a new feed. The Feed Details tab contains all details about your feed: the feed URL that you can add to the list of package sources in Visual Studio, your API key (which can be used to push packages from the NuGet command line or from NuGet Package Explorer), and some other information. The other tabs are also worth exploring—for example, Feed Security contains all settings related to who may access your feed and what privileges one has on the feed.

On the Feed Details tab, find the URL to your NuGet feed. My feed URL is `www.myget.org/F/pronuget-sample/`. As shown in Figure 5-15, you can simply register this feed in the NuGet Visual Studio extension's list of available package sources. After doing so, you can consume your own NuGet feed in the same manner as you would any other NuGet feed: search packages, install and uninstall packages, and so on.

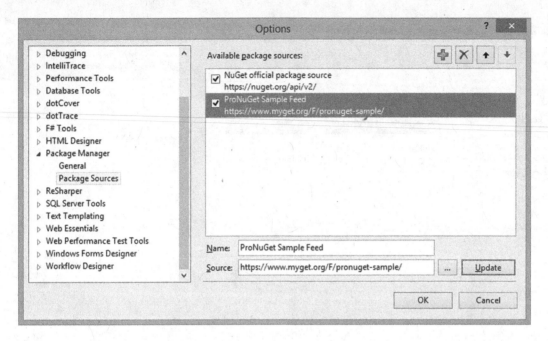

Figure 5-15. *Adding a NuGet feed hosted on MyGet to the NuGet Visual Studio extension list of available package sources*

Congratulations, you've now created your first NuGet feed by using MyGet!

Mirroring Packages from the Official NuGet Package Source

When we first developed MyGet, our idea was nothing more than a web application that enables you to mirror packages from the official NuGet package source. There are plenty of reasons for doing this: it allows you to essentially filter the official NuGet package source and displays only packages you've selected to be on your feed. If you want to provide your developers access to approved packages that have been tested and validated for use in your company's software projects, it's easy to create a NuGet feed containing only those packages.

Packages on the official NuGet package source are maintained by their respective package authors and not by Microsoft or any other party. This means external people have control over dependencies used in your software projects! Whenever a package author updates a NuGet package or removes a package from the official NuGet package source, your developers may have difficulties consuming existing NuGet package references. The easy way to solve this is to mirror packages from the official NuGet package source. And that's what we'll do in this section.

After logging in to your MyGet account, navigate to the list of packages in a feed you've created. If you haven't created a feed yet, start by creating one using the steps outlined in the previous section.

Clicking the Add a Package button will take you to the screen shown in Figure 5-16. This screen has several options to add packages to your MyGet feed. We'll be using the From NuGet option, which allows you to add a package from the official NuGet package source. The other options, From an Uploaded Package and From Packages.config, will be demonstrated later in this chapter.

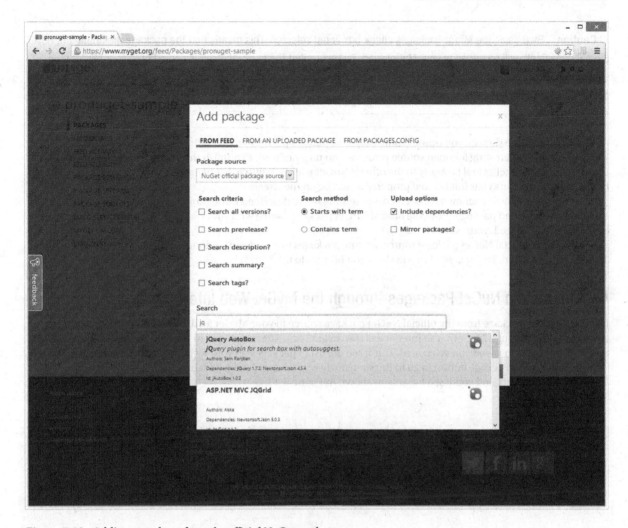

Figure 5-16. *Adding a package from the official NuGet package source*

■ **Note** The From Packages.config tab allows you to upload the `packages.config` file from a project you've created and will add multiple packages from the official NuGet package source at once. This is by far the quickest way to mirror a series of packages that are required in your project(s).

The From NuGet tab offers a rich search interface: packages from the official NuGet package source can be searched for by using a number of criteria. For example, you can choose to search only in the latest versions of packages or in earlier versions. You can search titles, summaries, and tags, as well as define how the search should be performed (Starts with Term or Contains Term).

In the Search box, start typing a keyword related to the package you want to mirror onto your MyGet feed, or simply enter the package identifier if you know it. After a second, search results will come in, and you'll be able to select a package to add to your MyGet feed. Make sure to select the Mirror Packages check box and click the Add button to add a package to your MyGet feed. In Figure 5-16, we've searched for the package identifier jQuery and clicked the Add button.

■ **Caution** By default, the Mirror Packages check box is not selected. This means that the package metadata, but not the package itself, will be added to your MyGet feed. To ensure that the package itself is copied onto your MyGet feed, we recommended selecting the Mirror Packages check box. This ensures that a package author deleting a package from the official NuGet package source does not affect your MyGet feed.

In Chapter 4, we showed you how to contribute and publish packages to the official NuGet package source. While doing so is interesting for open source projects, you may not want to publish the frameworks developed by your company or other intellectual property to the official NuGet package source. Everyone can consume packages from that feed, which means your intellectual property would be on the streets.

A solution is to host your own NuGet feed, something we've described throughout this chapter. Using MyGet, you can combine mirrored packages from the official NuGet package source with your own NuGet packages—all gathered in the same NuGet feed, your NuGet feed.

As with the official NuGet package source, adding packages to a feed can be done using a web interface and the NuGet command line. The next section will show you how to do this.

Adding Custom NuGet Packages through the MyGet Web Interface

Just like adding a package from the official NuGet package source to your MyGet feed, adding a custom NuGet package is done through MyGet's web interface at www.myget.org. After logging in to your MyGet account, navigate to the list of packages in a feed you've created. You'll see the list of packages on your feed under the Packages tab.

Click the Add a Package button to go to the screen where packages can be added. Navigate to the From an Uploaded Package tab, and you'll see the screen shown in Figure 5-17.

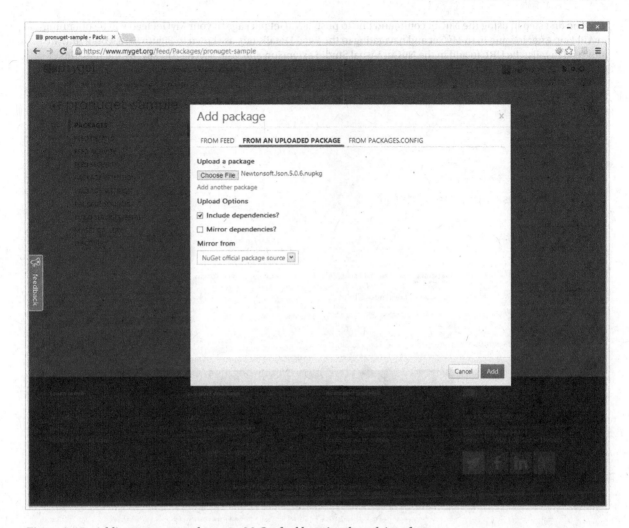

Figure 5-17. *Adding a custom package to a MyGet feed by using the web interface*

This screen allows you to select one or multiple packages from your local hard disk. Optionally, dependencies can be included as well as mirrored. For example, if you create a package that depends on one or more packages from the official NuGet package source, selecting the Include Dependencies check box will add those packages to your MyGet feed, next to the packages you are uploading. Optionally, these packages can also be mirrored, as we explained in the previous section.

Clicking the Upload button will send the packages you've selected to upload to your MyGet feed. When the upload succeeds, your feed will show all packages you've added previously as well as any packages just uploaded.

Adding Custom NuGet Packages by Using the NuGet Command Line

When doing a lot of work with NuGet, you may prefer to use the NuGet command line to push packages to your MyGet feed. Also, when automating package creation and publishing (for example, on a build server), using the NuGet command line may come in handy. This section will show you where to find the MyGet API key and how to push a package to a MyGet feed by using that key.

The first step in using the NuGet command line to push a NuGet package to your MyGet feed will be obtaining an API key. After logging in to MyGet and navigating to the Feed Details tab, as shown in Figure 5-18, you'll find all your feed details: the URL to add in the NuGet Visual Studio extension and your MyGet API key. By the time this book is in your hands, this tab will also display all information related to integrating MyGet and SymbolSource.org (refer to Chapter 4 to learn more about SymbolSource).

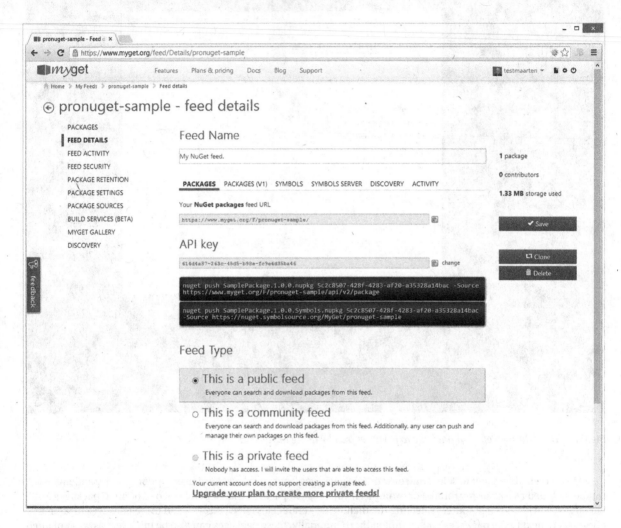

Figure 5-18. The Feed Details tab displaying all sorts of integration information

The API key displayed on the Feed Details tab is 5c2c8507-428f-4283-af20-a35328a14bac (in our case—yours will be different). As you saw in Chapter 4, most NuGet commands support the –Source switch. The nuget push command supports this switch as well and supports pushing packages to feeds other than the default official NuGet package source. The following command pushes a package named ProNuGetStringExtensions to the pronuget feed on MyGet, using the API key obtained from the Feed Details tab:

```
nuget push ProNuGetStringExtensions.1.0.nupkg 5c2c8507-428f-4283-af20-a35328a14bac -Source
http://www.myget.org/F/pronuget-sample
```

Obviously, this API key can also be used in the NuGet Package Explorer (NPE) to publish NuGet packages directly from the user interface to any MyGet feed on which you are allowed to publish packages.

Applying Security Settings to Your Feed

One of the reasons listed at the beginning of this chapter for setting up your own NuGet feed was security. *Security* is a large word with many nuances and possible scenarios, many of which are supported by MyGet. For example, some users can manage users and packages, while some can only manage packages, and others can only consume packages. This section will guide you through MyGet's security model and show you how to set up security and permissions in MyGet.

Using MyGet's Security Model

MyGet features a rich security model for your feeds. You, as a feed owner, always have the richest set of permissions possible. You can assign privileges to specific users with an account on MyGet. Table 5-2 lists all possible permissions and what they mean.

Table 5-2. *MyGet's Permissions*

Permission	Description	Requires a MyGet Account?	Requires Username/Password to Consume the Feed?
Owns this feed	This privilege can be assigned only to the feed owner, who can manage the feed, users, and packages in the feed.	Yes	No*
Can manage users and all packages for this feed	Allows the user to manage all packages and all user permissions on the feed. Similar to Owns This Feed except that deleting the feed is not permitted.	Yes	No*
Can manage all packages for this feed	Allows the user to manage all packages on the feed.	Yes	No*
Can contribute own packages to this feed	Allows the user to publish packages on the feed. Users with this privilege will be able to manage only their own packages. This security setting is identical to the security settings on the official NuGet package source.	Yes	No*
Can consume this feed	Allows the user to consume packages.	No	No*
Has no access to this feed	Denies access to the feed for the specific user.	Not applicable	Yes

* Unless the feed is a private feed, available in MyGet's paid plans

All of these privileges can be combined at will to create your unique security configuration. A common scenario is creating a private feed (which by default only the feed owner can access). Imagine you want to give some colleagues the privilege to consume packages after logging in by using their MyGet usernames and passwords. The following configuration should do the trick:

- You: Owns this feed (This cannot be changed.)

- Colleague X: Can consume this feed

- Colleague Y: Can consume this feed

If you want to allow Colleague X to manage all packages on this feed, you can assign that user the Can Manage All Packages for This Feed privilege. Optionally, the Can Manage Users and All Packages for This Feed privilege will enable thus user to manage user permissions as well.

Inviting Other Users to Your Feed

To give other users certain privileges, they have to be invited to your MyGet feed. This can be done on the Feed Security tab for your feed. This tab lists all users who currently have access to your feed as well as a list of pending users, that is, users who have been invited to your feed but haven't confirmed yet. An example of the Feed Security tab is shown in Figure 5-19.

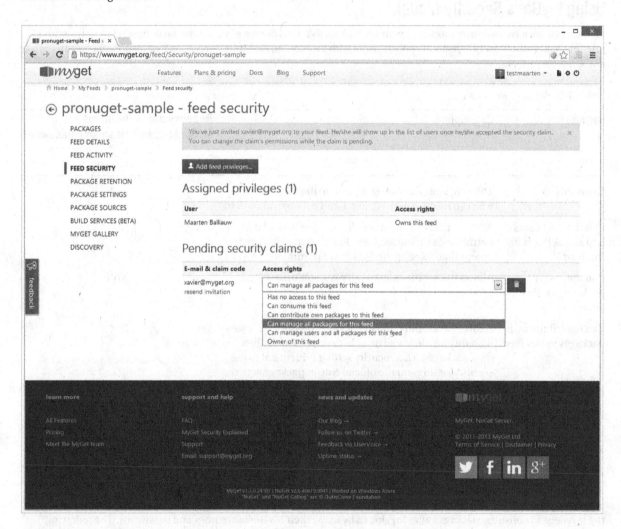

Figure 5-19. *The Feed Security tab enables you to assign specific privileges to other users*

The Add Feed Privileges button will open a dialog box that allows you to invite a user to your feed by entering a known username or an e-mail address. You can immediately assign a privilege to this user to ensure that the correct privilege will be assigned once the user confirms the invitation. Figure 5-20 shows an invitation for maarten@maartenballiauw.be to whom, once the invitation is confirmed, the Can Manage All Packages for This Feed privilege will be assigned.

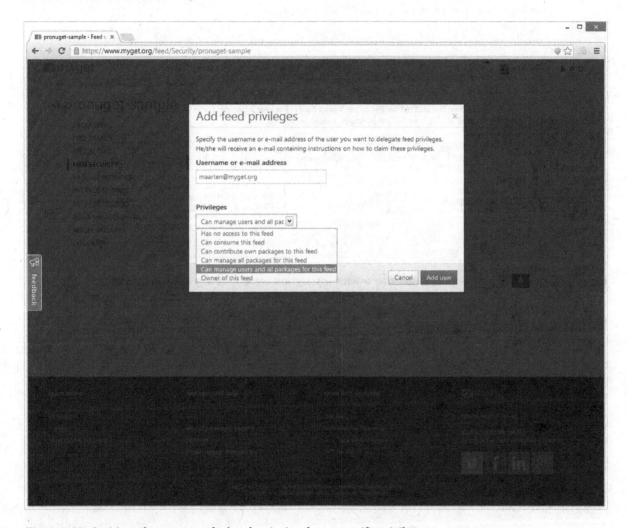

Figure 5-20. *Inviting other users to a feed and assigning them a specific privilege*

Once you've clicked the Add User button, an e-mail will be sent to the e-mail address provided. The user being added to your feed will receive this e-mail and can choose to claim the privileges you've assigned or to simply ignore the invitation. An example e-mail is shown in Figure 5-21. Once the user confirms this e-mail by clicking the link provided in the e-mail body, the user will be granted access to your feed with the privileges chosen in the Add Feed Privileges dialog box.

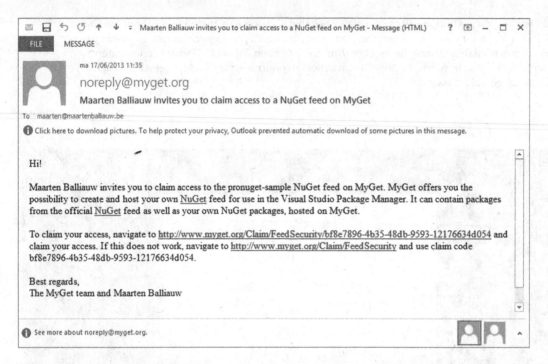

Figure 5-21. *The invitation e-mail sent to a user whenever you grant specific privileges on your private feed*

Managing User Permissions

After inviting a user to your feed, you can change the privileges previously assigned. For example, a user who could previously only consume packages may now be granted the privilege of contributing packages to your feed. Also, a user who could previously manage all packages on the feed can be locked down into a privilege where only consuming packages, not managing them, is permitted.

The Feed Security tab for your feed lists all users who currently have access to your feed as well as a list of users who have been invited to your feed but haven't confirmed their privileges yet. The drop-down list next to a user's name allows you to modify the currently assigned privilege (see Figure 5-22).

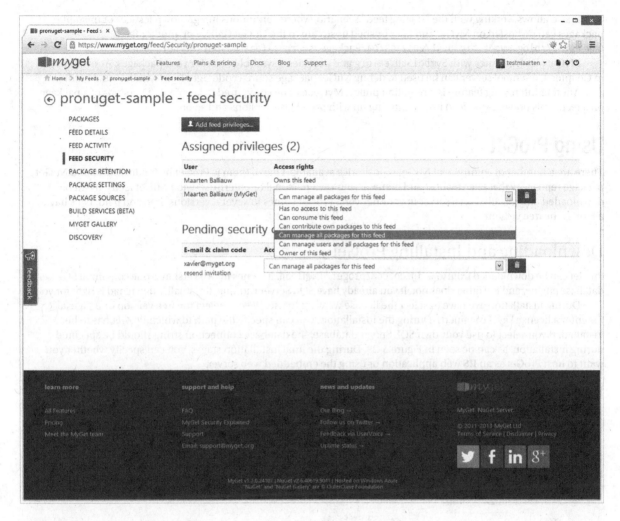

Figure 5-22. Managing user privileges

■ **Note** When you're assigning the Has No Access to This Feed privilege to a certain user, the user will be removed from the list of users. If, afterward, you want to assign a different privilege to this user, the user should be sent a new invitation by using the Add Feed Privileges button.

What Else Is There?

MyGet is probably one of the most mature NuGet repositories out there. It offers a lot of functionality around managing packages, feeds, and security. Depending on your subscription plan, it provides private feeds and integration with your Active Directory. It also comes with a feature called Build Services, which enables you to link a Git, Mercurial, Subversion, GitHub, Bitbucket, or CodePlex repository and automatically compiles your source code into NuGet packages.

It also allows working with the "staging feed" scenario, where continuous integration packages or unstable packages can be hosted on MyGet and later pushed upstream to the NuGet Gallery or another feed (see http://blog.myget.org/post/2013/03/04/Package-sources-feature-out-of-beta.aspx).

MyGet also integrates with SymbolSource.org and provides a symbol server for your packages. As described in Chapter 4, a symbol server can be used to debug NuGet package source code right from within Visual Studio.

Another interesting feature is a retention policy. MyGet can be configured to keep only x versions of a package on a feed. This prevents the feed from cluttering up with prerelease versions and so on.

Using ProGet

There are a number of commercial NuGet repositories available. One of them is ProGet by Inedo. ProGet is a NuGet package repository that lets you host and manage your own personal or enterprise-wide NuGet feeds. It can be downloaded and installed on a server in your network. ProGet comes in several versions: free and paid. Let's have a look at the free version.

Downloading and Installing ProGet

ProGet can be downloaded from www.inedo.com/proget/download. It comes in two versions; one contains a SQL Server database engine, and the other does not. If you already have SQL Server running, the smaller download is right for you.

During installation, we have to select the license we want to use. We can select the free version or try a trial (or enter a license key if obtained). During the installation, you can specify the path to which ProGet has to be installed. If you select to use your own SQL Server database, the database connection string should be specified during installation, as can be seen in Figure 5-23. During the final installation stages, you can specify whether you want to host ProGet as an IIS web application or using the embedded web server.

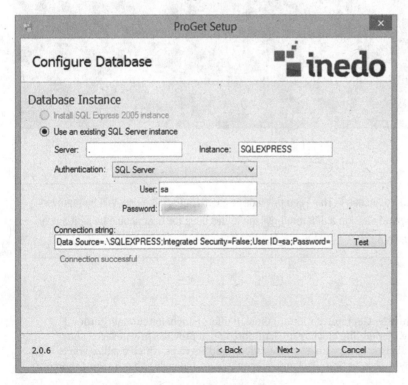

Figure 5-23. *ProGet database connection settings*

After installation, ProGet will be opened in your browser. Since an unregistered ProGet version will work for only six days, we want to make sure our license key is entered into the system. A license key should be sent to your e-mail address after installation. Click the Administration link and log in with username `Admin` and password `Admin`. Next, navigate to the Licensing and Activation option and enter the key sent to you by e-mail. Figure 5-24 shows an example of a correctly configured license key.

Figure 5-24. *License key validation with ProGet*

From the administration dashboard, you may want to change the default username and password for the administrator user as well.

Consuming NuGet Packages by Using ProGet

ProGet provides the ability to create multiple feeds. It comes with a default feed, but additional feeds can be created through the administration area. The default feed URL is `http://localhost:8885/nuget/Default` (the port number may be different in your situation) and can be registered in Visual Studio, as you can see in Figure 5-25.

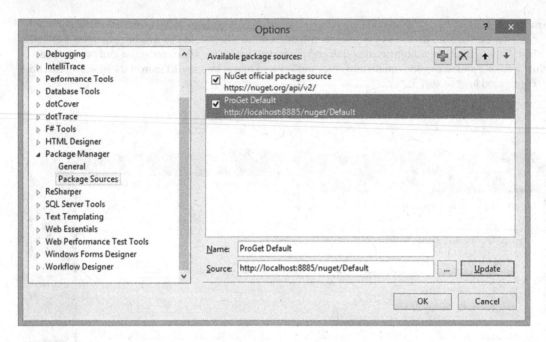

Figure 5-25. *Registering the ProGet feed in Visual Studio*

You can now add NuGet packages from the ProGet feed. By default, ProGet will proxy all packages from the official NuGet package source. This means that in Visual Studio you will see the exact same packages as can be seen in the official NuGet package source.

ProGet can cache packages from NuGet.org so that they are available from ProGet even if there is no Internet connection available. This behavior can be enabled for all packages in the feed through the administration area, or by cherry-picking the packages that should be available directly from the ProGet server. When navigating to a package in the ProGet interface, the Pull to ProGet button can be used to download a copy of the upstream package, as can be seen in Figure 5-26.

Figure 5-26. *Pull the package to ProGet*

As you've seen so far, ProGet does a great job at proxying the official NuGet package source. It also supports adding your own packages, as we will see in the next section.

Adding Your Own NuGet Packages

So far, we have used ProGet for mirroring and proxying packages from the official NuGet package source. It is also possible to add your own packages. This can be done from the ProGet interface by clicking the Add Package button.

After clicking the button, you will be presented with several options. Packages can be added by uploading them through the web interface, by pushing them using the NuGet command line, or by creating a new package through the web interface. Figure 5-27 shows how a package can be uploaded to the ProGet server.

Figure 5-27. *Uploading a package to ProGet*

As you've seen, ProGet allows mixing packages from the official NuGet package source and your own packages on one feed.

What Else Is There?

ProGet comes with several other features. Depending on the license (free vs. commercial), ProGet comes with LDAP support and a symbol server. Hosting multiple feeds on one ProGet server is supported, as well as linking more upstream package sources than just the official NuGet package source.

If you notice that your team is consistently pulling the same project from a remote feed, you can download the package to your local ProGet package source to cache it instead. Entire feeds can be downloaded to ProGet to have an onsite cache/backup of external dependencies.

ProGet also offers an SDK and an API, which allow you to integrate with their product. For example, by using the SDK, a custom store for feeds can be created.

Using TeamCity as a NuGet Repository

Many organizations make use of TeamCity (www.jetbrains.com/teamcity) as their build- and continuous integration server. It comes with several features around NuGet: builds can generate NuGet packages, and TeamCity can push these out to an external NuGet feed. Another option is to expose generated artifacts as NuGet packages by using TeamCity's built-in NuGet server.

While TeamCity comes with great NuGet support, it is focused around continuous integration. For example, the built-in NuGet feed can be used to expose build artifacts from TeamCity but does not support adding custom packages.

Pushing Packages to a NuGet Feed

When a build configuration in TeamCity creates NuGet packages as part of the build process, you can push these packages out to a NuGet server such as NuGet Gallery, MyGet, or ProGet. This makes perfect sense: when building software components that you want to use during development, TeamCity can build these components, run unit tests for them, and once successful, publish generated NuGet packages to a NuGet server for consumption by team members or customers.

Build configurations in TeamCity consist of one or more build steps. In TeamCity 7, several NuGet-related build steps have been introduced: installing NuGet packages, creating NuGet packages, and pushing NuGet packages. Let's have a look at that last one.

Before being able to push packages to an external NuGet server, at least one version of NuGet should be installed into TeamCity. From the TeamCity portal, you can do this under Administration ➤ NuGet Settings under the NuGet Commandline tab. The versions of NuGet installed here will be made available in the NuGet build steps afterward. As can be seen from Figure 5-28, we can select the version of nuget.exe to install, and you can upload your own version of NuGet as well.

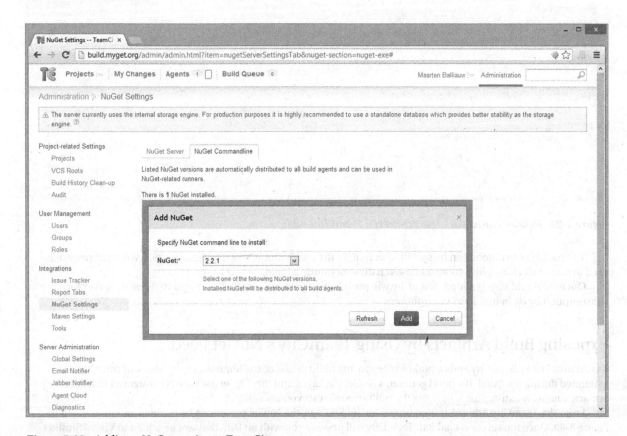

Figure 5-28. *Adding a NuGet version to TeamCity*

After at least one NuGet version has been installed, you can make pushing NuGet packages to an external feed a part of your build process. From any build configuration, you can add a new build step of the type NuGet Publish. This build step is able to upload packages created during the build to an external NuGet server. You can select the version of nuget.exe to use and specify the feed to which the package(s) have to be pushed. The API key for pushing packages has to be specified as well. An example configuration of this build step can be seen in Figure 5-29.

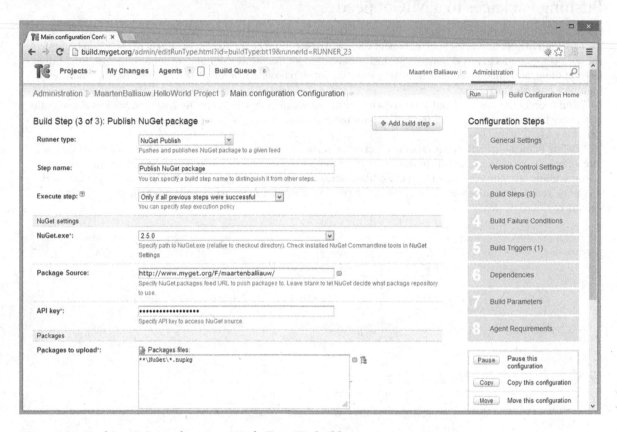

Figure 5-29. *Pushing NuGet packages as part of a TeamCity build*

The packages to upload can be specified as well. In the configuration seen in Figure 5-29, a wildcard pattern is used to match all .nupkg files created in a given directory during build.

Once this build step is added, TeamCity will push NuGet packages created to an external NuGet server for consumption by team members or customers.

Exposing Build Artifacts by Using TeamCity's NuGet Feed

As you may know, TeamCity ends a build with exposing build artifacts, the libraries, executables, or other items generated during the build. If a build generates NuGet packages and the NuGet package is configured as a build artifact, TeamCity can expose it by using the built-in NuGet server.

From the TeamCity Administration under NuGet Settings, the NuGet server can be enabled, as can be seen in Figure 5-30. Once the server is enabled, TeamCity will provide you with an URL that can be added to Visual Studio in order to consume the packages hosted on TeamCity. If guest access is enabled, TeamCity will provide you with a second URL that provides anonymous access to NuGet package build artifacts that are publicly available.

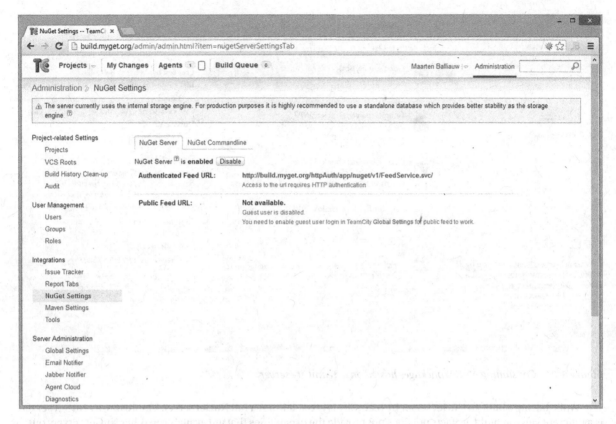

Figure 5-30. *Enabling the TeamCity built-in NuGet server*

The URL shown in the TeamCity portal can be used in Visual Studio. If guest access is disabled, you will have to provide credentials when consuming the feed. Figure 5-31 shows a list of packages fetched from TeamCity's NuGet server.

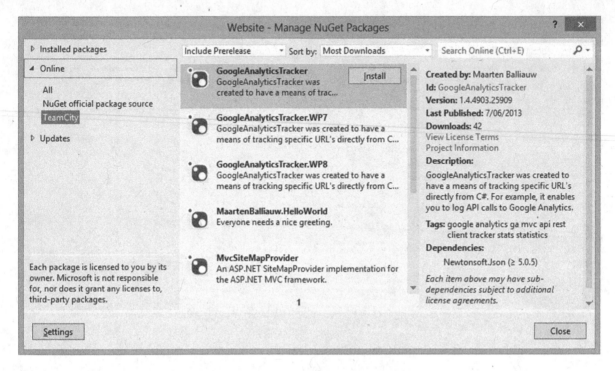

Figure 5-31. *Consuming NuGet packages hosted on a TeamCity server*

While having a built-in NuGet server in TeamCity is great, it is not a full NuGet server. The TeamCity NuGet server is a different view on build artifacts but does not provide the capabilities that are available in other NuGet servers out there. If you are using TeamCity for builds and continuous integration, it does, however, make perfect sense to either push packages created to an external NuGet server or to consume prerelease packages from TeamCity's built-in feed directly.

Using Other NuGet Repositories

So far, we've seen there are several free and commercial NuGet repository servers available. Next to network shares, NuGet.Server, the NuGet Gallery, MyGet, ProGet, and TeamCity, other solutions exist.

A free open source NuGet repository called NuRep is available from `https://bitbucket.org/thinkbeforecoding/nurep`. It comes with support for one feed and can host your own NuGet packages. It also comes with a symbol server so that you can debug NuGet packages in Visual Studio.

Other commercial NuGet repositories are JFrog Artifactory (available from `www.jfrog.com`) and Sonatype Nexus (available from `www.sonatype.org/nexus`). Both these repositories were originally built for Java and Maven repositories but also provide NuGet capabilities.

As you can see, there are a lot of different options available for hosting your own NuGet package repositories. Covering them all would be beyond the scope of this book. We did want to give you an overview of some of the available solutions out there, as a development process in which NuGet is leveraged will not do without having a NuGet server, whether free or commercial.

Preventing Disruptions in the Continuum

Just as a source repository is designed for working with sources, a package repository is designed to work with packages. It is commonly understood that it is important to keep the source repository operational and available to the development teams at all times. If they can't collaborate on their source repository, they are disabled in their work.

The importance of a NuGet feed should not be underestimated. NuGet package repositories are the home of your software dependencies, required to build your software. They're also the release catalog for those who want to consume your own packages. Depending on a NuGet feed implicitly turns it into a critical system for software development. This is especially true but not limited to those who use NuGet package restore.

If a package can't be restored during the build because the package source is unavailable, the build will fail. If a project team needs to consume a specific package from your NuGet feed in order to continue their work while the feed is unavailable, the team is blocked. It's obvious that package source availability is key to preventing disruptions in the work of development teams.

This effectively means you should treat all your NuGet package sources as critical systems, very similar to the way you treat your source repositories: high availability, data retention, backups, SLA, and security are words that come to mind. This is where MyGet really shines: you can mirror packages from external repositories onto MyGet feeds, backups and data retention options are offered as a service, and there's a granular security system for you to configure.

Nevertheless, whenever you depend on a package source, even if you solely depend on the NuGet Gallery or MyGet feeds, you should consider the implications of what happens when the flow is disrupted. There's always a possibility that you will lose connectivity, and this can be caused on your side, on the server side, or anywhere in between. Mirroring and caching are good strategies to ensure you always have a fallback scenario in place.

Summary

In this chapter, we've gone further than simply consuming packages and publishing packages to the official NuGet package source. We've shown you a variety of reasons that you may want to have your own NuGet feed.

The reasons for hosting your own NuGet feed are as simple as filtering the official NuGet package source and mirroring packages from it, and as complex as advanced scenarios involving security, privacy, and protecting intellectual property.

A lot of different options for creating and hosting your own NuGet package repositories are available. We've covered several options of creating your own NuGet feed. The easiest solution was using a folder or network file share to distribute packages. The NuGet.Server package and the NuGet Gallery allowed you to expose NuGet feeds and packages through an URL and allow you to expose your own NuGet feed to the Internet or intranet if you want.

We've also seen commercial options. MyGet, a hosted private NuGet feed solution, allows you to set up your own NuGet feed in seconds and provides a rich set of security options to configure your feed according to your needs. ProGet can be installed in your own network and comes with features such as proxying external NuGet feeds.

Many companies are already using TeamCity for their continuous integration. TeamCity comes with a built-in NuGet server that exposes build artifacts as a NuGet feed.

We've ended this chapter with some considerations to make when using NuGet in your development environment. Introducing a package source into the development flow also introduces a new critical system. A system all development teams depend on should comply with the highest SLA one can offer to prevent disruptions in their work: availability, retention, and security are key aspects to consider.

In this chapter, the fun began—we've gone beyond consuming and creating packages, to hosting your own NuGet feed. The next chapters will go even further as they explore some scenarios for integrating NuGet in your software development process as well as show how to leverage NuGet in other scenarios than pure package management.

CHAPTER 6

■■■

Continuous Package Integration

Having read the previous chapters of this book, you have now reached the point where you can start supporting processes in your development environment by using NuGet. You know how to create and publish packages and you have also learned how to set up your own NuGet feeds. Great! Now, let's fit the pieces together and streamline our development processes, because from a business point of view, that's one of the main reasons to introduce a package manager into a development organization.

You may already be using some common concepts and techniques to mitigate the risks of development, such as continuous integration and unit testing, perhaps even integration testing and automated deployments, or maybe a fully streamlined continuous delivery process. If you don't do any of these already, now would be a very good time to start.

This chapter will demonstrate how you can use NuGet in your development environment to support these processes. We'll focus primarily on supporting good practices for the application life cycle. We'll discuss whether or not NuGet packages belong in source control and look at the options available to facilitate both scenarios. Ensuring that packages flow from development to release without modification or rebuild is a typical scenario that deserves some attention as well; we'll call it *package promotion* later in this chapter.

Using a No-Commit Strategy

When it comes to source control, it is very interesting to see how development teams approach external software dependencies, or software dependencies in general. Many of us use a dedicated folder to store them in source control, often called `ReferencedAssemblies`, `References`, `Lib`, or something similar. This is a well-known strategy for keeping solution-level software dependencies close to the source code.

Many developers have been applying this good practice for years, yet there is no single convention on how the folder should be named or structured or where it should be located. This kind of information is typically defined in the corporation's naming conventions and guidelines documentation. It is strange to see a multitude of different guidelines, often with variations in underlying reasons, solving a common problem we all share. NuGet offers an opportunity to have a standardized location and name for those references by using the default `$(SolutionDir)\packages` folder. Even though this default can be overridden, it is a step toward a common direction.

In addition to this rather cosmetic annoyance (something many developers experienced when trying to figure out conventions while joining a new project or team), you might also experience issues with your version control system. Team Foundation Server (TFS) is a common victim of rants against its behavior for merging binary files. Ever had the task of upgrading a dependency and trying to check it into TFS source control, only to be prompted by a dialog box stating that TFS did not see any changes and leaving you with no other option but to undo your pending changes for that binary file?

Although blaming a tool is always easier than questioning the process, you have to realize that a version control system is not designed to version binary files but rather to track textual files such as source code.

The bigger issue that comes with storing all those software dependencies in source control is the amount of disk space required to store all those files, which are often duplicated in multiple project repositories. What's the point in storing NHibernate version 2.2.0 in source control, next to all of your 37 solutions? All of them are the same. What kind of history will you keep in your version control system for these files? You won't change them yourself, so all you keep track of is that, at a certain point in time, you added, removed, or changed the version of a dependency. The amount of useful information, in bytes, is almost nil compared to the amount of storage required for the dependency itself. Agreed, disk space is inexpensive nowadays, but we all want our sources to be safe from failure, right? Redundant, fail-safe storage that is backed up at regular intervals contributes to requiring even more disk space.

Also, do the binaries for these external dependencies belong in your source code repository? Is the actual binary a requirement for your software? Or would an identifier for it, such as a name and version number, be enough to rebuild a specific version of your software?

In NuGet terms, all you need is a package ID and a package version. The information stored in the `packages.config` file in your project contains everything you need to manage your dependencies. You store it in a version control system (VCS), after all.

Does this mean that you can choose to no longer commit packages into your VCS? Yes! But before you do, you need to put in place a good process supporting this scenario. It's not a lot of work; it's not overcomplicated, and it's quite fast to set up.

Keep in mind that we don't want to break any other established good practices by banning NuGet packages from source control. If you want to keep storing those packages next to your sources, that's fine. It's your choice. We don't want to force you in any way. But if you do want to get out of the comfort zone and gain insights into an alternative approach, you might want to give it a try and see for yourself. In fact, we want to make sure that every single build you do, based on a given revision or changeset of your sources, even without the required NuGet packages in source control, always produces the same output. The end result of building with or without NuGet packages in source control must be the same. The no-commit strategy outlined in the following sections explains how to achieve this while not storing those dependencies in source control.

Source Control Layout

As stated before, NuGet has a default setting as to where packages are being located relative to the Visual Studio solution. Depending on the VCS tool you use, there are various ways to keep NuGet packages out of your source control repository. We'll stick to the default package installation directory of `$(SolutionDir)\packages`. Conceptually, all you need to do is to ignore the entire directory, except for the `repositories.config` file.

The next sections will describe ignoring the `$(SolutionDir)\packages` directory when using some popular VCS tools such as Mercurial, Git, Subversion, and TFS.

Using Mercurial

When using the Mercurial (HG) source control system, you can add this directory to your ignore file. The Mercurial system uses a file called `.hgignore` in the root directory of a repository to control its behavior when it searches for files it is not currently tracking. More information about its syntax can be found at the following URL: `www.selenic.com/mercurial/hgignore.5.html`.

■ **Tip**   If you're not familiar with the `.hgignore` file, you can easily install a base `ignore` file for each of your projects by using NuGet (what else?). Simply install the HgIgnore NuGet package by running the `Install-Package HgIgnore` command in the NuGet Package Manager Console.

A good baseline for an .hgignore file when doing .NET development looks as follows:

```
syntax: glob

TestResults/*
*[Bb]in/
*[Dd]ebug/
*[Oo]bj/
*[Rr]elease/
*_[Rr]e[Ss]harper.*/
*.docstates
*.user
*.suo
*.xap
```

This is also the default one that is contained in version 1.4 of the HgIgnore NuGet package. However, this one still keeps track of the NuGet packages installed into the $(SolutionDir)\packages folder, which is the default location defined by NuGet.

To make sure you track only the $(SolutionDir)\packages\repositories.config file and no NuGet packages, you should add the following to your .hgignore file:

```
syntax: regex
^packages/(?!repositories.config)
```

Another way is to use the HgIgnore NuGet package we created for you, available on the Pro NuGet MyGet feed of this book. Install it by executing the following command in the NuGet Package Manager Console:

```
Install-Package HgIgnoreNuGet -Source https://www.myget.org/F/pronuget
```

Using Git

Git has a very similar concept for ignoring files and folders in source control, by using a .gitignore file. You can define ignore settings globally, on a per repository basis, or even on the folder level. Detailed information about how Git handles the .gitignore file can be found at the following URL: http://help.github.com/ignore-files/.

To prevent NuGet packages from being tracked by the Git VCS, you can put an .ignore file in the $(SolutionDir)\packages folder with the following contents:

```
# ignore everything in this folder
*

# do not ignore the .gitignore file
!.gitignore

# track the repositories.config file as well
!repositories.config
```

If you prefer having just one global `.gitignore` file in the root of the repository, adding two lines to that file will do:

```
# ignore nuget packages
packages/

# but not repositories.config
!packages/repositories.config
```

Using Subversion

Subversion (SVN) also supports ignoring files. However, it does not use any ignore file to achieve this. Instead, SVN works with ignore lists and SVN properties, which makes ignoring the `$(SolutionDir)\packages` folder, except the `repositories.config` file, a bit more cumbersome. We will use TortoiseSVN in our example, because it is the most popular SVN utility out there.

TortoiseSVN has Windows Explorer shell integration. When you open a local source folder with an SVN repository, you'll have SVN functionality readily available in the right-click contextual menu in Windows Explorer. When using SVN, you have to reverse your logic a bit. Instead of ignoring, we'll be adding only the files we want to the repository. To track the `$(SolutionDir)\packages\repositories.config` file, you simply right-click the `$(SolutionDir)\packages` folder in Windows Explorer and choose the Add option in the contextual menu that appears, as shown in Figure 6-1.

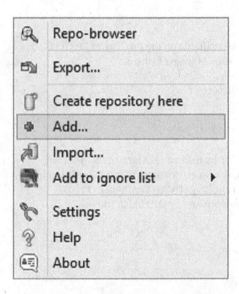

Figure 6-1. *Adding an item to the SVN repository by using TortoiseSVN*

After doing so, you'll be prompted with a dialog box, where you'll have more options to specify what exactly you want to track in your SVN repository, as shown in Figure 6-2.

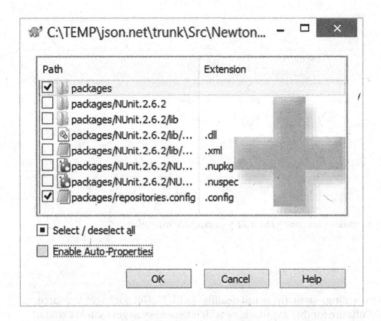

Figure 6-2. *Selecting what to add to the SVN repository using TortoiseSVN*

By selecting only the $(SolutionDir)\packages folder and the repositories.config file, we are not keeping track of everything else inside the package installation directory. All other contents will be treated as unversioned.

Using Team Foundation Server

TFS does not deal with ignore files as such. You have to think in terms of workspaces and cloaking, which might make you feel a bit like Darth Vader designing the Death Star. It is, however, quite easy to achieve the same result once you know where to look.

The no-commit strategy tells you not to commit any NuGet packages into your VCS, but as most people using TFS have mapped the entire branch to their workspace, this causes issues. Whenever we install a package through Visual Studio into a mapped workspace folder, Visual Studio tells TFS to add these files to source control. We want to keep track of the repositories.config file but not of the actual packages, which are, by default, being installed into the same $(SolutionDir)\packages folder. Respecting NuGet's convention-over-configuration approach, we want to keep these defaults.

The workaround is not very straightforward when looking at the UI, yet it's not hard to do from the workspace mapping dialog box. If you thought you could map only folders, think again! You can map single files as well! Knowing this is half of the work; the other part is just setting the correct workspace mapping, as shown in Figure 6-3.

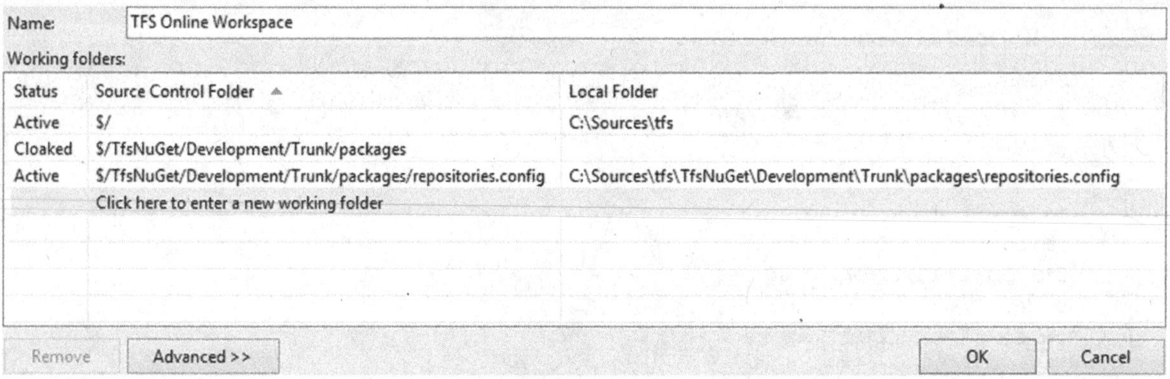

Name:	TFS Online Workspace	

Working folders:

Status	Source Control Folder ▲	Local Folder
Active	$/	C:\Sources\tfs
Cloaked	$/TfsNuGet/Development/Trunk/packages	
Active	$/TfsNuGet/Development/Trunk/packages/repositories.config	C:\Sources\tfs\TfsNuGet\Development\Trunk\packages\repositories.config
	Click here to enter a new working folder	

Remove	Advanced >>		OK	Cancel

Figure 6-3. *Cloaking the packages folder (except repositories.config) in a TFS workspace mapping*

Exploring Trade-offs

The no-commit strategy is a specific approach to dealing—actually, to not dealing—with NuGet packages in source control. You might be wondering what the trade-offs are for this approach, or which benefits you get vs. what kind of drawbacks to expect. As with everything, criticism is justified. Every approach has its benefits and its drawbacks. It's only a matter of picking the approach that works best for you in your situation.

Let's discuss the aspect of storage. One could say that disk space is inexpensive nowadays. And as a matter of fact, that is very true! If you have abundant storage, and you have no issue in duplicating those references over and over again, one could very easily agree with you. But again: you do want to make sure that source code is on fail-safe storage, preferably on redundant disks and being backed up at regular intervals, making the storage requirements a lot bigger all of a sudden.

Even when space is abundant, you might consider a no-commit strategy in any case. There is, however, one thing that is not cheap, and most likely will never be. It's usually left out of the picture in these kinds of discussions—time. Time is expensive. In fact, we often find ourselves lacking time. Duplicating your binaries in source control not only requires disk space but relies on processing power as well. What happens if you branch your project? Are those binary files copied into the new branch? Or is your VCS tracking only the delta of those files? Do you know the answer to this question with absolute certainty, without looking it up on the Internet? As usual, it depends. It depends on the source control system you are using. Distributed version control systems (DVCSs), such as Git or Mercurial, tend to behave very differently than centralized version control systems, such as TFS. The way your VCS will deal with those binaries during a branch (or merge) operation heavily depends on its (in)capability of tracking history on those files. For instance, TFS cannot track any differences for a .dll file; hence it cannot calculate the delta between two changes. Because of that, it will do a full copy of this file when it is branched. On the other hand, it will most likely not be able to merge changes for those files as well. You'll have to choose between the server version and your local version. This, again, takes time—time from the CPU tracking your sources, as well as time from the developers dealing with this kind of problem. Did we mention the time needed to perform backups of your source repository? Extrapolate the impact of time on your operational costs, and you might have found another compelling argument to convince your manager to consider another approach. Also, bear in mind that you don't want to track history on the actual content of those binary files, especially for external dependencies. What you really want to track is its metadata: the package ID and version information.

What would you say if centralizing your dependencies could save you time? Some teams already took a similar approach in the pre-NuGet era. They usually dedicated some network share to store all binary references and pointed all their projects to reference assemblies directly from that location. And the funny thing is that most of them are complaining about the time it takes to build. A significant delay is experienced when building your projects referencing binaries located somewhere on the network. This is obviously caused by the amount of network traffic required to fetch those binaries during the build process.

NuGet, however, has built-in support for caching of NuGet packages. By default, every new package you fetch from a NuGet feed is cached on the local machine. This is true both for your development machine and for any build server that fetches a NuGet package. This is a significant benefit over the custom solution of referencing binaries directly from a network share. Instead of downloading the binaries upon every single compilation of your project, you now need to download them only once. Every subsequent build of your project referencing those exact same packages will not experience the delay caused by network traffic and will fetch those packages from the local cache.

In addition to the caching optimization, NuGet packages are also compressed. As we mentioned earlier, a NuGet package is an archive file, which you can uncompress using any popular archive tool out there, such as our favorite, 7-Zip (www.7-zip.org). This is another optimization to increase the speed at which packages are downloaded, or in other words, decrease the amount of time required to fetch those NuGet packages.

So far, the trade-offs give the no-commit strategy the benefit of the doubt—a centralized location for your references, less disk space required to store them, and less time spent on tracking changes, dealing with conflicts, or across the wire generating unnecessary amounts of network traffic.

There is, however, one subtle dependency for this approach, which, at the same time, is its major drawback: a network connection to the package source is required. When the package source cannot be queried for the necessary packages required to build your project, compilation will fail—obviously because of the missing references. Note that after checking the package hash with the package source, the local cache will be used to install packages if they are present there. If we analyze the impact of this drawback, it is rather limited.

A build server needs a connection to your source repository as well, so on that level, your build server and source control repository share the same risk. If the package repository is on a different server than your sources, you just added another point of failure, because you now have two different connections that can fail. You have various options, though, for hosting your package repository: on the same server as your sources, on the build server (if you only have one), or even in the cloud (MyGet).

Your development machines share the exact same drawback as the build server. If a developer cannot build the solution because his laptop cannot connect to the NuGet repository, he has an issue. Developers don't like issues. Developers like good (or better) practices. The developer's workstation does not need to be connected with the NuGet package repository all the time, though. As with the build server, the connection is required only if the developer is performing operations against the NuGet repository. The actions a developer typically performs against a NuGet repository are limited as well:

- Updating a NuGet dependency to a newer version
- Installing a new NuGet dependency
- Fetching a NuGet package that is not yet available in the local cache
- Pushing or publishing a package to the NuGet repository (Shouldn't this be done as part of the release process, through an automated build, for instance?)

If you analyze the use cases in the preceding list, you should notice that none are actions a developer performs every day. Preferably, these actions are well planned and at least have some kind of standardized process. Updating a NuGet dependency or installing a new one should not be an ad hoc decision. Neither is releasing a package to the repository, ready for consumption by everyone pointing to it. This is not something you will do when working on the train home.

The use case of fetching a NuGet package that is not yet available on the local cache of the developer's workstation, however, is one to keep in mind, because it might happen more often than you think. Imagine that someone else in your team upgraded a NuGet dependency or installed a new package, and you just got the latest version out of your VCS, eager to continue coding on that same train home. If you did not build your solution and fetched those new NuGet packages before leaving the office, you'd be in for a frustrating ride.

As such, we want to introduce a good practice: whenever you fetch the latest sources from your VCS, rebuild your solution, and make sure you have all packages required for compilation to succeed. There's an even better approach: communicate changes in project dependencies to the team! Make it part of the process of updating or installing new dependencies. If you don't have a process, then this is the minimum. Communication is key!

NuGet in its most pure form, the command line and its packages, do not rely on Visual Studio or PowerShell. If you check the installed NuGet packages into your VCS, not a single developer is required to have any NuGet tooling installed on his system. That is good! We don't want to break this by requiring all developers to have this tooling installed on their systems. Even though it is very easy to get up and running fast, we consider it clean. When applying a no-commit strategy, we need to respect that. You'll read later on in this chapter how to do so.

Tracking Package Metadata

In a nutshell, all we want to have in our VCS is a trace of which dependencies we have and which versions we depend on. In NuGet terms, we're talking about package IDs and package versions. This happens to be exactly what is being stored into the `packages.config` files that NuGet produces when managing NuGet packages in a project or solution. Next to that, there's also the `repositories.config` file, by default located under the `$(SolutionDir)\packages` folder. The `repositories.config` file, as its name suggests, keeps track of the different NuGet repositories that your solution projects rely on and is thus pointing to all `packages.config` files for a given solution. This is the kind of meta-information we want to keep track of.

The information contained within these files is everything you need to fetch the required NuGet packages before building your project. This form of tracking your dependencies is very elegant. Every VCS is able to deal with XML files, which are just simple textual files, so we benefit from the comparison and tracking capabilities. The few merge conflicts you might encounter on these files will be very easy to resolve, as you'll be able to actually compare the contents of these files.

The main reason that we do want to track this information lays in one of the most important principles behind the continuous integration process: a given changeset in your VCS must always produce the same build output. This effectively means there is no room for tampering with any file you get from source control before unleashing the compiler on it to produce its build output.

Another key practice is to use only trusted sources when continuously integrating your product on the build server. That's the only way to ensure that no one else has modified any input to the build server. The need for this practice is very obvious for your source code files, which are being tracked in your VCS: you can easily view the history of your sources and track changes made to your build server. This is less obvious but equally as important for NuGet packages that come from outside your VCS. Make sure you can trust the NuGet package source you are using for your builds. This could result in limiting write permissions on the package source you are using—for instance, a network share, an internal NuGet server, or a secured MyGet feed. This could also mean you want to track who modified what in your NuGet repository, through RSS activity feeds, for instance, or custom logging you implemented in your NuGet server. In addition, this could even mean that every project has its own NuGet repository, which again is very easy to achieve using MyGet.

■ **Tip** If you experience issues connecting to an internal VCS and an external NuGet repository, or vice versa, whether on the build server or local machine, you might need to add both of them to the Trusted Sites list in Internet Options. This is definitely the case when your development workstation or build server is behind a corporate proxy.

Another great opportunity resides in the fact that software dependencies are now easily discoverable in these XML configuration files. Any decent software factory wants to know the answers to the following questions at any time:

- Who is using version X of component Y?

- Which versions of component Z are in use (and which not)?

- What dependencies does application A have and to which versions?

Answering these questions typically requires someone to maintain a spreadsheet with dependency matrices. What if you could just analyze these files with a tool and automate the generation of a package dependency matrix?

■ **Tip** In an attempt to automate dependency matrices, Xavier has built a proof-of-concept NuGet command-line extension that allows you to analyze a TFS or filesystem repository for NuGet package dependencies. It is open source and available on GitHub (patches and feedback are much appreciated):

https://github.com/xavierdecoster/NuGet.Analyze.

Try it out by using the following commands in the NuGet Package Manager Console:

```
Install-Package NuGet.InstallCommandLineExtension
Install-CommandLineExtension NuGet.Analyze
```

Enabling Package Restore

To perform continuous integration on your sources that depend on NuGet packages that are not in your VCS, we need to restore those packages before building. This is what we call *continuous package integration*.

An example process flow for continuous package integration can be found in Figure 6-4.

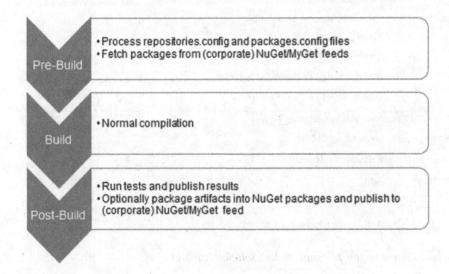

Figure 6-4. *A basic continuous package integration process flowchart*

Up to version 1.5 of NuGet, this could be achieved using David Fowler's NuGetPowerTools package (Install-Package NuGetPowerTools), which you can find at www.nuget.org. Because of the success of this approach, the NuGet team decided to integrate this functionality in NuGet starting from version 1.6, making it unnecessary for you to reinstall the NuGetPowerTools package for every single solution. And with version 2.7, a new approach to package restore was introduced. In there, it's enabled by default and completely transparent.

We will not cover the NuGetPowerTools package, but since not everyone may already be using NuGet 2.7 we will cover the pre-2.7 era and the post-2.7 era.

Package Restore Prior to NuGet 2.7

The Enable Package Restore feature built into NuGet 1.6 and above allows you to very easily set up the prebuild part of the workflow. To do so, right-click the solution node in Visual Studio's Solution Explorer, and click the Enable NuGet Package Restore option. If you do, and you still don't see this menu item appear, you either already enabled this option, or you have a folder named .nuget in your solution directory. Figure 6-5 illustrates this option.

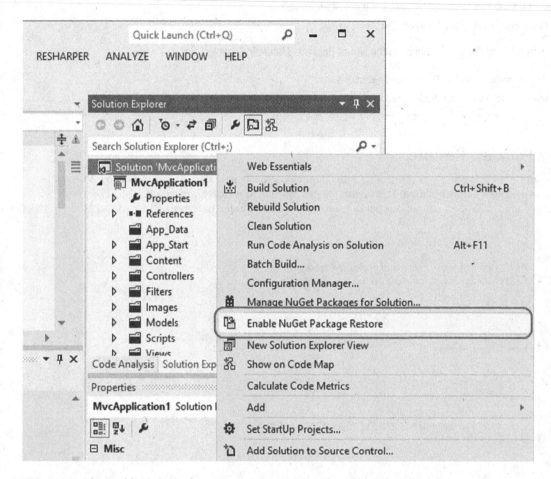

Figure 6-5. *The Enable NuGetPackage Restore option in Visual Studio's Solution Explorer*

Visual Studio will prompt with a dialog box explaining what is about to happen ("A .nuget folder will be added to the root of the solution that contains files that enable package restore. Are you sure?"). Simply confirming with Yes sets up NuGet package restore. You can now delete all subfolders of your package installation directory, by default $(SolutionDir)\packages, except for the repositories.config file, and your solution should still compile properly. During compilation, you should see NuGet installation traces in the Visual Studio output window, and you should see the required NuGet packages reappear in the package installation directory as well.

Although it is very easy to set this up, we encourage you to read further and get to know the details of how this works. If you ever run into issues (due to a merge conflict, for instance) and notice strange behaviors, it helps you a lot if you know what is going on.

After enabling NuGet package restore, you'll notice a .nuget folder in your solution directory containing three files: the NuGet command line (nuget.exe), a nuget.config file, and an MSBuild file called nuget.targets.

■ **Caution** Do not forget to check the .nuget folder into your VCS, because your solution now depends on it to be able to compile successfully.

If you know that your Visual Studio project files are MSBuild files as well, you conceptually already know what's going on. What happens is that, when enabling NuGet package restore, NuGet will iterate over all your solution's projects that contain NuGet package dependencies and add an import statement in the project file. The import statement will import the nuget.targets MSBuild file. It will also add a RestorePackages property to your project and set it to true. Listing 6-1 shows you the most meaningful parts of the nuget.targets task, allowing you to understand what's going on.

Listing 6-1. Partial NuGet.targets MSBuild Task Used for Package Restore

```xml
<?xml version="1.0" encoding="utf-8"?>
<Project ToolsVersion="4.0" xmlns="http://schemas.microsoft.com/developer/msbuild/2003">
    <PropertyGroup>
        <SolutionDir Condition="$(SolutionDir) == '' Or $(SolutionDir) == '*Undefined*'">
            $(MSBuildProjectDirectory)\..\
        </SolutionDir>

        <!-- Enable the restore command to run before builds -->
        <RestorePackages Condition="  '$(RestorePackages)' == '' ">false</RestorePackages>

        <!-- Property that enables building a package from a project -->
        <BuildPackage Condition="  '$(BuildPackage)' == '' ">false</BuildPackage>

        <!-- Determines if package restore consent is required to restore packages -->
        <RequireRestoreConsent
            Condition=" '$(RequireRestoreConsent)' != 'false' ">true</RequireRestoreConsent>

        <!-- Download NuGet.exe if it does not already exist -->
        <DownloadNuGetExe Condition=" '$(DownloadNuGetExe)' == '' ">false</DownloadNuGetExe>
    </PropertyGroup>

    <ItemGroup Condition=" '$(PackageSources)' == '' ">
        <!-- Package sources used to restore packages. By default,
registered sources under %APPDATA%\NuGet\NuGet.Config will be used -->
        <!-- The official NuGet package source (https://nuget.org/api/v2/) will be excluded
if package sources are specified and it does not appear in the list -->
        <!--
            <PackageSource Include="https://nuget.org/api/v2/" />
            <PackageSource Include="https://my-nuget-source/nuget/" />
        -->
    </ItemGroup>

    ...

</Project>
```

It helps if you are a bit familiar with MSBuild, but it's not really needed. Just know that an additional RestorePackages target, triggering a command-line nuget install packages.config, is going to be executed as part of every build, for each Visual Studio project that has the property RestorePackages set to true. You can easily access this file from within Visual Studio in the .nuget solution folder that got added to your solution, as shown in Figure 6-6.

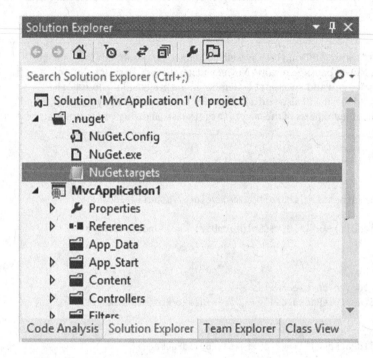

Figure 6-6. *The .nuget solution folder added by the Enable NuGet Package Restore feature*

Tweaking the NuGet.targets File

The NuGet.targets file contains all the logic for making package restore possible. It contains a series of MSBuild properties that can be changed, as well as the actual package restore target that calls into nuget.exe. Table 6-1 lists the MSBuild properties you may want to change.

Table 6-1. *NuGet.targets MSBuild Properties*

Property	Default value	Description
SolutionDir	$(MSBuildProjectDirectory)\..\	The solution directory for the solution in which NuGet package restore will run.
RestorePackages	false	Is package restore enabled? Each project file will typically override this variable and decide whether package restore is enabled.
BuildPackage	false	Should a NuGet package be created for every project? This can be overridden in the project file.

(continued)

Table 6-1. *(continued)*

Property	Default value	Description
RequireRestoreConsent	true	Should consent be given for package restore? By default, NuGet package restore will prompt the user for license acceptance, essentially blocking the restore process for input. If you want to run NuGet package restore on a build server, change the value of the RequireRestoreConsent element to false. This will ensure no license prompts block the NuGet executable.
DownloadNuGetExe	false	Should a copy of nuget.exe be downloaded from the Internet?

Next to these MSBuild properties, you can also specify the feed(s) from which packages should be downloaded by modifying the PackageSources setting. If you want, for instance, to fetch NuGet packages from the ProNuGet feed on MyGet, you could use the following:

```
<PackageSources>https://www.myget.org/F/pronuget</PackageSources>
```

By default, the package sources defined in the nuget.config file will be used. However, we prefer explicitly indicating the package source in this file, even when you are using only the NuGet.org feed, so you can track changes to it. It is also the only way to ensure that no external changes can break your build and to ensure that you always get the same output for a given changeset. If any external influence changes the nuget.config file on the machine that compiles your project, NuGet might be redirected to a different package source than the one you intended.

It is important to point out that the NuGet package restore feature will install the exact same package version as defined in the project's packages.config file: it will not perform any upgrades for the exact same reasons.

Package Restore and Build Targets Originating from a NuGet Package

Package restore may sound like the Holy Grail to some, but it also comes with a caveat: you have to know what you're doing—but then again, isn't that the case with everything?

Imagine you are making use of a package that contains custom build targets, a feature we described in Chapter 3. An example of such a package is the Microsoft.Bcl.Async package, which adds support for async/await in .NET 4.0, Silverlight, and Windows Phone 7.5 projects. Somewhere in its dependency chain (in the Microsoft.Bcl. Build package, to be precise), it adds an MSBuild target file to your project to be able to do all compiler magic that is required for making async/await work.

■ **Note** If you haven't heard of async/await or are interested in what happens behind the curtains, Dino Esposito has a great introductory article on this at www.simple-talk.com/dotnet/.net-framework/syntactic-sugar-and-the-async-pill/.

The `Microsoft.Bcl.Build.targets` file injected into your project is located under the `packages` folder. Now guess what happens if we enable package restore and don't add the contents of the packages folder to our source control system. Depending on how the package was created, one of two things will happen:

- If the package was not created using the `\build` folder convention introduced with NuGet 2.5 (see Chapter 3) and hasn't been properly added to the project file, the project will no longer load in Visual Studio.

- If the package follows the `\build` folder convention, NuGet will restore the `.targets` file and nothing bad will happen.

Unfortunately, a lot of packages are still not making use of this new package convention, resulting in not being able to load a project in Visual Studio or failing builds on a build server. There is a simple solution to this problem, though, which consists of making a small modification to the project file referencing the MSBuild `.targets` file by checking whether the `.targets` file exists.

You can open the project file that isn't loading by using a text editor like Notepad or Notepad++ and find the `<Import />` element in which the `.targets` file is referenced. For the `Microsoft.Bcl.Build` package (version 1.0.7), this element looks like the following:

```
<Import Project="..\packages\Microsoft.Bcl.Build.1.0.7\tools\Microsoft.Bcl.Build.targets" />
```

We can modify the statement by adding a condition to it, checking whether the file exists on disk. The added attribute is shown in bold:

```
<Import Project="..\packages\Microsoft.Bcl.Build.1.0.7\tools\Microsoft.Bcl.Build.targets" Condition=
"Exists('$(SolutionDir)\packages\Microsoft.Bcl.Build.1.0.7\tools\Microsoft.Bcl.Build.targets')" />
```

If you save the project file and load it again in Visual Studio, at least the project will load. However, depending on what features in the imported `.targets` file are being used, it may not be sufficient to get package restore working. The only option there is to run package restore before the build kicks off, by running `nuget.exe install packages.config`. On a build server you can do this by running the following batch file to build the project:

```
REM Package restore
.nuget\nuget.exe install MySolution\packages.config -OutputDirectory %cd%\packages -NonInteractive

REM Build
%WINDIR%\Microsoft.NET\Framework\v4.0.30319\msbuild MySolution.sln /p:Configuration="Release" /m
/v:M /fl /flp:LogFile=msbuild.log;Verbosity=Normal /nr:false
```

The easiest solution to the problem described in this section is probably just making sure the imported `.targets` file is stored in your version control system. With NuGet shipping new releases, most packages adding MSBuild targets will hopefully start respecting the `\build` folder convention, making this fix obsolete by the next edition of this book. And when using NuGet 2.7's package restore feature, this fix is already obsolete.

Package Restore with NuGet 2.7 and Beyond

The NuGet team started doing things differently with NuGet 2.7. Before that version, package restore was essentially a hack of the Visual Studio project file, sneaking in a custom build target that ran `nuget.exe install`. As we've seen in the previous section, running package restore during the build instead of prior to it sometimes caused trouble.

With the release of NuGet 2.7, package restore is no longer the responsibility of the Visual Studio project file but of the build system. Or in other words: Visual Studio or your build server are now responsible for running package restore prior to starting the build.

The NuGet Visual Studio extension does this by default, but this behavior can be changed through the options, under Tools ä Options ä Package Manager ä General. Figure 6-7 shows this dialog box and relevant settings.

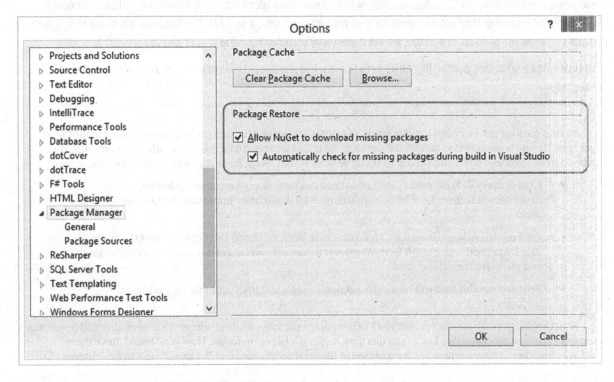

Figure 6-7. *Package restore options in Visual Studio*

As you can see, the new package restore functionality is much easier to use and comes with less hassle: no longer do you have to commit a `nuget.config` file and a copy of the NuGet command-line tool to your source control system.

When enabled, Visual Studio will run package restore before starting the actual build of the project files. Essentially, it calls into the NuGet command line behind the scenes, running `nuget.exe restore <your solution file>.sln`. As such, this is the key to package restore with NuGet 2.7 and beyond: calling into the `nuget.exe restore` command. If you need package restore on your build server, call into this command prior to the actual build. If you are writing your own build system, call into this command prior to the actual build. There are some additional options that can be specified on the call to `nuget.exe restore`. These are described in Appendix A.

Promoting Packages

NuGet packages, just like any other release vehicle (binaries, installers, and so forth), need to undergo rigorous testing and quality assurance before being released to the masses. One cannot just build a complex NuGet package, complete with custom PowerShell hook points, push it to the repository, and assume everything will work as expected, every single time, over and over again. If you're that good, you should be able to convince your managers to code directly onto the production servers.

We like Eric S. Raymond's approach of release early, release often. This is exactly what you should do with your NuGet packages as well. You release not only the package contents, but also the package itself. It is your release vehicle. That is why your continuous integration builds should be producing NuGet packages as well if you intend to ship your product as a NuGet package (or multiple NuGet packages).

■ **Note** The concept of release early, release often (or RERO, in short) actually has another part of the sentence: "and listen to your customers." Besides ensuring quality, anticipating your customer's needs and gathering feedback are among the most important requirements for your product to become a success. Continuously delivering high-quality releases enables you to do so. In addition, it's the fastest way of delivering value to your clients.

Phil Haack has a great blog post on this topic: `http://haacked.com/archive/2011/04/20/release-early-and-often.aspx`.

As your package goes through various stages of testing, you want to ensure nothing gets changed in those packages. No one is permitted to modify the package file or its contents. To facilitate the different teams that are involved in this process, one could choose to set up various NuGet feeds. An example setup is as follows:

- *CI feed*: Every CI build pushes its output onto this feed, ready for consumption by development teams who want to play around with it, but more important, for QA teams to test them.

- *QA feed*: All packages from the CI feed that have been validated and approved by QA could then be pushed onto the QA feed. Whenever a release needs to get out, you can pick a version and push it to the Release feed.

- *Release feed*: This feed will be used for general consumption of your officially released packages.

With this setup, you have a very short track of releasing a package, while ensuring optimal quality and respecting the normal release processes. We like to call this flow *NuGet package promotion*. How you should move these packages from repository to repository is explained in the section "Phasing Out Packages" later in this chapter.

Prereleasing Packages

Next to package restore, NuGet v1.6 also introduced the concept of prerelease packages. A prerelease NuGet package is considered unstable, and thus not ready yet for general consumption. A prerelease package is often indicated by the commonly used terms *alpha*, *beta*, *RC*, and so on. The concept of prereleases does not fit well with the concept of release fast, release often that we discussed in the previous section. If we cannot modify the package contents (for example, the version number), and we don't know up front whether our package will make it through the QA gate, how do we know when to tag our package with a certain release number? This is contradictory and counterintuitive. Then why does NuGet support prerelease tags at all?

Let's look at things from another perspective. We all know requirements change. Quite often, this happens very fast, and it occasionally impacts planning as well. Well, it nearly always impacts planning. It could be in the time dimension, resulting in shifting release dates. It could be in the scope dimension, resulting in adjusted functionality for a milestone. It could also have another impact on planning in the broader meaning of the word, any type of planning, including capacity or resource planning.

If planning is affected in the time dimension, you can choose to pick the latest QA-approved package and give it a prerelease tag before pushing it onto the Release feed. Probably more commonly, the opposite can happen as well, usually when changes have been made in scope: pick a prerelease package from QA, drop all version information after the dash (thus removing prerelease information), and push it out as an official release.

As explained in Chapter 3, NuGet also respects the SemVer notation and meaning of a prerelease package. Prerelease information is appended to the patch number, prefixed with a dash, as shown here:

```
major.minor.patch-prereleasetag (e.g. 1.0.0-RC1)
```

In our opinion, even prereleases are official releases. They indicate only a notion of potential instability or potential feature incompleteness. Prereleases should be considered milestones and be planned accordingly. A prerelease has a specific purpose—you want to get early feedback from your customers. This means that, ideally, your prerelease tags in the version information of your package should already be present in the CI build output.

Phasing Out Packages

In an enterprise environment, it is quite common to stop supporting an older, or maybe obsolete, framework. The same thing can happen to one or more of your NuGet package dependencies. If you want to discontinue a NuGet package, you either want to make sure that no one is still depending on it or that at least you can provide them with a working upgrade path.

A good example is the NuGet.org feed: in the past, package owners could delete a package from the gallery. A package owner had no idea who depended on that package and had no way of learning that either. A package owner could guess purely on the download count and, if by keeping track of this number over time, spot a trend in the usage of the package. However, a declining trend still does not justify the rude deletion of the package from a publicly available package source. Some package owners deleted their packages, essentially breaking other people's development and builds. This is the reason why the NuGet.org gallery now supports only "unlisting" packages instead, keeping them available for download but just no longer showing them in search results. This decision made it possible for package owners to still retract their package from search results but not break anyone's process.

What should enterprises do with their desire to block certain packages from being installed by their development teams? Deleting any already listed packages from your package source can have a significant impact. As with anything, communication is key. Communicating that support for a certain package (version) will be discontinued is a better practice. At least, your developers are aware that they should mitigate the risk associated with this pending change.

If you are using multiple package sources, you could add one for archiving those old or obsolete packages. If you delete a package without keeping a copy just in case, you're in for trouble. Archiving a package, after communicating its retirement, doesn't sound like a bad thing to us.

You could easily perform these actions by just moving the .nupkg file from one location to another, assuming you have enough permissions on both package sources. Moving those packages from filesystem path to filesystem path is straightforward. Moving a package from a feed to a filesystem path implies that you can download the package, store it on the archiving location, and delete it from the originating feed. This requires many more security permissions to be set properly. No matter how you move a package from one feed to another, you'll need all these permissions. This is a clear indication of how big an impact this action can have on your package consumers. Be cautious.

You could reuse Rob Reynold's command-line extension for NuGet, the NuGet.copy.extension package. You can install it by executing the following commands in the NuGet Package Manager Console:

```
Install-Package NuGet.InstallCommandLineExtension
Install-CommandLineExtension NuGet.copy.extension
```

After installing this extension, your NuGet command-line instances should have a new command available: the copy command. This command allows you to copy a package from one feed to another, by specifying the package ID (with optional version number), a source, a destination, and optionally an API key for the destination.

An example usage of the copy command follows:

```
nuget copy jQuery -Version 1.9.1 -Source https://www.myget.org/F/pronuget -Destination
 https://www.myget.org/F/pronugetarchive
```

When you are using MyGet feeds, you might as well benefit from the built-in package retirement feature. MyGet gives you the option to set, on a per package basis, whether the package is listed or not, without actually deleting it from the feed. By unlisting a package, you are preventing it from being consumed. Any newer versions of the package that are listed will still be available—older ones as well, but you should probably ask yourself why you didn't unlist those too. This effectively means you are no longer supporting a specific package (version) while maintaining an upgrade path to a newer version for those who still rely on it. Remember, you should communicate a package retirement so people can take appropriate actions, such as mirroring the package you are about to retire or even check it into source control as a temporary measure. This is a nice, soft phase-out of a package. In fact, you give your consumers a polite and gentle push toward upgrading this dependency.

■ **Caution** Continue respecting core principles of software craftsmanship: package owners can decide when to stop support for a certain package, but it is still the consumer's decision when and if to upgrade to a newer version!

Listing or unlisting a package on a MyGet feed is the same as toggling support on or off for that package. When navigating to the package details page on MyGet.org, you'll see a button next to each package version in the Package History listing, as shown in Figure 6-8.

Package history

List ▾	Unlist ▾	Delete ▾				
Version	**Size**	**Last updated**	**Downloads**	**Listed?**		
MvcSiteMapProvider 4.0.9	3 KB	Sunday, August 11, 2013	0	yes	⊕ Push ⌀ Unlist 🗑 Delete
MvcSiteMapProvider 4.0.8	3 KB	Sunday, August 11, 2013	0	yes	⊕ Push ⌀ Unlist 🗑 Delete
MvcSiteMapProvider 4.0.7	3 KB	Sunday, August 11, 2013	0	yes	⊕ Push ⌀ Unlist 🗑 Delete
MvcSiteMapProvider 4.0.6	3 KB	Sunday, August 4, 2013	2	yes	⊕ Push ⌀ Unlist 🗑 Delete
MvcSiteMapProvider 4.0.5	3 KB	Thursday, August 1, 2013	0	yes	⊕ Push ⌀ Unlist 🗑 Delete
MvcSiteMapProvider 4.0.4	3 KB	Thursday, August 1, 2013	0	yes	⊕ Push ⌀ Unlist 🗑 Delete

Figure 6-8. Listing and unlisting NuGet packages on a MyGet feed

If you toggle the state of a package version from listed to unlisted, you'll be prompted by a dialog box warning you about the impact of your action, which you'll have to confirm, as shown in Figure 6-9.

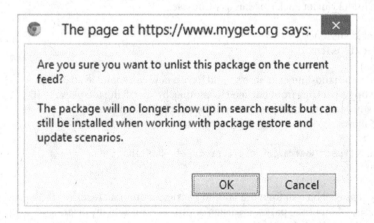

The page at https://www.myget.org says: ✕

Are you sure you want to unlist this package on the current feed?

The package will no longer show up in search results but can still be installed when working with package restore and update scenarios.

OK   Cancel

Figure 6-9. A dialog box will warn you and ask for confirmation when unlisting a package on MyGet

In addition, because of the soft implementation of this functionality, the operation of unlisting a package can be undone, as opposed to deleting the package from the feed.

Summary

In this chapter, we focused on supporting the development environment and processes, as well as the application and package life cycle. We've explained how NuGet can live in perfect symbiosis with established techniques such as continuous integration.

We have provided you with guidance on how you can set up a no-commit strategy using various version control systems and considered a different approach of dealing with software dependencies outside your VCS. We discussed both benefits and drawbacks of the no-commit strategy and highlighted some of the trade-offs being made.

Using a NuGet package as a release vehicle of our product, we discussed how packages should respect a correct flow and how versioning and package promotion can help you in doing so. We've touched on the enterprise scenario of gently phasing out old or obsolete packages as well.

The next chapter will change perspectives from continuously integrating to continuously delivering and discuss optimizations in the field of automated delivery, using NuGet.

■ ■ ■

## CHAPTER 7

Automated Delivery

Did you know that NuGet is more than just a tool to manage dependencies in your software projects? Since NuGet is both a tool and a means of publishing and consuming packages, those packages may be used for scenarios other than the ones we've already covered. Agreed, packages will mostly contain assemblies, but they can also contain PowerShell scripts and other files. What if there were tools out there leveraging this idea?

Meet Octopus Deploy and Chocolatey. Both projects started during the earliest NuGet release wave and started using NuGet for more than it was originally intended. We'll cover both tools in this chapter, because they are great for optimizing your deployments. Octopus Deploy can be used to deploy your application packages to various environments (think of test, staging, and production environments) and to automate deployment to web and database servers. Chocolatey, on the other hand, is leveraging NuGet to distribute and install software packages on the system level, distributed through a NuGet feed.

Both tools distribute software, but each does so in its own way and with its own goals. This chapter will explain how you can use Octopus Deploy to deploy your .NET solutions, packaged as a NuGet package, to your test, staging, and production servers. We'll also cover Chocolatey and how you can use it to install software prerequisites on either your machine or your servers.

Deploying Artifacts with Octopus Deploy

Let's start with some background. Imagine you have a web application, and you need to deploy it to test, staging, and production environments. How do you deploy your application today? Most people are using one or more of the following solutions:

- The application is copied to a USB drive or DVD and given to a system administrator, who copies all files to the target machine.

- The web application is built on one of the developer's machines. That developer connects to the target server by using FTP, Remote Desktop, or a file share and then copies over all files, either manually or using a batch file.

- A batch script runs on the build server and copies all files to the target machine.

- Microsoft's Web Deploy is used to deploy the web application to the target servers.

All the methods we've just mentioned (and probably a lot more) are valid ways of deploying an application. Unfortunately, most of them are not standardized through the use of either a process or a tool supporting that process.

We've seen this all before. If you look a few years back, the same story could be told about builds. Some shops let one lead developer create the final build. Others had a script in place that could be run either locally or on a server. Build processes are becoming more and more standardized. Most software developers have some sort of build server in place—think TeamCity, Team Foundation Server (TFS) build, and CruiseControl.NET. These build servers are all focusing on one thing: making it easy to create builds in a standardized manner.

Today, deployments are in the situation builds were a few years ago. Some teams do it manually; some have a script; some have a code monkey to deploy their product. Why not make deployments easy as well? Why not standardize them so every deployment is exactly the same? Microsoft is trying to do this by using Web Deploy; others are creating different solutions, including Octopus Deploy, the deployment solution based on NuGet that we'll describe in this section.

What Is Octopus Deploy?

Octopus Deploy is a tool supporting a conventions-based process of automating deployments. It can be downloaded from www.octopusdeploy.com. The general idea is to create your source code and check it into source control, making use of standard conventions like web.config transforms and using appSettings. Your build server, such as TeamCity or TFS, compiles this source code and packages this project into a NuGet package. This package is then published on a NuGet feed.

This is the moment where Octopus Deploy comes into play: you define a project and its target machines and environments. Octopus Deploy will then download the latest release of your software from a NuGet feed. It uploads each package to the target machines, which run a small agent called a Tentacle.

On each machine you plan to deploy to, the Tentacle agent accepts the NuGet package from Octopus Deploy and installs it by using a set of conventions, such as configuration file transforms and calling PowerShell scripts. A schematic overview of Octopus Deploy's deployment flow is shown in Figure 7-1.

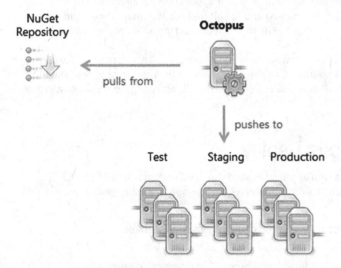

Figure 7-1. *High-level overview of Octopus Deploy deployment process (image courtesy of* http://octopusdeploy.com/documentation/getting-started)

In this chapter, we will not cover all options and conventions available in Octopus Deploy. We will only explain the basics of getting a deployment server up and running and how to deploy a simple application. All details—conventions, ways to configure your build server, and more—can be found on the Octopus Deploy web site at http://octopusdeploy.com/documentation/.

Installing Octopus Deploy

This section will guide you through installing Octopus Deploy. Since Octopus Deploy consists of the web portal for configuring and creating new deployments (Octopus Server) as well as agents to perform the actual deployments (Tentacle), we'll split this section into two parts.

■ **Note** To make things easy and for the purpose of demonstration, we'll install both Octopus Server and Tentacle on the same machine. In production environments, you would ideally deploy the server component to one server where you can manage deployments and releases, and install the tentacles to every machine on which software will be deployed.

Starting the Installation

Octopus Deploy comes with an installer that can be downloaded from the official web site (http://octopusdeploy.com/downloads). This page lists two downloads: Octopus Server and Octopus Tentacle. We'll download the Octopus.<some version>.msi file. Save this file to disk, and double-click the installer.

You'll be greeted by a friendly Octopus Deploy Server Setup Wizard, a favor you can return by just clicking Next until you have to click Install. If you stick to the defaults, after clicking the Install button, Octopus Deploy Server will be installed into %ProgramFiles%\Octopus. At the end of the installation, you'll have the opportunity to immediately run the configuration wizard. Make sure you leave this option selected, and click Finish. This is where the real work comes in, as shown in Figure 7-2: Welcome to Octopus!

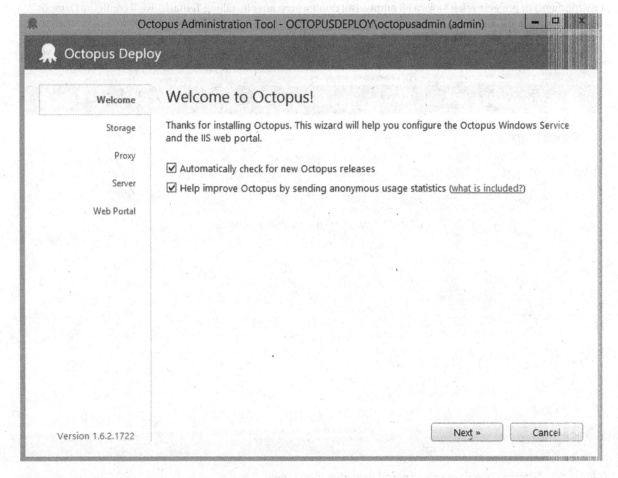

Figure 7-2. *Welcome to Octopus configuration screen*

The Octopus Deploy Configuration wizard has a few steps, allowing you to configure the fresh installation of Octopus Deploy Server:

- *Storage*: Octopus Deploy uses an embedded RavenDB database to store its data. You can change the location where the data is saved. By default, Octopus Deploy Server will store its data in `C:\Octopus\Data`.

- *Proxy*: If the server on which you deployed Octopus Deploy Server is behind a network proxy, you'll need to configure it manually in this wizard. By default, Octopus Deploy Server will use the proxy settings as configured in Internet Explorer.

- Octopus Deploy Windows Service: Has to be installed to push out deployments. Click the Install button to do so.

- Web Portal: Has to be installed to use the web portal to configure deployments and releases. You can configure your preferred authentication method and the IIS port number. Click the Create Site button to create the web portal and take note of the public URL.

If installation succeeds, you are good to go, and Octopus Deploy will be available on the URL you've just created. Browsing that URL displays the Octopus Deploy portal shown in Figure 7-3. Since we have not configured any environments or projects yet, it looks a bit empty. But don't worry: after installing Tentacle, we'll configure Octopus Deploy further.

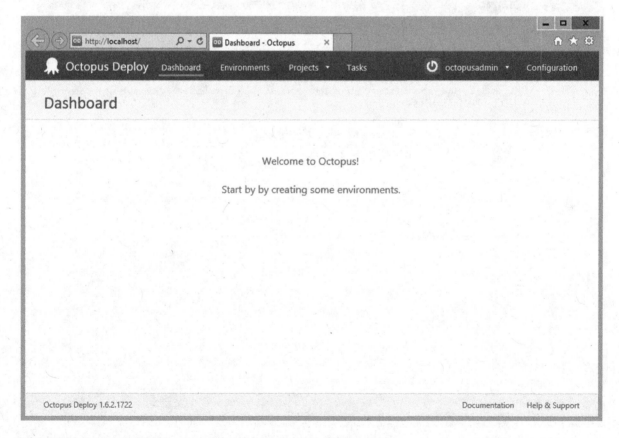

Figure 7-3. *Octopus Deploy Server web portal right after installation*

■ **Note** If for some reason you have issues with your installation, you might want to check the Octopus server installation instructions on the documentation web site (http://octopusdeploy.com/documentation/install/octopus).

Installing and Configuring a Tentacle

Octopus Tentacle comes with a very similar installer, which can also be downloaded from the official web site at www.octopusdeploy.com/Download. Recall that this page lists different downloads. This time, we'll download the Octopus.Tentacle.<some version>.msi file. Save this file to disk, and double-click the installer.

Again, a friendly Octopus Deploy screen welcomes you to the installation. After accepting the license agreement, you'll be able to configure the installation path. By default, Tentacle gets installed into %ProgramFiles%\Octopus Tentacle\. After clicking the Install button, the Tentacle Administration tool is shown because you now need to connect the server to its Tentacles.

Octopus Deploy uses certificates to secure the connection and create a trust relationship between the server and a Tentacle. Each Octopus Tentacle has its own Tentacle thumbprint, as shown in Figure 7-4.

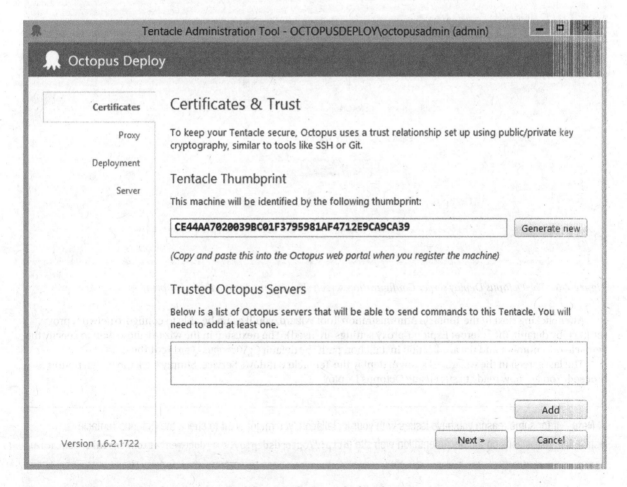

Figure 7-4. The Tentacle Administration tool showing the Tentacle thumbprint

To create the trust relationship, you'll need to add a trusted Octopus server. To do so, click the Add button. The Tentacle Administration tool will prompt to you for a thumbprint that identifies the Octopus Deploy server you want to trust.

The Octopus Deploy server thumbprint can be found in the web portal Configuration section. Click the Configuration link in the top menu and select the Certificates tab. You'll find the thumbprint presented onscreen, as shown in Figure 7-5. Copy this value in the Tentacle Administration tool prompt and click OK.

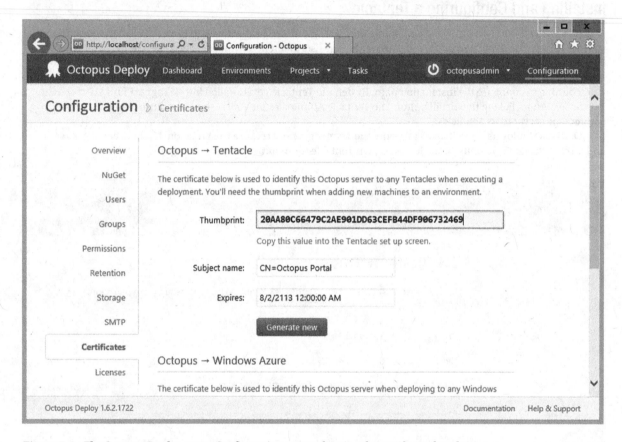

Figure 7-5. The Octopus Deploy server Configuration screen showing the certificate thumbprint

After clicking Next in the Tentacle Administration Tool Wizard, you'll again be able to configure network proxy settings (by default, the Internet Explorer proxy settings are used). The next step in the wizard allows you to specify the Tentacle port number and the application installation path (by default C:\Octopus\Applications).

The last screen in the wizard asks you to deploy the Tentacle Windows Service. Simply click the Install button to proceed. You are now ready to start using Octopus Deploy.

■ **Note** If for some reason you have issues with your installation, you might want to check the Octopus Tentacle installation instructions on the documentation web site (http://octopusdeploy.com/documentation/install/tentacle).

Deploying a Project by Using Octopus Deploy

This section will walk you through your first Octopus Deploy deployment. We'll start by setting up our Internet Information Services (IIS) environment to make sure Octopus Deploy knows where to deploy our web application. Next, we'll create a simple HelloWorld web application that we'll package by using NuGet. Finally, we'll use Octopus Deploy to deploy this application to a web server.

Let's start off with listing all Octopus Deploy conventions to give you some background on why we are doing certain things.

Performing Convention-Based Deployments

Octopus Deploy relies heavily on conventions, a set of rules to which your environment and packages must adhere, in order to make it easier for Octopus Deploy to discover all tasks it should execute when deploying an application. The following are the major conventions:

- The XML configuration convention assumes that your configuration files all have a filename ending with .config and that they are XML files. Octopus Deploy will update these files when deploying and also updates connection strings and application settings. More details about this convention can be found at http://octopusdeploy.com/documentation/features/xml-config.

- The PowerShell convention defines that the Octopus Tentacle will look for PreDeploy.ps1, Deploy.ps1, and PostDeploy.ps1 PowerShell scripts in the root folder of your NuGet package. If found, they will be executed. This convention can be useful to add configuration scripts into a NuGet package. More details about this convention can be found at http://octopusdeploy.com/documentation/features/powershell.

- The IIS WebSite convention defines that the Octopus Tentacle will install the NuGet package containing your application to the web site with a name matching the name of your package. More about this convention can be found at http://octopusdeploy.com/documentation/features/iis.

The IIS WebSite convention is the most important to take into account. It states that if we create a NuGet package named HelloWorld, we should also make sure that the IIS web site to which we'll deploy must be named HelloWorld, as shown in Figure 7-6. Note that the web root of your web site does not matter; Octopus Deploy will update this for every deployment.

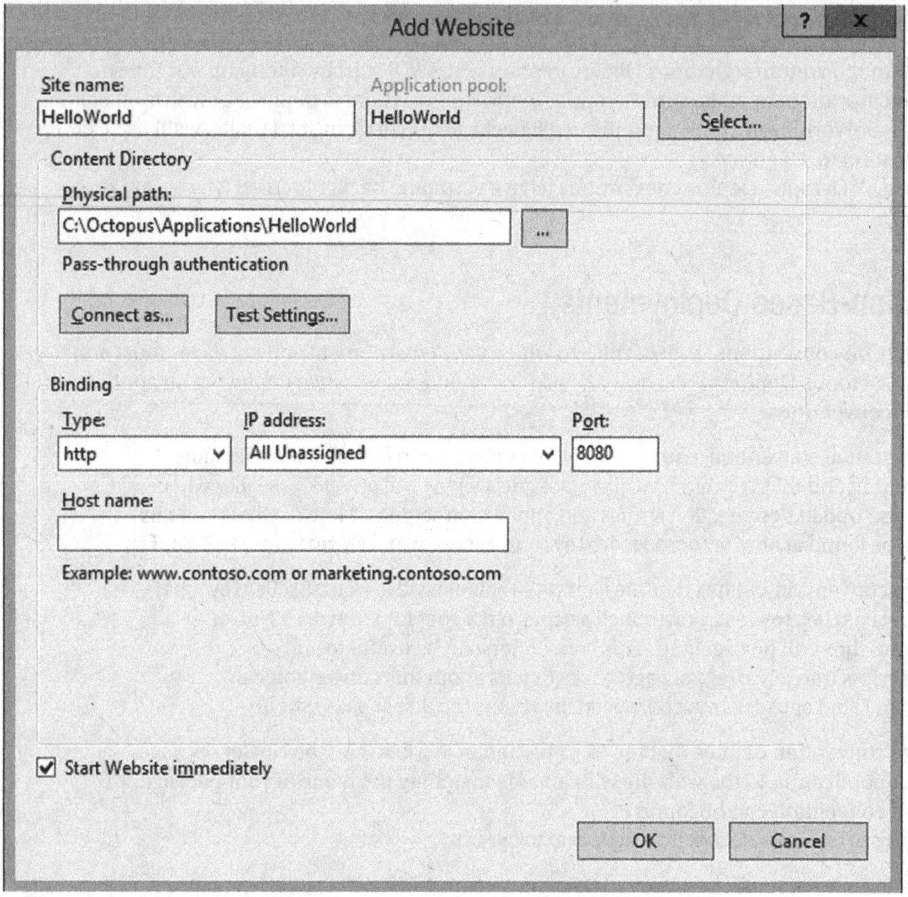

Figure 7-6. *An IIS web site name must be identical to the NuGet package identifier*

Shipping an Application in a NuGet Package

To deploy a web application by using Octopus Deploy, your application should be shipped as a NuGet package. This means creating a NuGet package containing your project's assemblies and artifacts. One way to do this is to publish your application to a local folder and package the application from there, either manually or using a build server.

There is another method that we slightly prefer because it is easier to set up. But before we go there, let's set up a quick sample. Create a new ASP.NET MVC application in Visual Studio, and make sure it is named HelloOctopus. This application will be the one we'll ship using NuGet, a task that can be done using the excellent OctoPack package. In the Package Manager Console, issue the following command:

```
Install-Package OctoPack
```

This will inject the tools and instructions in your Visual Studio solution required to create an Octopus-compatible NuGet package from your project. The OctoPack package adds a new build target to your project that is typically located under your solution root, `.octopack\OctoPack.targets`.

We're not quite finished yet. OctoPack will look for a `HelloWorld.nuspec` file in your project, a package manifest like the ones we have created several times before over the course of this book. Add the `HelloOctopus.nuspec` file to your project, and copy the code from Listing 7-1. Make sure you don't use any replacement tokens, as those are not supported by the OctoPack command-line tool.

Listing 7-1. NuGet package manifest for the HelloWorld application

```xml
<?xml version="1.0"?>
<package >
  <metadata>
    <id>HelloOctopus</id>
    <version>2.0.0.0</version>
    <title>HelloOctopus</title>
    <authors>Xavier Decoster &amp; Maarten Balliauw</authors>
    <owners> Xavier Decoster &amp; Maarten Balliauw </owners>
    <description>Hello World from Octopack!</description>
    <requireLicenseAcceptance>false</requireLicenseAcceptance>
    <copyright>Copyright 2011 - 2013</copyright>
  </metadata>
</package>
```

In order for the OctoPack package to be created, you'll need to instruct the build system to do so. This can be done in several ways. If you look at the `octopack.targets` MSBuild file, you'll notice the following MSBuild property setting:

```xml
<RunOctoPack Condition="'$(RunOctoPack)'==''">false</RunOctoPack>
```

The default value is `false`, so no package will be created. You can set it to `true`, or you can pass the `RunOctoPack=True` property to an MSBuild command line, or you might come up with something similar depending on the build context. You'll find a recipe in Chapter 8, where we'll use TeamCity to automate Octopus Deploy package creation and deployments. For now, you can simply set it to `true`, which will ensure that each compilation also creates an OctoPack package.

After compilation, you should see a `HelloOctopus.2.0.0.0.nupkg` file in your application's bin folder. Note that you can change the configuration in which OctoPack produces the package by adjusting the `OctopusPackageConfiguration` element in the `OctoPack.targets` file. Ensure that all assemblies and content are copied into the NuGet package. Figure 7-7 shows our package's contents in NuGet Package Explorer.

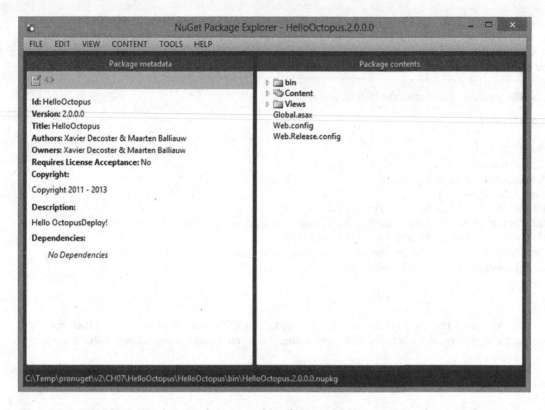

Figure 7-7. Using NuGet Package Explorer to verify package contents

The final step in shipping an application through NuGet is of course to push it to a NuGet feed. We've pushed the HelloOctopus package to our ProNuGet feed on MyGet, `www.myget.org/F/pronuget/`. Feel free to use that one when configuring Octopus Deploy if you don't want to create a package yourself.

Configuring the Octopus Deploy Environment

Before we can deploy an application to a web server by using Octopus Deploy, we'll have to define five things in Octopus Deploy. Don't worry; this is just some initial configuration, so there's no need to run through these steps on every deployment you want to create.

- Which environments do we have?

- Which servers are in those environments?

- Which NuGet feed has to be used to pull shipped applications from?

- Which projects do we have?

- Which packages have to be deployed for this project?

After making sure these items are configured, Octopus Deploy can be used to easily deploy an application across multiple environments.

Log in to the Octopus Deploy web portal. As a first step, we're going to configure a deployment environment. This is a logical unit of servers, typically named test, staging, and production. Of course, more than one environment can be created, and if you have a chucknorris environment as well, feel free to configure it. Click the Add Environment button, and provide a name and description for it.

After creating an environment, one or more servers should be added to it. Click the Add Machine button to configure a server on which Octopus Tentacle is installed. By default, Tentacles are listening on port 10399, which means we can simply add our localhost Octopus Tentacle by entering http://localhost:10399 in the Tentacle URL. You'll also need to provide a thumbprint for the Tentacle URL to be used on that machine. You can find it in the Octopus Deploy Tentacle Administration tool. This server will serve as an IIS server and host our deployed web applications, so adding the IIS role (or whatever name you prefer) makes it recognizable. Figure 7-8 shows you an example of a machine being added to the production environment.

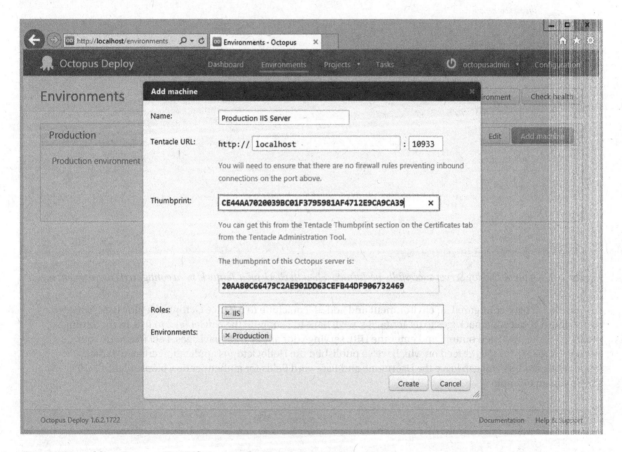

Figure 7-8. *Adding Octopus Tentacle to a production environment*

To verify connectivity and a trust relationship between Octopus Deploy Server and the Tentacle on this environment, click Check Health to schedule a task that will perform the health check for you. If all is good, you should see a green confirmation icon next to the server in your environment, as shown in Figure 7-9.

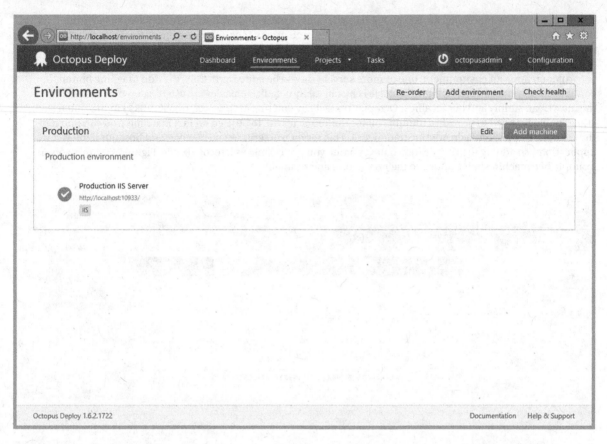

Figure 7-9. *Octopus Deploy Server succesfully performed a health check on a Tentacle for a configured environment server*

So far, we have configured an environment and added a machine to it. Since Octopus Deploy uses NuGet to distribute application packages to its Tentacles, we'll have to configure the NuGet feed to use. In the Settings menu, click the Add Feed button, and enter the URL serving your application packages. Feel free to use our www.myget.org/F/pronuget feed on which we've published the HelloOctopus application created earlier. It is a public feed, so you can leave the Username and Password fields for authentication blank. Figure 7-10 shows you an example.

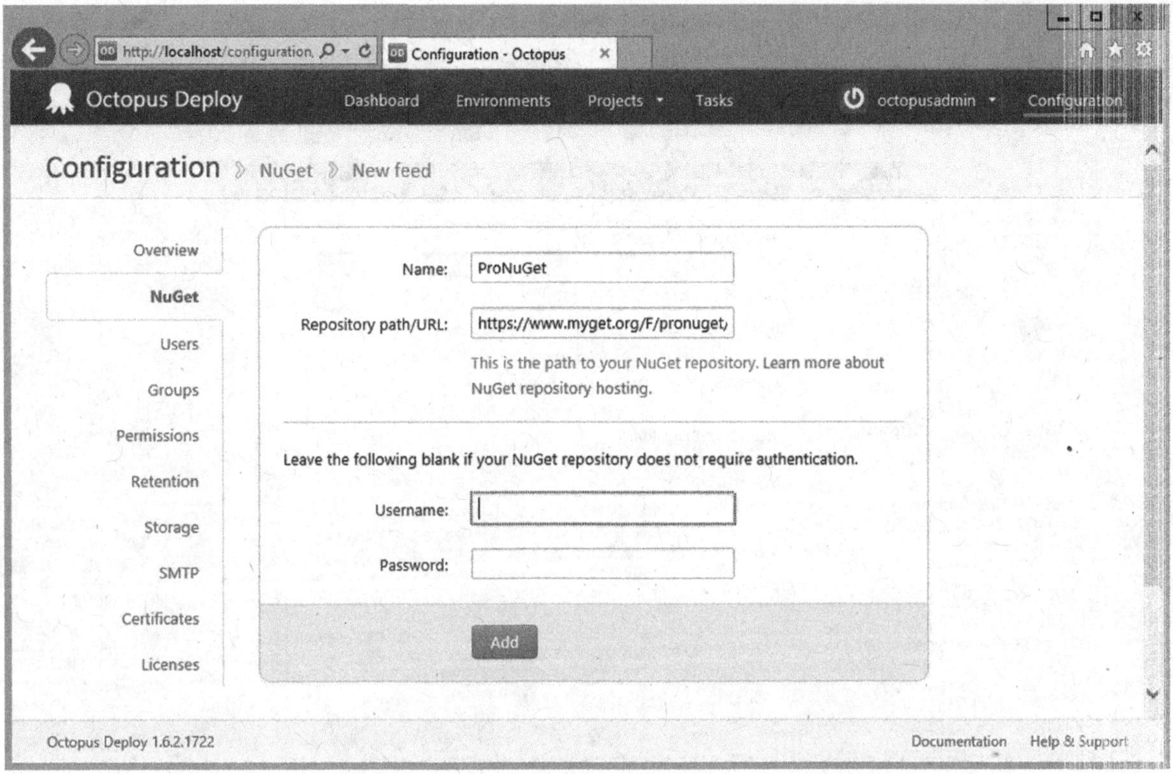

Figure 7-10. *Defining the NuGet feed to pull application packages from*

We're almost good to go now. The only thing missing is a project and a deployment. A project in Octopus Deploy is a logical unit of packages. For example, if you are building a three-tier application, the project will group all three tiers. There is no need to create a new project per tier! Also, there's no need to create a project for each environment either: Octopus Deploy can deploy a project to an environment of choice in a later step.

On the Projects page, click the Add Project Group button. Provide a name and then click the Create button, as shown in Figure 7-11.

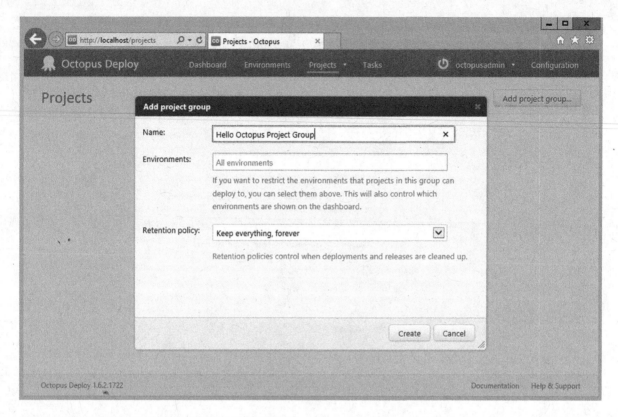

Figure 7-11. *Adding a project group in the Octopus Deploy web portal*

Next, click the Create Project button within this newly created project group. Enter a project name and description and then click the Add button to add it to your project group, as shown in Figure 7-12.

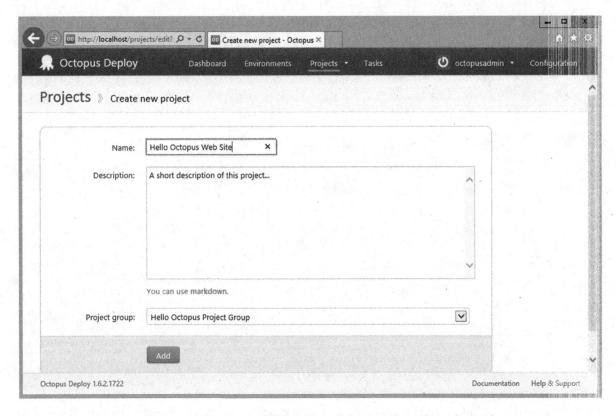

Figure 7-12. *Create a new project and add it to a project group in the Octopus Deploy web portal*

The newly created project will appear in the Projects page and drop-down menu. When you navigate to this project, you will notice that the project Overview page is rather empty. The reason for that is the project does not know which application packages should be deployed. Navigate to the project's Steps page and click the Add Step button to add a deployment step to your project. A deployment step indicates that a certain package from a certain feed should be deployed to a web, application, or database server. Figure 7-13 shows that we'll choose the Deploy a NuGet Package step type.

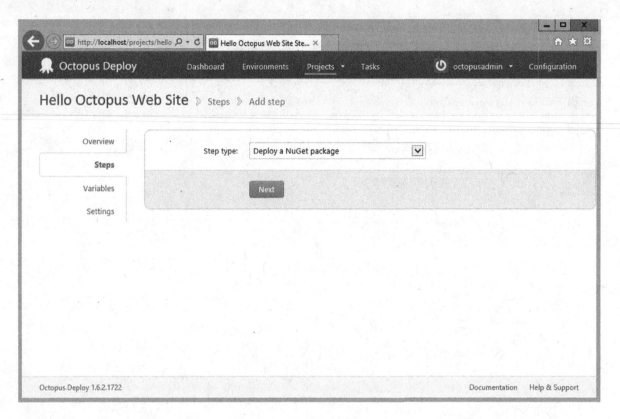

Figure 7-13. *Add a new deployment step to an Octopus Deploy project in order to configure deployment of a NuGet package*

Figure 7-14, Figure 7-15, and Figure 7-16 illustrate how we configure this deployment step: we'll fetch the HelloOctopus package from the ProNuGet feed and make sure we deploy it to the correct installation path as configured in IIS. In addition, we'll choose to delete all files present in the target location before this step executes to ensure we have a clean deployment every single time. Speaking of environment, we specify the IIS role to ensure this step gets executed only on a server configured with the IIS role, as we did in Figure 7-8. We have no specific XML configuration transformations so far, but we can live with the default settings. If we ever decide to make use of this feature, our deployment step will already pick them up.

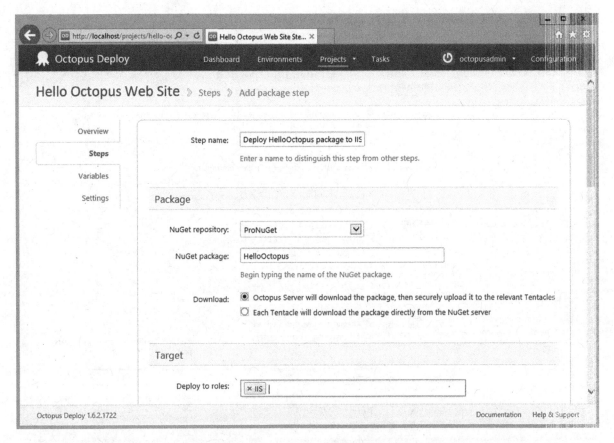

Figure 7-14. *Configuring a package deployment step in the Octopus Deploy web portal*

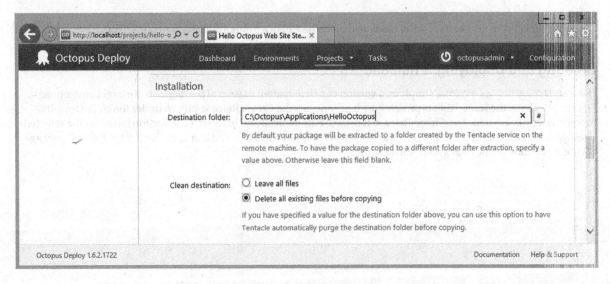

Figure 7-15. *Configuring an installation path for a package deployment step in the Octopus Deploy web portal*

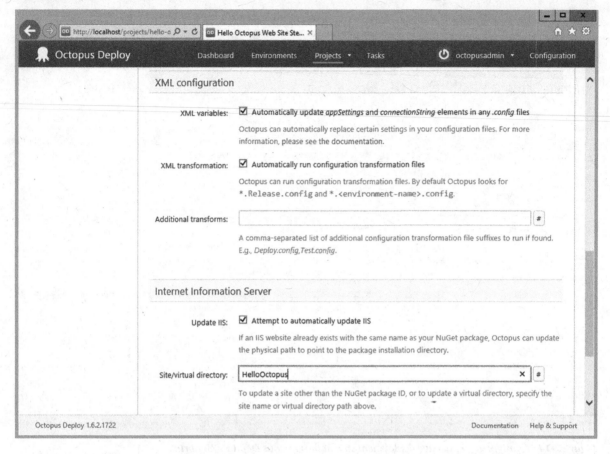

Figure 7-16. *Configuring XML transformations and IIS for a package deployment step in the Octopus Deploy web portal*

After clicking the Add button, we're ready to deploy the HelloOctopus application to our servers.

Creating and Deploying a Release

Octopus Deploy defines a *release* simply as a version of a deployment of several packages to the target environment. Figure 7-17 shows the screen that is presented when you click the Create Release button under the HelloOctopus project we've just created. The Create Release form will automatically fill in the release version based on the selected package that should be deployed. This is the place where NuGet comes in: you can select a package from all package versions available on the configured NuGet feed.

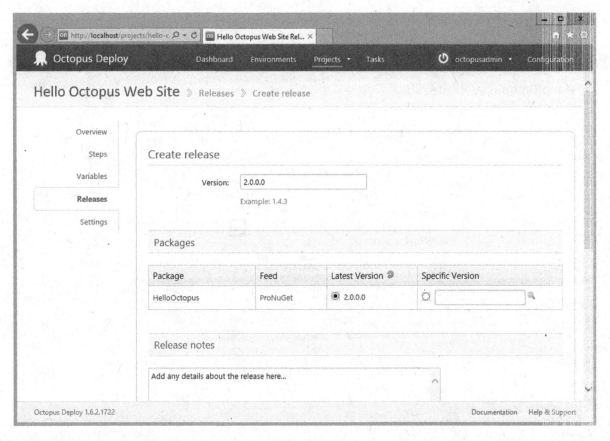

Figure 7-17. *Creating a release*

When you click the Create Release button at the bottom of the page, the actual deployment is not executed yet. Your release is queued, and a release manager in your team can still inspect the release before deployment through the web portal shown in Figure 7-18. Once a release is approved, you can click the Deploy This Release button to trigger the actual deployment of your web application to an environment of choice.

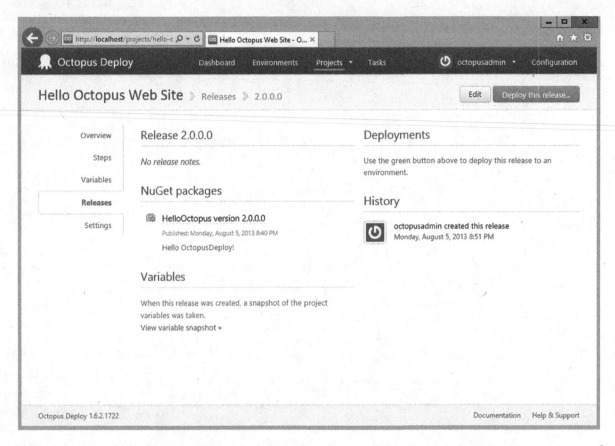

Figure 7-18. *A new release waiting to be deployed in the Octopus Deploy web portal*

During deployment, just as with a build server, you can see what Octopus Deploy is doing: a release log is created, where you can see all steps of a deployment as well as eventual warnings or errors. Note that release logs are kept in Octopus Deploy's database. Just as with builds, it's important to be able to roll back a release and/or to inspect what happened during a certain release. Part of this release log is shown in Figure 7-19. Note that the HelloOctopus 2.0.0.0 package is downloaded from a NuGet feed and then sent off to an Octopus Deploy Tentacle. Packages deployed using Octopus Deploy cannot have dependencies on other packages.

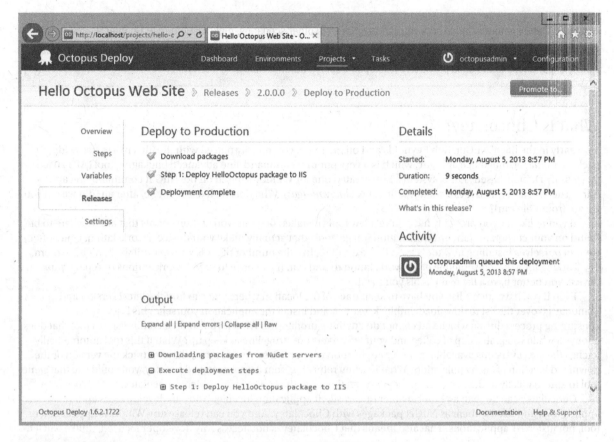

Figure 7-19. *The Octopus Deploy release and deployment details*

If the release yields "Success!", your application will be deployed to the IIS web site configured earlier. Note that Octopus Deploy automatically applied any configuration transforms to the web site, starting from web.config (or app.config). Octopus Deploy always applies the web.release.config first, and if the package is being deployed to an environment different from your release environment, it will also apply any available web.(environment).config transformations. For example, when you deploy to an environment with the name QA, Octopus Deploy will transform the web.config file by first applying the transformations of web.release.config, followed by web.QA.config.

The big benefit of Octopus Deploy is that you can simply release a single package and deploy it to multiple different environments without having to create a new release version in Octopus Deploy. This also means that no modifications to the package can be done between various stages of the deployment pipeline, ensuring that what you deploy to the acceptance environment is exactly what will get deployed onto production as well.

Deploying Software with Chocolatey

The first part of this chapter focused on deploying a NuGet package remotely, but we'll now do the opposite and look at a very interesting way of installing a NuGet package locally—no, not within your code base, but on your system. Obviously, these NuGet packages will contain something of interest for the entire system. How about an application? That's right, an application! You can wrap an application installer into a NuGet package and have a common means of distributing those applications to various systems.

■ **Note** If you are interested in how you can use NuGet in other scenarios, make sure to read Chapter 9, where we explain how to use NuGet as a protocol for delivering content and how you can use the NuGet.Core assembly to create similar experiences to the ones provided by Octopus Deploy and Chocolatey.

What Is Chocolatey?

Very early in the life of NuGet, Rob Reynolds and others in the community played with the idea of a systemwide package manager, much like apt-get, which is a very popular command-line advanced packaging tool (APT) used on (mainly Debian-based) Linux systems. Rob created one for Windows based on the NuGet command line and infrastructure, and called it Chocolatey (after *chocolatey nougat*). Who doesn't like chocolate, after all (did we tell you we are from Belgium)?

If you're like us, you probably have quite a few tools installed on your workstation—tools that are nowhere to be found on your corporate standard workstation image, tools that actually make your device a workstation. Quite often, we find ourselves installing new tools as well. We don't realize the number of tools we use until we don't have them. Try working for a day on someone else's workstation to find out. If you have to switch workstations or repave your device, you better have a list of the tools you need.

Even if you have such a list, you have to keep track of the location where you can find the latest version and manually go over the list to download, unblock, extract, and install the application yourself. This is a very time-consuming process during which you cannot do anything productive. What if you could feed this list to a tool that does it for you while you grab a cup of coffee and your coworkers are struggling to keep up? What if this tool automatically fetches the latest versions available for every application in your list, so you no longer have to track the version or the download location of each application? What if, when returning from a well-deserved holiday, you could use that same tool to automatically update all your applications on the list to the latest version? Meet Chocolatey.

Chocolatey can be seen as a tool enabler or as a silent application installer. You can develop tools and applications and release them as NuGet packages with Chocolatey. And you can release any Windows application or tool, not just .NET applications. That also means that Chocolatey is not necessarily developer focused, unlike NuGet.

■ **Tip** To get an instant Chocolatey experience, you can watch a video on YouTube showing Chocolatey in action: http://bit.ly/chocolateyVideo.

Installing Chocolatey

Chocolatey has very few requirements. You have to have the .NET 4 Framework and PowerShell 2 installed. Installing Chocolatey really takes only a matter of seconds. You have multiple installation options, so just pick the one you prefer. Chocolatey itself exists as a NuGet package, so if you get a hold of the package, you get an opportunity to install it.

As of v1.0, Chocolatey installs by default into the %SystemDrive%\Chocolatey folder. Older versions target %SystemDrive%\NuGet instead. If you are not OK with that, you can define the desired installation directory before running the installation. To do so, adjust the user environment variable named ChocolateyInstall, and set it to the folder you want Chocolatey to install to.

Using PowerShell

Using PowerShell is the easiest installation method. Because of PowerShell's security strategy, make sure you have set your execution policy to Unrestricted before installing Chocolatey. You can check your current execution policy by running the Get-ExecutionPolicy command in any PowerShell console. If it returns anything other than

Unrestricted, you should run the `Set-ExecutionPolicy Unrestricted` command. To change the PowerShell execution policy, you should open a PowerShell console with elevated privileges, so run it as Administrator. On Windows 7, you simply right-click the PowerShell icon in the Start menu, and select Run as Administrator. Figure 7-20 illustrates how to change the PowerShell execution policy.

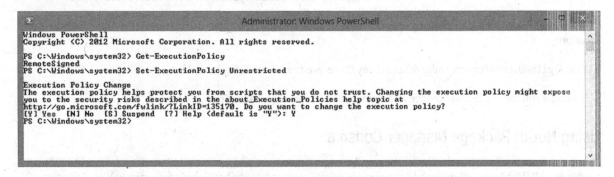

Figure 7-20. *Ensuring the PowerShell execution policy is set to Unrestricted*

If your PowerShell execution policy is set to Unrestricted, you can run the following one-liner to install the latest version of Chocolatey on your system; Figure 7-21 shows you the Chocolatey installation process in a PowerShell console.

```
iex ((New-Object Net.WebClient).DownloadString("http://bit.ly/psChocInstall"))
```

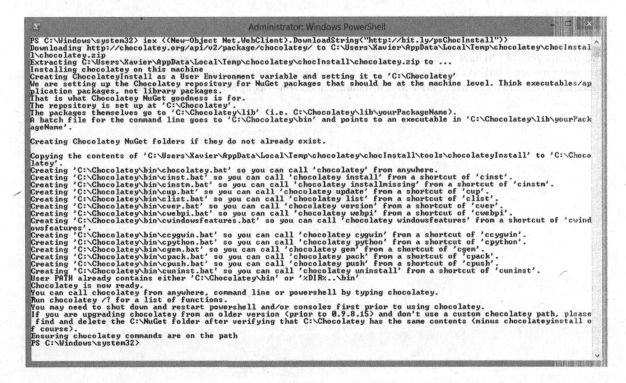

Figure 7-21. *Installing Chocolatey from within PowerShell*

If you have PowerShell ninja skills and want to find out what happens behind the scenes, you can take a look at the install script on GitHub (yes, Chocolatey is open source as well!). The install script can be found at the following location:

```
https://raw.github.com/chocolatey/chocolatey/master/chocolateyInstall/InstallChocolatey.ps1
```

Another way to install Chocolatey is by downloading the two files from the GitHub repository at the following location:

```
https://github.com/ferventcoder/chocolatey/tree/master/chocolateyInstall
```

Simply run the installChocolatey.cmd batch file to finish the installation.

Using NuGet Package Manager Console

By now, you are familiar with the NuGet Package Manager Console, so you can install Chocolatey from within Visual Studio as well. This installation method is no one-liner and requires you to have a solution open in Visual Studio. Don't forget to select the NuGet.org feed as the package source.

Whereas the PowerShell installation method executed the remote unsigned install.ps1 script directly from the GitHub repository, the NuGet Package Manager Console installation method will make use of the Chocolatey NuGet package, available from the NuGet.org feed.

To install Chocolatey by using the Package Manager Console, simply run the following commands:

```
Install-Package Chocolatey
Initialize-Chocolatey
Uninstall-Package Chocolatey
```

Figure 7-22 shows you the output of running the Install-Package Chocolatey command. If you read the instructions, you see you have to run Initialize-Chocolatey once, and after that, you can safely uninstall the package by using the Uninstall-Package Chocolatey command. If you read the output a bit more carefully, you'll notice there is another, alternative method of installing Chocolatey—using NuGet outside Visual Studio.

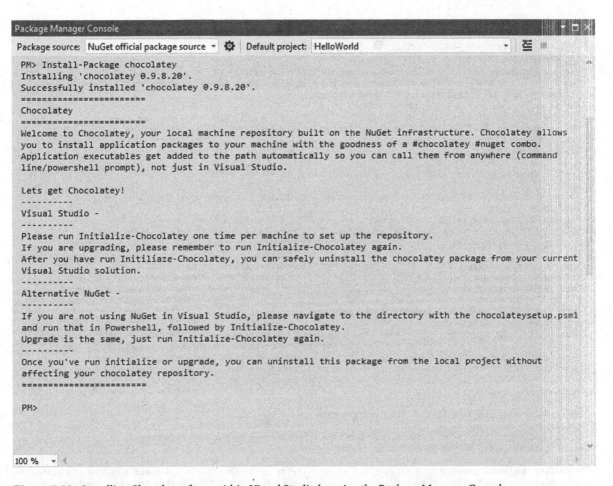

Figure 7-22. *Installing Chocolatey from within Visual Studio by using the Package Manager Console*

After installing Chocolatey, it has to be initialized. Figure 7-23 shows the output for the `Initialize-Chocolatey` command, which adds Chocolatey's installation directory to your system's PATH environment variable. It also creates several shortcut commands, for example cup which is a shortcut for chocolatey update.

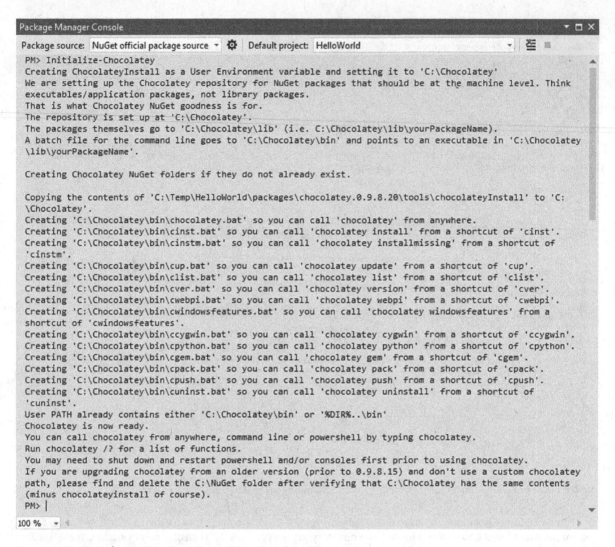

Figure 7-23. *Initializing Chocolatey from within Visual Studio*

If you installed the Chocolatey package by using the nuget.exe command line, for instance, you can run the ChocolateySetup.psm1 file in a PowerShell console, followed by the Initialize-Chocolatey command.

The initialization of Chocolatey also mentioned another interesting thing: every tool or application you install by using Chocolatey will be automatically available from within every command prompt on that system, because the install path is in the system environment path. You also get a glimpse of the various commands that Chocolatey exposes. Let's see what tasty ingredients Chocolatey has to offer.

Using Chocolatey

Chocolatey is a command-line tool that exposes quite a few options for managing applications. You can install a single application or batch the installation of an application list. You can update a single application or update all applications that have been installed using Chocolatey at once. Let's take a look at the various commands.

■ **Tip**   For the latest up-to-date Chocolatey commands reference, you can visit the following URL:
https://github.com/chocolatey/chocolatey/wiki/CommandsReference.

Installing Tools and Applications

We are going to use Chocolatey to install Notepad++, our favorite replacement for the Windows built-in Notepad text editor. We can do this because Notepad++ is also available as a NuGet package on the Chocolatey Gallery feed at http://chocolatey.org (see Figure 7-24).

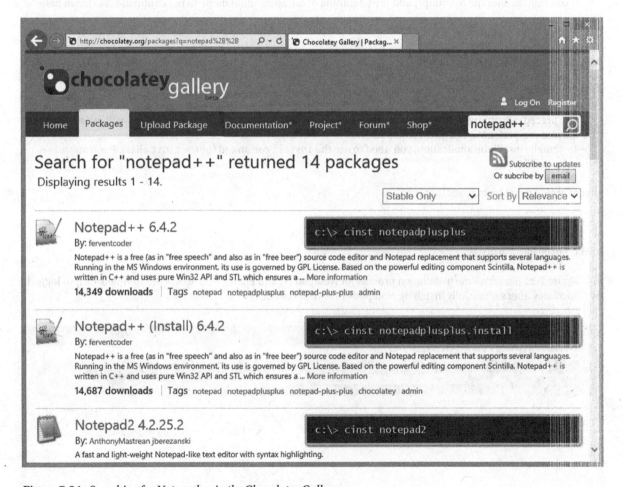

Figure 7-24. *Searching for Notepad++ in the Chocolatey Gallery*

Another way to find out whether your favorite tool or application has been packaged and made available on Chocolatey is by using the Chocolatey command line. Chocolatey has a `chocolatey list` command (or `clist` for short) that you could use for that. To list all available packages in the Chocolatey Gallery, you can run the following command (this might take a while to finish):

```
chocolatey list
```

or

```
clist
```

If you want to filter the list, simply add the beginning of the application name to the command, as shown here:

```
chocolatey list notepad
```

or

```
clist notepad
```

The preceding command will yield results for both Notepad2 and Notepad++ (or NotepadPlusPlus), so you can pick the one you prefer. We will go for Notepad++.

To actually install the application, you need to use the `install` command (or the `cinst` alias). For Notepad++, this looks as follows:

```
chocolatey install notepadplusplus
```

or

```
cinst notepadplusplus
```

Figure 7-25 illustrates the installation process for Notepad++, and Figure 7-26 shows the complete output logged by Chocolatey after successfully installing Notepad++ on your system.

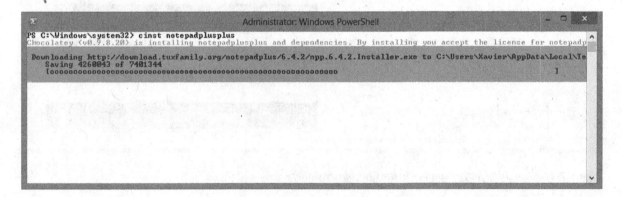

Figure 7-25. *Progress indication of the installation process of the Notepad++ Chocolatey package*

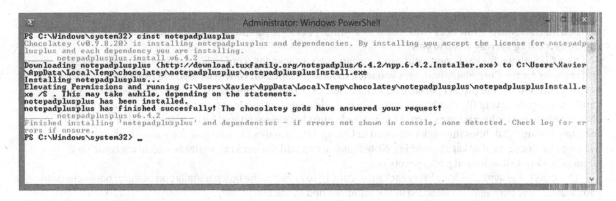

Figure 7-26. *The Chocolatey gods answered your request and successfully installed Notepad++*

What is interesting is that Chocolatey packages can have dependencies, and Chocolatey will also download and install these. For example, a graphical interface for Git can have a dependency on a command-line version of Git that is shipped as another Chocolatey package. Installing the first will bring down the latter as well.

As easy as it is to install a single application by using Chocolatey, you could actually batch the installation of multiple tools and applications at once. Because Chocolatey comes as a command-line tool and registers itself in the PATH environment variable, it is very convenient to call Chocolatey commands from any location on your system. Listing 7-2 shows how you can install a sequence of tools in one go by using Chocolatey. Save this listing into a script file (for example, installMyTools.ps1 or installMyTools.bat) to distribute it to your colleagues, who can then simply double-click the file to execute this script on their machines as well.

Listing 7-2. An Example Batch File to Sequentially Install Various Tools by Using Chocolatey

```
cinst sysinternals
cinst notepadplusplus
cinst adobereader
cinst msysgit
cinst fiddler
cinst filezilla
cinst putty -version 0.62
cinst tortoisesvn
cinst tortoisehg
cinst tortoisegit
cinst iisexpress -source webpi
```

Note that the install command will install the package unless the package is already installed on the system. If you want to reinstall the package, you should use the -force option. A few more options are available to pass on to the install command, and these are discussed in the "Distributing Chocolatey Goodness" section, when we will talk about configuring the native installer that is triggered by the Chocolatey package.

This is a very useful way of making sure your system is configured with the tools desired in one go. We've given the example of easily repaving your computer or quickly configuring a new system, but you could also use it to make sure all developers have the same (version of) specific tooling installed on their systems when working on your code base. By checking this script file into source control, everyone on the team can run it locally with ease.

In addition to manually creating batch files and duplicating a bunch of Chocolatey commands (cinst for instance) on every line, you could also just describe the packages you want and perform a single Chocolatey operation to process the file. Installing a list of packages would then result in a single install command, passing in a file containing your packages list to install. This also allows for internal optimization by Chocolatey to perform this operation.

What would be the best way to describe the packages you want to install onto your system? Think about the parallelism with NuGet: how does NuGet describe which packages should be installed into a project? Does the packages.config file ring a bell to you?

The Chocolatey install command supports targeting a packages.config file. Simply list the package IDs and versions for the Chocolatey packages you want to have installed on your system in the exact same XML format as NuGet does to denote project package dependencies. Chocolatey supports a tiny deviation from the default vanilla packages.config file that NuGet uses. You can add a very convenient source attribute to each of the package elements in the packages.config file, to indicate what source should be used to fetch the package. Listing 7-3 defines the packages listed in Listing 7-2. Save this file, and give it a name (for instance, MyFavoriteChocolateyPackages.config). Note that you can add the version attribute within each package element to denote the desired package version.

Use cinst MyFavoriteChocolateyPackages.config to perform the batch installation of these packages onto your system. The packages are installed in the order defined in the file.

Listing 7-3. An Example packages.config File to Sequentially Install Various Tools by Using Chocolatey

```xml
<?xml version="1.0" encoding="utf-8"?>
<packages>
  <package id="sysinternals" />
  <package id="notepadplusplus" />
  <package id="adobereader" />
  <package id="msysgit" />
  <package id="fiddler" />
  <package id="filezilla" />
  <package id="putty" version="0.62" />
  <package id="tortoisesvn" />
  <package id="tortoisehg" />
  <package id="tortoisegit" />
  <package id="iisexpress" source="webpi" />
</packages>
```

Last, but definitely not least, there is a third option to easily tell Chocolatey which packages you want to have installed on your system. What if you're like us and don't like messing around with script files, distributed over various systems, and trying to remember which one was the latest one? If you need to repave your system, or want to tell someone how to install a bunch of tools, you want to give simple instructions—a simple command, preferably a single line, with no files involved.

You might have guessed it: we will be using a feed for this. Chocolatey supports installing all listed packages directly from a custom feed. To do so, you need to create your own custom Chocolatey repository—you could use a MyGet.org feed for this—and target it in your commands. As such, you now have a central place to maintain your list of favorite tools and keep them up-to-date. Simply invite people to target your feed URL, and you can easily share this list with your colleagues and friends. Upload or mirror the packages you need on your feed, and off you go. The Chocolatey command involved is the following one:

```
cinst all -source [feedURL]
```

This is a great way of installing many tools at once, but what if one of those tools is not available as a package on the Chocolatey Gallery? What if you want to install a tool (for instance, IIS Express) using the Microsoft Web Platform Installer? You could use Web PI, the Web Platform Installer command-line tool, but you might not have this additional tool yet on the system. No problem for the Chocolatey gods: Chocolatey has built-in support for Web PI. In fact, webpi is a command available in Chocolatey:

```
chocolatey webpi IISExpress
```

or

```
cwebpi IISExpress
```

Another way to install applications by using Web PI as a source instead of the Chocolatey NuGet Gallery is by using the –source switch of the Chocolatey install command.

```
cinst IISExpress -source webpi
```

■ **Tip** Once you have installed the Web PI command-line tool (using cinst webpicommandline, for instance), you could use Chocolatey to list the available applications for the Web Platform Installer, using the clist -source webpi command.

It goes without saying that Chocolatey has been influenced and inspired by tooling outside the .NET community, such as apt-get or RubyGems. If you want to benefit from Chocolatey goodness while working with Ruby, you'll be happy to learn that Chocolatey also has built-in support for RubyGems. According to Wikipedia, "RubyGems is a package manager for the Ruby programming language that provides a standard format for distributing Ruby programs and libraries (in a self-contained format called a *gem*), a tool designed to easily manage the installation of gems, and a server for distributing them" (http://en.wikipedia.org/wiki/RubyGems).

To install RubyGems by using Chocolatey, use the chocolatey gem or cgem command, followed by the package name. This command defaults to the latest version of the package available, so if you want to get a specific version of the package, you should use the –version option. The command to install the latest version of RubyGems (for instance, GemCutter) using Chocolatey would look as follows:

```
chocolatey gem gemcutter
```

or

```
cgem gemcutter
```

Much as you could for the built-in Web PI support, you could also install RubyGems by using the install command and specifying Ruby as the source to be used, as follows:

```
cinst gemcutter -source ruby
```

This command will result in the exact same operation being performed as when using the cgem command.

Keeping Your Tool Belt Up-to-Date

Of course, you don't want to simply install a bunch of tools and applications and then work with those happily ever after. Those applications evolve, and your tools have updates—a good reason to keep those installed applications up-to-date as well.

There's a very handy way of updating an application installed through Chocolatey. Simply use the update command, and target an installed package name to update that application to the latest version available. In addition, there is a very convenient short notation for the chocolatey update command: cup (as in *cup of Chocolatey*).

```
chocolatey update notepadplusplus
```

or

```
cup notepadplusplus
```

Just as easily as you can batch the installation of multiple packages on your system, you can keep all these tools up-to-date with one simple command:

```
chocolatey update all
```

or

```
cup all
```

Much as you can on the NuGet command line, you can also perform an in-place update of Chocolatey itself. Simply run the following command to update Chocolatey to the latest version:

```
chocolatey update
```

or

```
cup
```

If you want to determine whether an update is available for any of your installed Chocolatey packages without immediately triggering the actual update operation, you could use the version command. This command will output the found version and the latest version of those packages:

```
chocolatey version all
```

or

```
cver all
```

Again, this command can be used similarly to the update command. If you do not specify all or a package name, it will perform the action against the Chocolatey command-line tool itself. To check whether Chocolatey itself is up-to-date, run cver or chocolatey version.

Distributing Chocolatey Goodness

No, not distributing chocolates! At this point, we want you to contribute useful Chocolatey packages to the Chocolatey Gallery at http://chocolatey.org. That's right; you can produce packages yourself and make them available to the broader community as well.

Although you'll find quite a few useful packages already hosted on the Chocolatey Gallery, you might occasionally look for a missing one. If you ever find one of your favorite must-have tools or applications missing on the Chocolatey Gallery, you might consider creating and publishing a package for it yourself.

You know by now how to create various types of vanilla NuGet packages (Chapter 3 explained this in detail). There are a few things you should know about creating and publishing Chocolatey packages, however.

■ **Note** When we refer to *vanilla* NuGet packages, we are referring to the original NuGet packages, to make a clear distinction with Chocolatey NuGet packages.

As with NuGet vanilla, you'll need to start from a .nuspec file. Let's take a look at the Notepad++ Chocolatey package we just installed onto our system.

■ **Tip** To browse the Chocolatey packages installed on your system through Windows Explorer, simply navigate to the %SystemDrive%\Chocolatey\lib folder. You should notice a folder structure very similar to the $(SolutionDir)\packages folder that NuGet vanilla installs solution-level packages into.

Open notepadplusplus.6.4.2.nupkg (if you find a different version, note that version 6.4.2 was the latest version available at the time of this writing) by using NuGet Package Explorer. You should see something unusual: where's the Notepad++ installer? The package has almost no content at all, as shown in Figure 7-27.

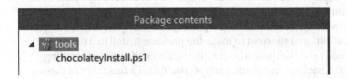

Figure 7-27. *The Chocolatey package for Notepad++ has no content except for the installation script*

You should notice, however, a single script file called chocolateyInstall.ps1 in the tools folder. Using this filename by convention allows Chocolatey to recognize a Chocolatey package and makes sure NuGet vanilla is not doing anything with this package inside Visual Studio. This file will contain the script that will install this package onto your system. So to create a Chocolatey package, you should start with having a chocolateyInstall.ps1 script file in the package's tools folder. Don't worry about the image file for now, because it is just the logo for the package to be displayed on the Chocolatey Gallery web site.

Taking a closer look at the contents of the chocolateyInstall.ps1 file, you might be surprised again: it contains only a single line of PowerShell! If you aren't surprised, probably things just got clearer to you. The reason a Chocolatey package is so small and has almost no content is because the content is usually hosted elsewhere. Most of these tools already have a download URL on their originating web sites. This allows the installChocolatey.ps1 script in your package to simply point to that URL and avoids copying the installers of the tool into your package. That's why Chocolatey packages are small, fast to download, and allow Chocolatey to provide immediate feedback during the installation process.

If we take a closer look at the one-liner in the installChocolatey.ps1 file, you'll see the following piece of code:

```
Install-ChocolateyPackage 'notepadplusplus' 'exe' '/S'
'http://download.tuxfamily.org/notepadplus/6.4.2/npp.6.4.2.Installer.exe'
```

It is calling the Install-ChocolateyPackage cmdlet and passing in some values to the following arguments:

- PackageName: notepadplusplus
- PackageType: exe
- SilentArgs: /S
- Url: http://download.tuxfamily.org/notepadplus/6.4.2/npp.6.4.2.Installer.exe

In short, the Install-ChocolateyPackage cmdlet will download a file from an URL and install it on your system. The PackageName argument is arbitrary. You can name it whatever you want, but it would make sense to use the NuGet package ID of the package you are currently creating. The PackageType should either be exe or msi, depending on the installer that will be downloaded, which is referenced in the Url parameter.

If you want to provide a silent installation experience, without any wizards popping up asking for user input (mostly true for automated installations), you should pass in some value for the SilentArgs parameter. If you don't pass any value for this argument, you'll experience the default installation of the target installer. Please use the notSilent tag in your package's NuGet metadata if you choose a nonsilent installation experience.

The SilentArgs arguments are being passed on to the exe or msi installer. For a PackageType of msi, this is easy: use /quiet. For an exe package, things are a bit different, because there is no standard format. Try any of these values to provide a silent installation experience: /s, /S, /q, /Q, /quiet, /silent, /SILENT, /VERYSILENT.

In addition to the arguments used by the NotepadPlusPlus package, you could use a few other arguments in your own packages. One of them is the Url64bit argument, which could point to an alternative URL for the installer of the x64 version of the tool or application.

The chocolatey install or cinst command also has a few additional options available for use when installing a Chocolatey package. You can, for instance, pass on a set of arguments to the native installer being triggered by the package installation. This could be useful if you know some of the arguments being used or have some custom ones defined for your own installer. You can pass on these arguments to the InstallArguments parameter. By default, this parameter is empty and will be appended to any arguments already passed in by the package installation script. If you do not want to append these arguments and want to override all arguments the package already passes in, you could use the OverrideArguments switch. There's one last, additional shortcut to make the package install in a nonsilent model: the NotSilent option. This will make the installer use the default interactive behavior, if any, disregarding any SilentArgs being passed on to it by the Chocolatey package installation script. You'll find a summary of these commands in Table 7-1.

Table 7-1. *Passing Arguments to a Native Installer via Chocolatey*

Option	Description	Alternative Notation
InstallArguments	Specifies the installation arguments to be passed on to the native installer. Default behavior is to append these arguments to any arguments being passed on in the installChocolatey.ps1 script.	-ia -installArgs
OverrideArguments	Specifies whether InstallArguments should be appended or overrides any arguments being passed internally in the package.	-o -overrideArgs
NotSilent	Specifies that the native installer should be run in nonsilent mode, whatever the value of the SilentArgs parameter inside the installChocolatey.ps1 script.	

■ **Caution**   You can actually include executables in your Chocolatey packages if you have the right to distribute. If you feel uncertain about this, make sure you check out https://github.com/chocolatey/chocolatey/wiki/Legal for more information on legalities and distributions.

So, to create a Chocolatey package, you only have to create a .nuspec manifest, reference the installChocolatey.ps1 file in its tools folder, and call the Install-ChocolateyPackage cmdlet within the script to point to the URL of your favorite tool's installer. Listing 7-4 shows how the .nuspec manifest could look (metadata shortened for clarity):

Listing 7-4. An Example NuGet Manifest for Creating a Chocolatey Package

```xml
<?xml version="1.0"?>
<package xmlns="http://schemas.microsoft.com/packaging/2010/07/nuspec.xsd">
  <metadata>
    <id>notepadplusplus</id>
    <version>6.4.2</version>
    ...
    <description>Notepad++ is a free ...</description>
    <summary>Notepad++ is a free ...</summary>
    <tags>notepad notepadplusplus notepad-plus-plus chocolatey</tags>
  </metadata>
  <files>
    <file src="tools\chocolateyInstall.ps1" target="tools\chocolateyInstall.ps1" />
  </files>
</package>
```

In addition to the Install-ChocolateyPackage cmdlet, you might find the following helpers useful:

- Install-ChocolateyPowerShellCommand

- Install-ChocolateyZipPackage

All of these helper methods have built-in error handling, so there's no need to check for errors yourself when calling them from within installChocolatey.ps1. For more information on these helpers, check https://github.com/chocolatey/chocolatey/wiki/CreatePackages. This web page also provides information regarding some other helper methods you could use supporting some more-advanced scenarios.

To create the Chocolatey package itself, the .nupkg file, Chocolatey exposes a chocolatey pack command, or cpack for short. Similar to the NuGet pack command, simply call cpack myPackage.nuspec (or chocolatey pack myPackage.nuspec if you like typing a lot), and out comes a Chocolatey package.

All that is left now is to make it available to the public for consumption. To do so, use the chocolatey push command, or cpush for short. Note that you must be a registered user on http://chocolatey.org and have a valid API key to be able to push your package to the Chocolatey Gallery. The package will be pushed, not published. Publishing will happen shortly, after the package has been reviewed by the Chocolatey gods.

Summary

We've looked at two projects in the NuGet ecosystem that focus on distributing applications using NuGet rather than distributing dependencies.

Octopus Deploy can be used to deploy your application packages to a variety of test, staging, and production environments and to automate deployment to web and database servers. You learned that Octopus Deploy is the next step in formalizing the development process; build servers were introduced to automate and manage builds, and now, software like Octopus Deploy tries to provide a solution for the next step in the process: deployments.

We switched sides from remote deployments using NuGet packages to installing applications and tools, shipped in NuGet packages, using the Chocolatey command line. We touched briefly on how Chocolatey builds a bridge between NuGet and the Microsoft Web Platform Installer and RubyGems. You also learned how you can automate software installations, even in batches, and how you can keep those packages up-to-date with minimal effort. We also shed light on how easy it is to create and distribute tools and applications yourself by using Chocolatey.

In the next chapter, we'll look at extending NuGet, a logical next step in creating software using NuGet in a tailor-made process.

CHAPTER 8

■ ■ ■

NuGet Recipes

So far, we've seen a lot of details about NuGet. We've seen how we can consume packages, create them, work with package restore and so on. But how does NuGet fit in popular tools that are used by many development teams? How do you create a NuGet package during a build on Team Foundation Server or TeamCity? How to work with authenticated feeds and credentials in a continuous integration environment?

This chapter will give you some recipes for common scenarios when working with NuGet. We'll explore how things fit together and what some third-party tools have to offer to make working with NuGet a smooth experience.

Of course, we'll not be able to cover all tools and scenarios out there. For an overview of all players (both open-source and commercial) in the NuGet space, refer to http://docs.nuget.org/docs/reference/ecosystem. This page contains links to various tools that provide NuGet integration.

Team Foundation Server/Service

At the time of writing this book, Microsoft Team Foundation Server (TFS) did not have any built-in support for NuGet package creation and publishing. That does not mean you can't leverage NuGet in your automated builds on TFS. How you will leverage NuGet depends on how you want to tackle the problem: as a TFS administrator or as an isolated project team. To put it simple: either you customize TFS to support NuGet features, or you tweak your project's MSBuild instructions without modifications to the TFS templates.

The TFS Build Definition templates can be tweaked in such way that they leverage the NuGet Command Line tool in pre- and post-build steps. If you are familiar with TFS Build Definition Template customization and designing workflow activities, then you can easily build this yourself, given you have the appropriate TFS permissions of course. Instead of reinventing the wheel, we highly recommend you to take a look at the *TFS NuGetter* template which you can freely download from CodePlex at https://nugetter.codeplex.com/. It is even better when used in combination with the *TFS Versioning* template found on https://tfsversioning.codeplex.com/.

The TFS NuGetter build process defines the following steps in order of precedence:

1. *Compilation:* during this step, a single or multiple solutions are compiled, and optionally the assemblies are versioned (using the TFS Versioning customization).

2. *PrePackage:* a PowerShell script can be invoked to organize the files and NuGetter passes in the folder locations (drop, sources and binaries). This is convenient if you want to order your package contents by convention (lib, content, tools, build, target frameworks/platforms).

3. *Package:* This step allows for passing in NuGet.exe as part of the build process. This means that the NuGet command line does not need to be installed on every build agent: it can be fetched from source control during the build process. A NuSpec manifest is used to direct the packaging instructions. Packages are also versioned during this step.

4. *Push and Publish:* an API key is used, either passed in directly or through a remote file, to push and publish the package to the configured package repository (local folder, network share or feed URL).

215

5. ***Test:*** as soon as the build completes, the package is ready for testing.

6. ***Repeat:*** this process can repeat for every build.

To configure TFS NuGetter within Team Foundation Service, Microsoft's hosted version of TFS, you'll need to download the template and check it into TFS source control. Download the latest version of the TFS NuGetter build process template and extract the archive. You'll find two XAML files and one assembly (the XX in the filename is the version number):

- NuGetterMultiPkgBuildTemplateXX.xaml: the standalone NuGetter build process template.

- NuGetterMultiPkgBuildVersionedTemplate20.xaml: the NuGetter build process template that is integrated with the TFS Versioning template. Use this one if you have installed the TFS Versioning template as well.

- TfsBuild.NuGetter.Activities.dll: the code behind the TFS NuGetter workflow activities. This assembly needs to be installed in the GAC of all build agents, or you need to configure the TFS Build Controller to look for the assembly in the source control location where you added the assembly.

Figure 8-1 shows you how you can add the required XAML templates and assembly to the BuildProcessTemplates folder of your TFS Team Project. Click Next to complete the wizard.

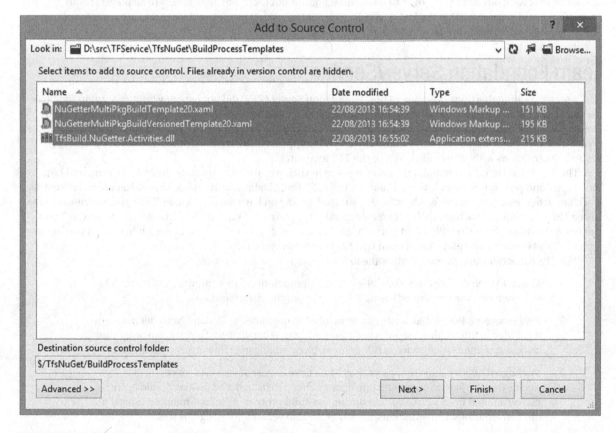

Figure 8-1. *Add TFS NuGetter build process template files to a Team Project*

Next, you'll need to commit your pending changes and push the change set to the server. Figure 8-2 shows you the pending changes for this commit.

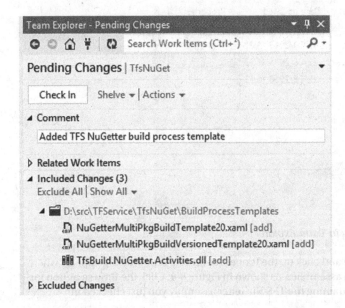

Figure 8-2. *Pending changes when adding the TFS NuGetter build process template to source control*

■ **Tip** If you haven't created a store for custom assemblies, a recommended approach is to create a TFS Team Project to store the custom assemblies and any custom build templates. This way you have a central location for the assemblies and build templates. All projects that need the build capability can access them and you won't have to copy anything into an application's project area. Maintenance is much easier this way.

Once the required build process template files are in source control, it is time to configure the TFS Build controller. To do so, select Builds in Team Explorer and choose Manage Build Controllers from the Actions menu item. A dialog appears listing all available Build Controllers, as shown in Figure 8-3.

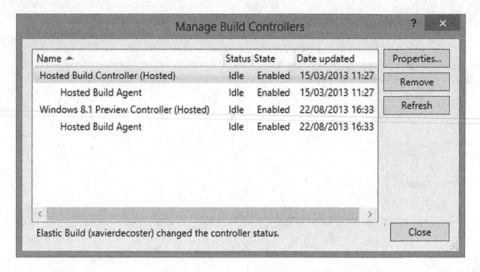

Figure 8-3. *The Manage TFS Build Controllers dialog in Team Explorer*

Select the build controller you want to configure and click on the Properties button. A new dialog appears where you can configure the version control path to custom assemblies, as shown in Figure 8-4. Click the Browse button for this setting and select the source control location containing the TFS NuGetter assembly you just checked in.

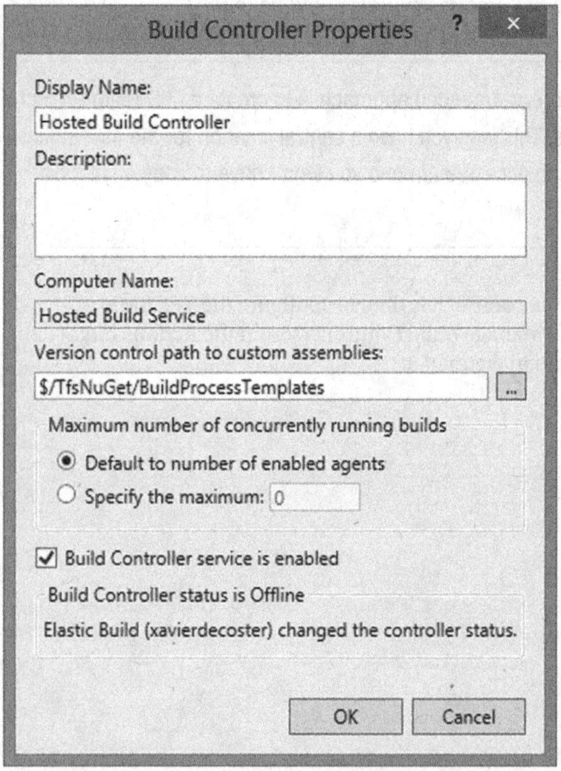

Figure 8-4. *Configure the version control path to custom assemblies in the Build Controller Properties dialog*

Close all dialogs to store your new configuration settings. It is now time to create the TFS Build Definition using our brand new build process template. Within Team Explorer, select Builds and click on New Build Definition to open the New Build Definition dialog in Visual Studio. Provide a name and trigger type: Continuous Integration doesn't sound too bad for this type of build. You can tweak the source control settings for the build definition but ensure you don't cloak the BuildProcessTemplates folder containing your build process templates. In the Build Defaults tab, ensure you select the correct build controller: the one that is configured to look for the TFS NuGetter assembly. The key step in this wizard is available in the Process tab: selecting the build definition process file. The label suggests it expects a XAML file. Since we just committed a new template to source control, it is unlikely that the TFS NuGetter template will appear in the dropdownlist. If it doesn't, then simply click on the New button which will prompt you to select a file from source control, as shown in Figure 8-5.

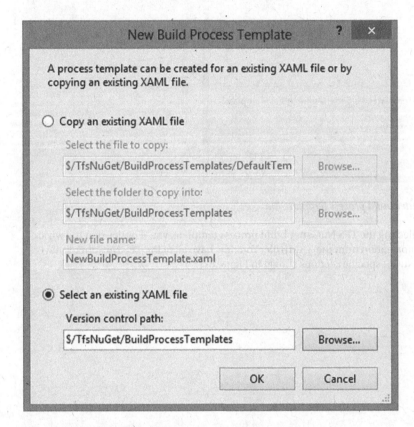

Figure 8-5. *Create or select an existing Build Process Template*

Notice we are selecting an existing template instead of creating a copy, because in our scenario there's no separate TFS Team Project for the templates. You're free to manage this however you prefer, but the key is to select the appropriate TFS NuGetter build process template file, as shown in Figure 8-6.

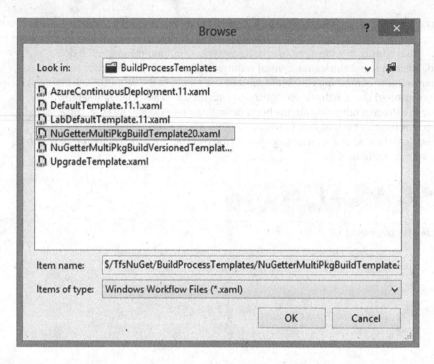

Figure 8-6. *Select the default TFS NuGetter build process template file*

When you close the dialogs after selecting the TFS NuGetter build process template, you'll notice that the wizard reloads the Process tab using the new information from the XAML file. You now have all of the TFS NuGetter build settings at your disposal, including the NuGet specific sections shown in Figure 8-7.

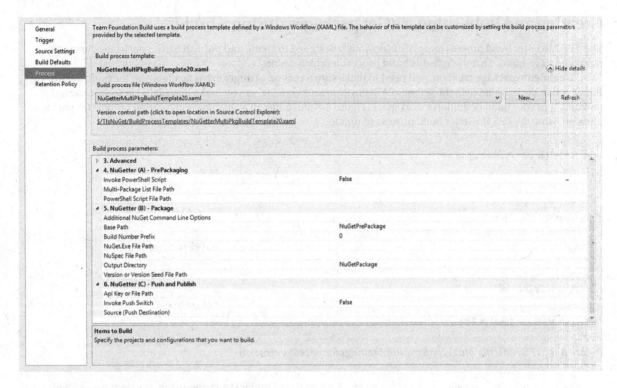

Figure 8-7. *The TFS NuGetter build process settings*

This recipe will not explain all possible configurations and options of this template but will rather focus on how you can easily restore, create and publish packages during an automated build. If you've downloaded the latest version of TFS NuGetter from CodePlex, then you'll find a pretty exhaustive manual inside the archive.

Working with NuGet package restore

NuGet version 2.7 introduced a completely redesigned package restore workflow. The core NuGet team and Team Foundation Server product team are working closely on making TFS call nuget.exe restore prior to compilation. This makes it very easy to configure NuGet package restore: the build agent will perform package restore for you, and all you need to tweak the NuGet settings is a solution-local nuget.config file (or any other NuGet configuration file picked up in the hierarchy).

On TFS, it is advised to make use of the msbuild-based package restore or to create an extra solution with a project that calls into nuget.exe restore (v2.7+) or nuget.exe install (prior to v2.7). If you configure this solution to build prior to the one you actually want to build, then the restore step will be completed before compilation of the second solution starts. This is just a workaround however, so we strongly encourage you to update your TFS installation as soon as the update supporting NuGet package restore is available.

Also check the Windows Azure Web Sites recipe for more information about how you can restore NuGet packages using MSBuild.

Creating and Publishing NuGet packages during a build

The TFS NuGetter build process template is obviously designed to create and publish NuGet packages during an automated TFS build. That's where this build process template shines!

To configure package creation, you need to make sure a version of nuget.exe is available on the build agents. Either you make it available in the server's PATH environment variable, or you make it available in source control and map it in your build definition's workspace. Figure 8-8 illustrates all available configuration options for package creation using the TFS NuGetter build process template.

⊿ **4. NuGetter (A) - PrePackaging**	
Invoke PowerShell Script	False
Multi-Package List File Path	
PowerShell Script File Path	
⊿ **5. NuGetter (B) - Package**	
Additional NuGet Command Line Options	
Base Path	NuGetPrePackage
Build Number Prefix	0
NuGet.Exe File Path	
NuSpec File Path	
Output Directory	NuGetPackage
Version or Version Seed File Path	

Figure 8-8. *TFS NuGetter build configuration settings for package creation*

The pre-packaging step allows you to create convention-based folder structures using a custom PowerShell script. This script in which you can organize project output for packing is run prior to the packaging step.

The actual packaging step has several options in which you can define the versioning scheme to be used, the path to the NuGet Command Line, the NuSpec file path, the packaging base path and output directory and additional command line options for nuget.exe. For a full specification of these settings, please read the manual that comes with the TFS NuGetter build process template.

To configure package publication, you need to modify three build settings as shown in Figure 8-9:

- Invoke Push Switch: true. Simply tell the build process that the package publication activity should be executed.

- API key or File Path: either provide the API key or provide the path to a file (relative to the Sources folder in the workspace or an absolute source control path) that contains the API key.

- Source (push destination): the URL of the NuGet feed or a network share path you want to push the packages to.

⊿ **6. NuGetter (C) - Push and Publish**	
Api Key or File Path	a2e18223-75e8-480a-8bd1-6a8c24496e46
Invoke Push Switch	**True**
Source (Push Destination)	**https://www.myget.org/F/tfsnuget/**

Figure 8-9. *TFS NuGetter build configuration settings for the push and publish NuGet packages step*

Although a custom TFS build process template can extend the build server's featureset to support common NuGet operations, we don't feel this is a compelling story to tell: asking our Dear Reader to go talk to corporate IT and ask for elevated permissions to change something server-wide on a TFS Build Controller is just not an ordinary thing to do.

TeamCity

Many development teams make use of JetBrains' (awesome) continuous integration solution: TeamCity. It provides everything you need to build software projects, run unit tests, code coverage, deploy to target systems, versioning and so on. It has a rich plugin ecosystem which enhances TeamCity's capabilities even more.

TeamCity provides a number of NuGet-related features out of the box. In chapter 5, we've already seen some of these featues. It can create and publish NuGet packages during builds, consume and restore packages from NuGet feeds. It even comes with a basic NuGet server which provides access to build artifacts through its own NuGet feed.

Let's dive into a number of these features. For more information about TeamCity, refer
`www.jetbrains.com/teamcity`.

Installing NuGet to TeamCity Build Agents

TeamCity provides a server component, in which build can be configured and reviewed, as well as one or more build agents which are the place where it all happens: build agents run the actual build, creating build artifacts from source control. While TeamCity server and a build agent can be colocated on one machine, typically they are installed separately. With only one build agent it is easy to download and install `NuGet.exe` on the build agent machine, but how would you go about that in a build farm with a larger number of build agents? Or what if some builds require different `NuGet.exe` versions?

Through the administration interface on the TeamCity server, we can specify which versions of the NuGet Command Line have to be made available on the build agent(s). Under Administration ➤ NuGet Settings ➤ NuGet Command Line, one or more NuGet versions can be downloaded to the build agents. Figure 8-10 shows this interface in action.

Figure 8-10. *Installing a NuGet Command Line version to build agents*

Once one or more versions of NuGet.exe are available on build agents, you can start using the other NuGet features in TeamCity. Note it is best to assign a default NuGet version, this will make it easier to upgrade to newer versions in all build configurations when needed.

NuGet Build Runners

Every build configuration in TeamCity exists of one or more build steps, each using a build runner to do things like compiling a Visual Studio solution, running MSBuild, running unit tests and so on. TeamCity comes with several NuGet build runners that can be used in a build step:

- NuGet Pack - similar to the NuGet pack command, can be used to create a NuGet package.

- NuGet Publish - similar to the NuGet push command, can be used to push packages to a NuGet feed.

- NuGet Installer - similar to the various NuGet commands for installing packages (install, update, restore), can be used to download and install NuGet packages during the build.

Let's see what we can do with these runners.

The NuGet Pack Build Runner

NuGet packages can be created during a TeamCity build. For example, after building your software library and running unit tests on it, it may make sense to distribute this software library as a NuGet package. This can be done using the NuGet Pack build runner.

When selecting the NuGet Pack build runner from the dropdown when creating a new build step, you can provide several options with regards to how the package should be created. Figure 8-11 shows a number of these options.

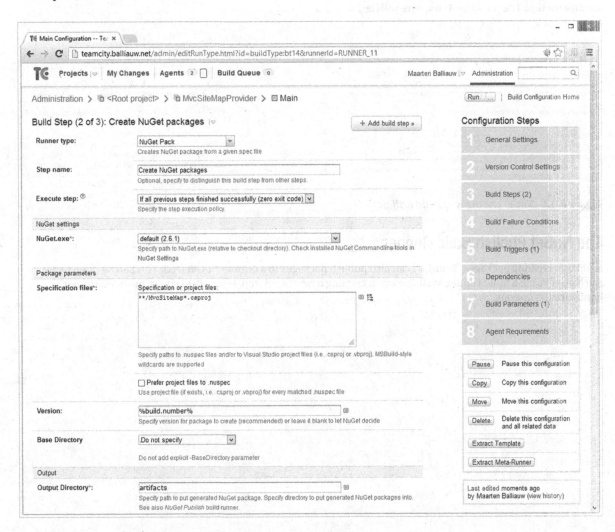

Figure 8-11. *The NuGet Pack build runner configuration in TeamCity*

You can specify the NuGet version to use when running this build step. The dropdown will list all NuGet.exe versions installed through the administration interface earlier. The NuGet Pack build runner can create multiple packages at once. The Specification Files text area allows you to specify the paths to all project files or .nuspec files for which a NuGet package should be created in the build.

The Version specification will be used to provide NuGet package versions. If this has to be the same version as the version number generated for the build by TeamCity, the `%build.number%` variable can be used.

For Output Directory, the folder in which the NuGet package has to be created should be given. This will typically be a path that you will also want to include in the build artifacts path so that NuGet packages can be downloaded from the TeamCity server.

Optionally, symbols packages can be created. You can also provide additional command line parameters, if needed.

After running a build, the packages created during build will be listed as build artifacts. Figure 8-12 shows an example of this. The packages listed here will be

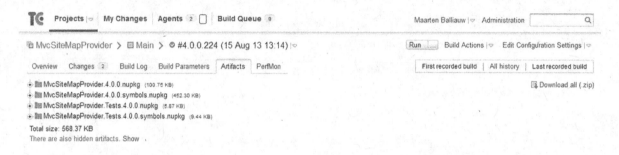

Figure 8-12. *NuGet packages as build artifacts*

The NuGet Publish Build Runner

Similar to creating packages, TeamCity can also publish packages to a remote NuGet feed. This can be done using the NuGet Publish build runner, available when creating a new build step. Figure 8-13 shows the build runner's configuration options.

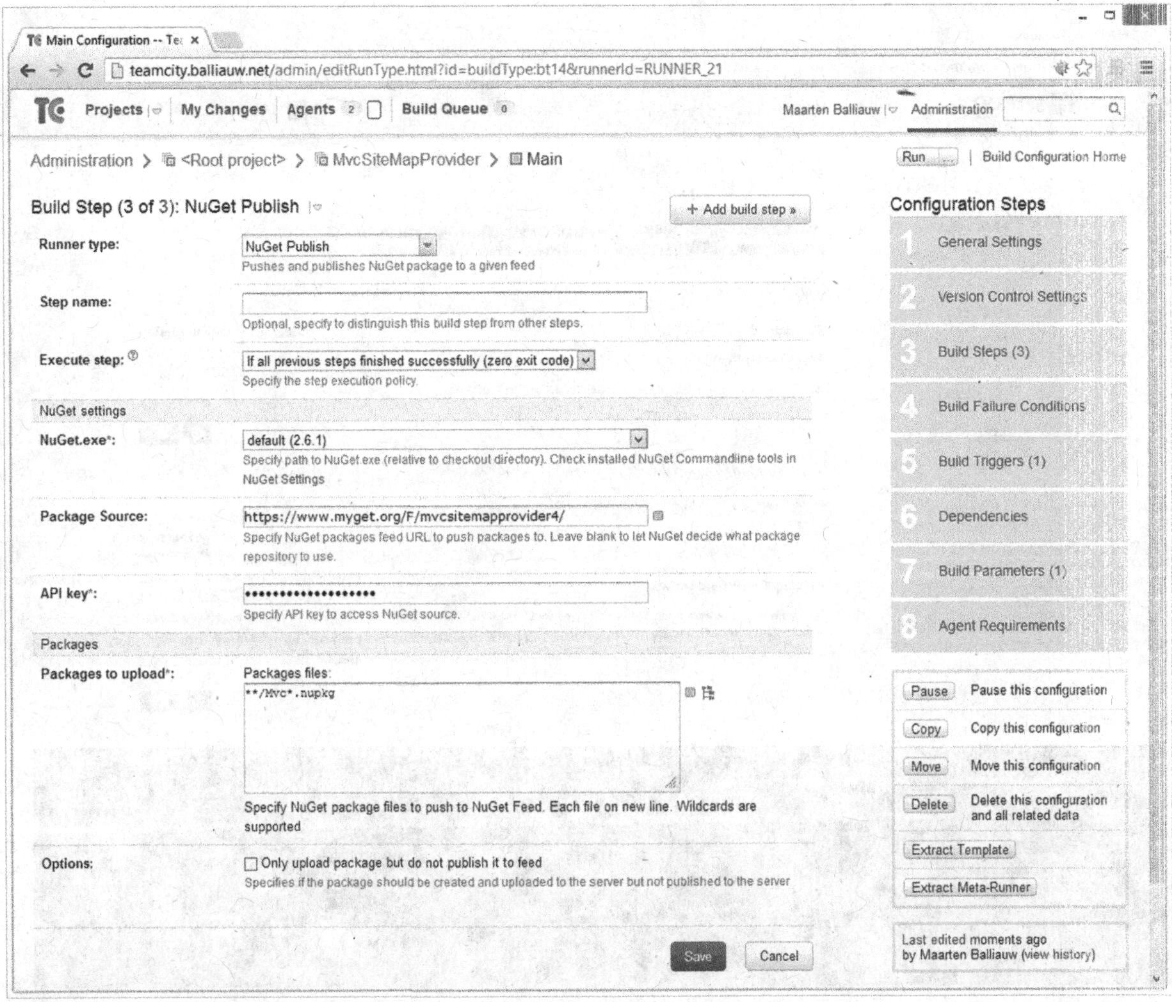

Figure 8-13. *NuGet Publish build runner configuration*

Again, you can select the NuGet version to be used when pushing the package to a feed. You will also have to specify the feed's URL as well as the API key to use when publishing. The example shown in Figure 8-13 pushes the generated NuGet packages to a feed on MyGet from where they can be consumed by clients later on.

Of course, specifying the packages to upload is an important step. Note that wildcard paths can be used here, for example **/Mvc*.nupkg to find all NuGet packages named Mvc*.nupkg in every folder of your build.

Optionally, you can choose to only upload the package to the remote feed but not list it. This is the same as pushing an unlisted package to a NuGet feed and may make sense in some cases.

After running the build, packages will be pushed to the remote NuGet feed as can be seen in Figure 8-14.

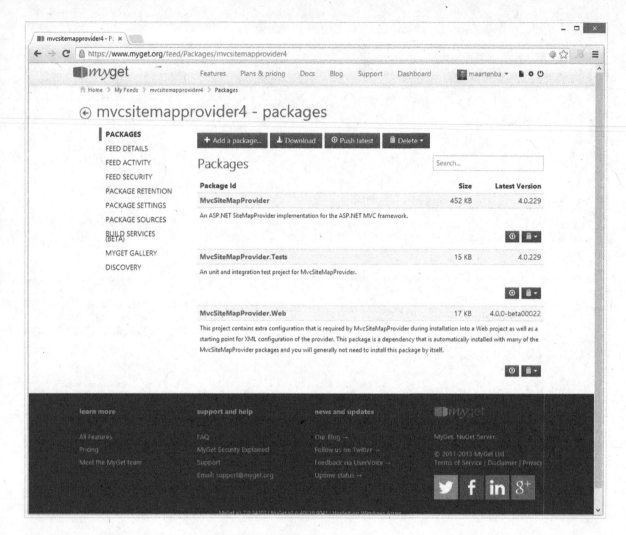

Figure 8-14. *Packages pushed to a NuGet feed from TeamCity*

The NuGet Installer Build Runner

Another build runner in TeamCity is the NuGet Installer build runner. Using this build runner, NuGet packages can be installed during a build on TeamCity. But wait, isn't that the same as using NuGet package restore? It is! Mostly, as there is an interesting and very useful side effect of using the NuGet Installer build runner. We'll have a look at that in a minute, let's first add a new build step using the NuGet Installer. Figure 8-15 shows the build runner's configuration parameters.

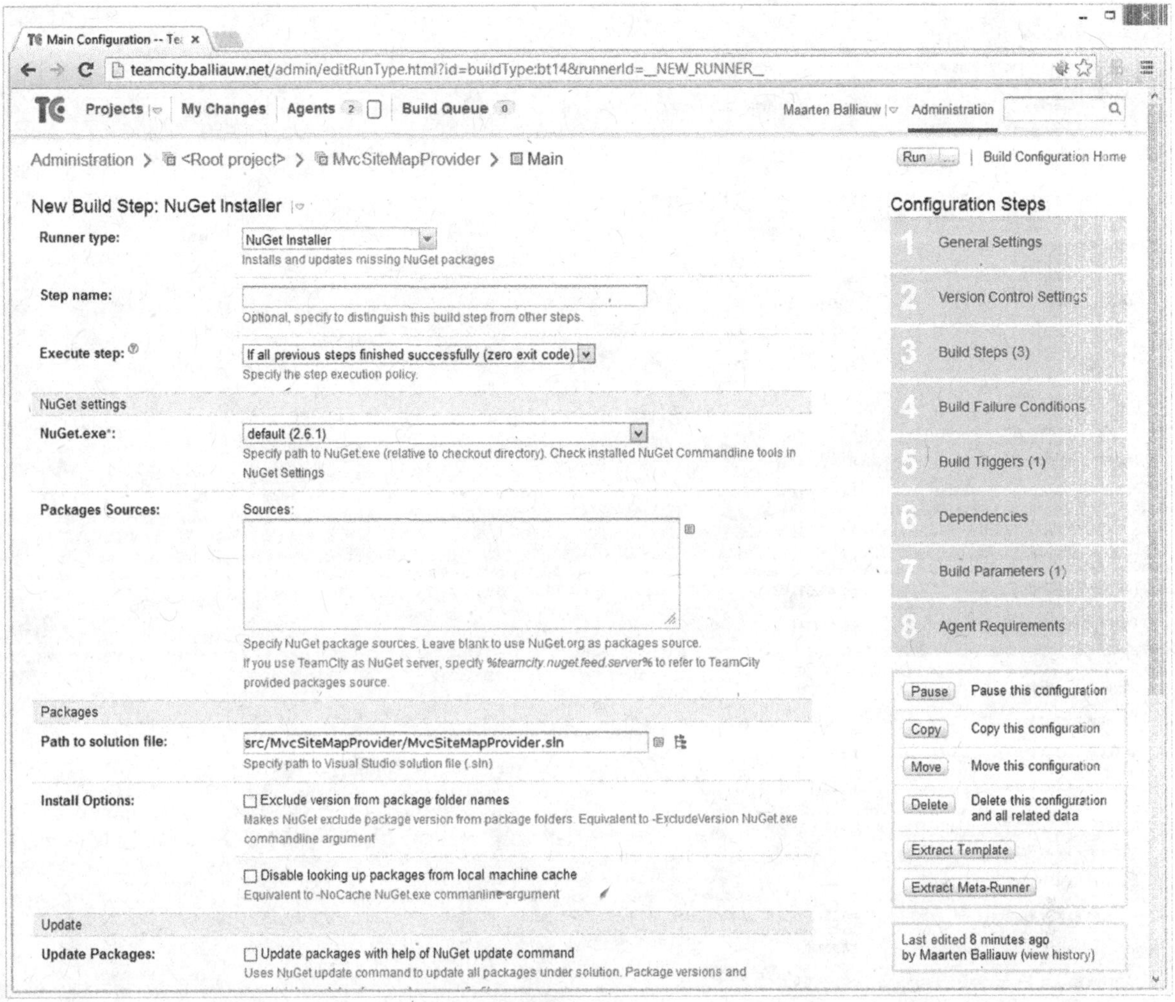

Figure 8-15. *NuGet Installer build runnr configuration page*

You will have to specify the NuGet Command Line version to run so TeamCity uses the correct version of NuGet.exe for your build configuration. Optionally, package sources like your own NuGet feed can be specified. Note that if feeds that require authentication are used, the NuGet Feed Credentials build feature should be used as well. More on that one later on.

The NuGet Installer build runner will do its work based on the solution file that is specified. It provides some additional options like disabling the NuGet local cache on the build agents.

Farther down the configuration, you can also enable auto-updating of NuGet packages for the solution. As described in earlier chapters, we recommend against doing this as a build may no longer be reproducible. But in case you do need it, it's there.

What's interesting about using the NuGet Installer build runner as opposed to plain package restore, is that TeamCity provides a listing of the NuGet packages used during build. Figure 8-16 shows this report in action, which can be consulted from the build overview page.

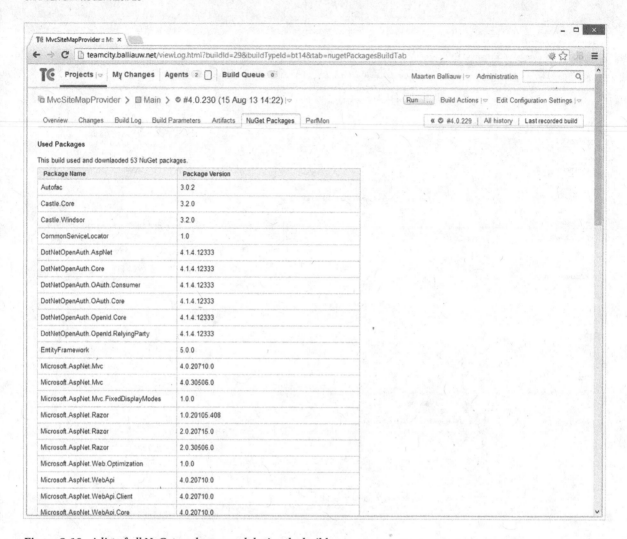

Figure 8-16. *A list of all NuGet packages used during the build*

NuGet Feed Credentials Build Feature

When consuming NuGet packages from an authenticated feed during a build, the last thing you want to do is add credentials for connecting to that authenticated feed to source control. TeamCity provides a build feature which enables you to consume packages from feeds that require authentication.

From the build configuration, this build feature can be added. In the dialog that is opened, the feed URL should
• be specified as well as credentials to connect to the feed, as can be seen from Figure 8-17.

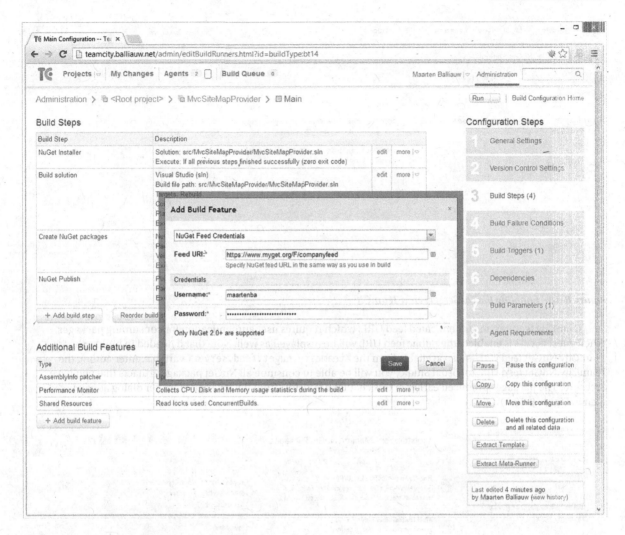

Figure 8-17. *NuGet Feed Credentials buildfeature*

Enabling the TeamCity NuGet feed

TeamCity provides various methods of consuming build artifacts. From the TeamCity server, guests or authenticated users can navigate to the builds they have access to and consult the artifacts tab to download executables, documentation, NuGet packages or any other artifacts that have been created during build. There is also a plugin out there which seeds build artifacts using torrents, which can be useful for distributing builds across teams. There is another way of consuming (specific) build artifacts: TeamCity contains a built-in NuGet feed!

From the TeamCity administration under NuGet Settings ➤ NuGet Server, the NuGet server can be enabled as you can see in Figure 8-18.

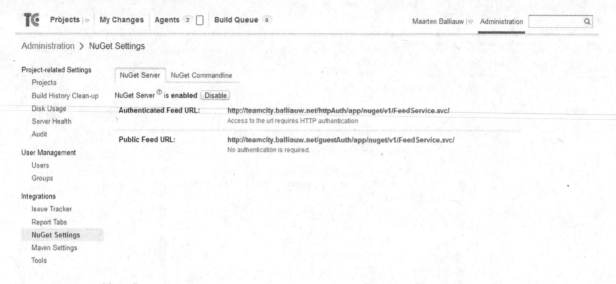

Figure 8-18. *Enabling the NuGet server in TeamCity*

TeamCity features an authenticated feed URL, which requires user authentication for consuming packages. When guest access is enabled, the public feed URL will be displayed as well. Note that if needed in builds, the TeamCity NuGet feed URL is also available from the `%teamcity.nuget.feed.server%` variable. After adding the TeamCity NuGet feed URL to Visual Studio, you will be able to consume all NuGet package artifacts that you have access to. The packages produced earlier in this chapter are visible from the Package Manager dialog as can be seen in Figure 8-19.

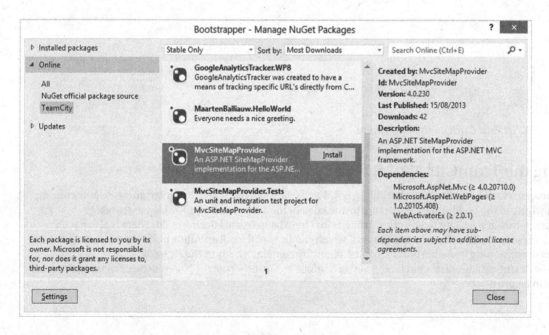

Figure 8-19. *Consuming the TeamCity NuGet feed from Visual Studio*

Now where do these NuGet packages come from? TeamCity publishes all build artifacts from all build configurations that are NuGet packages on this feed. Depending on the build configurations you have access to, the list of packages available from the TeamCity NuGet feed will be different.

Can you push your own packages to TeamCity's NuGet server and use it as a private feed? The TeamCity NuGet feed should not be seen as a full-fledged private NuGet server. Instead, it is a different method of accessing build artifacts in an automated fashion. The TeamCity NuGet feed can be consumed by developers, by tools like MyGet or OctopusDeploy and so on.

TeamCity and OctopusDeploy

In the previous chapter, you have seen how OctopusDeploy can be used to deploy applications by packaging them as NuGet packages and deploying them on web servers, database servers and so on. Why not run builds on TeamCity, run unit tests and deploy to target machines using OctopusDeploy in one go?

First of all, you should enable the TeamCity NuGet server and add the feed URL to OctopusDeploy as a package repository. Figure 8-20 shows an example of how this can be done.

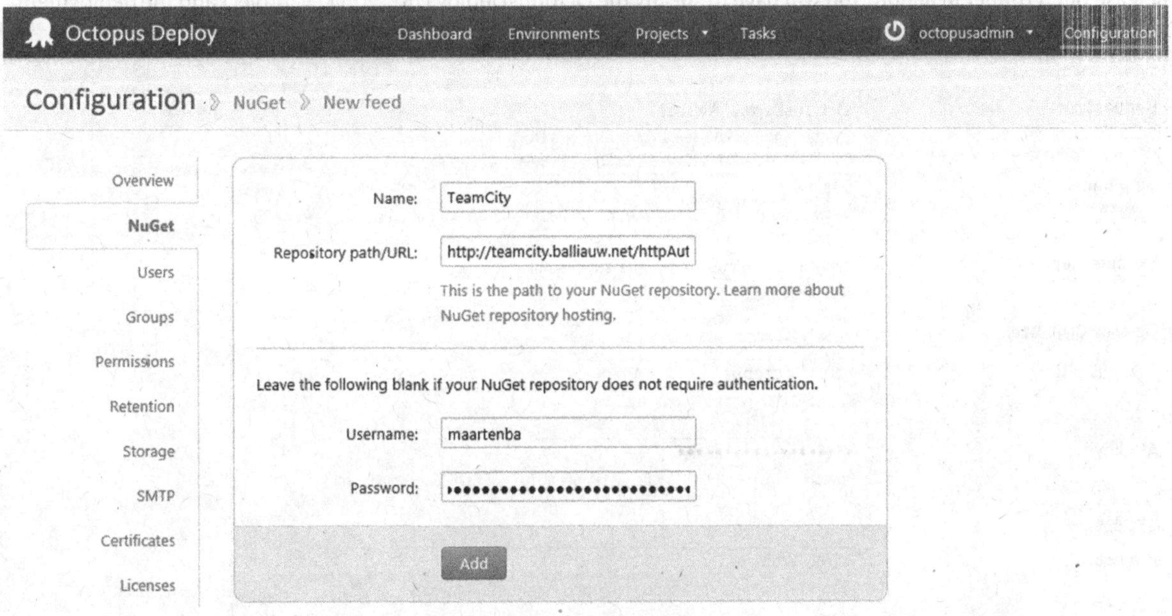

Figure 8-20. *Adding TeamCity as a package source to OctopusDeploy*

In OctopusDeploy, new deployments can now be triggered from the TeamCity NuGet feed. But what if we want to trigger a deployment as a final build step on TeamCity?

OctopusDeploy also has a plugin for TeamCity available which can be downloaded from `http://octopusdeploy.com/downloads` (installation instructions are available from `http://octopusdeploy.com/documentation/integration/teamcity`).

Once the OctopusDeploy plugin is installed into TeamCity, some new options will be available. Firstly, the OctoPack tool described in the previous chapter is available in MSBuild and Visual Studio build runners. These runners will show an additional option to run OctoPack as a part of the build on TeamCiy, as can be seen in Figure 8-21. This will produce a NuGet package for your application.

Octopus Packaging	
Run OctoPack:	☑
	If checked, any projects with OctoPack installed will be packaged.
OctoPack package version:	%build.number% ▦
	Package version number for NuGet packages created by OctoPack.

Figure 8-21. *OctoPack integration in TeamCity build steps*

The OctopusDeploy plugin for TeamCity introduces two additional build runners as well:

- `OctopusDeploy: Release`, which will trigger a release on OctopusDeploy.
- `OctopusDeploy: Promote`, which will promote a release from one environment to another.

For both build runners, some additional configuration must be given. Figure 8-22 shows the OctopusDeploy: Release build runner in action. You will have to specify the OctopusDeploy URL, API key, project and the deployment target environment.

Runner type:	OctopusDeploy: Release ▾
	Creates and deploys releases in Octopus Deploy
Step name:	Deploy
	You can specify a build step name to distinguish it from other steps.
Execute step: ⑦	Only if all previous steps were successful ▾
	You can specify step execution policy
Octopus Connection	
Octopus URL:*	http://octopus/ ▦
	Specify Octopus web portal URL
API key:*	••••••••••••••••••••
	Specify Octopus API key. You can get this from your user page in the Octopus w
Release	
Project:*	ACME Website ▦
	Enter the name of the Octopus project to create a release for
Release number:	%build.number% ▦
	The number to use for this release, e.g., 1.0.%build.number%.
Deployment	
Deploy to:	Test ▦
	Comma separated list of environments to deploy to. Leave empty to create a re
Wait for deployment to complete:	☑
	If checked, the build process will only succeed if the deployment is successful.

Figure 8-22. *The OctopusDeploy build runner configuration*

Note that NuGet packages created from your build won't appear in TeamCity until after the build completes. This means you'll usually need to configure a secondary build configuration, and use a snapshot dependency and build trigger in TeamCity to run the deployment build configuration after the first build configuration completes.

Windows Azure Web Sites and NuGet Package Restore

Windows Azure Web Sites (WAWS) is a great cloud computing feature of the Windows Azure Platform allowing you to quickly provision and deploy a web site with flexible scaling options. A great development flow consists of automatic deployments triggered by pushing some commits to your source code repository. Windows Azure Web Sites can perform such automated deployments from various hosted source code repositories, such as Team Foundation Service, CodePlex, GitHub, DropBox, BitBucket as well as any local Git repository.

Before your web site can be deployed, it needs to be built. This is handled by the service on WAWS. Obviously, this also means that package restore should happen as well in a pre-build step. If you are consuming NuGet packages from the NuGet.org gallery, then this will work without any special modifications. However, if you are consuming NuGet packages from a secured feed requiring authentication, then this can be a little more cumbersome in a locked-down environment such as WAWS, because you'll need to have a way to configure your feed credentials and have the Kudu service use them during package restore.

This recipe will show you how to configure NuGet package restore from a secured feed during automated deployments to Windows Azure Web Sites. This recipe will use a GitHub repository and a private MyGet feed, but you could replace both the source repository and package repository with the one you prefer.

Creating and Configuring the Windows Azure Web Site for Auto-Deployment from GitHub

You can replay the steps from this recipe by downloading the CloudSurvey sample application from the Windows Azure Toolkit. The sources of this application are hosted on GitHub, so you can simply fork the CloudSurvey repository and use that one as the source of your deployments. You can find the repository at https://github.com/WindowsAzure-Samples/CloudSurvey. A step by step tutorial on how to publish the application from your local machine can be found in the repository's readme file at https://github.com/WindowsAzure-Samples/CloudSurvey/blob/master/README.md.

For this recipe, we won't be publishing manually and rather trigger the deployment automatically using the GitHub post-commit HTTP Hooks. The following steps will get you started.

Log on to the Windows Azure Management Portal and select Web Sites in the left navigation menu. Click on the *New* button on the bottom left and select *Compute* ➤ *Web Site* ➤ *Custom Create* from the menu, as shown in Figure 8-23.

Figure 8-23. *Creating a custom Windows Azure Web Site in the Management Portal*

The dialog that appears will ask you to provide a URL and allow you to select a datacenter in a region you prefer to deploy the web site to. The CloudSurvey application requires a SQL database, so we will configure this as well in the next wizard step. We will also enable publishing from source control so make sure you check that checkbox as well to unlock the third step in the wizard. Figure 8-24 allows you to verify your configuration before clicking the arrow to move to the next step in the wizard.

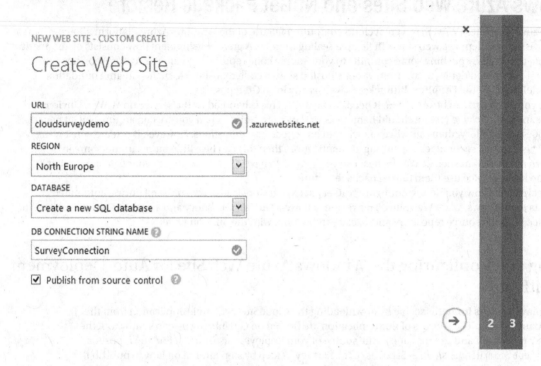

Figure 8-24. *Configuring deployment of a new Windows Azure Web Site*

The second step of the wizard will ask you to specify the database settings for this web site. We'll create a new database server, but if you already have one then you can obviously choose that server as well. Figure 8-25 shows the configuration used in this recipe. Make sure the connection string name equals SurveyConnection, as this is what is expected by the CloudSurvey application code.

NEW WEB SITE - CUSTOM CREATE

Specify database settings

NAME

cloudsurveydb

SERVER

New SQL database server

SERVER LOGIN NAME

cloudsurveyadmin

SERVER LOGIN PASSWORD   CONFIRM PASSWORD

●●●●●●●●●●●   ●●●●●●●●●●●

REGION

North Europe

☐ CONFIGURE ADVANCED DATABASE SETTINGS

1   3

Figure 8-25. *Configuring database settings for a new Windows Azure Web Site*

The next and final step in the wizard allows us to configure automated deployment from our source repository. Figures 8-26 and 8-27 illustrate how this recipe uses GitHub and lets the wizard set up the connection for you.

NEW WEB SITE - CUSTOM CREATE

Where is your source code?

Team Foundation Service

Local Git repository

GitHub

Dropbox

GitHub is the best place to share code with friends, co-workers, classmates, and complete strangers. Over three million people use GitHub to build amazing things together.

1   2

Figure 8-26. *Select a source repository to set up automated deployments to WAWS*

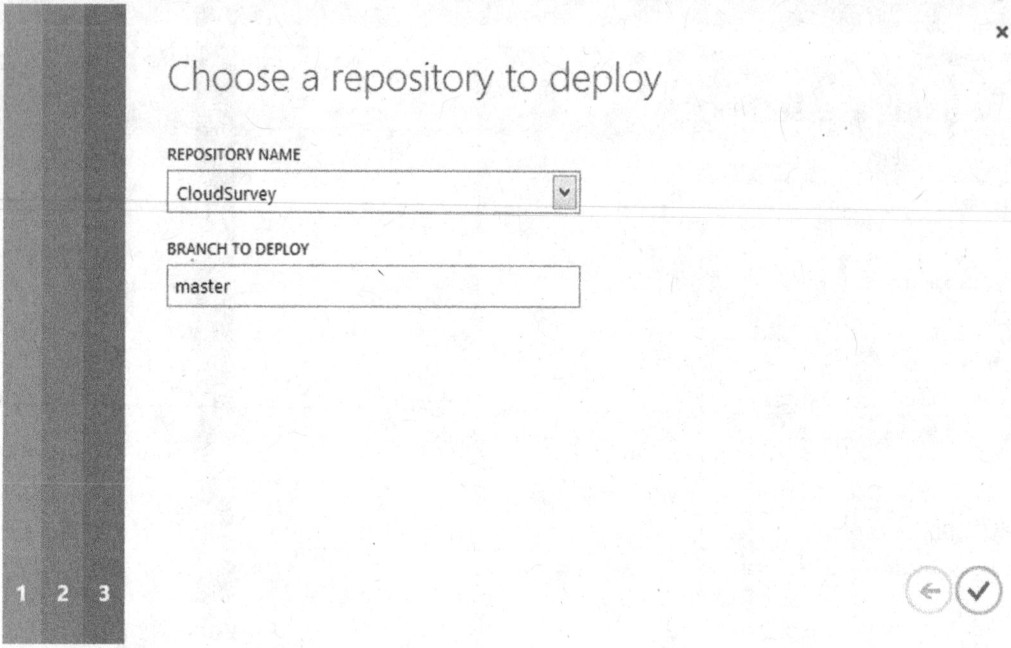

Figure 8-27. *Choose a repository to deploy to WAWS*

Click the finish checkmark to complete the wizard and in about a minute your brand new Windows Azure Web Site will be provisioned with a fresh deployment of the selected source repository. If all went well, you should be able to login to the web site using the default credentials for the application (username: 'admin', password: 'Contoso123!'). The login screen is shown in Figure 8-28.

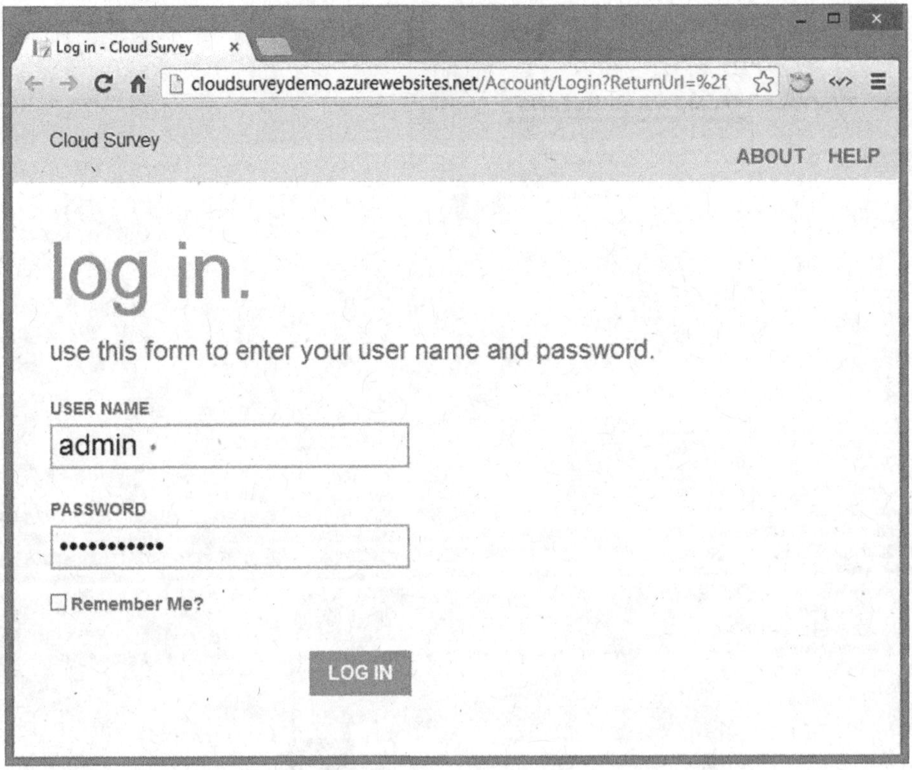

Figure 8-28. *The log in screen welcomes you after a successful deployment*

Configuring NuGet Package Restore from a Secured Feed

If you reached this point, you already restored NuGet packages during a WAWS deployment! That's right, this happened seemingless in the previous steps: the source repository is configured to restore NuGet packages from the NuGet.org gallery, which is publicly available and doesn't require any form of authentication to consume packages.

In this section, we will configure the solution to restore its packages from a secured MyGet.org feed. You can quickly create a feed containing all required packages by uploading the packages.config file to your MyGet feed, as shown in Figure 8-29.

Figure 8-29. *Upload a packages.config file to a MyGet feed*

Once all the required packages are hosted on the secured feed, it is time to change the package source to be used during restore. Look for a nuget.config file in the sources of the CloudSurvey repository or add one to the solution directory if it got removed from the repository (at the time of writing it is still there). Open the nuget.config file and edit it to have the same contents as shown in Listing 8-1. Replace the package source URL and credentials with the settings you'll be using.

Listing 8-1. The nuget.config file configured to restore packages from a secure package source.

```xml
<?xml version="1.0" encoding="utf-8"?>
<configuration>
  <solution>
    <add key="disableSourceControlIntegration" value="true" />
  </solution>
  <packageRestore>
    <!-- Allow NuGet to download missing packages -->
    <add key="enabled" value="True" />
    <!-- Automatically check for missing packages during build in Visual Studio -->
    <add key="automatic" value="True" />
  </packageRestore>
```

```
  <packageSources>
    <!-- Configure the feed URL -->
    <add key="MySecureFeed" value="https://www.myget.org/F/securedpackagerestore/" />
  </packageSources>
  <packageSourceCredentials>
    <!-- Configure credentials for a given package source key -->
    <MySecureFeed>
      <add key="Username" value="xavierdecoster" />
      <add key="ClearTextPassword" value="secret" />
    </MySecureFeed>
  </packageSourceCredentials>
</configuration>
```

At the time of writing, this project was configured against a version of nuget.exe older than v2.7, so you'll have to make a few more adjustments to make it work.

First you'll need to adjust the RestoreCommand in the <path to solution>/.nuget/nuget.targets file to make it point to the nuget.config file. Optionally, you can also add the -Verbosity detailed switch to get more detailed output as seen in Listing 8-2.

Listing 8-2. Make sure the RestoreCommand is using the nuget.config file.

```
<RestoreCommand>$(NuGetCommand) install "$(PackagesConfig)" -source $(PackageSources) -o
"$(PackagesDir)" -ConfigFile "$(NuGetToolsPath)/nuget.config"</RestoreCommand>
```

When you rebuild the solution, you should see a build log similar output as shown in Listing 8-3.

Listing 8-3. Extract of build output from a secure package restore operation.

```
1>------ Rebuild All started: Project: CloudSurvey, Configuration: Debug Any CPU ------
1> Using credentials from config. UserName: xavierdecoster
1> GET https://www.myget.org/F/securedpackagerestore/FindPackagesById()?id='jQuery'
1> GET https://www.myget.org/F/securedpackagerestore/FindPackagesById()?id='Microsoft.AspNet.Mvc'
1> Installing 'jQuery 1.6.4'.
1> Successfully installed 'jQuery 1.6.4'.
...
```

Next, you should also update nuget.exe itself. This can easily be done by opening a command prompt and executing the following commands:

```
cd <path-to-solution>/.nuget
nuget.exe update -self
```

In order to kick off your deployment to WAWS with these new settings, all you need to do is to push your commit to your source repository. A few seconds later, you'll see a new active deployment appear in the deployment history of your Windows Azure Web Site, as shown in Figure 8-30.

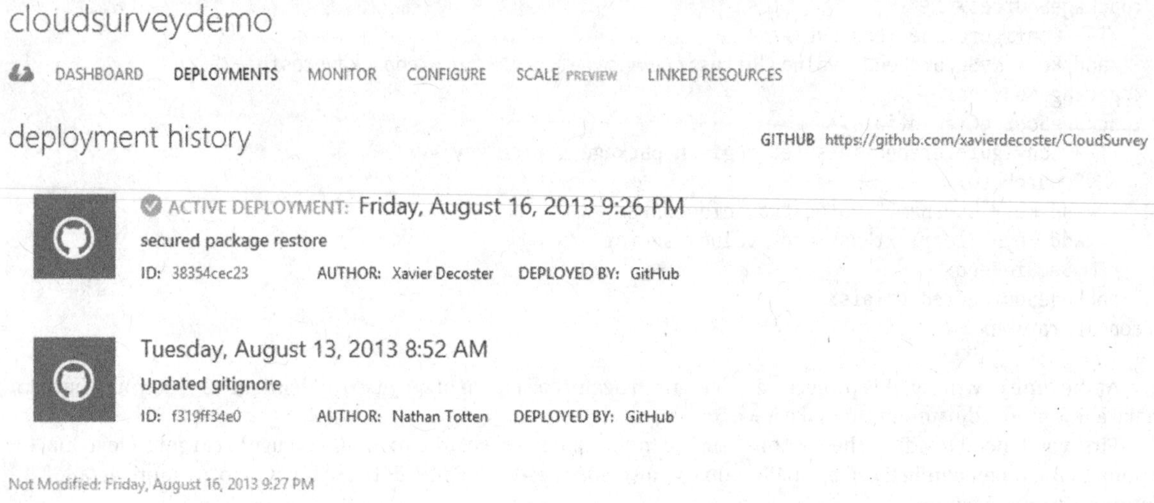

cloudsurveydemo

DASHBOARD   **DEPLOYMENTS**   MONITOR   CONFIGURE   SCALE PREVIEW   LINKED RESOURCES

deployment history

GITHUB   https://github.com/xavierdecoster/CloudSurvey

✅ ACTIVE DEPLOYMENT: Friday, August 16, 2013 9:26 PM
secured package restore
ID: 38354cec23   AUTHOR: Xavier Decoster   DEPLOYED BY: GitHub

Tuesday, August 13, 2013 8:52 AM
Updated gitignore
ID: f319ff34e0   AUTHOR: Nathan Totten   DEPLOYED BY: GitHub

Not Modified: Friday, August 16, 2013 9:27 PM

Figure 8-30. *A new active deployment of a WAWS triggered by a GitHub service hook*

■ **Warning**   As you made use of the ClearText password feature, please make sure that the nuget.config file is not exposed to anyone that should not know the package source's credentials!

NuGet and MyGet

We have been using MyGet throughout this book to set up some samples and illustrate some good practices. MyGet makes it super simple to create and publish NuGet packages, even for first-time NuGet users. This chapter provides some recipes for success when using MyGet as your NuGet platform.

Next to hosting private feeds, MyGet also comes with Build Services, an easy way of converting source code into a NuGet package. Let's see how we can leverage private feeds, build services and some of the other features available in a NuGet workflow.

Using MyGet Build Services

After creating a feed on MyGet, you can add one or more build sources to that feed. A build source is a build configuration for one of your hosted source repositories that make use of Git, Mercurial (Hg) or Subversion.

MyGet Build Services is not intended to be a replacement for a professional Continuous Integration server like TeamCity. It is there to help facilitating package creation and making it easier to convert source code into a NuGet package.

When triggered, MyGet Build Services will start a build of the source code available from your repsoitory.

Adding a build source

To create a build source for a GitHub repository, browse to your feed on the MyGet web site and select build sources in the navigation menu on the left. The toolbar shown on the build sources page, shown in Figure 8-31, allows you to add a build source. The first button will enable you to manually specify settings for the source code repository, the others launch a step-by-step configuration wizard that connects MyGet to either GitHub, BitBucket or CodePlex. Upon completion of the wizard you'll have successfully added a new build source to your MyGet feed.

Figure 8-31. *Add a new build source to a MyGet feed*

Once added, a new build can be triggered manually by clicking the Build button, or using an HTTP post hook, a concept which we'll cover in a bit.

Build conventions

Build services used a best-effort approach to compile and package your sources, but the build process can be influenced. MyGet Build Services will scan the contents of your source control repository and look for a file which it can work with. In order of precedence, the following files are searched for:

- `build.bat`, `build.cmd` or `build.ps1`
- `MyGet.sln`
- Any other `*.sln` file
- `*.csproj` (and `*.vbproj`, etc)
- `*.nuspec`

Following these conventions, you can influence what is being built. If you want to only build certain projects, adding a `MyGet.sln` file that holds only those projects will make sure only those are built. If you want full control over your build, using a `build.bat` file allows scripting a custom build.

Build services evolves quite rapidly, an up-to-date overview of all conventions can be found in the documentation pages at `http://docs.myget.org/docs/reference/build-services`.

Continuous Delivery of NuGet packages

In addition to manually triggering a build within the MyGet user interface, it is also possible to automatically trigger a build every time code commits are pushed to your source control repository, by making use of an HTTP POST hook URL.

If you are using a hosted source control service such as GitHub, BitBucket or Codeplex, then you can leverage MyGet's Build Services to set up continuous delivery for NuGet packages: every code change you push to your source repository will result in a new package being built and published on MyGet. This is a great workflow as it enables a super fast delivery cycle of new development builds, nightly builds, prereleases or releases.

MyGet Build Sources and HTTP POST URL

Once you have fully configured a build source for your MyGet feed, you will be able to manually trigger a build whenever you like. However, if you are trying to adopt the Continuous Integration Software Development Practice, then automatically triggering a MyGet Build whenever you push some code changes to your Source Code Repository is one of the first steps in doing this.

To connect MyGet Build Services to your source repository service, you'll need to configure a so-called Post-Receive hook. This HTTP POST Hook URL is a mechanism to allow your Source Code Repository to notify the MyGet Build Service (via an HTTP POST to the given URL) when a commit has been pushed. As soon as this has happened, a MyGet Build will be added to the Build Queue, which will then go and grab the latest code from the Source Code Repository, and execute the Build. Figure 8-32 shows you where you can find your MyGet feed's HTTP POST URL you'll need to use. The HTTP POST Hook URL is clearly visible on this page (the GUID at the end of the URL has been obscured simply because this is unique to each MyGet feed). Click the copy button (indicated by the arrow) to grab the URL ready for adding into your Source Code Repository.

Figure 8-32. Each build source of a MyGet feed has a HTTP POST hook

Setting up GitHub

To configure your GitHub repository to trigger your build source configuration on MyGet Build Services, you'll need to copy the HTTP POST hook from MyGet into your GitHub repository settings. Follow these steps to set up GitHub for this scenario.

1. Log into GitHub and navigate to the repository that is to be configured.

2. In the top right corner of the page, click the *Settings* button.

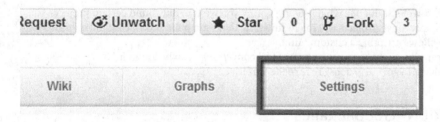

3. Within the Settings page, click on the *Service Hooks* button, located down the left side of the page

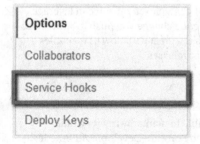

4. Within the Service Hooks page, click on the *WebHook URLs* link

5. Using the form that appears, paste in the HTTP POST Hook URL that was copied from MyGet above into the *URL* field and click the *Update settings* button

6. To verify that this has been set up correctly, you can then click the Test Hook button. Doing this should trigger a Build straight away within MyGet.

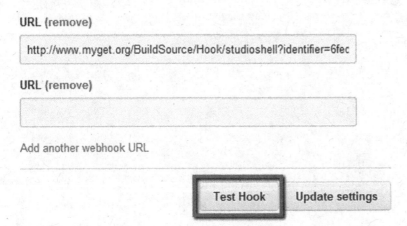

Setting up BitBucket

Very similar to GitHub, BitBucket repositories also support HTTP POST hooks. The following steps will help you configure your BitBucket repository to trigger MyGet Build Services for every push to the source repository.

1. Log into BitBucket and navigate to the repository that is to be configured.

2. In the right hand corner of the page, click the *Settings* button.

3. Within the Settings page, click on the *Services* link, located down the left hand side of the page.

4. Within the Services page, find the POST option within the *Select a service*... drop down list, and click the *Add Service* button.

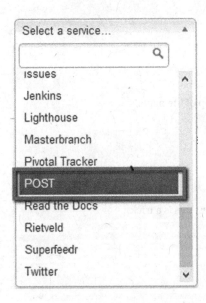

5. Using the form that appears, paste in the HTTP POST Hook URL that was copied from MyGet above into the *URL* field and click the *Save* button.

6. At the time of writing this book, there was no automatic way of testing to ensure that the URL that you have entered works correctly. In order to achieve this though, you can follow the Troubleshooting Bitbucket Service page (`https://confluence.atlassian.com/display/BITBUCKET/Troubleshooting+Bitbucket+Services`) on the Atlassian Wiki. In addition, make sure to add comments on the issue that has been raised at `https://bitbucket.org/site/master/issue/4667/add-ability-to-test-services-bb-5436` to add this feature to Bitbucket to show that it is popular.

Setting up CodePlex

If you are using Codeplex, then you'll need to apply a little trick in the Service Hooks settings for your repository. You can make use of the AppHarbor Service Hook and paste the MyGet build source URL instead. The following 6 steps provide information about how to use the MyGet HTTP POST Hook URL within a CodePlex project.

1. Log into CodePlex and navigate to the project that is to be configured.

2. In the right hand corner of the page, click the *Settings* link.

3. Within the Settings page, click on the *Services* link, located at the top of the page.

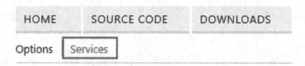

4. Within the Services page, click the *AppHarbor* option on the left (yes, this is a trick).

Service Hooks

5. Using the form that appears, check the *Enable code change events* option and paste in the HTTP POST Hook URL that was copied from MyGet above into the *URL* field and click the *Save* button.

APPHARBOR

AppHarbor is a fully hosted .NET Platform as a Service. AppHarbor can deploy and scale any standard .NET application to the cloud.

■ ENABLE CODE CHANGE EVENTS
This integration will continuously deploy to AppHarbor as you push updates to your project. Learn more.

URL
https://www.myget.org/BuildSource/Hook

A button to copy the 'Build URL' is found on your AppHarbor application's main page.

SAVE

6. At this point in time, there is no automatic way of testing to ensure that the URL that you have entered works correctly other than commiting code to your CodePlex repository.

The package promotion flow

The continuous delivery of NuGet packages requires a proper workflow to process the resulting packages. There's no point in stacking up packages on a feed for every code change you do, unless you have a mechanism in place for triage. It makes a lot of sense to promote pacakges through the various stages of the release process based on quality or acceptance criteria.

Typically, you'll promote a development build to the testing team, and later on to a staging area before releasing it into production. The same can be done with NuGet packages: you can support this release cycle by promoting packages from a Continuous Integration (CI) feed to a Quality Assurance (QA) feed before prereleasing or releasing the package onto a production feed. This is what is meant by a *package promotion flow*.

To support this natural flow of packages, MyGet feeds have the concept of *upstream package sources*. Package sources play a key role in the MyGet Build Services workflow. By default, the NuGet Gallery is configured as an upstream package source. You could obviously also configure Chocolatey, an Orchard feed, or your own MyGet feed, or all of them!

These upstream package sources allow you to reference or mirror packages onto your own feed. It also allows you to easily push packages from your feed to the upstream package source, given you configured your API key in the package source configuration.

Adding a package source

To configure a package source for your MyGet feed, navigate to the feed settings and browse the Package Sources tab. Then click Add Package Source.

A dialog will prompt your for package source information and will also expose a few common presets for you to take advantage of, as shown in Figure 8-33.

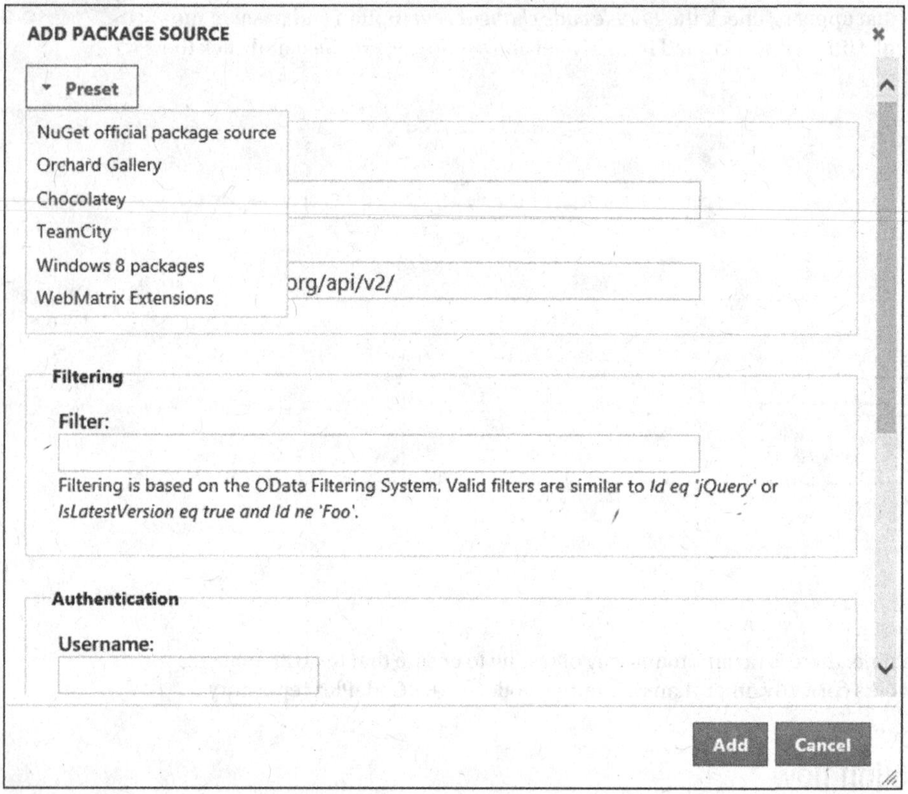

ADD PACKAGE SOURCE   ✕

▾ Preset

NuGet official package source
Orchard Gallery
Chocolatey
TeamCity
Windows 8 packages
WebMatrix Extensions

org/api/v2/

Filtering

Filter:

Filtering is based on the OData Filtering System. Valid filters are similar to *Id eq 'jQuery'* or
IsLatestVersion eq true and Id ne 'Foo'.

Authentication

Username:

[Add] [Cancel]

Figure 8-33. *Add a Package Source to a MyGet feed*

Pushing a package upstream

A major scenario made possible by using package sources is the package promotion workflow: pushing a package
from one feed to another.

Choose the package you want to promote and with a click of a button you can push it upstream. A dialog will
provide you with additional options, e.g. configure the package version to be used upstream, as shown in Figure 8-34.

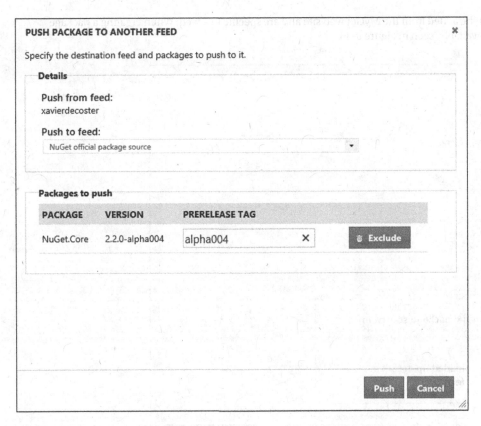

Figure 8-34. *Pushing a package upstream to one of the feed's package sources*

To set up your preferred release cycle for NuGet packages, simply chain up a series of feeds using the package sources system and you'll be able to promote packages within the constraints imposed by this flow with a click of a button.

Working with aggregate feeds

Another scenario for package sources is making MyGet your only NuGet feed. By forwarding package searches and proxying upstream packages, your MyGet feed is a one-stop feed for all packages you are using in your projects.

Figure 8-35 shows this concept in action: all your developers will connect to only one feed, which can hold custom packages, search results and packages from upstream feeds, packages from your TeamCity server and so on. Additionally, upstream packages can be automatically mirrored, making the MyGet feed an ideal backup of all the packages that are being consumed in your projects.

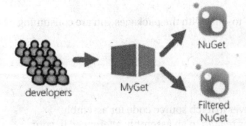

Figure 8-35. *Using a single MyGet feed to proxy various upstream package sources*

Package sources can be added from the MyGet web site and are specific to a feed. When creating a package source, two options are available, seen in Figure 8-36.

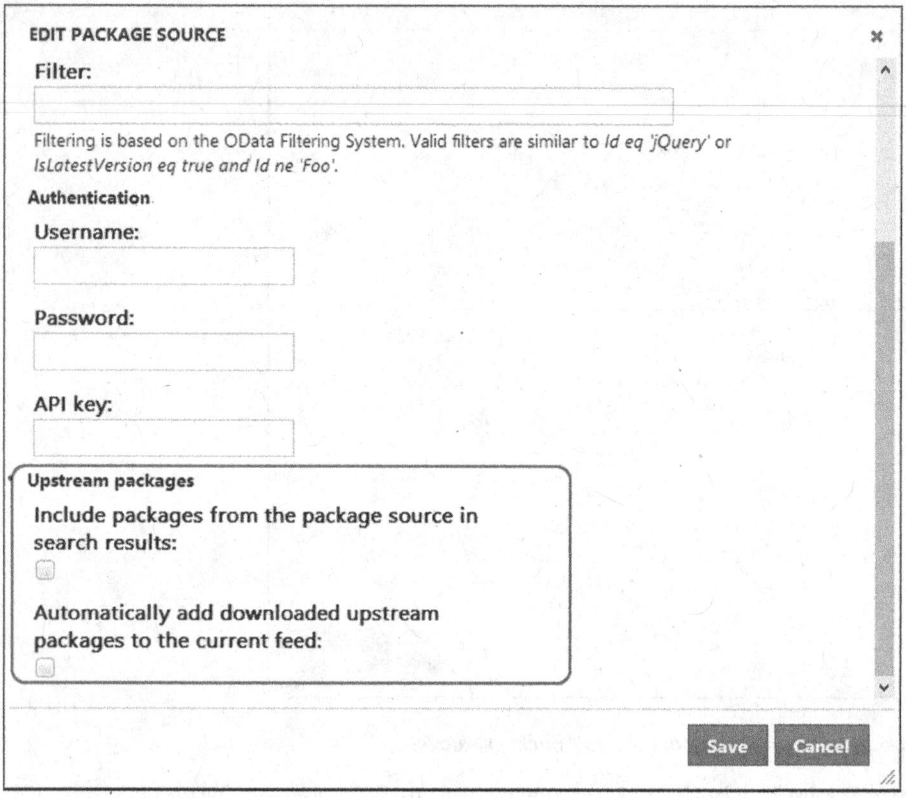

Figure 8-36. *Configuration options for upstream packages in a MyGet feed's package source*

- ***Include packages from the package source in search results:*** the upstream package source will be searched and packages that match the search will be displayed when consuming the feed from Visual Studio. Packages from the upstream source can be installed into a project but will be downloaded from the upstream package source.

- ***Automatically add downloaded upstream packages to the current feed:*** when the above option is enabled, packages that are downloaded will automatically be mirrored on your feed, ensuring the package is available all the time (even when the upstream package source experiences an outage).

Enabling both options will ensure that the MyGet feed is always up-to-date with the packages you are consuming in your organization.

Setting up a Private Symbol Server

In chapter 4, we've seen that Visual Studio can make use of a symbol server to fetch source code for assembly references that you want to debug into. Symbol servers host the .pdb files related to an assembly referenced in your project. When working with NuGet.org, MyGet or ProGet, a symbol server is offered to host symbols for the NuGet packages you publish. But what if you are hosting your own NuGet Server? Or want to have a symbol server that hosts symbols for packages hosted on TeamCity's NuGet server?

You could tinker with Microsoft's Source Server (http://msdn.microsoft.com/en-us/library/ms680641%28v=vs.85%29.aspx), but that would require quite some effort to get up and running in a secure and automated way. The people at SymbolSource.org have a solution! Next to their hosted symbol server, they offer a free-to-use NuGet package which enables you to create your own symbol server which hosts debugger symbols added through NuGet packages. In this section, we will see how to get a symbol server up and running.

Installing prerequisites

The symbol server provided by SymbolSource.org has one dependency which should be installed on your system (or on the server which will host the symbol server): the Debugging Tools for Windows. These can be downloaded from http://msdn.microsoft.com/en-us/windows/hardware/gg463009. These Debugging Tools contain a number of executables that are required for any symbol server to work.

Once downloaded, install the Debugging Tools for Windows by enabling the checkbox for them as seen in Figure 8-37. You can install the other components as well if you need them but for the symbol server you will only need the Debugging Tools.

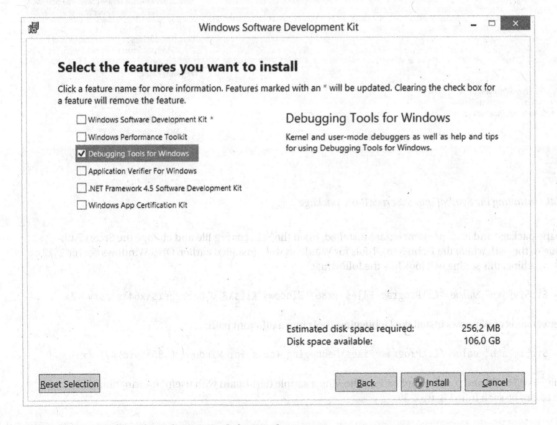

Figure 8-37. Installing the Debugger Tools for Windows

Setting up the Symbol Server

If you have tried creating your own NuGet server in Chapter 5 using the NuGet.Server package, you will find creating a symbol server very similar. In Visual Studio, create a new ASP.NET MVC application using the Empty project template. Once Visual Studio finished project creation, install the SymbolSource.Server.Basic package. As Figure 8-38 shows, this package contains a symbol server and brings down a number of dependencies.

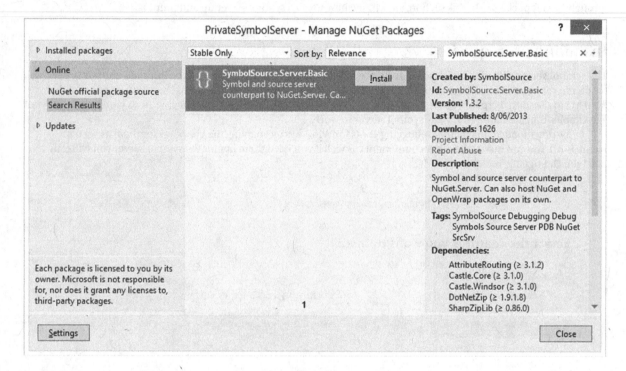

Figure 8-38. *Installing the SymbolSource.Server.Basic package*

Once the package and its dependencies are installed, open the Web.config file and change the SrcSrvPath setting value to the path where the Debugging Tools for Windows were installed earlier. On a Windows Server 2012 or Windows 8 machine, this setting will look like the following:

```
<add key="SrcSrvPath" value="C:\Program Files (x86)\Windows Kits\8.0\Debuggers\x64\srcsrv" />
```

Earlier versions of Windows install the Debugging Tools into a different path:

```
<add key="SrcSrvPath" value="C:\Program Files\Debugging Tools for Windows (x86)\srcsrv" />
```

Hitting F5 will build and run the application, showing a simple dashboard with useful information on the homepage as can be seen from Figure 8-39.

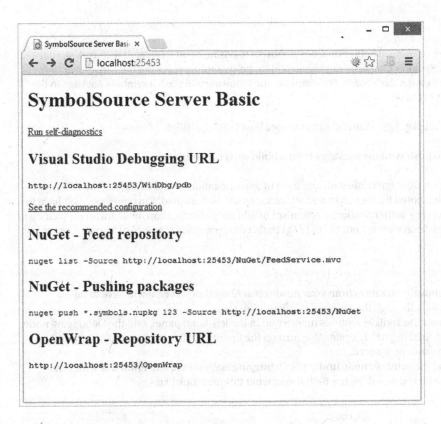

Figure 8-39. SymbolSource server dashboard

Every URL that is available from the symbol server is listed on the application's start page:

- Visual Studio Debugging URL - You need to configure this URL in the Debug settings of your Visual Studio development environment. This configuration cn be done following the steps outlined in chapter 4 of this book.

- NuGet Symbols Packages Repository URL - This is the NuGet package repository where you should push your symbols packages to.

- OpenWrap Repository URL - OpenWrap is another package manager which is supported by SymbolSource.

- Self-diagnostics - This link will help you verify whether the prerequisite is installed and your Web site is configured correctly to provide a fully functioning SymbolSource basic server.

■ **Caution** The SymbolSource basic server comes with no security enabled by default. Make sure to shield the dashboard and self-diagnosis pages from the outside world. Since ELMAH is installed, also follow the best-practices outlined on their wiki at `http://code.google.com/p/elmah/wiki/SecuringErrorLogPages` to ensure logs cannot be accessed by unauthorized users.

Pushing Symbols

Once you have your symbol server running, whether on a development machine or on a server, it will work similar to how SymbolSource.org works. Symbols packages can be pushed to the symbol server using the NuGet Symbols Packages Repository URL outlined on the dashboard. For example, the following will push a symbols package to the server hosted at http://localhost:25453:

```
nuget push MyPackage.symbols.nupkg 123 -Source http://localhost:25453/NuGet
```

The same URL can be used to push symbols packages from a build server, whether Team Foundation Server, TeamCity, Jenkins or other.

Be aware that the symbol server does not come with any form of authentication or authorization: the API key (123 in the above example) will be ignored by the server and all packages will be accepted. Currently, you will have to resort to making use of the web server's authentication mechanism or add an authentication mechanism on your own by downloading and modifying the source code from https://github.com/SymbolSource/SymbolSource.Community.

Consuming Symbols

In order to be able to consume debugging symbols from your newly created symbol server, it will have to be configured in Visual Studio. Let's walk through the required configuration steps.

Open the Options dialog (under the Tools ➤ Options menu) and in the left-hand panel, find the Debugging node. Under General, turn off the option Enable Just My Code. Also turn on the option "Enable source server support." The warning that may pop up can safely be ignored.

Still in the options dialog, find the Symbols node under the Debugging node on the left. From this window, the URL to your symbol server can be registered. Figure 8-40 shows what this may look like.

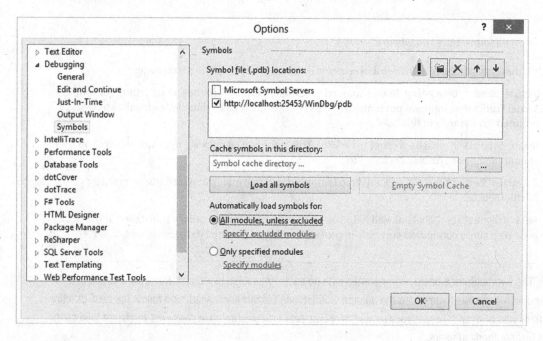

Figure 8-40. *Configuring the symbol server*

From now on, you will be able to debug into installed NuGet packages if debugger symbols are available from your symbol server.

Package Source Discovery

How do you know which feeds are available in your company? How do you know if an open source project provides additional NuGet feeds, for example with nightly builds of their NuGet packages?

NuGet Package Source Discovery (PSD) tries to solve this problem. It allows for NuGet-based clients tools to discover the feeds that are hosted by a user or organization by using the blog or website URL. NuGet Package Source Discovery is an attempt to remove friction from the following scenarios:

- An individual user may have several NuGet feeds spread across the Internet. Some may be on NuGet.org (including curated feeds), some on MyGet and maybe some on my corporate network. How do I easily point my Visual Studio to all my feeds accross different machines? And how do I maintain this configuration?

- An organization may have several feeds internally as well as one on MyGet and some CI packages on TeamCity. How can this organization tell his developers what feeds they can/should use?

- An organization may have a NuGet server containing multiple feeds. How will developers in this organization get a list of available feeds and services?

For all scenarios, a simple feed discovery mechanism could facilitate this. Such feed discovery mechanism could be any URL out there (even multiple per host). As an example of PSD, which has a full spec available at http://psd.myget.org/, try running the following from the Package Manager Console:

```
Install-Package DiscoverPackageSources
Discover-PackageSources -Url "https://www.myget.org/gallery"
```

If you close and re-open Visual Studio and check your package sources, you will see a number of additional NuGet feeds have been registered. This is because https://www.myget.org/gallery provides support for NuGet Package Source Discovery. Glimpse, a popular open-source projects which allows you to peek into what happens on the server when running your ASP.NET application, also makes use of PSD. When discovering feeds from www.getglimpse.com, their nightlies feed as well as a feed which contains various plugins for Glimpse will be added to your package sources.

Now how does this work? By adding one or more simple link elements in the form of `<link rel="nuget" href=http://your.psd.manigest.url />`, PSD can discover feeds. This link element points to a Package Source Discovery manifest, an XML document which describes the feed that can be added. For example, MyGet produces the manifest shown in Listing 8-4 on an anonymous call to https://www.myget.org/Discovery/Feed/googleanalyticstracker.

Listing 8-4. An example PSD manifest.

```
<?xml version="1.0" encoding="utf-8"?>
<rsd version="1.0" xmlns:dc="http://purl.org/dc/elements/1.1/" xmlns="http://archipelago.phrasewise.com/rsd">
  <service>
    <engineName>MyGet</engineName>
    <engineLink>http://www.myget.org/</engineLink>
    <dc:identifier>https://www.myget.org/F/googleanalyticstracker/</dc:identifier>
    <dc:owner>maartenba</dc:owner>
    <dc:creator>maartenba</dc:creator>
    <dc:title>Staging feed for GoogleAnalyticsTracker</dc:title>
    <dc:description>Staging feed for GoogleAnalyticsTracker</dc:description>
```

```
    <homePageLink>http://www.myget.org/Feed/Details/googleanalyticstracker/</homePageLink>
    <apis>
      <api name="nuget-v2-packages" blogID="" preferred="true" apiLink="http://www.myget.org/F/
googleanalyticstracker/" />
      <api name="nuget-v1-packages" blogID="" preferred="false" apiLink="http://www.myget.org/F/
googleanalyticstracker/api/v1/" />
    </apis>
  </service>
</rsd>
```

This manifest can contain several API endpoints, such as the feeds available or the URL to the symbol server. By providing these manifests, it is easier for developer to configure the feeds they need to work with.

More examples and a complete listing of available elements and options can be found at `http://psd.myget.org/`.

Summary

Throughout this chapter, we've seem how NuGet fits in popular tools that are used by many development teams. Creating and publishing a NuGet package during a build on Team Foundation Server or TeamCity, using Windows Azure Web Sites and package restore, working with authenticated feeds and credentials in a continuous integration environment and much more.

Working with these recipes, you should be able to get started with NuGet in your development process with some of the third-party tools out there.

A full overview of the NuGe ecosystem and links to further documentation can be found at `http://docs.nuget.org/docs/reference/ecosystem.`.

■■■

## CHAPTER 9

Extending NuGet

In the previous chapters, we've shown you how you can leverage NuGet in more-advanced scenarios and how NuGet can be the tool of preference for managing external dependencies in your software projects. We've even touched on some alternative scenarios, where NuGet can be used to distribute releases and deploy them onto your server infrastructure.

While all of this is great, there are some use cases we haven't covered yet. The power of NuGet is its simplicity: it enables you to publish and consume packages. There are three major clients that work with NuGet. And all three of them can be extended to give you more power. For example, wouldn't you like to know how you can make yourself or your development team more productive? Or how you can get a grasp on what external dependencies are being used in your projects?

This chapter will focus on these questions and will provide the required starting points to extend NuGet on your machine, or the machines of your team, to make software development more fun. We'll start with a quick *why* before we dive into the more technical part, where we'll be creating plug-ins and extensions for all three clients—simple, basic things that you can extend or build upon to achieve super powers.

Why Extend NuGet?

The enthusiast software developer in you may answer the question of why one should extend NuGet with an energetic "because I can!" While that is a valid reason (and also the reason why we started looking into extending NuGet), there are some better reasons to do so as well.

If you've heard about Git, a distributed version control system (DVCS) that gained enormous popularity in the open source world thanks to GitHub.com, you may be aware that Git offers various extensions. In fact, the Git source control system is fairly easy and does not contain a lot of commands at its core. The real value of Git as a source control system comes from its easy-to-create extensions, of which a lot are available.

A parallel can be drawn to NuGet. Out of the box, the NuGet command line knows the commands list, pack, push, setApiKey, install, restore, upgrade, and uninstall. Those commands give you a great base set of functionality; you can do everything you probably want to do with them. But what about copying a package from one feed to another? A nuget copy command would come in handy there. What about knowing about all packages and their dependencies without having to open every single project in Visual Studio? Wouldn't nuget analyze be useful?

Similarly, for the NuGet Package Manager Console, it's great to have some functionality out of the box. Knowing that the Package Manager Console is just a PowerShell console with some added variables (such as $dte, an object representing Visual Studio) makes it an incredibly powerful tool to extend your development process. What about creating Team Foundation Server (TFS) work items or YouTrack issues from the Package Manager Console? What about writing packages that add some to-do tasks to your list of work items? What about adding code generation or even a Bing search in there?

NuGet Package Explorer (NPE) is a great tool to work with NuGet packages and inspect what is going on in there. The lib folder in NuGet packages typically contains only an assembly and not source code. How about creating an NPE plug-in that allows you to decompile assemblies in a NuGet package and browse through the source code of the packages you download?

We've just scratched the surface in this section: all tools are there for you to use; all extension points are available. This chapter will give you some starters on how to extend the various tools, but we'll leave the implementation of the cool stuff to you. And when you're finished, why not publish your extensions on NuGet so everyone can use them?

Extending the NuGet Command Line

The NuGet command-line tool is built in a very extensible fashion. For starters, every command that the command-line tool exposes implements the same ICommand interface. In addition, the tool is using the Managed Extensibility Framework (MEF) to import (actually ImportMany) these commands within the scope of the application's lifetime. It does this by scanning its own assemblies and a special extensions folder defined by the command-line tool. It is the exact same folder used when deploying a custom package analysis rule. This special extensions folder can be found in the following location on your system:

```
%LocalAppData%\NuGet\Commands
```

Because the NuGet command line is scanning this extension folder upon startup, it will automatically detect any assembly within that directory or any of its subdirectories that contains an export of a well-known type.

■ **Note**   The NuGet command-line tool is a very nice example of how one could design an application open for extensibility, by making good use of the Managed Extensibility Framework (MEF). MEF is an interesting topic on its own and has shipped as part of the .NET Framework since version 4.0. If you haven't heard about it before, we highly recommend you read up on MSDN (http://msdn.microsoft.com/en-us/library/dd460648.aspx). And you can also dive into the sources and examples on CodePlex (http://mef.codeplex.com).

Some of the exports that will be scanned for are implementations of NuGet's ICommand interface. The ICommand interface is decorated with MEF's InheritedExport attribute, as shown in Listing 9-1, declaring that any implementing type will be exported as an implementation of type ICommand.

Listing 9-1. The NuGet Command-Line ICommand Interface

```
[InheritedExport]
public interface ICommand
{
    CommandAttribute CommandAttribute { get; }
    IList<string> Arguments { get; }
    void Execute();
}
```

To be able to create your own custom ICommand implementation, you'll have to add a reference in your project to the nuget.exe file—that's right, to the NuGet command-line tool itself! All you need to do is implement the interface, compile your assembly that exports your custom commands, and deploy it into the NuGet extensions directory. The concept is very simple yet so powerful.

■ **Tip** The commands available in NuGet are implemented in the same way as a command-line extension is created for NuGet. This means that, if you want to create a command similar to the existing NuGet commands, you can easily peek at the NuGet source code. Also, if you want to borrow code that accesses an external package source, many good examples can be found in the NuGet source code.

One such example is the `nuget install` command, for which you can find the sources at `https://nuget.codeplex.com/SourceControl/latest#src/CommandLine/Commands/InstallCommand.cs`.

Creating a Custom NuGet Command

Creating a custom NuGet command is as easy as implementing the ICommand interface or its easy-to-use companion, the Command class. This interface (and companion class) can be found in the nuget.exe assembly. Here are the steps required to get started in Visual Studio:

1. Create a new Visual Studio solution, and add a class library project by using the full .NET 4.0 Framework.

2. Add a NuGet reference to Nuget.CommandLine (Install-Package Nuget.CommandLine).

3. Manually add a reference to nuget.exe. You'll find it in your solution's packages folder, where you installed Nuget.CommandLine in the previous step. Adding a reference to nuget.exe gives you access to the ICommand interface, the Command class, and the CommandAttribute class.

4. Add a reference to System.ComponentModel.Composition (the Managed Extensibility Framework).

The ICommand interface is very straightforward to implement, as it contains only one method, Execute, and a read-only property, IList<string> Arguments. Obviously, the Execute method executes the command, and the Arguments property gives you access to any command-line arguments received by the console.

To make things even easier for you, you can also inherit from a base class implementing this ICommand interface and providing you with some common NuGet command behavior, such as integrated help from the command line. This integrated help gives your custom command support for the help (or ?) option, so you can output some help information to the user instead. This way, you can provide guidance to users requesting help by executing the command nuget help or nuget help myCustomCommand. The base class we refer to is called Command and can be found in the NuGet.Commands namespace of the nuget.exe assembly.

■ **Tip** We really encourage you to reuse this base class and benefit from its integrated help functionality to provide your users with a consistent NuGet command-line experience.

To get started, take a look at the NuGet.Analyze package, which provides some analysis functionality on top of source code repositories consuming NuGet packages. The package is a first attempt to automate the creation of a dependency grid for a given project, which is currently a manual and time-consuming task, often forgotten or allowed to become out-of-date. However, NuGet stores all your dependencies in a nice XML file (the packages.config file) relative to each Visual Studio project, as well as storing a reference to all these XML files in a central repositories.config file in the solution's packages folder. This is very useful information stored in a well-known format, so analysis of these files should be pretty straightforward.

For any solution that is consuming NuGet packages, you can find out which module of the product (or project of the solution) has which dependencies, even without parsing the information inside the source code itself. Therefore, one should be able to point NuGet to a solution file and get a real-time view on its dependencies. The output could be used as a generated dependency matrix for the given target solution.

The NuGet.Analyze package has support for both Team Foundation Server source control and local (or remote) file system folders. This should cover most source control systems in a first attempt. Of course, as the entire thing is open source as well, feel free to contribute your own ideas and send a pull request. The source code can be found at https://github.com/xavierdecoster/NuGet.Analyze.

Let's take a closer look at AnalyzeCommand, which you can find in the source code. You'll notice the usage of a few attributes in that class, as shown in Listing 9-2.

Listing 9-2. Implementing a Custom NuGet Command-Line Command

```
[Command(typeof(AnalyzeCommandResources), "analyze", "AnalyzeCommandDescription",
UsageSummaryResourceName = "AnalyzeCommandUsageSummary",
MinArgs = 0, MaxArgs = 1,AltName = "analyse")]
public class AnalyzeCommand : Command
{
    public override void ExecuteCommand()
    {
        ...
    }
}
```

To create a basic command, you simply inherit from Command and implement the abstract ExecuteCommand method. However, you still need to expose a little metadata for the NuGet command line to know how to deal with this command. That's where CommandAttribute comes in, which you can see decorated on top of the class declaration. Nuget.exe will process this information and learn that the analyze command corresponds to the AnalyzeCommand type. An alternative name for the command has been provided as well: analyse.

Helpful information, such as a usage summary, can be found in the AnalyzeCommandResources file by using the key AnalyzeCommandUsageSummary. Figure 9-1 shows you what the AnalyzeCommandResources file looks like.

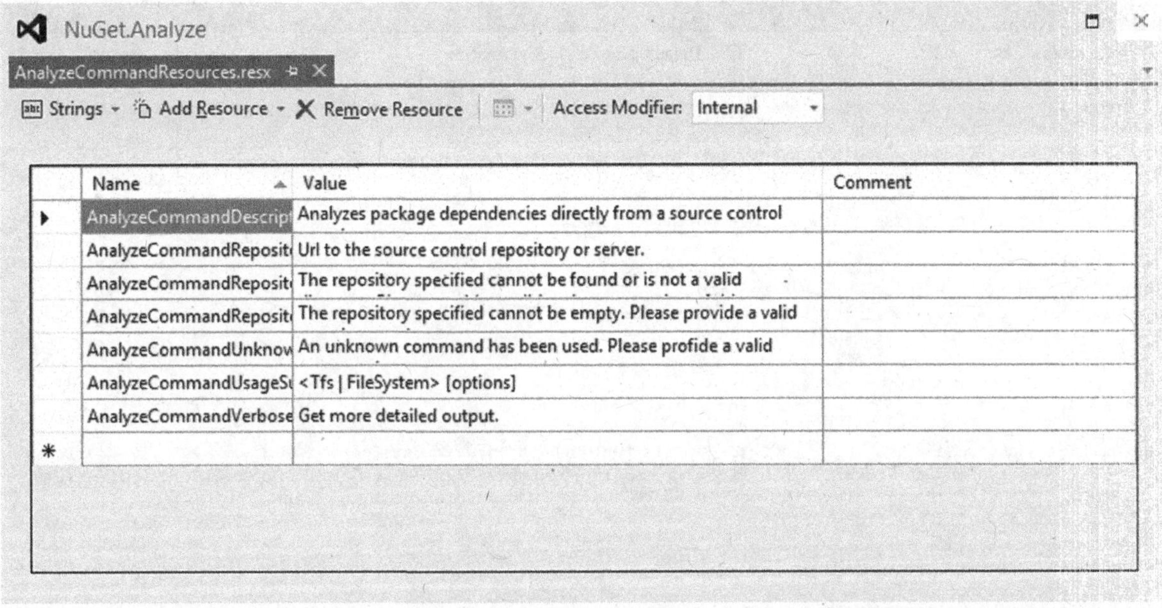

Figure 9-1. *The AnalyzeCommandResources file containing all messages related to the Analyze command we are creating*

Using the `CommandAttribute`, the NuGet command line also knows that zero or one argument can be passed to this command. That's a lot of information in a single attribute, but it gives you a lot of flexibility to implement your command as you want, without needing to take care of plumbing your command into the command-line tool to make it integrate nicely.

We already mentioned that you inherit support for the help option when deriving from `Command`, but you can create additional options or flags that can give an extra meaning or different behavior to your custom command. For example, Listing 9-3 implements an argument as a simple property, decorated with the `OptionAttribute`. Figure 9-1 contains the messages referred to by the `OptionAttribute` as well.

Listing 9-3. Implementing an Optional Flag for a Custom Command

```
[Option(typeof(AnalyzeCommandResources), "AnalyzeCommandVerboseDescription")]
public bool Verbose { get; set; }
```

Installing a Custom NuGet Command

You now have learned all there is to extending the NuGet command line with your own custom commands: inherit `Command` and distribute the compiled assembly to the NuGet extensions directory. The classical way of installing a command-line extension is shown in Listing 9-4.

Listing 9-4. Installing a NuGet Command-Line Extension the Classical Way

```
nuget.exe install /excludeversion /outputdir "%LocalAppData%\NuGet\Commands" MyCustomExtension
```

How do you feel about distributing those assemblies? What if we could make NuGet extend itself and distribute NuGet command-line extensions by using NuGet packages?

Luckily for you, there is a package for that! It's called `NuGet.InstallCommandLineExtension` and is available at NuGet.org. Figure 9-2 shows `NuGet.InstallCommandLineExtension` in action.

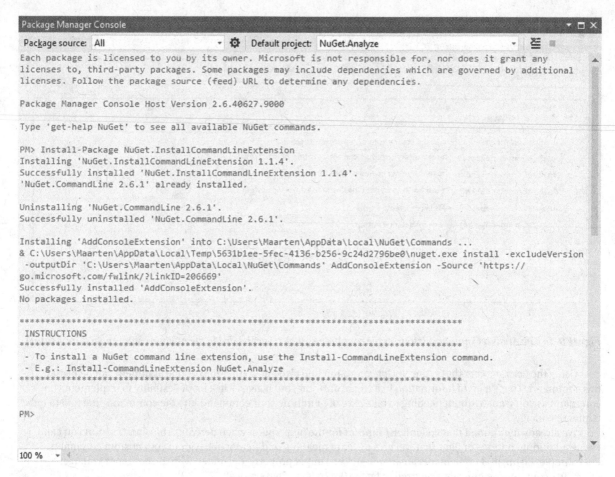

Figure 9-2. Installing the NuGet.InstallCommandLineExtension package using the NuGet Package Manager Console

Installing the NuGet.InstallCommandLineExtension package performs two actions: it will install a first NuGet command-line extension, called AddConsoleExtension, and it will install a custom PowerShell cmdlet into the Package Manager Console, called Install-CommandLineExtension. This gives you two different ways of extending the NuGet command line in a way you already know and love—by using NuGet itself.

Now let's install the NuGet.Analyze extension containing the nuget analyze command. From the Visual Studio Package Manager Console, we can execute the following command:

```
Install-CommandLineExtension NuGet.Analyze
```

Once our NuGet command-line extension is installed, we are able to run it. We even get help information, by running the nuget help analyze command. Figure 9-3 shows the help command in action.

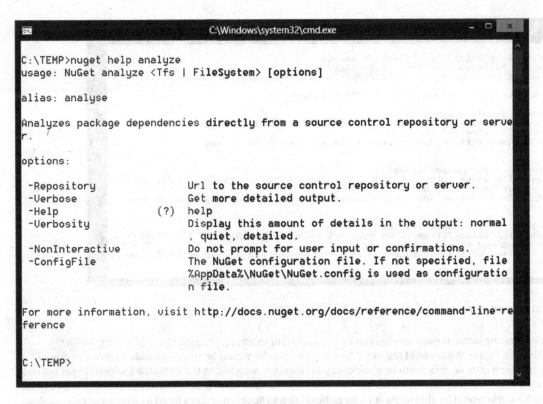

```
C:\Windows\system32\cmd.exe                                          _  □  ×

C:\TEMP>nuget help analyze
usage: NuGet analyze <Tfs | FileSystem> [options]

alias: analyse

Analyzes package dependencies directly from a source control repository or serve
r.

options:

 -Repository              Url to the source control repository or server.
 -Verbose                 Get more detailed output.
 -Help              (?)   help
 -Verbosity               Display this amount of details in the output: normal
                          , quiet, detailed.
 -NonInteractive          Do not prompt for user input or confirmations.
 -ConfigFile              The NuGet configuration file. If not specified, file
                          %AppData%\NuGet\NuGet.config is used as configuratio
                          n file.

For more information, visit http://docs.nuget.org/docs/reference/command-line-re
ference


C:\TEMP>
```

Figure 9-3. *Help information for our NuGet command-line extension*

Go on and create your own extensions! Maybe an extension to clean the NuGet cache would be nice. Or one that copies NuGet packages from one feed to another. Or one that downloads all packages from a given feed to create a backup.

▪ **Note** The NuGet Package Source Discovery (PSD) protocol that is described at https://github.com/myget/ PackageSourceDiscovery also offers a custom NuGet command. NuGet PSD allows for NuGet-based clients' tools to discover the feeds that are hosted by a user or organization by using the blog or web site URL. For example, if you have a blog, you could add a simple <link /> tag to your site (such as <link rel="nuget" type="application/rsd+xml" title="GoogleAnalyticsTracker feed on MyGet" href="https://www.myget.org/discovery/feed/ googleanalyticstracker"/>). By installing the PSD extension to the NuGet command line, users of your custom NuGet feed will be able to automatically discover the feed URL and its name by running nuget discover -Url "http://yoursite.com. Source code for this extension can be found at https://github.com/myget/PackageSourceDiscovery/tree/master/ src/Extension.

Creating Custom Package Analysis Rules

When creating NuGet packages by using the NuGet command line, you may have encountered warnings. For example, when you are working with a generated .nuspec file and don't make any changes, chances are you might be seeing a lot of these warnings. Figure 9-4 shows what we mean by them.

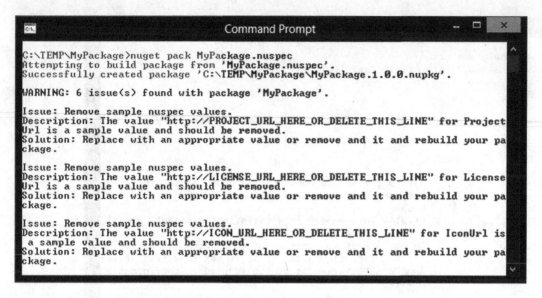

Figure 9-4. *A number of warnings when creating a NuGet package*

What is interesting is that these warnings can be extended. For example, imagine you are building NuGet packages inside your team. What would happen if, say, a certificate file would be shipped inside a NuGet package? Perhaps you require a `.cer` or `.pfx` file to be present in your local working folder, but if this file happens to get packed into a NuGet package, that may turn into a disaster: all team members would suddenly have this certificate. Or even worse, the entire world would be able to use it when publishing it to `NuGet.org`. Let's build a custom package analysis rule that prevents us from adding certain file extensions to our packages.

Just as when creating custom NuGet commands, you have to create a new class library project targeting the .NET 4.0 Framework, reference the `System.ComponentModel.Composition` namespace in which MEF resides, install `NuGet.CommandLine` into the project, and add an assembly reference to the `nuget.exe` file it installed.

Once all that is done, we can start creating our custom validation rule. First of all, you'll have to implement the `IPackageRule` interface, which is located in the `nuget.exe` file that is referenced. Also add `ExportAttribute` to the class, which will hold the custom package analysis rule, so `nuget.exe` will be able to pick it up and run it when creating a NuGet package.

```
[Export(typeof(IPackageRule))]
public sealed class CertificateRule : IPackageRule
{
    public IEnumerable<PackageIssue> Validate(IPackage package)
    {
        // code will go here
    }
}
```

The actual package validation logic will go in the `Validate` method. This method will be called by `nuget.exe` when creating a NuGet package and receives all package data: metadata such as package ID and version, as well as the files included in the package, their names, and data. If you don't want `.cer` or `.pfx` files included in a NuGet package, simply scan for any file that matches these extensions and yield a `PackageIssue` instance, which can return either a warning or an error. The full code for the `CertificateRule` class that holds our custom validation can be seen in Listing 9-5.

Listing 9-5. *A Custom Package Analysis Rule for NuGet That Scans the Package for Forbidden File Extensions*

```
[Export(typeof(IPackageRule))]
public sealed class CertificateRule : IPackageRule
{
    private readonly string[] _forbiddenExtensions = { ".cer", ".pfx" };

    public IEnumerable<PackageIssue> Validate(IPackage package)
    {
        // Loop through all files and match them with _forbiddenExtensions
        foreach (var packageFile in package.GetFiles())
        {
            if (_forbiddenExtensions.Any(
                extension => extension == Path.GetExtension(
                                        packageFile.Path).ToLowerInvariant()))
            {
                yield return new PackageIssue(
                    "Forbidden file extension found",
                    string.Format("The file {0} is of a forbidden file extension and may not be
                                    included in a NuGet package.", packageFile.Path),
                    "Remove it from the package folder.",
                    PackageIssueLevel.Error);
            }
        }
    }
}
```

If you compile the project and copy its assemblies into the %LocalAppData%\NuGet\Commands folder on your system, the NuGet command line will pick up the package validation rule. This folder can hold NuGet command-line extensions as well as custom package analysis rules. If you now try to create a NuGet package that holds a .cer or .pfx file, a package issue will be shown, as can be seen in Figure 9-5.

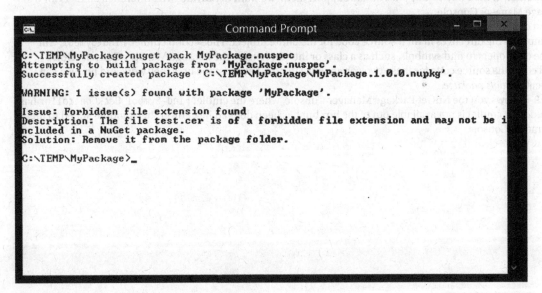

Figure 9-5. *A custom package analysis rule in action, scanning for forbidden file extensions*

■ **Note** Xavier has written a package analysis rule that ensures the package version complies with semantic versioning. It can be found on his blog at www.xavierdecoster.com/nuget-package-analysis-encouraging-semantic-versioning. This is a good example of a useful package analysis rule, and we think every package author should have it installed.

Extending the Package Manager Console

So far, you've seen how you can extend the NuGet command line. While handy, NuGet extensions of this type worked only from the command prompt. What about extending Visual Studio? The Package Manager Console is just a PowerShell console with additional variables such as $dte, an object representing Visual Studio itself.

NuGet already speeds up your development in terms of dependency management, but having the Package Manager Console at hand, inside Visual Studio, makes NuGet incredibly powerful for extending your Visual Studio environment as well.

This section will guide you through the creation of PowerShell cmdlets that can be run in the Package Manager Console. It starts with some simple cmdlets that (of course) will be distributed through NuGet. After that, we'll create a more advanced cmdlet that also includes tab completion to make using the cmdlet even easier.

■ **Tip** An interesting Package Manager Console extension we've found is Steve Sanderson's MvcScaffolding package. It adds PowerShell cmdlets to the NuGet Package Manager Console and enables you to generate code in ASP.NET MVC.

Creating and Distributing a Package Manager Console Extension

Let's start the creation of a NuGet Package Manager Console extension by defining what we want to achieve. Visual Studio exposes a lot of functionality hidden in menus and keyboard shortcuts. Some developers are very keyboard-oriented in their day-to-day jobs, and to support them, we want to provide two PowerShell cmdlets for use in the Package Manager Console.

The first cmdlet, Remove-Usings, will enable any developers who have installed the extension we're creating to sort and remove using directives in their source code for the entire project. The second cmdlet, Find-Symbol, will enable those developers to find symbols, such as a class or interface, using the Package Manager Console. Don't worry: we'll cover the source code for these two commands later on. Let's first see how they work and how we can create a so-called *tools package*.

Figure 9-6 shows you the NuGet Package Manager Console, where the cmdlet Find-Symbol DeckController has been invoked. This cmdlet is not available out of the box but has been defined in a PowerShell module added to the Package Manager Console.

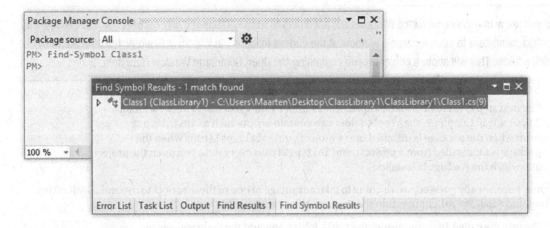

Figure 9-6. *The Package Manager Console executing a custom cmdlet named Find-Symbol*

Creating a NuGet Package Folder Structure

The Package Manager Console extension we are creating will be distributed through NuGet, so we'll have to create a NuGet package for that. In this section, we'll be using a simple approach to create a NuGet package: create a folder, create a NuGet package manifest, and invoke the nuget pack command.

Let's do that step by step.

1. First of all, create a folder on your hard drive that will mimic the NuGet package contents. Maarten has created C:\Temp\VsCommands for that, but the exact location does not really matter.

2. Next, open a command prompt and run the nuget spec VsCommands command. This will create a NuGet package manifest (the .nuspec file) named VsCommands.nuspec. Open the file in Notepad (or any other text editor) and update the XML to something along the lines of Listing 9-6.

Listing 9-6. The NuGet Package Manifest for Our Package Manager Console Extension

```xml
<?xml version="1.0"?>
<package>
  <metadata>
    <id>VsCommands</id>
    <version>1.0.0</version>
    <authors>Maarten Balliauw</authors>
    <owners>Maarten Balliauw</owners>
    <requireLicenseAcceptance>false</requireLicenseAcceptance>
    <description>Adds cmd-lets NuGet PowerShell Console.</description>
    <releaseNotes>Adds cmd-lets to the NuGet PowerShell Console.</releaseNotes>
    <copyright>Copyright Maarten Balliauw 2011</copyright>
    <tags>nuget powershell pronuget apress</tags>
  </metadata>
</package>
```

■ **Tip** Did you know that Windows (since Windows 95, according to http://support.microsoft.com/kb/126449) has a hidden context menu item to open a console window at the current location? In Windows Explorer, hold the Shift key and right-click a folder. This will show a context menu containing the Open Command Window Here item.

3.   The next step is to create a folder called \tools under your VsCommands folder structure. As you saw in Chapter 3, the \tools folder can contain scripts such as install.ps1 (runs when the package is installed into a project), uninstall.ps1 (runs when the package is uninstalled from a project), and init.ps1 (runs every time you open the project into which the package is installed).

As you may have already guessed, we're going to take advantage of one of these scripts to dynamically load our Remove-Usings and Find-Symbol cmdlets into the Package Manager Console.

4.   Create a file called init.ps1 under the tools folder, and add the code you see in Listing 9-7. This code is a (short) PowerShell script that will be executed every time Visual Studio loads a project containing the VsCommands NuGet package we are creating.

Listing 9-7. The init.ps1 PowerShell Script for our Package Manager Console Extension

```
param($installPath, $toolsPath, $package)
Import-Module (Join-Path $toolsPath VsCommands.psm1)
```

There are two important things to note in the init.ps1 script. The first line of code accepts some parameters the Package Manager Console hands to our PowerShell script. These contain the installation path to your package, the tools path, and the package itself. You are not obliged to use them, but there are scenarios where you may want to use this data to take action. For example, you can use the $installPath parameter to write additional files into the project.

The second line of code imports a PowerShell module into the Package Manager Console. As you can see, we're loading the module named VsCommands.psm1. Aha! This is where the actual Package Manager Console extension is defined. The VsCommands.psm1 file is a regular PowerShell module, which is simply being imported into the Package Manager Console PowerShell host.

5.   Create a new file named VsCommands.psm1 in the tools folder.

■ **Note** Advice on writing PowerShell script modules, as we will be doing in the VsCommands.psm1 file, is worth a book in itself. If you want to know everything about it, or just want to dive into specifics such as providing output when the Get-Help cmdlet is invoked on your extensions, refer to the MSDN pages at http://msdn.microsoft.com/en-us/library/dd878340(v=VS.85).aspx. Also, the Apress book *Pro Windows PowerShell* by Hristo Deshev (ISBN: 978-1-59059-940-2) may come in handy.

Creating the Package Manager Console Extension

In the previous section, we created the required NuGet package folder structure. The VsCommands.psm1 file in the tools folder is still empty. In this section, we'll add the required PowerShell code that implements our Remove-Usings and Find-Symbol cmdlets.

The VsCommands.psm1 script will have access to the NuGet Package Manager Console and therefore to global variables such as $dte, an object representing Visual Studio. Cmdlets you already know (and love?) such as

Get-Project and Install-Package are available as well; the complete list of available NuGet PowerShell cmdlets can be found in Appendix C.

Given the fact that we have access to the $dte object, the Package Manager Console has access to the Visual Studio environment. This opens the possibility we are looking for: to interact with Visual Studio.

■ **Tip** A list of properties and methods available on the $dte object can be found on the MSDN page at http://msdn.microsoft.com/en-us/library/envdte.dte.aspx. James Chambers also did a great job collecting some PowerShell snippets in various NuGet packages and posted a list of $dte interactions and other samples at http://jameschambers.com/blog/powershell-script-examples-for-nuget-packages.

Let's start with implementing the Remove-Usings cmdlet. Since it will accept no parameters, it's just a PowerShell function that executes a method on the $dte object. Here's the definition of the Remove-Usings cmdlet:

```
function Remove-Usings {
    $dte.ExecuteCommand("ProjectandSolutionContextMenus.Project.RemoveandSortUsings")
}
```

When the Remove-Usings command is executed, the $dte object's ExecuteCommand method is called, passing the Visual Studio command name we expect to be executed. A list of possible Visual Studio commands is hidden inside Visual Studio: open the Tools ➤ Options menu and find the Environment ➤ Keyboard tab. This will give you a searchable list of all commands available in Visual Studio.

The Find-Symbol cmdlet for our VsCommands Package Manager Console extension will accept a parameter: if we want to find a class or interface, it'll be crucial to know what to search for. Here's the code for the Find-Symbol cmdlet:

```
function Find-Symbol {
    param(
        [parameter(ValueFromPipelineByPropertyName = $true)]
        [string]$Name
    )

    $dte.ExecuteCommand("Edit.FindSymbol", $Name)
}
```

Again, we're simply delegating the actual work to Visual Studio. The Edit.FindSymbol cmdlet exposed by the $dte object's ExecuteCommand method will search for the symbol.

There is one missing part in our VsCommands.psm1 file: we need to tell PowerShell to expose all cmdlets to the outside world. In their current state, the only place where Remove-Usings and Find-Symbol can be executed is inside the VsCommands.psm1 file itself. Solving that is easy: PowerShell's Export-ModuleMember cmdlet will allow you to expose all (or some specific) functions to the Package Manager Console PowerShell host.

The complete source code for VsCommands.psm1, including the call to Export-ModuleMember at the bottom, can be seen in Listing 9-8.

Listing 9-8. The VsCommands.psm1 File Containing the Actual Implementation of the Package Manager Console Extension

```
function Remove-Usings {
    $dte.ExecuteCommand("ProjectandSolutionContextMenus.Project.RemoveandSortUsings")
}
```

```
function Find-Symbol {
    param(
        [parameter(ValueFromPipelineByPropertyName = $true)]
        [string]$Name
    )

    $dte.ExecuteCommand("Edit.FindSymbol", $Name)
}

Export-ModuleMember -Function *
```

Distributing the Package Manager Console Extension

Now that the PowerShell scripts for our Package Manager Console extension are ready, it's time to gather everything as a NuGet package and get the extension out there. Packaging the extension is easy; by now, you should know the nuget pack command. Distributing the package is easy as well; nuget push should do the trick.

In the folder containing the VsCommands.nuspec file, open a command prompt and run the nuget pack command. After you've run this command, a NuGet package for your Package Manager Console extension has been created.

The VsCommands.1.0.0.nupkg file can be pushed to NuGet.org or to your private NuGet feed. For this book, Maarten has pushed the package to a feed on MyGet that we've created for this book, https://www.myget.org/F/pronuget. Feel free to add this package source in Visual Studio and install the VsCommands package. Figure 9-7 shows the output for both the nuget pack and nuget push commands.

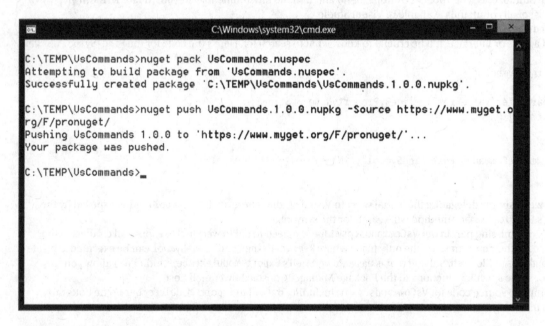

Figure 9-7. Results of packaging and publishing the VsCommands.1.0.0.nupkg package

Adding Tab Expansions to Package Manager Console Extensions

The VsCommand commands we created in the previous section were simple to create and use. There was no need for a lot of documentation or samples because both cmdlets were straightforward. Things are different if you create more-complex cmdlets.

One of the things you may have noticed when using the NuGet Package Manager Console is the support for tab expansions, an idea similar to the IntelliSense you know and love when editing code in Visual Studio. Figure 9-8 shows you an example of tab expansion. When working with the Get-Package cmdlet, every option available features a menu of possible values when pressing the Tab key.

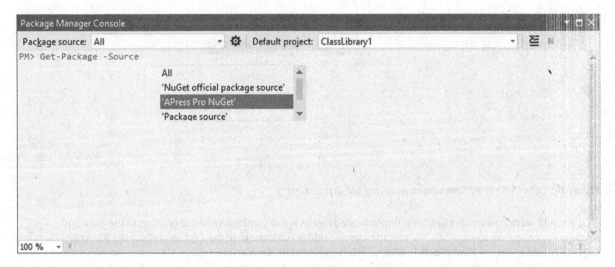

Figure 9-8. *Tab expansion in action after pressing the Tab key in the Package Manager Console*

For this section, find the source code related to this book on the Apress website at www.apress.com/9781430260011 or in our GitHub repository at www.github.com/myget/pronuget. We won't dive into creating a Package Manager Console extension from scratch again; instead, we'll have a quick look at the TfsCommands.psm1 PowerShell module, which you can download from the Apress web site. If you just want to test the TfsCommands commands, find them on the www.myget.org/F/pronuget NuGet feed for this book.

The TfsCommands extension features several PowerShell cmdlets that can be used when your project is added to a Team Foundation Server (TFS) server and a connection to that server has been established in Visual Studio. It features the following cmdlets:

- Get-CurrentTfsCollectionUri: Returns the URL for the TFS server to which you are currently connected

- Get-CurrentTfsProjectName: Returns the TFS project name to which you are currently connected

- Get-TfsProjectNames: Returns all projects for the TFS server to which you are currently connected

- Get-WorkItemTypes: Returns the work item types available in the TFS project to which you are currently connected

- Add-WorkItem: Creates a TFS work item in a specified project

The Add-WorkItem cmdlet is hard to use in the Package Manager Console. It requires you to specify a number of parameters (-Title, -Description, -WorkItemType, -TfsCollectionUri, and -Project). Wouldn't it be great to have tab expansions for these cmdlets? Figure 9-9 shows you what we are aiming for.

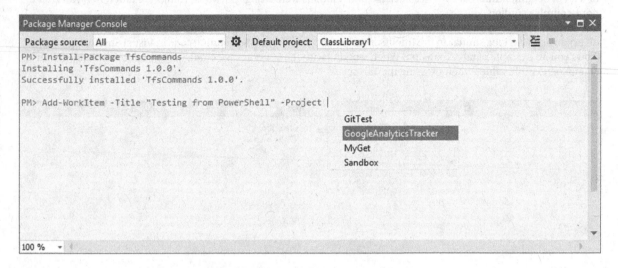

Figure 9-9. *Our Add-WorkItem cmdlet featuring tab expansions*

The Add-WorkItem cmdlet has been implemented just as we've implemented the cmdlets in the previous section. To achieve tab expansions, we've added some code at the bottom of the TfsCommands.psm1 file. Using the Register-TabExpansion PowerShell cmdlet, which is provided by the NuGet Package Manager Console, we can instruct the Package Manager Console to enable tab expansions for a given cmdlet. Listing 9-8 shows you how to do this.

Tab expansions can be static, based on an array of possible values, or dynamic, querying for data through other PowerShell cmdlets or remote servers. In Listing 9-9, note the Title and Description tab expansions will simply return a list of strings containing some sample data of what the user may pass into these cmdlet parameters. The WorkItemType, TfsCollectionUri, and Project tab expansions are slightly more complicated: these call into another PowerShell cmdlet to retrieve their data.

Listing 9-9. The Tab Expansion Registration

```
Register-TabExpansion 'Add-WorkItem' @{
    'Title' = {
        "Implement feature X",
        "Verify bug Y"
    }
    'Description' = {
        "Please implement feature X",
        "Bug Y has not been verified yet. Please take care of it."
    }
    'WorkItemType' = { Get-WorkItemTypes | Select -ExpandProperty Name }
    'TfsCollectionUri' = { Get-CurrentTfsCollectionUri }
    'Project' = { Get-TfsProjectNames | Select -ExpandProperty Name }
}
```

PUTTING TOGETHER THE MODULE'S CODE

In this section, you'll find the complete source code for this module.

```
function Get-CurrentTfsCollectionUri {
    [System.Reflection.Assembly]::LoadWithPartialName(
        "Microsoft.VisualStudio.TeamFoundation") | Out-Null

    if ($dte -ne $null) {
        $tfs = $dte.GetObject(
            "Microsoft.VisualStudio.TeamFoundation.TeamFoundationServerExt")
        $tfs.ActiveProjectContext.DomainUri
    }
}

function Get-CurrentTfsProjectName {
    [System.Reflection.Assembly]::LoadWithPartialName(
        "Microsoft.VisualStudio.TeamFoundation") | Out-Null

    if ($dte -ne $null) {
        $tfs = $dte.GetObject(
            "Microsoft.VisualStudio.TeamFoundation.TeamFoundationServerExt")
        $tfs.ActiveProjectContext.ProjectName
    }
}

function Get-TfsProjectNames {
    [System.Reflection.Assembly]::LoadWithPartialName(
        "Microsoft.VisualStudio.TeamFoundation") | Out-Null

    if ($dte -ne $null) {
        $tfs = $dte.GetObject(
            "Microsoft.VisualStudio.TeamFoundation.TeamFoundationServerExt")
        $TfsCollectionUri = $tfs.ActiveProjectContext.DomainUri

[psobject]$tfs = [Microsoft.TeamFoundation.Client.TeamFoundationServerFactory]::GetServer(
 $TfsCollectionUri)
    $wit = $tfs.GetService(
            [Microsoft.TeamFoundation.WorkItemTracking.Client.WorkItemStore])

return $wit.Projects
    }
}

function Get-WorkItemTypes {
    param(
        [parameter(Mandatory = $false)]
        [string]$TfsCollectionUri,
        [parameter(Mandatory = $false)]
        [string]$Project
    )
```

```
    [System.Reflection.Assembly]::LoadWithPartialName(
        "Microsoft.VisualStudio.TeamFoundation") | Out-Null
    [System.Reflection.Assembly]::LoadWithPartialName(
        "Microsoft.TeamFoundation.Client") | Out-Null
    [System.Reflection.Assembly]::LoadWithPartialName(
        "Microsoft.TeamFoundation.WorkItemTracking.Client") | Out-Null
    [System.Reflection.Assembly]::LoadWithPartialName(
        "Microsoft.TeamFoundation.WorkItemTracking.Client.WorkItemStore") | Out-Null

    if ($TfsCollectionUri -ne $null -and $dte -ne $null) {
        $tfs = $dte.GetObject(
            "Microsoft.VisualStudio.TeamFoundation.TeamFoundationServerExt")
        $TfsCollectionUri = $tfs.ActiveProjectContext.DomainUri
    }

    if ($Project -eq $null -ne $null -and $dte -ne $null) {
        $tfs = $dte.GetObject(
            "Microsoft.VisualStudio.TeamFoundation.TeamFoundationServerExt")
        $Project = $tfs.ActiveProjectContext.ProjectName
    }

    [psobject]$tfs =[Microsoft.TeamFoundation.Client.TeamFoundationServerFactory]
        ::GetServer($TfsCollectionUri)
    $wit = $tfs.GetService(
        [Microsoft.TeamFoundation.WorkItemTracking.Client.WorkItemStore])
    return $wit.Projects[$Project].WorkItemTypes
}

function Add-WorkItem {
    param(
        [parameter(ValueFromPipelineByPropertyName = $true)]
        [string]$Title,
        [parameter(Mandatory = $false)]
        [string]$Description,
        [parameter(Mandatory = $false)]
        [string]$WorkItemType = "Task",
        [parameter(Mandatory = $false)]
        [string]$TfsCollectionUri,
        [parameter(Mandatory = $false)]
        [string]$Project
    )

    [System.Reflection.Assembly]::LoadWithPartialName(
        "Microsoft.VisualStudio.TeamFoundation") | Out-Null
    [System.Reflection.Assembly]::LoadWithPartialName(
        "Microsoft.TeamFoundation.Client") | Out-Null
    [System.Reflection.Assembly]::LoadWithPartialName(
        "Microsoft.TeamFoundation.WorkItemTracking.Client") | Out-Null
    [System.Reflection.Assembly]::LoadWithPartialName(
        "Microsoft.TeamFoundation.WorkItemTracking.Client.WorkItemStore") | Out-Null
```

```
    if ($TfsCollectionUri -ne $null -and $dte -ne $null) {
        $tfs = $dte.GetObject(
            "Microsoft.VisualStudio.TeamFoundation.TeamFoundationServerExt")
        $TfsCollectionUri = $tfs.ActiveProjectContext.DomainUri
    }

    if ($Project -eq $null -ne $null -and $dte -ne $null) {
        $tfs = $dte.GetObject(
            "Microsoft.VisualStudio.TeamFoundation.TeamFoundationServerExt")
        $Project = $tfs.ActiveProjectContext.ProjectName
    }

    [psobject]$tfs = [Microsoft.TeamFoundation.Client.TeamFoundationServerFactory]
        ::GetServer($TfsCollectionUri)
    $wit = $tfs.GetService(
        [Microsoft.TeamFoundation.WorkItemTracking.Client.WorkItemStore])
    $workItem = new-object Microsoft.TeamFoundation.WorkItemTracking.Client.WorkItem(
        $wit.Projects[$Project].WorkItemTypes[$WorkItemType])
    $workItem.Title = $Title
    if ($Description -ne $null) {
        $workItem.Item("System.Description") = $Description
    }
    $workItem.Save()
}

Register-TabExpansion 'Add-WorkItem' @{
    'Title' = {
        "Implement feature X",
        "Verify bug Y"
    }
    'Description' = {
        "Please implement feature X",
        "Bug Y has not been verified yet. Please take care of it."
    }
    'WorkItemType' = { Get-WorkItemTypes | Select -ExpandProperty Name }
    'TfsCollectionUri' = { Get-CurrentTfsCollectionUri }
    'Project' = { Get-TfsProjectNames | Select -ExpandProperty Name }
}

Export-ModuleMember -Function *
```

Extending NuGet Package Explorer

If you often use NuGet Package Explorer, you're probably doing some repetitive work without even paying too much attention to it. For example, you might need to take a look at the sources of a given assembly inside a NuGet package. We personally like to use ILSpy, a free and open source .NET assembly browser and decompiler, to disassemble binaries and investigate their inner workings. If you want to do this for an assembly inside a NuGet package you opened in NuGet Package Explorer, you would first need to extract it, save it to disk (and remember its location), open ILSpy, and open the assembly you just saved. This is too much manual effort, and if you do this a lot, you can easily consume too much valuable time.

When dealing with scenarios like these, it's worth considering whether a plug-in could help you with this task. That's exactly what Xavier's ILSpy plug-in for NuGet Package Explorer does! We will use this plug-in as an example of how to create plug-ins, and we'd like to invite you to create your own and share them with the world. The ILSpy plug-in is open source and can be found at `http://npeilspy.codeplex.com`.

NuGet Package Explorer has been designed to support plug-ins by making good use of the Managed Extensibility Framework. It has a full-blown plug-in manager built in, allowing you to add plug-ins from within the application itself. Starting from version 2.5, it has pushed the limit even further by supporting plug-ins to be delivered through NuGet packages, hosted on a dedicated NuGet feed on `MyGet.org`, available at `https://www.myget.org/F/npe`. As such, NuGet Package Explorer supports both local and feed plug-ins. You can see the dialog box for adding a plug-in in Figure 9-10.

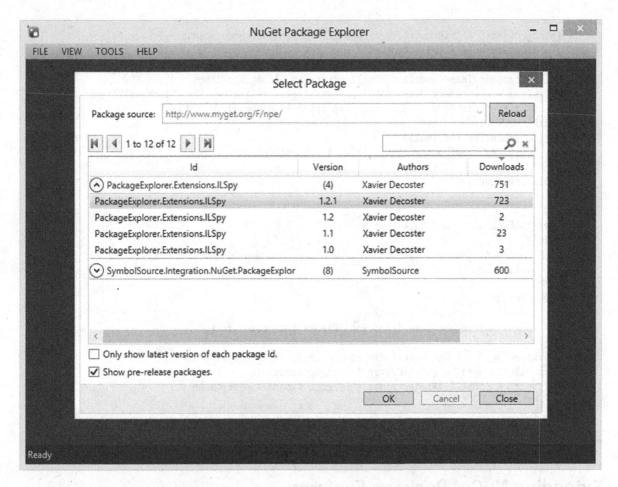

Figure 9-10. *Adding a feed plug-in in NuGet Package Explorer's built-in plug-in manager*

NuGet Package Explorer features three different types of extensions:

- Content viewer extensions provide support for visualizing files in NuGet packages. For example, if you open a package containing an image, the standard NPE image visualizer will show you a preview of the selected image.

- Package validation rules provide the ability to analyze packages you create using NPE. When a user clicks the Analyze Package command, your custom package validation rules will be activated to check that the package you are creating conforms to the rules you define for creating packages.

- Package commands provide support to add menu items and actions to the NPE application. For example, if you always publish a package to a specific feed using the exact same API key, why not create a `PublishToMyFeed` command to do exactly that without interrupting you with other dialog boxes?

Creating any of these three types of extensions is done using the same pattern:

1. Create a new Visual Studio Solution and add a class library. (Make sure you target the .NET 4.5 Framework.)

2. Add a NuGet reference to the `NuGetPackageExplorer.Types` package, which will come from NuGet.org (`Install-Package NuGetPackageExplorer.Types`).

This will make sure your project has the required references and will install some sample code files into your project, ready for modification to suit your needs.

Creating a Custom Content Viewer

The main purpose of the NuGet Package Explorer content viewer plug-in is to attach custom visualizers to certain file types. By default, NuGet Package Explorer does not handle every possible file extension, except for the most common NuGet package contents. Whenever a user triggers the View Content command on a certain file (by double-clicking it, for instance), NuGet Package Explorer scans the application for a command that can handle the requested file extension.

After installing the `NuGetPackageExplorer.Types` package, described in the previous section, the installer has injected your project with a class named `MyCustomContentViewer`, shown in Listing 9-10. This class is a sample content viewer that you can adjust to suit your needs. For starters, you might want to pick a proper file extension to tell the tool what kind of files your plug-in will target. Notice that your plug-in can register itself for more than one extension at the same time. The integer parameter of the `PackageContentViewerMetadata` attribute sets your plug-in's priority. The lower the value, the higher its priority.

Listing 9-10. Default Sample of a Custom Content Viewer for NuGet Package Explorer

```
// TODO: replace '.extension' with your custom extension
[PackageContentViewerMetadata(0, ".extension", ".anotherextension")]
internal class MyCustomContentViewer : IPackageContentViewer
{
    public object GetView(string extension, Stream stream)
    {
        throw new NotImplementedException();
    }
}
```

The content viewer has only one significant method—`GetView`. It returns an object, but please bear in mind that NuGet Package Explorer is a WPF application and will put the result of this method into a `ContentPresenter` control's `Content` property. Therefore, you can return either a simple `string` or any deriving object of the `Visual` class. The `GetView` method has access to information regarding the file it will need to handle: its file extension and its content stream.

A simple sample is shown in Listing 9-11. This is an NPE content viewer plug-in that handles .txt files and simply returns their content stream as a string.

Listing 9-11. A Simple .txt file Content Viewer Example

```
[PackageContentViewerMetadata(0, ".txt")]
internal class TextFileContentViewer : IPackageContentViewer
{
    public object GetView(string extension, Stream stream)
    {
        StreamReader reader = new StreamReader(stream);
        return reader.ReadToEnd();
    }
}
```

The ILSpy plug-in for NuGet Package Explorer goes a little further and works with a modal WPF dialog box showing a custom ConfigurationControl, as shown in Listing 9-12. Because it targets files with a .dll or .exe extension and has a priority of 0, it will be used as the default content viewer for assembly files inside a NuGet package.

Listing 9-12. A Content Viewer Using a Custom WPF Control in a Modal Dialog Box

```
[PackageContentViewerMetadata(0, ".dll", ".exe")]
internal class ILSpyPackageContentViewer : IPackageContentViewer
{
    private ConfigurationControl configControl;
    private Window dialog;

    public object GetView(string extension, Stream stream)
    {
        try
        {
            configControl = new ConfigurationControl(extension, stream);
            dialog = new Window();
            dialog.Content = configControl;
            dialog.Topmost = true;
            dialog.Width = 300;
            dialog.Height = 120;
            dialog.ResizeMode = ResizeMode.NoResize;
            dialog.WindowStartupLocation = WindowStartupLocation.CenterOwner;
            dialog.ShowInTaskbar = false;
            dialog.ShowDialog();

            return configControl.Assembly.FullName;
        }
        catch (Exception exception)
        {
            return exception.ToString();
        }
    }
}
```

If you have the ILSpy plug-in installed in NuGet Package Explorer, double-clicking an assembly inside a NuGet package will prompt the user for the path to ILSpy, as shown in Figure 9-11.

Figure 9-11. *The configuration control of NuGet Package Explorer's ILSpy plug-in*

After choosing the correct path to your ILSpy executable and clicking the OK button, you'll see ILSpy opening up the requested file, as shown in Figure 9-12.

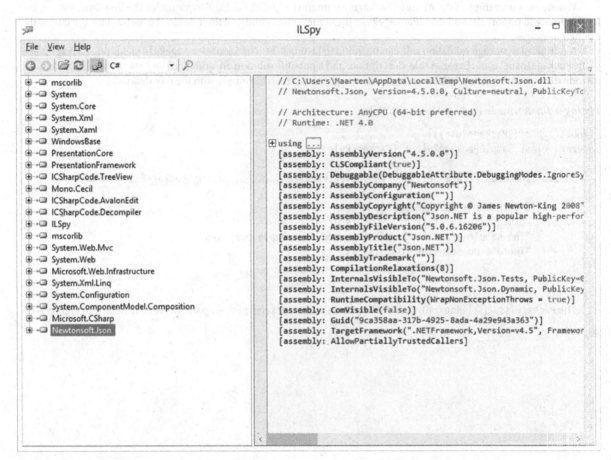

Figure 9-12. *Browsing and decompilling a .dll assembly with ILSpy*

Creating a Custom Package Validation Rule

You'll notice that after installing the NuGetPackageExplorer.Types package, two more classes were injected into your project, in addition to a custom content viewer. One of them, the MyCustomPackageRule class, is implementing IPackageRule, which allows you to add your own validation logic for NuGet packages—for example, to enforce that all packages produced in your company have correct copyright information and a proper logo in the manifest. Do not forget to export these package rules by marking them with the Export attribute, as shown in Listing 9-13.

Listing 9-13. Default Sample of a Custom Package Rule for NuGet Package Explorer

```
[Export(typeof(IPackageRule))]
internal class MyCustomPackageRule : IPackageRule
{
    public IEnumerable<PackageIssue> Validate(IPackage package)
    {
        throw new NotImplementedException();
    }
}
```

Whenever a user triggers the Analyze Package command in NuGet Package Explorer for the first time, the application will import all available `IPackageRule` implementations and call their `Validate` method for the currently opened package.

A sample of a package validation rule can be found in Listing 9-14. The `SamplePackageRule` yields one `PackageIssue` of the `PackageIssueLevel.Error`. A title, description, and a possible solution are added to the `PackageIssue` object to provide the user running this validation rule with enough information to comply with the rule defined.

Listing 9-14. A Sample Package Validation Rule

```
[Export(typeof(IPackageRule))]
internal class SamplePackageRule : IPackageRule
{
    public IEnumerable<PackageIssue> Validate(IPackage package, string packageFileName)
    {
        yield return new PackageIssue(
            PackageIssueLevel.Error, "Sample error",
            "The sample error is just being used for sample purposes.",
            "There's no solution to this.");
    }
}
```

The `PackageIssue(s)` being returned will be shown in the package analysis pane of NPE, as shown in Figure 9-13.

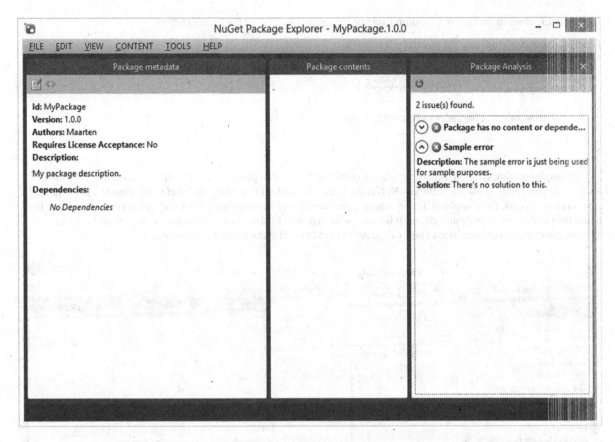

Figure 9-13. NuGet Package Explorer displaying an error message created by a package validation rule

---

■ **Warning** Do not store any state into your custom rule classes, because all package rules will be instantiated only once per session of the NuGet Package Explorer application. As such, all package rule instances are likely to be shared among multiple invocations of the Analyze Package command.

Creating a Custom Package Command

The third piece of code that has been added to your project after installing the NuGetPackageExplorer.Types package is a sample custom package command. A custom package command has access to the opened package and appears as a menu item in the Tools menu. A custom package command implements the IPackageCommand interface and exposes some metadata through the PackageCommandMetadata attribute, as shown in Listing 9-15.

Listing 9-15. Default Sample of a Custom Package Command for NuGet Package Explorer

```
[PackageCommandMetadata("My custom command")]
internal class MyCustomPackageCommand : IPackageCommand
{
    public void Execute(IPackage package)
    {
        throw new NotImplementedException();
    }
}
```

By implementing your own custom package commands, you can plug your own useful commands into NuGet Package Explorer and reuse them for any NuGet package—for instance, a command that easily clones a package and saves a copy on disk. Or how about adding a menu item under the Tools menu that can open the current package in a different tool, such as JetBrains' decompiler, dotPeek? Figure 9-14 shows what this menu entry could look like. The code for this menu entry would be a call to Process.Start with the correct parameters.

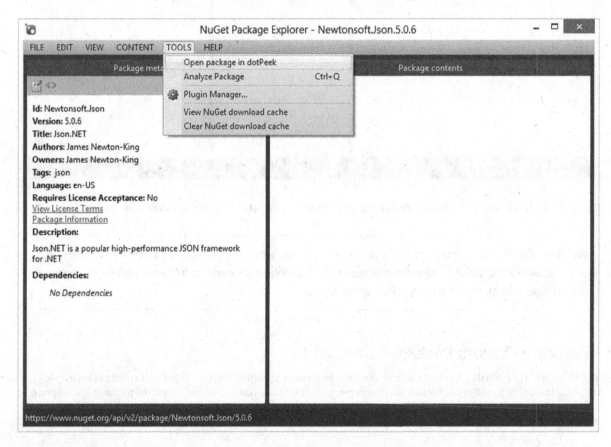

Figure 9-14. NuGet Package Explorer showing a new menu entry loaded from a plug-in

NuGet Package Explorer offers you a lot of extensibility in three different domains: file content viewers, package validation rules, and custom package commands. Each of them are useful on their own, and combined, they can possibly be a huge asset in your NuGet tool belt. Here are some ideas for extensions to NuGet Package Explorer we would like to see:

- A content viewer that shows decompiled assembly sources straight within NuGet Package Explorer.

- A custom validation rule that checks NuGet.org to see whether the package version you are creating already exists. (I hate it when I have to repackage because of this.)

- Maybe a tool menu that finds the GitHub project for a package and loads the readme file on demand?

There is more we can think of, and we are pretty sure that you might come up with some great plug-ins as well.

Invoking NuGet Services from Inside Visual Studio

There is one other extensibility point for NuGet. When creating your own Visual Studio extensions, some NuGet services can be used to interact with NuGet. For example if you are creating a unit test runner plug-in for Visual Studio, the NuGet services can be used to install the unit-testing framework. Or if you are creating a Visual Studio extension with additional features for a specific open source project, the related NuGet package can be installed (or upgraded) from within that extension.

NuGet exports several interfaces that can be used in your own Visual Studio extension (after installing the NuGet.VisualStudio package into your extension project):

- IVsPackageInstaller: Contains methods to install NuGet packages into projects.

- IVsPackageInstallerEvents: Offers events that raise when packages are installed and uninstalled in the current solution.

- IVsPackageInstallerServices: Contains a method to retrieve installed packages in the current solution, as well as methods to check whether a specified package ID is installed in a project.

- IVsPackageUninstaller: Contains methods to uninstall NuGet packages from projects.

- IConsoleInitializer: Triggers eager initialization of the NuGet Package Manager Console.

- IVsTemplateWizard: This interface is designed for project/item templates to include preinstalled packages, and is not meant to be invoked from code.

For more information regarding these services, check out the documentation at http://docs.nuget.org/docs/reference/invoking-nuget-services-from-inside-visual-studio.

Summary

In this chapter, we covered the power of NuGet: its simplicity (it enables you to publish and consume packages) and its extensibility (the three mayor clients to work with NuGet can be extended with more power).

We've created extensions for all three clients. We've extended the NuGet command line with custom package analysis rules and a custom analyze command. We've seen how to install these extensions as well.

The Package Manager Console was extended with several cmdlets—some simple commands that instruct Visual Studio to search for symbols or remove and sort using directives. We've covered how to create more-complex commands with tab expansion support for creating an experience similar to IntelliSense for the users of your extensions.

NuGet Package Explorer can also be extended. We've demonstrated this with a plug-in providing you with ILSpy integration, allowing you to disassemble binary package content right from within NuGet Package Explorer. No need to extract the desired assembly from the package, open Windows Explorer windows to find ILSpy.exe, and then manually drag the assembly onto the ILSpy window. It is a much better experience to automate such things.

We have also seen that it is possible to invoke NuGet services from inside Visual Studio when creating our own Visual Studio extensions.

If you find yourself executing repetitive tasks when working with any of these NuGet client tools, consider whether writing a simple extension or plug-in could help you out and save you, and others, lots of time in the future.

In the next chapter, we'll go one step further. NuGet is great for managing packages, but if we change perspective, you'll see that NuGet can be considered a protocol too—a protocol that enables you to automatically update your applications or to extend your own applications with plug-ins that are distributed through NuGet. And that's exactly what we'll do in the next chapter.

■ ■ ■

## CHAPTER 10

NuGet as a Protocol

So far, you've seen how to consume and create NuGet packages and how to host your own feed containing packages. Using NuGet, we've managed to set up a means of continuous package delivery and extended the NuGet command line and Package Manager Console.

The concepts and techniques demonstrated in the previous chapters focused on using NuGet as a means of managing dependencies when developing software using Visual Studio. We've looked at NuGet as a package manager. How about we change our perspective and look at NuGet as a protocol for distributing packages?

You've already seen that complete deployments can be shipped as NuGet packages and that complete software installations can be distributed through NuGet (see Chapter 7). Why not leverage these techniques ourselves? All NuGet components have been built around one central assembly, NuGet.Core, which provides the base functionalities used in NuGet: working with feeds (or repositories) and installing and uninstalling packages based on such feeds.

This chapter will demonstrate how you can use NuGet.Core in your applications. If you are working with any form of plug-ins that users can install into your application or want to work with a self-updating executable (much like nuget.exe update -self), the techniques described in this chapter will be of use to you. In this chapter, we'll create a simple ASP.NET Model-View-Controller (MVC) application that supports loading plug-ins from external assemblies, and we'll distribute these plug-ins through NuGet.

Understanding Protocols

Let's have a look at Wikipedia's definition for a protocol:

> A communications protocol is a system of digital message formats and rules for exchanging those messages in or between computing systems and in telecommunications. A protocol may have a formal description.
>
> Protocols may include signaling, authentication, and error detection and correction capabilities.
>
> Wikipedia, http://en.wikipedia.org/wiki/Communications_protocol

If we break down the definition for a protocol, there are two important concepts to note: exchanging messages and formal description. When you think of NuGet, it supports exactly that: NuGet provides a means of exchanging messages through the use of a feed containing packages. These feeds conform to the OData feed format, a formal description of what a feed should look like. Packages are also created according to a format description: the Open Packaging Conventions are used to create a compressed archive containing multiple files and the relations between them. The NuGet package manifest adds a layer of information to these packages, containing data such as package authors, versioning information, and tags.

That leaves one conclusion to make: NuGet is a protocol—not a low-level protocol like TCP, but a high-level protocol for exchanging packages between a server and a client. If you take into account that packages can be pushed onto a feed, that also means an exchange between client and server is possible. Whereas TCP packages transport only a few bytes, NuGet packages can potentially transport gigabytes of data. NuGet provides a protocol for distributing those packages through a feed.

To make this explanation more clear, let's look at an example. Paint.NET, a well-known image editor written in .NET and available freely at `www.getpaint.net`, has plug-ins. If you want to create an image effect filter that performs specific actions on the input image, you can do so. It's a pity, though, that community-contributed plug-ins are available only on a bulletin board, from which you have to manually download the plug-in and copy it into Paint. NET's installation directory.

Of course, this could be done by using a web site where a zip file containing a plug-in is available for download. Using some C# or VB.NET code, it would be easy to download these files and copy them to a specific folder. But why go through all the hassle of supporting proxies and authentication and creating conventions on how a plug-in should be compressed?

It would make sense to use NuGet as a protocol in this situation. If the members of the team behind Paint.NET chose NuGet as a protocol, they could provide a user interface enabling users to pick the plug-ins to install from a feed (a NuGet feed, but that fact would be invisible to the user). Using NuGet under the cover, Paint.NET would be able to download the plug-in packages and copy the contents to the Paint.NET plug-ins folder. Authors of plug-ins could publish their plug-ins to the same NuGet feed to share their work with the world. All the infrastructure to establish this scenario is available in `NuGet.Core`!

Similarly, in the next section, we'll create an ASP.NET MVC application supporting plug-ins and distribute these plug-ins through a NuGet feed.

Creating a Pluggable Application by Using NuGet

This chapter will make use of a sample application called SearchPortal, for which you can find the source code in the Source Code/Download area of the Apress web site (`www.apress.com`). SearchPortal is a web application written in ASP.NET MVC, which can be installed in any company and serves as a portal to one or more search engines. As Figure 10-1 demonstrates, anyone navigating to the SearchPortal home page can enter a string to search for, select a search engine, and perform a web search based on that information.

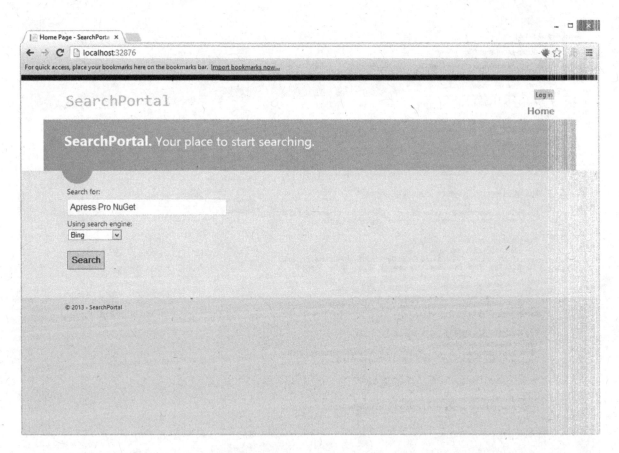

Figure 10-1. *SearchPortal home page, allowing a user to specify a search string and select a search engine that should be used to perform the search*

The list of search engines that can be used is specific to the IT department installing SearchPortal on its servers. Some companies may choose to allow searches using only Bing, while others may allow Bing, Google, and maybe even their own internal search engine. Figure 10-2 shows you a search for *Apress Pro NuGet* after selecting Bing from the list of search engines.

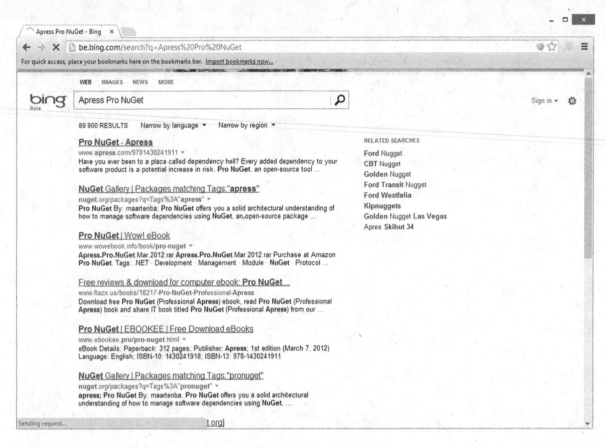

Figure 10-2. *Using Bing to search for Apress Pro NuGet*

An administrator can log in to the administration area of the application (conveniently located at /administration). As Figure 10-3 shows, the administration area features a list of available search engines that can be installed or uninstalled. Using this page, the administrator picks the search engines to be shown in the drop-down list on the SearchPortal home page.

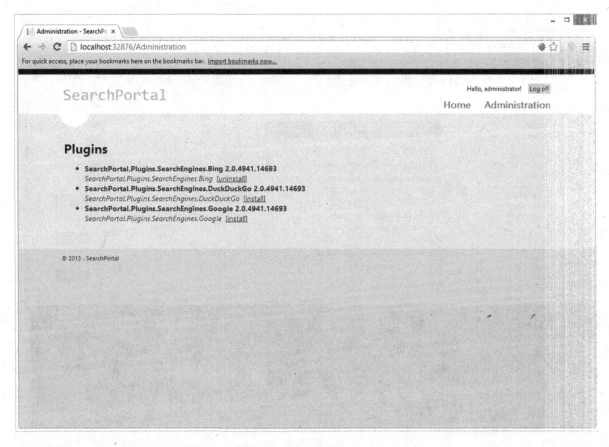

Figure 10-3. *The SearchPortal administration area*

The Plugins list shown in the administrative area is based on a NuGet feed located at www.myget.org/F/pronuget, the same feed that we've used as a sample in previous chapters. All plug-ins for SearchPortal are, in fact, NuGet packages containing a search engine that can be plugged into SearchPortal. This enables any user of SearchPortal to create a search engine plug-in that can be installed in any SearchPortal deployment by administrators of SearchPortal. The list of packages on the MyGet feed can be seen in Figure 10-4.

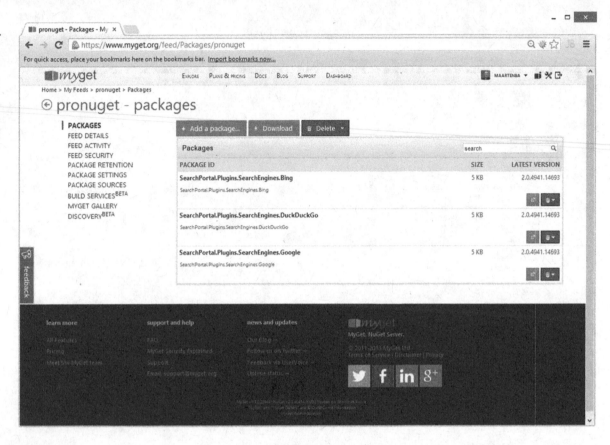

Figure 10-4. *The pronuget feed hosted on MyGet and listing three SearchPortal search engine plug-ins*

Defining Architecture and Technologies

Before we dive into how SearchPortal is developed, it is important to identify a suitable architecture and pick suitable technologies to support that architecture. SearchPortal uses two concepts that require a well-thought-out architecture:

- SearchPortal has to be extensible. The application architecture should support loading plug-ins from assemblies that were not originally shipped with the SearchPortal installation files. Extensions should be discovered and loaded by the application and integrated at runtime.

- Plug-ins should be easily discoverable. Distributing plug-ins to SearchPortal administrators should be simple and easy to do.

To build SearchPortal, we will make use of the following technologies:

- ASP.NET MVC will be used to develop the web interface for SearchPortal.

- Microsoft's Managed Extensibility Framework (MEF) will be used to make the application extensible. Living in the `System.ComponentModel.Composition` namespace, MEF is a framework that enables your application to load external assemblies at runtime and integrate them into your application.

- NuGet will be used for plug-in distribution. Plug-ins containing additional search engines will be compiled into an assembly and packaged into a NuGet package.

■ **Tip**   If you are not familiar with the Managed Extensibility Framework (MEF), refer to Maarten's MEF Is Cool as ICE blog post at http://blog.maartenballiauw.be/post/2010/03/04/MEF-will-not-get-easier-its-cool-as-ICE.aspx. Using MEF, classes can import dependencies by adding the [Import] attribute to a property. These imports are satisfied by composing the application and looking for matching exports, which have an [Export] attribute. Have a look at this blog post to quickly grasp the ideas and principles behind MEF.

Figure 10-5 shows a schematic view of the SearchPortal architecture. The SearchPortal.Web application will be created as an ASP.NET MVC application using Visual Studio. It will make use of MEF to load search engine plug-ins such as Bing or Google. These plug-ins will be distributed using NuGet and can be installed through an administration area, which makes use of the NuGet.Core assembly.

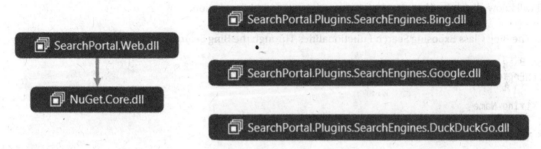

Figure 10-5. *Schematic view of the SearchPortal architecture*

Defining the ISearchEngine Interface

As discussed in the previous section of this chapter, SearchPortal will make use of MEF to load and integrate plug-ins at runtime. Since MEF is part of the .NET Framework, it is easy to make an application support a form of plug-ins:

- Add an assembly reference to System.ComponentModel.Composition.
- Create an interface for the search engines plug-ins.

The first part, adding a reference to a .NET Framework assembly to a Visual Studio project, should be easy. Let's do something more interesting; let's define an interface for search engine plug-ins.

The ISearchEngine interface in Listing 10-1 shows you an interface that exposes a property and a method. This interface has to be implemented by the plug-ins to be discoverable by the SearchPortal application. The Name property should return the name of the search engine plug-in—for example, *Bing*. The GenerateSearchUri method should return a Uri object based on a given searchTerm. For example, when searching for *Pro NuGet*, the GenerateSearchUri should return an URL in the form of www.bing.com/search?q=Pro%20Nuget. This URI can then be used by SearchPortal to initiate the actual search on the selected search engine.

Listing 10-1. The ISearchEngine Interface

```
[InheritedExport]
public interface ISearchEngine
{
    string Name { get; }

    Uri GenerateSearchUri(string searchTerm);
}
```

Note that the ISearchEngine interface has the [InheritedExport] attribute, which will tell MEF that any class implementing the ISearchEngine interface will be exposed as a plug-in and can be loaded at runtime. This is the basis for the plug-in architecture in SearchPortal.

An example ISearchEngine implementation is shown in Listing 10-2. The Bing class implements the ISearchEngine interface, and because that interface was attributed with the [InheritedExport] attribute, SearchPortal will know about the Bing class being a search engine implementation.

Listing 10-2. The Bing Class Exposing Search Functionalities Through the Bing Search Engine

```
public class Bing
    : ISearchEngine
{
    public string Name
    {
        get { return "Bing"; }
    }

    public Uri GenerateSearchUri(string searchTerm)
    {
        return new Uri(string.Format("http://www.bing.com/search?q={0}", searchTerm));
    }
}
```

Importing Search Engines

In the previous section, we defined the ISearchEngine interface. This interface defined what a search engine plug-in should look like and how MEF can discover implementations of this interface.

MEF will look for implementations of the ISearchEngine interface in a so-called catalog of components. This catalog is created once when the application starts and is exposed through a CompositionContainer. The catalog and container will be created just once, at application startup. It is an expensive operation in terms of performance, and you are advised to do this only once, when explicitly needed.

The initialization code will be added to the Application_Start() method of the Global.asax file so it runs only at application startup. This code does all the MEF wiring in the SearchPortal application. A trimmed-down version of it is shown in Listing 10-3. If you want the full source code for this class, see the related source code download for this book.

Listing 10-3. Global.asax Application_Start() Method

```
namespace SearchPortal.Web
{
    public class MvcApplication : System.Web.HttpApplication
    {
        public static CompositionContainer Container { get; private set; }

        protected void Application_Start()
        {
            // Load plugins
            ShadowCopyPlugins();

            var catalog = new AggregateCatalog(
                new AssemblyCatalog(typeof(MvcApplication).Assembly),
                new
RecursiveDirectoryCatalog(HostingEnvironment.MapPath("~/App_Data/ShadowedPlugins")));
            Container = new CompositionContainer(catalog);
            Container.ComposeParts(this);

            // ...
        }

        // ...
    }
}
```

In the Application_Start() method, a call to the ShadowCopy() method is done. We'll have a look at that method later in this chapter. Next, an AggregateCatalog is created, in which MEF will look for plug-ins. This AggregateCatalog is an aggregate of two other catalogs, an AssemblyCatalog that scans for plug-ins in the application's assembly (perhaps you want to ship some search engines out of the box) and a RecursiveDirectoryCatalog that scans the ~/App_Data/ShadowedPlugins folder and automatically registers the plug-ins that are installed through NuGet.

From now on, we can easily retrieve a list of all ISearchEngine implementations that are found by MEF. For example, the HomeController for SearchPortal can query the MEF container for all ISearchEngine implementations in its constructor, which is illustrated in Listing 10-4. The resulting IEnumerable will contain all ISearchEngine implementations discovered by MEF, if there are any, and can be used by the HomeController to decide which search engines should be shown in the drop-down list on the home page. The bold sections in Listing 10-4 illustrate using this IEnumerable. On a side note, we are querying the MEF container here directly. Many Inversion-of-Control (IoC) containers have support for automatically injecting the ISearchEngine implementations whenever the controller is instantiated.

Listing 10-4. The HomeController Querying the Container for all ISearchEngine Implementations

```
public class HomeController : Controller
{
    private readonly IEnumerable<ISearchEngine> _searchEngines;
    public HomeController()
    {
        _searchEngines = MvcApplication.Container
            .GetExportedValues<ISearchEngine>();    }
```

```
public ActionResult Index()
{
    var viewModel = new SearchFormViewModel();
    viewModel.SearchTerm = "";
    viewModel.SearchEngine = _searchEngines.Select(e => e.Name).FirstOrDefault();
    viewModel.AvailableSearchEngines = _searchEngines.Select(
        e => new SelectListItem()
                {
                    Text = e.Name,
                    Value = e.Name
                }).ToList();

    return View(viewModel);
}

[HttpPost, ActionName("Index")]
public ActionResult Index_Post(SearchFormViewModel model)
{
    if (ModelState.IsValid)
    {
        var searchEngine = _searchEngines.FirstOrDefault(
            e => e.Name == model.SearchEngine);
        if (searchEngine != null)
        {
            return Redirect(
                searchEngine.GenerateSearchUri(model.SearchTerm).ToString());
        }
    }

    return View(model);
}
}
```

Installing Plug-ins into SearchPortal

SearchPortal features an administration area that enables administrators to install a search engine plug-in from a list of available search engines that can be installed or uninstalled. Using this page, the administrator picks the search engines to show in the drop-down list on the SearchPortal home page.

The administration area of the application is located at /administration. If you are running the sample code, administrator is the username and password is the password. This administrative interface has been developed as a dedicated ASP.NET MVC controller, the AdministrationController.

Listing 10-5 shows the source code for the AdministrationController class. The AdministrationController class consists of three action methods:

- Index: This method queries an IPluginManager interface for a list of available and installed plug-ins. The IPluginManager interface and its implementation will be covered later in this section.

- Install: This action method instructs the IPluginManager implementation to install a specific plug-in into the SearchPortal application.

- Uninstall: This action method instructs the IPluginManager implementation to uninstall a specific plug-in from the SearchPortal application.

Listing 10-5. The AdministrationController Enabling the Administrator of SearchPortal to List, Install, and Uninstall Search Engine Plug-ins

```
[Authorize]
public class AdministrationController : Controller
{
    private readonly PluginManager _pluginManager;

    public AdministrationController()
    {
        _pluginManager = new PluginManager();
    }

    public ActionResult Index()
    {
        var plugins = _pluginManager.ListPlugins();

        var viewModel = new AdministrationViewModel();
        viewModel.Plugins = plugins
            .Select(p => new PluginViewModel()
            {
                PackageId = p.PackageId,
                PackageVersion = p.PackageVersion,
                PackageDescription = p.PackageDescription,
                IsInstalled = p.IsInstalled
            })
            .ToList();

        return View(viewModel);
    }

    public ActionResult Install(string packageId, string packageVersion)
    {
        _pluginManager.Install(packageId, packageVersion);

        return RedirectToAction("Index");
    }

    public ActionResult Uninstall(string packageId, string packageVersion)
    {
        _pluginManager.Uninstall(packageId, packageVersion);

        return RedirectToAction("Index");
    }
}
```

The IPluginManager interface is a simple interface that enables its consumers to ListPlugins and to Install or Uninstall a plug-in. Listing 10-6 is the source code for this interface, which serves as an abstraction used by the AdministrationController.

Listing 10-6. The IPluginManager Interface Used by the AdministrationController

```
public interface IPluginManager
{
    IEnumerable<PluginModel> ListPlugins();
    void Install(string packageId, string packageVersion);
    void Uninstall(string packageId, string packageVersion);
}
```

Of course, no NuGet magic will happen if we don't implement the IPluginManager interface. This implementation will do the actual integration with the NuGet.Core namespace. The NuGet.Core assembly can be installed through NuGet itself. Simply use Install-Package NuGet.Core.

Among other classes, NuGet.Core features two interesting types:

- The IPackageRepository interface is used to query a NuGet feed for information.

- The PackageManager class manages installing, updating, and uninstalling packages to a local folder based on an IPackageRepository instance to retrieve a list of packages.

We'll use both of these types in the constructor for our PluginManager class:

```
public class PluginManager
    : IPluginManager
{
    private readonly string _pluginFolder;
    private readonly IPackageRepository _packageRepository;
    private readonly PackageManager _packageManager;

    public PluginManager()
    {
        _pluginFolder = HostingEnvironment.MapPath("~/App_Data/Plugins");
        _packageRepository = PackageRepositoryFactory.Default
            .CreateRepository("https://www.myget.org/F/pronuget/");
        _packageManager = new PackageManager(_packageRepository, _pluginFolder);
    }
}
```

First of all, a plug-in folder is determined. This folder will hold all installed search engine plug-ins. We've chosen the /App_Data/Plugins folder for this. We're using the HostingEnvironment class's MapPath() method to determine the absolute path to this folder.

Next, a package repository reference is created. NuGet.Core features a default PackageRepositoryFactory, which can create a repository by simply passing the URL of the feed to consume. We're passing in www.myget.org/F/pronuget, because this is the URL to the NuGet feed that holds search engine plug-ins.

Finally, a PackageManager instance is created, linking the package repository to a local folder where installed packages will be stored. In essence, this is the inner working of all NuGet components such as the NuGet command line and the Package Manager Console.

We still have some methods to implement. Let's start with the ListPlugins() method:

```
public IList<PluginModel> ListPlugins()
{

    return _packageManager.SourceRepository.GetPackages()
        .Where(p => p.Tags.ToLower().Contains("searchportalplugin"))
        .OrderBy(p => p.Id)
```

```
    .Select(p => new { Id = p.Id, Version = p.Version, Description = p.Description})
    .ToList()
    .Select(p => new PluginModel()
        {
            PackageId = p.Id,
            PackageVersion = p.Version.ToString(),
            PackageDescription = p.Description,
            IsInstalled = _packageManager.LocalRepository.Exists(p.Id, p.Version)
        })
    .ToList();
}
```

Using the PackageManager created in the constructor of our PluginManager class, we query the source repository for all packages having the tag "searchportalplugin". Of course, other queries are possible here as well. You can search any property a NuGet package has in this query: you can look for packages having a specific ID, containing a search string in their title or summary, a specific package version, and so on. Be as creative as you want here.

The ListPlugins() method returns an IList of PluginModel instances. The PluginModel class is a simplified representation of a NuGet package that will be used by the AdministrationController mentioned earlier in this section. The PluginModel class contains only the package ID, the package version, the description, and a Boolean that tells SearchPortal whether the package is installed.

To check whether a package is installed, call PackageManager's local repository method Exists.

Finally, the PluginManager should be able to install and uninstall NuGet packages. The Install method consists of only two lines of code:

```
public void Install(string packageId, string packageVersion)
{
    _packageManager.InstallPackage(packageId, new SemanticVersion(packageVersion));

    HostingEnvironment.InitiateShutdown();
}
```

As you can see, the Install method calls into the PackageManager's Install method with the package ID and package version to install. From then on, the PackageManager will take care of downloading the package from the NuGet feed at www.myget.org/F/pronuget and extracting the package to the /App_Data/Plugins folder.

The second line of code in the Install method is interesting and is required only when working with web applications. The HostingEnvironment.InitiateShutdown() method requests the web server—for example, Internet Information Server (IIS)—to shut the running down instance of SearchPortal and to restart the application pool in which SearchPortal is running. We have two good reasons for doing this:

- The MEF catalog containing all available plug-ins is created only once, at startup of the SearchPortal application. This catalog is rebuilt when the application is restarted, and only then is our newly installed search engine plug-in discovered.

- The Common Language Runtime (CLR), .NET's runtime, locks the assemblies loaded at runtime. This means that if we install a search engine plug-in, the CLR will lock the assembly containing the search engine plug-in. We will never be able to remove the assembly again, because the file will be in use by the CLR. In addition to restarting the application pool, we'll be using a technique called *shadow copying*, which will be explained in the next section.

The complete source code for the PluginManager class which can list, install and uninstall packages from a specific NuGet feed is in Listing 10-7.

Listing 10-7. The PluginManager Class

```
public class PluginManager
    : IPluginManager
{
    private readonly string _pluginFolder;
    private readonly IPackageRepository _packageRepository;
    private readonly PackageManager _packageManager;

    public PluginManager()
    {
        _pluginFolder = HostingEnvironment.MapPath("~/App_Data/Plugins");
        _packageRepository = PackageRepositoryFactory.Default
            .CreateRepository("https://www.myget.org/F/pronuget/");
        _packageManager = new PackageManager(_packageRepository, _pluginFolder);
    }

    public IList<PluginModel> ListPlugins()
    {
        return _packageManager.SourceRepository.GetPackages()
            .Where(p => p.Tags.ToLower().Contains("searchportalplugin"))
            .OrderBy(p => p.Id)
            .Select(p => new { Id = p.Id, Version = p.Version, Description = p.Description})
            .ToList()
            .Select(p => new PluginModel()
                {
                    PackageId = p.Id,
                    PackageVersion = p.Version.ToString(),
                    PackageDescription = p.Description,
                    IsInstalled = _packageManager.LocalRepository.Exists(p.Id, p.Version)
                })
            .ToList();

    }

    public void Install(string packageId, string packageVersion)
    {
        _packageManager.InstallPackage(packageId, new SemanticVersion(packageVersion));     }

    public void Uninstall(string packageId, string packageVersion)
    {
        _packageManager.UninstallPackage(packageId, new SemanticVersion(packageVersion));

        HostingEnvironment.InitiateShutdown();
    }
}
```

Loading Installed Plug-ins into MEF's Catalog

So far, we've downloaded search engine plug-ins from a NuGet feed and installed them into the ~/App_Data/Plugins folder. Now, it's time to make sure they can be loaded by our application.

As mentioned earlier, Application_Start() creates a catalog containing possible plug-ins. This catalog uses a RecursiveDirectoryCatalog to load plug-ins from disk. If you've watched carefully, there is a mismatch in the directories we have been using: plug-ins are installed into the ~/App_Start/Plugins folder, while MEF loads them from the ~/App_Data/ShadowedPlugins folder. Listing 10-8 shows the relevant lines of code again.

Listing 10-8. Adding the Installed Search Engine Plug-ins to MEF's Catalog

```
// Load plugins
ShadowCopyPlugins();

var catalog = new AggregateCatalog(
    new AssemblyCatalog(typeof(MvcApplication).Assembly),
    new RecursiveDirectoryCatalog(HostingEnvironment.MapPath("~/App_Data/ShadowedPlugins")));
Container = new CompositionContainer(catalog);
Container.ComposeParts(this);
```

There is a good reason for adding the ~/App_Start/ShadowedPlugins folder to the catalog instead of the ~/App_Start/Plugins folder, where the PluginManager installs its packages. The CLR locks the assemblies loaded at runtime. This means that all assemblies in the ~/App_Start/Plugins folder would be locked, and we would be unable to uninstall packages once installed.

To overcome this problem, we'll use a technique called shadow copying, which is also used by Microsoft to make it possible to compile ASP.NET web pages at runtime without being affected by CLR locks. Shadow copying may sound difficult, but it isn't. It consists of creating a copy of the original assemblies and using that copy instead of the original assemblies. Doing this allows us to modify the original set of assemblies by, for example, installing or uninstalling a search engine plug-in. The shadow copy is then updated whenever the application pool is restarted.

Listing 10-9 shows a simple technique to create a shadow copy of the ~/App_Data_Plugins folder to a folder called ~/App_Data/ShadowedPlugins.

Listing 10-9. Creating a Shadow Copy of the /App_Data/Plugins Folder to Overcome CLR Locks

```
private static void ShadowCopyPlugins()
{
    var shadowedPlugins = new DirectoryInfo(
        HostingEnvironment.MapPath("~/App_Data/ShadowedPlugins"));

    // Remove old shadow copies
    if (shadowedPlugins.Exists)
    {
        shadowedPlugins.Delete(true);
    }
    shadowedPlugins.Create();

    // Shadow copy plugins (avoid the CLR locking DLLs)
    var plugins = new DirectoryInfo(HostingEnvironment.MapPath("~/App_Data/Plugins"));
    if (plugins.Exists)
    {
        plugins.Copy(shadowedPlugins);
    }
}
```

Creating and Publishing Plug-ins

Until now, we've discussed only making the SearchPortal application pluggable. To make use of it, we'll have to create some search engine plug-ins. You can do this by creating a new class library project in Visual Studio. Name the project `SearchPortal.Plugins.SearchEngines.Google`.

To ensure that the ISearchEngine interface is known by our plug-in, add a reference to the `SearchPortal.Web` project, which you can find in the downloads for this book. This project contains the ISearchEngine interface that we'll use to implement a Google search engine plug-in for SearchPortal.

Add a class named Google to the project, and add the code in Listing 10-10 to it.

Listing 10-10. Source Code for the Google Search Engine Plug-in

```
using System;
using SearchPortal.Web.Code.Contracts;

namespace SearchPortal.Plugins.SearchEngines.Google
{
    public class Google
        : ISearchEngine
    {
        public string Name
        {
            get { return "Google"; }
        }

        public Uri GenerateSearchUri(string searchTerm)
        {
            return new Uri(string.Format("http://www.google.com/search?q={0}", searchTerm));
        }
    }
}
```

To publish this plug-in to a NuGet feed, we'll have to package it. Open a command prompt in the root folder of the newly created project `SearchPortal.Plugins.SearchEngines.Google`, and run the nuget spec command. This will create a file named `SearchPortal.Plugins.SearchEngines.Google.nuspec` that contains a package manifest for the Google search engine plug-in we are creating. Listing 10-11 lists the markup for the package manifest that will be used to create a NuGet package for this plug-in. Note that the tags element contains a tag named searchportalplugin; this is the tag we've specified in the PluginManager, because we want to show only packages having this tag in the SearchPortal application.

Listing 10-11. The Package Manifest Used to Package the Google Search Engine Plug-in

```
<?xml version="1.0"?>
<package >
  <metadata>
    <id>$id$</id>
    <version>$version$</version>
    <title>$title$</title>
    <authors>Maarten Balliauw, Xavier Decoster</authors>
    <owners>Maarten Balliauw, Xavier Decoster</owners>
    <requireLicenseAcceptance>false</requireLicenseAcceptance>
```

```
    <description>$description$</description>
    <copyright>Copyright Maarten Balliauw and Xavier Decoster 2013</copyright>
    <tags>pronuget apress plugin searchportalplugin</tags>
  </metadata>
</package>
```

From now on, you can use the knowledge you have gained from this book to package your project. Run the nuget pack command to create a package from the Google plug-in project, and publish this package to a NuGet feed of choice. If you have an account on MyGet.org, you can also push to the www.myget.org/F/pronuget feed by using your MyGet API key.

■ **Tip**   As an alternative to manually running the nuget pack command, you can also Install-Package NuGet.Build and edit the NuGet.targets file's <BuildPackage> element value to true. This will change the project file for the SearchPortal.Plugins.SearchEngines.Google project and will trigger the nuget pack command automatically on every build.

Creating a Self-Updating Application by Using NuGet

In addition to distributing plug-ins, why not distribute your application itself through NuGet? In fact, the NuGet command line is nothing more than a small bootstrapper downloading the NuGet.CommandLine package from NuGet.org on first run. The nuget update -self command does the exact same thing and updates the NuGet.CommandLine package to its latest version. It's a good example to take a closer look at.

The NuGet Command Line as Example

In this section, we'll use the NuGet source code that you can find at https://git01.codeplex.com/nuget. You can clone this URL by using Git. To clone the NuGet repository, simply run the following command, using the git executable in a command prompt, while making sure you are in the directory into which you want to clone the remote repository.

```
git clone https://git01.codeplex.com/nuget
```

This command will work only if you have a Git client installed. If not, use Chocolatey (described in Chapter 7), and invoke the cinst git command. If you don't want to install a Git client, you can also navigate to the www.codeplex.com/nuget URL in your browser and browse through the NuGet source code online.

Let's look at the nuget update command. The source code for this command is in the NuGet repository at /src/CommandLine/Commands/UpdateCommand.cs. This class contains a method named SelfUpdate, for which you can see the source code in Listing 10-12.

Listing 10-12. Source Code for NuGet's UpdateCommand SelfUpdate Method

```
private const string NuGetCommandLinePackageId = "NuGet.CommandLine";
private const string NuGetExe = "NuGet.exe";
private const string PackagesFolder = "packages";

internal void SelfUpdate(string exePath, SemanticVersion version)
{
    Console.WriteLine(NuGetResources.UpdateCommandCheckingForUpdates,
        NuGetConstants.DefaultFeedUrl);
```

```
// Get the nuget command line package from the specified repository
IPackageRepository packageRepository =
    RepositoryFactory.CreateRepository(NuGetConstants.DefaultFeedUrl);

IPackage package = packageRepository.FindPackage(NuGetCommandLinePackageId);

// We didn't find it so complain
if (package == null)
{
    throw new CommandLineException(NuGetResources.UpdateCommandUnableToFindPackage,
        NuGetCommandLinePackageId);
}

Console.WriteLine(NuGetResources.UpdateCommandCurrentlyRunningNuGetExe, version);

// Check to see if an update is needed
if (version >= package.Version)
{
    Console.WriteLine(NuGetResources.UpdateCommandNuGetUpToDate);
}
else
{
    Console.WriteLine(NuGetResources.UpdateCommandUpdatingNuGet, package.Version);

    // Get NuGet.exe file from the package
    IPackageFile file = package.GetFiles().FirstOrDefault(f =>
        Path.GetFileName(f.Path).Equals(NuGetExe, StringComparison.OrdinalIgnoreCase));

    // Get the exe path and move it to a temp file (NuGet.exe.old)
    // so we can replace the running exe with the bits we got
    // from the package repository
    string renamedPath = exePath + ".old";
    Move(exePath, renamedPath);

    // Update the file
    UpdateFile(exePath, file);

    Console.WriteLine(NuGetResources.UpdateCommandUpdateSuccessful);
}
}
```

The SelfUpdate method contains a simple code flow that does the following:

1. Get the NuGet.CommandLine package from NuGet.org.

2. Compare the current version and the new version of this package to verify whether an update is required.

3. Rename the current nuget.exe to nuget.exe.old.

4. Extract the package (in memory), and extract the nuget.exe file from it to the current path.

These four simple steps are all it takes to create a self-updating application using NuGet.

An Application Bootstrapper That Checks for Updates

Now that we know how NuGet updates itself, we can also create our own application bootstrapper that checks for updates. Since the update check and installation are fairly common, we can abstract this into a stand-alone executable that checks for updates for your custom application.

Imagine we have an application called `Bootstrapper.SampleApp` that we package as a NuGet package. The executable and all its libraries are packaged into the `lib` folder of the NuGet package. Figure 10-6 shows what the contents of this package may look like.

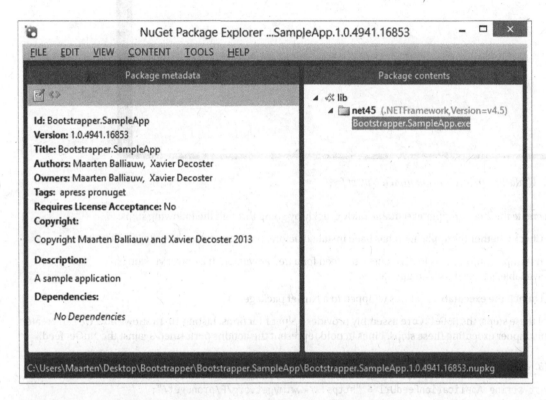

Figure 10-6. *A NuGet package containing an executable*

When distributing this application to our users, we don't distribute the actual `Bootstrapper.Sample.exe` executable, but we distribute a simple bootstrapper. This simple bootstrapper will download the package from a NuGet feed if it wasn't downloaded yet, and update it if a newer version exists. Figure 10-7 shows the output of our bootstrapper executable when a newer version of our application package exists.

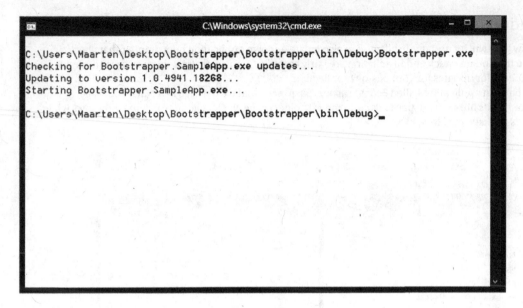

```
C:\Windows\system32\cmd.exe                                               - □  ×

C:\Users\Maarten\Desktop\Bootstrapper\Bootstrapper\bin\Debug>Bootstrapper.exe
Checking for Bootstrapper.SampleApp.exe updates...
Updating to version 1.0.4941.18268...
Starting Bootstrapper.SampleApp.exe...

C:\Users\Maarten\Desktop\Bootstrapper\Bootstrapper\bin\Debug>_
```

Figure 10-7. *Updating an application from a NuGet feed*

We can create this bootstrapper executable fairly quickly by going through the following steps:

1. Check whether the application has been installed before. If not, use NuGet.Core to install it.

2. If the application exists in disk, check the feed for a newer version. If a newer version is available, proceed with an update.

3. Launch the executable that was wrapped in a NuGet package.

For all of these steps, the NuGet.Core assembly provides helper functions. Listing 10-13 shows how we can create a simple bootstrapper executing these steps. Lines in bold represent the actions performed against the NuGet feed.

Listing 10-13. An Application Bootstrapper for Applications That Checks for Updates on Startup

```csharp
private const string ApplicationFeedUrl = "https://www.myget.org/F/pronuget/";
private const string ApplicationPackageName = "Bootstrapper.SampleApp";
private const string ApplicationFolder = "application";
private const string ApplicationExecutableName = "Bootstrapper.SampleApp.exe";

static void Main(string[] args)
{
    var packagesFolder = Path.Combine(AppDomain.CurrentDomain.BaseDirectory, ApplicationFolder);
    var packageRepository = PackageRepositoryFactory.Default
        .CreateRepository(ApplicationFeedUrl);
    var packageManager = new PackageManager(packageRepository, packagesFolder);
    var versionFile = Path.Combine(ApplicationFolder, "version.txt");

    if (!Directory.Exists(packagesFolder) || !Directory.EnumerateDirectories(
        packagesFolder, ApplicationPackageName + "*", SearchOption.AllDirectories).Any())
    {
        Console.WriteLine("Installing {0}...", ApplicationExecutableName);
        IPackage package = packageRepository.FindPackage(ApplicationPackageName);
```

```
        File.WriteAllText(versionFile, package.Version.ToString());
        packageManager.InstallPackage(package, true, false);
    }
    else
    {

        Console.WriteLine("Checking for {0} updates...", ApplicationExecutableName);

        var currentVersion = new SemanticVersion(File.ReadAllText(versionFile));
        IPackage package = packageRepository.FindPackage(ApplicationPackageName);
        if (package.Version > currentVersion)
        {
            Console.WriteLine("Updating to version {0}...", package.Version);
            packageManager.UpdatePackage(package, false, false);
            File.WriteAllText(versionFile, package.Version.ToString());
        }
        else
        {
            Console.WriteLine("No updates were found.");
        }
    }

    // Find executable
    var executablePath = Directory.EnumerateFiles(packagesFolder,
        ApplicationExecutableName, SearchOption.AllDirectories).FirstOrDefault();
    if (!string.IsNullOrEmpty(executablePath))
    {
        Console.WriteLine("Starting {0}...", ApplicationExecutableName);
        Process.Start(executablePath);
    }
    else
    {
        Console.WriteLine("Could not find {0} executable.",
            ApplicationExecutableName);
    }
}
```

The code from Listing 10-13 can be used in your applications as well to provide an auto-update functionality based on NuGet.

Summary

In this chapter, we've changed our perspective and looked at NuGet as a protocol for distributing packages. We've leveraged techniques used by all NuGet components: using its central assembly, NuGet.Core, we have created a plug-in system for an ASP.NET MVC application that makes use of NuGet's features for working with feeds (or repositories) and installing and uninstalling packages based on such feeds.

This technique is also used by NuGet Package Explorer, as you saw in Chapter 9. Plug-ins for NuGet Package Explorer are distributed through a NuGet feed, to which you can contribute your NuGet plug-ins.

You've also seen how the NuGet command-line tool is, in essence, also using this technique: when invoking the nuget update -self command from the command line, NuGet updates itself by querying NuGet.org for the NuGet.CommandLine package.

If you are working with any plug-ins that users can install into your application or want to work with a self-updating executable (much like nuget.exe update -self), the techniques described in this chapter will be of use to you. It's up to you to find a creative use case for these techniques.

■ ■ ■

Package Manifest Reference

In previous chapters, you've seen NuGet package manifests, or .nuspec files, being created a number of times. When creating packages, NuGet uses a convention-over-configuration approach. These conventions are rather simple by default, but relying on them may not be enough to mold the package you wish to create. A NuGet package manifest describes the contents and metadata of your package. It is included in each NuGet package, or .nupkg, file, and it is the file you'll need to create the actual package. In short, before you can create a package, you'll need to describe it.

This appendix covers all details about available options in the XML of a package manifest. It is largely based on the information available on the official NuGet web site at http://docs.nuget.org/docs/reference/nuspec-reference. NuGet documentation (from the Outercurve Foundation) is licensed under Creative Commons license BY 3.0 (http://creativecommons.org/licenses/by/3.0/).

■ **Note** Editing .nuspec files in Visual Studio or any XML editor can be made easier by using the XSD schema of the package manifest. This can be installed into a Visual Studio project by using NuGet: Install-Package NuGet.Manifest.Schema.

Creating the Metadata Section

The package manifest metadata section is a mandatory section within the package manifest. The metadata section itself also has a set of mandatory elements. These required elements must be specified before you can create a package based on the .nuspec manifest. Here is the list of all required metadata fields:

- ID
- Version
- Description
- Authors

Package Manifest Metadata elements

The first pieces of metadata your package exposes are the package ID and the package version. This pair of fields will uniquely identify your package on any NuGet feed. The package description and authors are used to search in the NuGet Gallery.

Table A-1 lists the possible elements in the package manifest metadata section and their descriptions.

Table A-1. *Elements in the Package Manifest Metadata Section*

Element	Required?	Description
id	Yes	The unique identifier for the package. This is the package name that is shown when packages are listed by using the Package Manager Console, and when installing a package using the Install-Package command within the Package Manager Console. Package IDs may not contain any spaces or characters that are invalid in an URL.
version	Yes	The version of the package in a format (for example, 1.2.3).
title	No	The human-friendly title of the package displayed in the Manage NuGet Packages dialog box. If none is specified, the ID is used instead.
authors	Yes	A comma-separated list of authors of the package code.
owners	No	A comma-separated list of the package creators. This is often the same list as in authors. This is ignored when uploading the package to the NuGet Gallery.
description	Yes	A long description of the package. This shows up in the right pane of the Manage NuGet Packages dialog box as well as in the Package Manager Console when listing packages by using the Get-Package command.
releaseNotes	No	A description of the changes made in each release of the package. This field shows up only when the Updates tab is selected and the package is an update to a previously installed package. It is displayed where the description would normally be displayed.
summary	No	A short description of the package. If specified, this shows up in the middle pane of the Add Package dialog box. If not specified, a truncated version of the description is used instead.
language	No	The locale ID for the package, such as en-us.
projectUrl	No	An URL for the home page of the package.
iconUrl	No	A URL for the image to use as the icon for the package in the Manage NuGet Packages dialog box. This should be a 32 × 32-pixel .png file that has a transparent background.
licenseUrl	No	A link to the license that the package is under.
copyright	No	Copyright details for the package.
requireLicenseAcceptance	No	A Boolean value that specifies whether the client needs to ensure that the package license (described by licenseUrl) is accepted before the package is installed.
dependencies	No	The list of dependencies for the package.

(continued)

Table A-1. (*continued*)

Element	Required?	Description
references	No	Names of assemblies under lib that are added as project references. If unspecified, all assemblies in lib are added as project references. When specifying a reference, specify only the name, not the path inside the package.
frameworkAssemblies	No	The list of .NET Framework assembly references that this package requires. These are references to assemblies that exist in the .NET Framework and thus should already be in the GAC for any machine. Specifying framework assembly references ensures these references are added when installing the package.
tags	No	A space-delimited list of tags and keywords that describe the package. This information is used to help make sure users can find the package by using searches in the Add Package Reference dialog box or filtering in the Package Manager Console window.
minClientVersion	No	Specifies the minimum version of the NuGet client that can install this package. This requirement is enforced by both the NuGet Visual Studio extension and the NuGet command line. Note that this attribute was introduced in NuGet 2.5 and has no effect in older versions.

Populating Replacement Tokens

NuGet package manifests can be generated based on either a compiled assembly or a project file (for example, MyProject.csproj). NuGet populates some replacement tokens within the metadata section of a package manifest with the data defined in the project's assembly name, AssemblyVersionAttribute, AssemblyCompanyAttribute, and AssemblyDescriptionAttribute. The MyProject.nuspec file adjacent to the MyProject.csproj file may contain the replacement tokens listed in Table A-2, which are populated by the values within the project.

Table A-2. *Package Manifest Metadata Section Replacement Tokens*

Token	Description
id	The assembly name of the project's output
$version$	The assembly (informational) version as specified in the project's AssemblyVersionAttribute
$title$	The assembly title as specified in AssemblyTitleAttribute
$author$	The company as specified in AssemblyCompanyAttribute
$company$	The company as specified in AssemblyCompanyAttribute
$description$	The description as specified in AssemblyDescriptionAttribute
$references$	This element contains a set of <reference> elements, each of which specifies an assembly that will be referenced by the project. The existence of this element overrides the convention of pulling everything in the lib folder.
e	The current configuration (for example, Debug or Release).

Referencing Dependencies

If your NuGet package depends on other NuGet packages, the listing of these dependencies will be generated based on the packages.config file found in your project, if any. External assemblies referenced in your project will also be added to the NuGet manifest based on the files contained in the lib folder. Adding a <dependencies> element for NuGet package references or a <references> element to add external assembly references allows adding additional dependencies for the package.

Specifying Dependencies

The <dependencies> element is a child element of the <metadata> element and contains a set of <dependency> elements. Each dependency element is a reference to another package that this package depends on. When installing a package that contains a list of package dependencies through NuGet, these package dependencies will be downloaded and installed as well. The following is an example list of dependencies:

```
<dependencies>
  <dependency id="RouteMagic" version="1.1.0" />
  <dependency id="RouteDebugger" version="1.0.0" />
</dependencies>
```

Note that dependencies can be specified for all target frameworks the package can be installed in, as well as on a per-framework basis using dependency groups. We will cover this later in this section.

Specifying Dependency Versions

NuGet supports using interval notation for specifying version ranges. This way, you can create a package that references another NuGet package based on a specific version, a range of versions, or any latest version of the package. Limiting the version ranges may limit dependency hell in your projects. The NuGet specification was inspired by the Maven Version Range Specification but is not identical to it. The following summarizes how to specify version ranges:

```
1.0 = 1.0 ≤ x
(,1.0] = x ≤ 1.0
(,1.0) = x < 1.0
[1.0] = x == 1.0
(1.0) = invalid
(1.0,) = 1.0 < x
(1.0,2.0) = 1.0 < x < 2.0
[1.0,2.0] = 1.0 ≤ x ≤ 2.0
empty = latest version (it's best to just omit the attribute in this case)
```

Working with Dependency Groups

Package dependencies can be specified to vary according to the framework profile of the target project. For example, when installed in a .NET 2.0 project, the package may have different package dependencies than when it would be installed in a .NET 4.5 project.

The <dependencies> element can contain a set of <group> elements. Each group contains zero or more <dependency> elements and a target framework attribute specifying the framework(s) in which the dependencies should be resolved. Here's an example:

```
<dependencies>
  <group>
    <dependency id="jQuery" />
  </group>

  <group targetFramework="net40">
    <dependency id="jQuery" />
    <dependency id="WebActivator" />
  </group>

  <group targetFramework="net45">
    <dependency id="jQuery" />
    <dependency id="WebActivatorEx" />
  </group>
</dependencies>
```

The preceding snippet specifies several dependencies. When the package is installed in the .NET 4 Framework, specified by the net40 value in the targetFramework attribute, the package requires the dependencies jQuery and WebActivator to be installed. For a .NET 4.5 target project (net45), the jQuery and WebActivatorEx packages are depended on and not the WebActivator package we had earlier. For all target project frameworks that are different, only the jQuery package is depended on. Table A-3 lists commonly used targetFramework attribute values.

Table A-3. *targetFramework Values*

Target	targetFramework Value
.NET Framework 4.5.1	net451
.NET Framework 4.5	net45
.NET Framework 4.0	net40
.NET Framework 4.0 Client Profile	net40-client
.NET Framework 3.5	net35
.NET Framework 3.5 Client Profile	net35-client
.NET Framework 3.0	net30
.NET Framework 2.0	net20
.NET Framework 1.1	net11
.NET Framework 1.0	net10
.NET Framework (unspecified version)	net
.NET Compact Framework 3.5	net35-cf
Windows 8 Store Apps	netcore45

(continued)

Table A-3. (*continued*)

Target	targetFramework Value
Silverlight 5.0	`sl5`
Silverlight for Windows Phone 7.0	`sl3-wp`
Silverlight for Windows Phone 7.1 Mango	`sl4-wp71`
Windows Phone 8	`wp8`
Portable class libraries	`portable-{frameworks}` (frameworks separated by +)
Native libraries	`native`

Note that when working with dependency groups, the `<dependencies>` element can contain only `<group>` elements. Mixing `<group>` and `<dependency>` elements is not allowed. However, by omitting the `targetFramework` attribute, the group will act as a fallback dependency group, which will be used when the target project cannot be matched against the other dependency groups in the package manifest.

Specifying Explicit Assembly References

Use the `<references />` element to explicitly specify assemblies that the target project should reference.

For example, if you add the following, only the `xunit.dll` and `xunit.extensions.dll` will be referenced from the appropriate framework or profile subdirectory of the `lib` folder, even if there are other assemblies in the folder. If this element is omitted, the usual behavior applies, which is to reference every assembly in the `lib` folder.

This feature supports design-time-only assemblies. For example, when using code contracts, the contract assemblies need to be next to the runtime assemblies that they augment so that Visual Studio can find them, but the contract assemblies should not actually be referenced by the project and should not be copied into the `bin` folder. Likewise, the feature can be used to unit test frameworks such as XUnit, which need its tool assemblies to be located next to the runtime assemblies, but excluded from project references.

```
<references>
    <reference file="xunit.dll" />
    <reference file="xunit.extensions.dll" />
</references>
```

Explicit assembly references can also be varied per target framework. Just as with package dependencies, the `<references>` element can contain one or more `<group>` elements that target a specific framework version. The `<reference>` and `<group>` elements cannot be mixed under the `<references>` element. A `<group>` element that omits the `targetFramework` attribute should be used in case a fallback is needed. Possible values for the `targetFramework` attribute can be found in Table A-3. Here's an example:

```
<references>
  <group>
    <reference file="xunit.dll" />
  </group>

  <group targetFramework="net40">
   <reference file="xunit.dll" />
   <reference file="xunit.extensions.dll" />
  </group>
</ references >
```

Specifying Framework Assembly References from the GAC

In some cases, a package may depend on an assembly that's in the .NET Framework. For example, your package may depend on the Managed Extensibility Framework (MEF), which is a .NET Framework assembly that should be added as a reference to a project explicitly. When specifying framework assembly references, NuGet will explicitly add a reference to a framework assembly when installing your NuGet package.

The <frameworkAssemblies> element, a child element of the <metadata> element, allows you to specify a set of <frameworkAssembly> elements pointing to a framework assembly in the Global Assembly Cache (GAC). Note the emphasis on *framework assembly*. These assemblies are not included in your package, because they are assumed to be on every machine as part of the .NET Framework.

```
<frameworkAssemblies>
    <frameworkAssembly assemblyName="System.ServiceModel" targetFramework="net40" />
    <frameworkAssembly assemblyName="System.Web" targetFramework="net40,net45" />
    <frameworkAssembly assemblyName="System.SomethingElse"  />
</frameworkAssemblies>
```

Table A-4 lists all attributes of the frameworkAssembly element.

Table A-4. Attributes for the framleworkAssembly Element

Attribute	Required?	Description
assemblyName	Yes	The fully qualified assembly name.
targetFramework	No	If specified, the specific target framework that this reference applies to. Multiple target frameworks can be specified, separated with a comma. For example, if a reference applies to only .NET 4.0, the value should be "net40". Possible values for the targetFramework attribute can be found in Table A-3. If the reference applies to all frameworks, omit this attribute.

Specifying Files to Include in a Package

By convention, you do not have to explicitly specify a list of files in the .nuspec file. In some cases, however, it may be useful to explicitly list the files in your project that should be included in the NuGet package. Do note that if you specify any files, the conventions are ignored, and only the files listed in the package manifest are included in the package.

The files element is an optional child element of the package element and contains a set of file elements. Each file element specifies the source and destination of a file to include in the package via the src attribute and target attribute, respectively.

Table A-5 lists the possible attributes of the file element.

Table A-5. *Attributes for the file Element*

Attribute	Required?	Description
src	Yes	The location of the file or files to include. The path is relative to the .nuspec file unless an absolute path is specified. The wildcard character (*) is allowed. Using a double wildcard character (**) implies a recursive directory search.
target	Yes	This is a relative path to the directory within the package where the source files will be placed.
exclude	No	The file or files to exclude. This is usually combined with a wildcard value in the src attribute. The exclude attribute can contain a semicolon-delimited list of files or a file pattern. Using a double wildcard character (**) implies a recursive exclude pattern.

Note that NuGet will never add assemblies that are named *.resources.dll. The reason for that is NuGet treats these as localization assemblies, in which case a localized package should be created.

Exploring File Element Examples

This section describes some example usages of the file element to give you a better understanding of how it's used in NuGet. Most of these use cases have been copied from the NuGet documentation at docs.nuget.org, but we've added a few as well.

Single Assembly

Copy a single assembly in the same folder as the .nuspec file into the package's lib folder:

```
<file src="foo.dll" target="lib" />
```

The source contains foo.dll.
The packaged result is lib\foo.dll.

Single Assembly with a Deep Path

Copy a single assembly into the package's lib\net40 folder so that it applies to only projects targeting the .NET 4 Framework:

```
<file src="assemblies\net40\foo.dll" target="lib\net40" />
```

The source contains foo.dll.
The packaged result is lib\net40\foo.dll.

Set of Assemblies

Copy a set of assemblies within the bin\release folder into the package's lib folder:

```
<file src="bin\release\*.dll" target="lib" />
```

The source contains one of these:

- `bin\releases\MyLib.dll`
- `bin\releases\CoolLib.dll`

The packaged result is one of these:

- `lib\MyLib.dll`
- `lib\CoolLib.dll`

Set of Assemblies, Excluding a Specific Assembly

Copy a set of assemblies within the `bin\release` folder into the package's `lib` folder, omitting one assembly:

```
<file src="bin\release\*.dll" target="lib" exclude="bin\release\CoolLib.dll" />
```

The source contains one of these:

- `bin\releases\MyLib.dll`
- `bin\releases\CoolLib.dll`

The packaged result is `lib\MyLib.dll`.

Assemblies for Different Frameworks

Copy a set of assemblies compiled for various versions of the .NET Framework:

```
<file src="lib\**" target="lib" />
```

Note that the double wildcard character implies a recursive search in the source for matching files.
The source contains one of these:

- `lib\net40\foo.dll`
- `lib\net20\foo.dll`

The packaged result is one of these:

- `lib\net40\foo.dll`
- `lib\net20\foo.dll`

Content Files

Copy content files from a source folder into a specific folder in a NuGet package:

```
<file src="css\mobile\*.css" target="content\css\mobile" />
```

The source contains one of these:

- `css\mobile\style1.css`
- `css\mobile\style2.css`

The packaged result is one of these:

- `content\css\mobile\style1.css`
- `content\css\mobile\style2.css`

Content Files with a Directory Structure

Recursively copy content files from a source folder into a NuGet package:

```
<file src="css\**\*.css" target="content\css" />
```

The source contains one of these:

- `css\mobile\style.css`
- `css\mobile\wp7\style.css`
- `css\browser\style.css`

The packaged result is one of these:

- `content\css\mobile\style.css`
- `content\css\mobile\wp7\style.css`
- `content\css\browser\style.css`

Content Files with a Deep Path

Copy content files from a source folder into a folder in a NuGet package that has a different folder hierarchy than the source files:

```
<file src="css\cool\style.css" target="Content" />
```

The source contains `css\cool\style.css`.
The packaged result is `content\style.css`.

Content Files Copied to a Folder with *Dot* in Its Name

Copy content files from a source folder into a folder in a NuGet package that has a *dot* in its name:

```
<file src="images\Neatpic.png" target="Content\images\foo.bar" />
```

Note that, because the `target` extension doesn't match the `src` extension, NuGet treats it as a directory.
The source contains `images\Neatpic.png`.
The packaged result is `content\images\foo.bar\Neatpick.png`.

Content File with a Deep Path and a Deep Target

Copy a content file from a source folder into a NuGet package by using either of the following two lines:

```
<file src="css\cool\style.css" target="Content\css\cool" />
<file src="css\cool\style.css" target="Content\css\cool\style.css" />
```

Because the file extensions of the source and target match, the target is assumed to be the file name, not a directory name.

The source contains css\cool\style.css.

The packaged result is content\css\cool\style.css.

Content File Copy and Rename

Copy a content file from a source folder into a NuGet package to a different filename in the NuGet package:

```
<file src="ie\css\style.css" target="Content\css\ie.css" />
```

The source contains ie\css\style.css.

The packaged result is content\css\ie.css.

Excluding Files from the Package Manifest

The <file> element within a .nuspec file can be used to include a specific file or a set of files, by using a wildcard character. When doing so, there's no way to exclude a specific subset of the included files. For example, suppose you want all text files within a directory except a specific one:

```
<files>
    <file src="docs\*.txt" target="content\docs" exclude="docs\admin.txt" />
</files>
```

Use semicolons to specify multiple files:

```
<files>
    <file src="*.txt" target="content\docs" exclude="admin.txt;log.txt" />
</files>
```

Use a wildcard character to exclude a set of files, such as all backup files:

```
<files>
    <file src="tools\*.*" target="tools" exclude="tools\*.bak" />
</files>
```

Or use a double wildcard character to exclude a set of files recursively across directories:

```
<files>
    <file src="tools\**\*.*" target="tools" exclude="**\*.log" />
</files>
```

■ **Note** By convention, NuGet ignores a series of files automatically. Every file starting with a dot (.) is ignored by default. The reason for this is that NuGet packages should not contain files and folders created by some source control clients for Subversion, Mercurial, or Git. If these files are required to be shipped in a NuGet package, make sure to explicitly add them by using the file element or specify the -NoDefaultExcludes command-line switch to the nuget pack command.

NuGet Command-Line Reference

In previous chapters, you've seen the NuGet command line being used. While we've covered most commands, this appendix lists all available commands from the NuGet command line. Parts of this appendix are based on the information available on the official NuGet web site at http://docs.nuget.org/docs/reference/command-line-reference. NuGet documentation (from the Outercurve Foundation) is licensed under Creative Commons license BY 3.0 (http://creativecommons.org/licenses/by/3.0/). Commands in this chapter are listed alphabetically.

The help Command

This command displays general help information and help information about other commands:

```
nuget help [command]
```

For example, retrieving help for the NuGet push command may be done by issuing the following command:

```
nuget help push
```

Available options are shown in Table B-1.

Table B-1. *Available Options for the NuGet help Command*

Option	Description
All	Print detailed information for all available commands.
Markdown	Print detailed help in markdown format.
Verbosity	Specifies the amount of detail in the output. Possible values are normal, quiet, detailed.
NonInteractive	Do not prompt for user input or confirmations.
Help	Help information for the command.

The config Command

The NuGet config command can be used to set values in a NuGet configuration file. More on configuration files can be found in Appendix D. Here's an example:

```
nuget config -Set <name>=<value>
```

Available options are shown in Table B-2.

Table B-2. *Available Options for the NuGet config Command*

Option	Description
Set	One or more key-value pairs to be set in config.
ConfigFile	The NuGet configuration file to use. If not specified, %AppData%\NuGet\NuGet.config is used as the configuration file.
Verbosity	Specifies the amount of detail in the output. Possible values are normal, quiet, detailed.
NonInteractive	Do not prompt for user input or confirmations.
Help	Help information for the command.

The delete Command

After publishing a package to a NuGet feed, the NuGet delete command enables a user to delete a package from the server. Note that some NuGet feeds, like the official NuGet Gallery at NuGet.org, may not allow package deletion. The reason for this is threefold:

- Other packages may depend on that package. Those packages might not necessarily be on the same feed.

- It ensures that folks who are not committing packages (package restore) will not have broken builds.

- It helps ensure that important community-owned packages are not mass deleted.

Here's an example:

```
nuget delete <package Id> <package version> [API Key] [options]
```

Available options are shown in Table B-3.

Table B-3. *Available Options for the NuGet delete Command*

Option	Description
Source	Specify the server URL.
NoPrompt	Do not prompt when deleting.
ApiKey	The API key used to connect to the server.
ConfigFile	The NuGet configuration file to use. If not specified, %AppData%\NuGet\NuGet.config is used as the configuration file.
Verbosity	Specifies the amount of detail in the output. Possible values are normal, quiet, detailed.
NonInteractive	Do not prompt for user input or confirmations.
Help	Help information for the command.

The install Command

The following command installs a package by using the specified sources:

```
nuget install packageId|pathToPackagesConfig [options]
```

If no sources are specified, all sources defined in %AppData%\NuGet\NuGet.config are used. If nuget.config specifies no sources, the default NuGet feed is used.

Note that when no package name is specified to the install command and instead package$.config is referenced, the install command will install all packages listed in packages.config. This may be very useful to restore a set of dependencies in a project without having to explicitly install all packages manually.

Available options are shown in Table B-4.

Table B-4. *Available Options for the NuGet install Command*

Option	Description
Source	Specify the server URL.
OutputDirectory	Specify the directory in which packages will be installed.
Version	The version of the package to install.
ExcludeVersion	If set, the destination folder will contain only the package name, not the version number.
PreRelease	Allow prerelease packages to be installed. This flag is not required when restoring packages from packages.config.
NoCache	When NoCache = true, NuGet contacts the configured package source to check for the existence of the requested package. When it has found the version, it will use the version from the cache if it's there or download a fresh copy if it's not. If the version no longer exists in the feed, the version from the cache is ignored.
RequireConsent	Checks whether package restore is granted before installing a package.
SolutionDirectory	Solution directory root used for package restore.
FileConflictAction	The action to take, when asked to overwrite or ignore existing files referenced by the project. Possible values: Overwrite, Ignore, None.
ConfigFile	The NuGet configuration file to use. If not specified, %AppData%\NuGet\NuGet.config is used as the configuration file.
Verbosity	Specifies the amount of detail in the output. Possible values are normal, quiet, detailed.
NonInteractive	Do not prompt for user input or confirmations.
Help	Help information for the command.

The list Command

The following command displays a list of packages from a given source:

```
nuget list [search terms] [options]
```

If no package sources are specified, all sources defined in %AppData%\NuGet\NuGet.config are used.
If nuget.config specifies no sources, the default NuGet feed is used.

Available options are shown in Table B-5.

Table B-5. *Available Options for the NuGet list Command*

Option	Description
Source	A list of package sources in which to search.
Verbose	Display detailed information for each package.
AllVersions	List all versions of a package. By default, only the last version is displayed.
PreRelease	Allow prerelease packages to be listed.
ConfigFile	The NuGet configuration file to use. If not specified, %AppData%\NuGet\NuGet.config is used as the configuration file.
Verbosity	Specifies the amount of detail in the output. Possible values are normal, quiet, detailed.
NonInteractive	Do not prompt for user input or confirmations.
Help	Help information for the command.

The pack Command

Create a NuGet package based on the specified .nuspec file, a project file, or an assembly name by using the pack command:

```
nuget pack <nuspec | project | assembly> [options]
```

Available options are shown in Table B-6.

Table B-6. *Available Options for the NuGet pack Command*

Option	Description
OutputDirectory	Specify the directory for the created NuGet package file. If none is specified, use the current directory.
BasePath	The base path of the files defined in the .nuspec file.
Verbose	Show verbose output for package building.
Version	Override the version number from the .nuspec file.
Exclude	Specify one or more wildcard patterns to exclude when creating a package.

(continued)

Table B-6. (*continued*)

Option	Description
Symbols	Determine whether a package containing sources and symbols should be created. When specified with a .nuspec file, create a regular NuGet package file and the corresponding symbols package.
Tool	Determine whether the output files of the project should be in the tools folder.
Build	Determine whether the project should be built before building the package.
NoDefaultExcludes	Prevent default exclusion of NuGet package files and files and folders starting with a dot (for example, .svn).
NoPackageAnalysis	Specify whether the command should not run package analysis after building the package.
IncludeReferencedProjects	Include referenced projects either as dependencies or as part of the package. If a referenced project has a corresponding nuspec file that has the same name as the project, that referenced project is added as a dependency. Otherwise, the referenced project is added as part of the package.
ExcludeEmptyDirectories	Prevent inclusion of empty directories when building the package.
Properties	Provide the ability to specify a semicolon-delimited list of properties when creating a package.
MinClientVersion	Set the minClientVersion attribute for the created package. This value will override the value of the existing minClientVersion attribute (if any) in the .nuspec file.
ConfigFile	The NuGet configuration file to use. If not specified, %AppData%\NuGet\NuGet. config is used as the configuration file.
Verbosity	Specifies the amount of detail in the output. Possible values are normal, quiet, detailed.
NonInteractive	Do not prompt for user input or confirmations.
Help	Help information for the command.

The push Command

The following command pushes a package to the server:

```
nuget push <package path> [API key] [options]
```

Depending on the NuGet feed you are pushing to, the package will immediately be published as well. Optionally, this behavior can be disabled by specifying the -CreateOnly option.

Available options are shown in Table B-7.

Table B-7. *Available Options for the NuGet push Command*

Option	Description
Source	The package source to publish to. By default, NuGet assumes you are pushing to a v2 feed and appends /api/v2/package to the specified package source URL. To overcome this or to push to a v1 feed, you have to explicitly specify the source URL. If omitted, NuGet.org will be used unless a DefaultPushSource configuration value is specified.
ApiKey	The API key for the server.
Timeout	Specifies the timeout for pushing to the server in seconds. Defaults to 300 seconds (5 minutes).
ConfigFile	The NuGet configuration file to use. If not specified, %AppData%\NuGet\NuGet.config is used as the configuration file, and then any nuget.config or .nuget\nuget.config starting from the root of the drive and ending in the current directory.
Verbosity	Specifies the amount of detail in the output. Possible values are normal, quiet, detailed.
NonInteractive	Do not prompt for user input or confirmations.
Help	Help information for the command.

The restore Command (NuGet >2.7)

The following command restores NuGet packages for a solution file or packages.config file specified. Note that it is available only in NuGet version 2.7 and newer.

```
nuget restore [solution | packages.config file] [options]
```

If a solution is specified, this command restores NuGet packages that are installed in the solution and in projects contained in the solution. Otherwise, the command restores packages listed in the specified packages.config file.

If no package sources are specified, all sources defined in %AppData%\NuGet\NuGet.config are used. If NuGet.config specifies no sources, the default NuGet feed is used.

Available options are shown in Table B-8.

Table B-8. *Available Options for the NuGet install Command*

Option	Description
Source	A list of package sources to use.
NoCache	If set, the NuGet package cache will not be used for restoring packages.
RequireConsent	Checks whether package restore is granted before installing a package.
DisableParallelProcessing	If set, parallel NuGet package restores are disabled.
PackagesDirectory (or OutputDirectory)	Specify the directory in which packages will be restored.
SolutionDirectory	Solution directory root used for package restore.
ConfigFile	The NuGet configuration file to use. If not specified, %AppData%\NuGet\NuGet.config is used as the configuration file.
Verbosity	Specifies the amount of detail in the output. Possible values are normal, quiet, detailed.
NonInteractive	Do not prompt for user input or confirmations.
Help	Help information for the command.

The setapikey Command

This command saves an API key for a given server URL:

```
nuget setapikey <API key> [options]
```

When no URL is provided, the API key for the official NuGet gallery is saved. API keys are stored in %AppData%\NuGet\NuGet.config.

Available options are shown in Table B-9.

Table B-9. *Available Options for the NuGet setapikey Command*

Option	Description
Source	The package source to store the API key for.
ConfigFile	The NuGet configuration file to use. If not specified, %AppData%\NuGet\NuGet.config is used as the configuration file.
Verbosity	Specifies the amount of detail in the output. Possible values are normal, quiet, detailed.
NonInteractive	Do not prompt for user input or confirmations.
Help	Help information for the command.

The sources Command

This command provides the ability to manage list of sources located in %AppData%\NuGet\NuGet.config:

```
nuget sources <List|Add|Remove|Enable|Disable> -Name [name] -Source [source]
```

Available options are shown in Table B-10.

Table B-10. *Available Options for the NuGet sources Command*

Option	Description
Name	Name of the source.
Source	Path to the package source.
Username	The username to be used when connecting to a server that requires authentication.
Password	The password to be used when connecting to a server that requires authentication.
StorePasswordInClearText	Do not encrypt the password when storing it in the configuration file. Note that by default, passwords will be encrypted with the computer's machineKey.
ConfigFile	The NuGet configuration file to use. If not specified, %AppData%\NuGet\NuGet.config is used as the configuration file.
Verbosity	Specifies the amount of detail in the output. Possible values are normal, quiet, detailed.
NonInteractive	Do not prompt for user input or confirmations.
Help	Help information for the command.

The spec Command

Generate a .nuspec for a new package with the following command:

nuget spec [package id]

If this command is run in the same folder as a project file (.csproj, .vbproj, or .fsproj), it will create a package manifest that uses replacement tokens, such as id, $version$, $description$, and $authors$.

Available options are shown in Table B-11.

Table B-11. *Available Options for the NuGet spec Command*

Option	Description
AssemblyPath	Assembly to use for metadata.
Force	Overwrite a .nuspec file if it exists.
ConfigFile	The NuGet configuration file to use. If not specified, %AppData%\NuGet\NuGet.config is used as the configuration file.
Verbosity	Specifies the amount of detail in the output. Possible values are normal, quiet, detailed.
NonInteractive	Do not prompt for user input or confirmations.
Help	Help information for the command.

The update Command

Update packages to latest available versions by using the following command, which also updates nuget.exe itself.

nuget update <packages.config|solution>

Available options are shown in Table B-12.

Table B-12. *Available Options for the NuGet update Command*

Option	Description
Source	A list of package sources to search for updates.
Id	Package IDs to update.
RepositoryPath	Path to the local packages' folder (location where packages are installed).
Safe	Looks for updates with the highest version available within the same major and minor version as the installed package.
Self	Update the running nuget.exe file to the newest version available from the server.
Verbose	Show verbose output while updating.
Prerelease	Allow updating to prerelease versions. This flag is not required when updating prerelease packages that are already installed.

(continued)

Table B-12. (*continued*)

Option	Description
FileConflictAction	The action to take, when asked to overwrite or ignore existing files referenced by the project. Possible values: Overwrite, Ignore, None.
ConfigFile	The NuGet configuration file to use. If not specified, %AppData%\NuGet\NuGet.config is used as the configuration file.
Verbosity	Specifies the amount of detail in the output. Possible values are normal, quiet, detailed.
NonInteractive	Do not prompt for user input or confirmations.
Help	Help information for the command.

APPENDIX C

■ ■ ■

NuGet Package Manager Console PowerShell Reference

Throughout this book, you've seen the NuGet Package Manager Console making use of PowerShell. Although those chapters already covered the most important NuGet commands, this appendix lists all available NuGet commands exposed in the NuGet Package Manager Console.

This appendix builds on top of the contents of this book and will provide references to other parts of this book as well. However, this appendix is not meant to be a full PowerShell reference; there are plenty of good books on that topic.

Parts of this appendix are based on the information available on the official NuGet web site at `http://docs.nuget.org/docs/reference/package-manager-console-powershell-reference`. The NuGet documentation (from the Outercurve Foundation) is licensed under Creative Commons license BY 3.0 (`http://creativecommons.org/licenses/by/3.0/`).

Support for Common Parameters

Note that the PowerShell commands listed in this appendix all support the following set of common PowerShell cmdlet parameters, indicated by the [`<CommonParameters>`] option:

- `Verbose`
- `Debug`
- `ErrorAction`
- `ErrorVariable`
- `WarningAction`
- `WarningVariable`
- `OutBuffer`
- `OutVariable`

For more-detailed information, you can simply type `Get-Help About_CommonParameters` in the NuGet Package Manager Console if the PowerShell help documents are installed on your system.

Adding Binding Redirects

This command adds binding redirects to the app.config or web.config file:

```
Add-BindingRedirect [-ProjectName] <string>
```

It has not been explicitly mentioned earlier in this book because, as of NuGet v1.2, this command is run automatically when needed during package installation. The available parameter for this command is shown in Table C-1.

Table C-1. *Available Option for the NuGet Add-BindingRedirect Command*

Option	Description	Required
ProjectName	Specifies the project to analyze and add binding redirects to.	True

Getting a Package or a Set of Packages

This command gets a package or a set of packages available from the package source:

```
Get-Package -Source <string> [-ListAvailable] [-Updates] [-ProjectName] [-Filter•
<string>] [-First <int>] [-Skip <int>] [-IncludePrerelease] [-AllVersions]
```

This command defaults to showing only the list of installed packages. Use the -ListAvailable flag to list packages available from the package source. Available options for this command are shown in Table C-2.

Table C-2. *Available Options for the NuGet Get-Package Command*

Option	Description	Required
Source	Specifies the URL or directory path for the package source containing the package to install. When set to a local file system path, Source can be either absolute or relative to the current directory. If omitted, NuGet looks in the currently selected package source to find the corresponding package URL.	No
ListAvailable	Gets packages available from the online package source.	False
ProjectName	Specifies the project to get installed packages from. If omitted, the command will return installed packages for the entire solution.	False
Updates	Gets the latest versions of packages that have an update available from the package source.	False
Filter	Specifies a filter string used to narrow down the list of packages returned. The filter is searched for in the package ID, the description, and tags.	False
First	Specifies the number of packages to return from the beginning of the list.	False
Skip	Skips (does not return) the specified number of packages, counting from the beginning of the list.	False
IncludePrerelease	Indicates whether to include prerelease packages in the returned results.	False
AllVersions	By default, only the latest version of a package is shown. This option displays all available versions of a package.	False

Using this command, you can easily loop through all installed packages on the MyProject project. The following command prints all installed package IDs for the current project into the Package Manager Console window:

```
Get-Package -ProjectName MyProject | % { Write-Host "$_.Id is installed" }
```

It can also be used to search for packages. The following example searches for the jQuery package from all configured package sources:

```
Get-Package -ListAvailable -Filter jQuery
```

The package source that should be queried can be specified explicitly. The following example searches for the jQuery package from the www.myget.org/F/pronuget feed:

```
Get-Package -ListAvailable -Filter jQuery -Source https://www.myget.org/F/pronuget
```

Getting Project Information

This command gets the specified project. If none is specified, it returns the default project (which is selected from the drop-down in the Package Manager Console toolbar). The project is returned as an EnvDTE.Project instance.

```
Get-Project [[-Name] <string>] [-All] [<CommonParameters>]
```

Available parameters for this command are shown in Table C-3.

Table C-3. *Available Options for the NuGet Get-Project Command*

Option	Description	Required
Name	Specifies the project to return. If omitted, the default project selected in the Package Manager Console is returned.	False
All	Returns every project in the solution that supports NuGet.	False

An example of calling Get-Project is shown in Figure C-1; it illustrates the output including the ProjectName, Type, and FullName properties of the object.

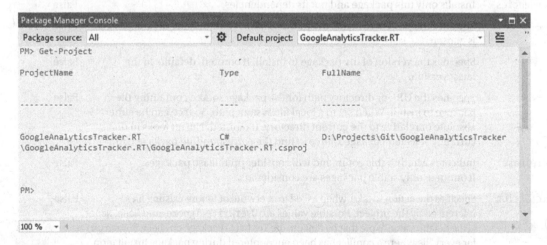

Figure C-1. *Example output of the Get-Project cmdlet in NuGet Package Manager Console*

This command opens up quite a few interesting opportunities to further automate the way we work with NuGet, and by extension, Visual Studio.

An example use case could be to install a package in multiple target projects at once, based on some selection criteria. For instance, let's say we want to install the NUnit package into all of our testing projects, which are named using the convention *Tests. This is not something you can easily achieve by using the user interface dialog boxes of the NuGet Visual Studio extension. Smart usage of the Get-Project command, however, allows you to achieve this very easily, as shown in Listing C-1.

Listing C-1. Installing a Package in Selected Target Projects by Using the Get-Project Cmdlet

```
Get-Project -All | Where { $_.Name.EndsWith("Tests ") } | Install-Package NUnit
```

When combining the Get-Project command with the Get-Package command, you could also list all installed packages for each project. Listing C-2 shows you how you can do this by using a single line in PowerShell.

Listing C-2. Listing All Installed Packages for All Projects in the Current Visual Studio Solution

```
Get-Project -All | % { Write-Host $_.ProjectName; Get-Package -ProjectName •
$_.ProjectName | % { Write-Host "  $_.Id is installed" } }
```

Installing Packages

This command installs a NuGet package and, by default, its dependencies into the target project:

```
Install-Package [-Id] <string> [-IgnoreDependencies] [-ProjectName <string>] [[-Version]
<string>] [[-Source] <string>] [-IncludePrerelease] [-FileConflictAction] [<CommonParameters>]
```

Available parameters for this command are shown in Table C-4.

Table C-4. Available Parameters for the NuGet Install-Package Command

Option	Description	Required
Id	Specifies the ID of the package to install.	True
IgnoreDependencies	Installs only this package and not its dependencies.	False
ProjectName	Specifies the project to install the package into. If omitted, the default project is chosen.	False
Version	Specifies the version of the package to install. If omitted, defaults to the latest version.	False
Source	Specifies the URL or directory path for the package source containing the package to install. When set to a local file system path, Source can be either absolute or relative to the current directory. If omitted, NuGet looks in the currently selected package source to find the corresponding package URL.	False
IncludePrerelease	Indicates whether this command will consider prerelease packages. If omitted, only stable packages are considered.	False
FileConflictAction	Specifies the action to take, when asked to overwrite or ignore existing files referenced by the project. Possible values are Overwrite, Ignore, and None. None is the default value. Note that by default, the Install-Package cmdlet will prompt for every file where a conflict has been encountered during package installation.	False

Opening Package Pages

This command will open the browser pointing to ProjectUrl, LicenseUrl, or ReportAbuseUrl of the specified package.

```
Open-PackagePage -Id <string> [-Version] [-Source] [-License] [-ReportAbuse] [-PassThru]•
[<CommonParameters>]
```

Available parameters for this command are shown in Table C-6.

Table C-6. *Available Parameters for the NuGet Open-PackagePage Command*

Option	Description	Required
Id	Specifies the ID of the NuGet package to search for.	False
Version	Specifies the version of the package to search for. If omitted, defaults to the latest version.	False
Source	Specifies the source of the repository to search for the package. If omitted, defaults to the selected source in the package source drop-down control.	False
License	Indicates that the cmdlet should open the LicenseUrl of the specified package. If neither LicenseUrl nor ReportAbuseUrl is set, the cmdlet will open the ProjectUrl by default.	False
ReportAbuse	Indicates that the cmdlet should open the ReportAbuseUrl of the specified package. If neither LicenseUrl nor ReportAbuseUrl is set, the cmdlet will open the ProjectUrl by default.	False
PassThru	If specified, the cmdlet will return the value of the requested URL.	False

Uninstalling Packages

This command uninstalls a NuGet package. If other packages depend on this package, the command will fail unless the –Force option is specified.

```
Uninstall-Package [-Id] <string> [-RemoveDependencies] [-Force] [-Version <string>]•
[-ProjectName <string>] [<CommonParameters>]
```

Available parameters for this command are shown in Table C-7.

Table C-7. *Available Parameters for the NuGet Uninstall-Package Command*

Option	Description	Required
Id	Specifies the package ID of the package to uninstall.	True
RemoveDependencies	Uninstalls the package and its dependencies that are not depended on by other packages.	False
Force	Forces uninstalling this package and its dependencies, whether they are used by other packages or not. This is the case only if -RemoveDependencies is set.	False
Version	Indicates the version of the package to uninstall. If omitted, defaults to the latest version.	False
ProjectName	Specifies the project to uninstall the package from. If omitted, the default project that is selected from the drop-down in the Package Manager Console is chosen.	False

Updating Packages

This command updates a package and its dependencies to a newer version:

```
Update-Package [-Id] <string> [-IgnoreDependencies] [-ProjectName <string>] [-Version•
  <string>] [-Safe] [-Source <string>] [-IncludePrerelease] [-FileConflictAction] • [-Reinstall]
[<CommonParameters>]
```

Available parameters for this command are shown in Table C-8.

Table C-8. *Available Parameters for the NuGet Update-Package Command*

Option	Description	Required
Id	Specifies the package ID of the package to update. If omitted, every package is updated.	False
IgnoreDependencies	By default, only the package specified is updated. Adding the -IgnoreDependencies switch updates all of the package's dependencies as well.	False
ProjectName	Specifies the project containing the package to update. If omitted, the package is updated in every project with the package installed.	False
Version	Specifies the version that the package will be upgraded to. If omitted, defaults to the latest version.	False
Safe	Constrains upgrades to newer versions with the same major and minor version components. For example, if version 1.0.0 of a package is installed, and versions 1.0.1, 1.0.2, and 1.1 are available in the feed, the -Safe flag updates the package to 1.0.2.	False
Source	Specifies the URL or directory path for the package source containing the packages to update. When set to a local file system path, Source can be either absolute or relative to the current directory. If omitted, NuGet looks in the currently selected package source to find the corresponding package URL.	False

(continued)

Table C-8. (*continued*)

Option	Description	Required
IncludePrerelease	Indicates whether to include prereleases when searching for updates. If omitted, only stable packages are considered.	False
FileConflictAction	Specifies the action to take, when asked to overwrite or ignore existing files referenced by the project. Possible values are Overwrite, Ignore, and None. Note that by default, the Update-Package cmdlet will prompt for every file where a conflict has been encountered during package installation.	False
Reinstall	Reinstalls the currently installed package versions. This can be very useful, for example, when switching target frameworks or when a project file is broken because of NuGet packages. The reinstall switch reinstalls the current version of the package; its dependencies may change depending on the version constraints specified in the depending package.	False

Chaining PowerShell Cmdlets

By chaining cmdlets, we can perform some very nice operations in our projects. How about retrieving all distinct license URLs for all packages that have been installed in a solution?

```
Get-Package | Open-PackagePage -License -WhatIf -PassThru | %{ $_.OriginalString }
```

Or maybe we want to create a list of all packages installed in our solution?

```
Get-Package | %{ $_.Id + " " + $_.Version } | Select-Object -unique
```

∎ ∎ ∎

NuGet Configuration File Reference

The NuGet Visual Studio extension, the NuGet Package Manager Console, and the NuGet command-line tool all make use of the NuGet configuration file, which by default is located under %AppData%\NuGet\NuGet.config. NuGet can make use of other configuration files as well. There are possibilities to work with machine-wide configuration files as well as with solution-specific configuration files.

This appendix describes the various configuration files available, as well as the possible configuration elements that can be specified therein. Parts of this appendix are based on the information available on the official NuGet web site at http://docs.nuget.org/docs/reference/nuget-config-file. NuGet documentation (from the Outercurve Foundation) is licensed under Creative Commons license BY 3.0 (http://creativecommons.org/licenses/by/3.0/).

Configuration File Locations

Throughout this book, we have always referenced the default NuGet.config file available from %APPDATA%\NuGet\NuGet.config. This configuration file is user specific and by default will be used by all NuGet clients. Additional configuration files can be created. For example, a NuGet.config file can be created in the Visual Studio solution, or a NuGet.config can be created for a specific Visual Studio version you have installed on your system.

The following locations will be traversed by NuGet when loading configuration files:

- The current directory and all its parents

- The user-specific config file located under %AppData%\NuGet\NuGet.config

- IDE-specific configuration files that can be stored under the following locations:

    - %ProgramData%\NuGet\Config\{IDE}\{Version}\{SKU}*.config (for example, %ProgramData%\NuGet\Config\VisualStudio\12.0\Pro\NuGet.config)

    - %ProgramData%\NuGet\Config\{IDE}\{Version}*.config

    - %ProgramData%\NuGet\Config\{IDE}*.config

    - %ProgramData%\NuGet\Config*.config

NuGet recursively loads settings from these files. If a package source named ABC is specified in a NuGet configuration file, and NuGet encounters the same package source name in another NuGet configuration file, the first occurrence's value will be used.

- After traversal, one special file is merged into the result: the machine-wide .config file located under %ProgramData%\NuGet\NuGetDefaults.config. Values from this file will be added to the configuration that was resolved using the preceding hierarchy.

- Each NuGet client will use a different set of folders it will scan, as you will see in the next section.

Which File Will NuGet Use?

With the various locations in which a NuGet configuration file can exist, let's go through some examples.

When running the NuGet command line from the `C:\Projects\MySolution\MyProject` folder, the following locations will potentially be searched for NuGet configuration files:

- `C:\Projects\MySolution\MyProject\NuGet.config`

- `C:\Projects\MySolution\NuGet.config`

- `C:\Projects\NuGet.config`

- `C:\NuGet.config`

- `%AppData%\NuGet\NuGet.config`

- `%ProgramData%\NuGet\Config\{IDE}\{Version}\{SKU}\*.config`

- `%ProgramData%\NuGet\Config\{IDE}\{Version}\*.config`

- `%ProgramData%\NuGet\Config\{IDE}\*.config`

- `%ProgramData%\NuGet\Config\*.config`

- Values from `%ProgramData%\NuGet\NuGetDefaults.config` are merged into the result from following the above chain.

If we run the NuGet command line from the `C:\Projects\MySolution\MyProject` folder, the following locations will be searched for NuGet configuration files:

- `C:\Projects\MySolution\MyProject\NuGet.config`

- `C:\Projects\MySolution\NuGet.config`

- `C:\Projects\NuGet.config`

- `C:\NuGet.config`

- `%AppData%\NuGet\NuGet.config`

- Values from `%ProgramData%\NuGet\NuGetDefaults.config` are merged into the result from following the above chain.

If we run the NuGet Visual Studio extension from Visual Studio 2012 Ultimate, having opened a project from the `C:\Projects\MySolution\MyProject` folder, the following locations will be searched for NuGet configuration files:

- `C:\Projects\MySolution\.nuget\NuGet.config`

- `C:\Projects\MySolution\NuGet.config`

- `C:\Projects\NuGet.config`

- `C:\NuGet.config`

- `%AppData%\NuGet\NuGet.config`

- `%ProgramData%\NuGet\Config\VisualStudio\11.0\Ultimate\*.config`

- `%ProgramData%\NuGet\Config\VisualStudio\11.0\*.config`

- `%ProgramData%\NuGet\Config\VisualStudio\*.config`

- `%ProgramData%\NuGet\Config\*.config`

- Values from `%ProgramData%\NuGet\NuGetDefaults.config` are merged into the result from following the above chain.

As you can see, different locations will be scanned by different NuGet clients.

Useful Scenarios

Knowing that NuGet searches various locations for NuGet configuration files, a number of useful scenarios can be thought of. For example, project-specific NuGet feeds can be distributed through source control. You can also create company-wide configuration files that apply to every developer. Let's have a look at these two scenarios.

Project-Specific Configuration Files

Since NuGet always starts its search for NuGet configuration files in the directory in which NuGet is invoked, you can add a NuGet.config file in the project directory and distribute it to a team of developers through source control.

Imagine that every project in your company uses its own specific NuGet feed. By adding a NuGet.config file like the following, a solution-specific feed can be added that will show up in Visual Studio only when that specific project is loaded.

```xml
<?xml version="1.0" encoding="utf-8"?>
<configuration>
  <packageSources>
    <add key="AlanParsons Project Feed" value="https://www.myget.org/F/alanparsonsproject" />
  </packageSources>
</configuration>
```

Using this approach, any configuration setting NuGet provides (see the Configuration File section further in this appendix) can be set in a project-specific way.

Company-Wide Configuration Files

Company-wide configuration files can be deployed to the machines of developers—for example, by using an Active Directory Group Policy.

Imagine that your company has a private MyGet feed on which internal frameworks are published as NuGet packages. There are several options to distribute the name and URL of this feed to all developers in a team:

- Tell them to manually add the package source on their machine.

- Tell them to use the NuGet Package Source Discovery protocol (see https://github.com/myget/PackageSourceDiscovery).

- Create a Group Policy that deploys a NuGet configuration file to the developer's machine under %ProgramData%\NuGet\NuGetDefaults.config.

The first two options require manual intervention from every team member. Using an Active Directory Group Policy, a NuGet configuration file can be placed at %ProgramData%\NuGet\NuGetDefaults.config. The following configuration file would automatically add a company-wide feed to all NuGet clients, make the default package source to push packages to the company-wide feed, make the company-wide feed the default, make NuGet.org the second feed to use, and disable NuGet.org.

```xml
<?xml version="1.0" encoding="utf-8"?>
<configuration>
  <config>
    <add key="DefaultPushSource" value="http://www.myget.org/F/acmecompany/api/v2/package" />
  </config>
  <packageSources>
```

```
      <add key="AcmeCompany" value="https://www.myget.org/F/acmecompany" />
      <add key="nuget.org" value="https://www.nuget.org/api/v2/" />
    </packageSources>
    <disabledPackageSources>
      <add key="nuget.org" value="true" />
    </disabledPackageSources>
</configuration>
```

The machine-wide configuration file can only:

- Add additional package sources
- Specify the default push source
- Enable/disable package sources

Do note that individual team members can override these settings by specifying them in a NuGet configuration file that is higher up the configuration file location chain.

Configuration File

The NuGet configuration file can hold several options. Table D-1 lists the various configuration elements available.

Table D-1. *NuGet Configuration File Elements*

Element	Description
`<config>`	Holds NuGet configuration values. The `<config>` element can contain `<add key="" value="">`, `<remove>`, or `<clear>` elements.
	Possible keys are as follows:
	• `repositoryPath`: Allows you to install the NuGet packages in the specified folder, instead of the default "$(SolutionDir)\Packages" folder.
	• `DefaultPushSource`: Used to specify the default source for the push command.
	• `http_proxy`: HTTP proxy server to use.
	• `http_proxy.user`: Proxy server username.
	• `http_proxy.password`: Proxy server password (encrypted).
	Note that these values can be set by using the NuGet `config` command—for example, `nuget config -Set repositoryPath=c:\packages`.
`<packageRestore>`	Holds settings for package restore. The `<packageRestore>` element can contain `<add key="" value="">`, `<remove>`, or `<clear>` elements.
	Possible keys are as follows:
	• `enabled`: When the value is set to `true`, allows you to restore missing packages from the NuGet source during the build.
	• `automatic`: When the value is set to `true`, Visual Studio will automatically check for missing packages during the build.

(continued)

Table D-1. *(continued)*

Element	Description
`<packageSources>`	Holds the list of package sources. The `<packageSources>` element can contain `<add key="" value="">`, `<remove>`, or `<clear>` elements.
	The key attribute should contain the name for the package source. The `value` attribute should contain the full URL to the package source. Note this can be a local folder, a UNC path, or an HTTP(S) URL.
	Note that these values can be set by using the NuGet sources command—for example, `nuget sources add -Name "Test feed" -Source "C:\temp"`.
`<disabledPackageSources>`	Holds the list of package sources that are disabled. The `<disabledPackageSources>` element can contain `<add key="" value="">`, `<remove>`, or `<clear>` elements.
	The key attribute should contain the name for the package source. The `value` attribute should contain the full URL to the package source. Note this can be a local folder, a UNC path, or an HTTP(S) URL.
`<activePackageSource>`	Holds the active package source. It should contain exactly one `<add key="" value="">` element.
	The key attribute should contain the name for the package source. The `value` attribute should contain the full URL to the package source. Note this can be a local folder, a UNC path, or an HTTP(S) URL.
	Note that to work with an aggregate of all package sources specified under the `<packageSources>` element, a value of "`(Aggregate Source)`" can be used. For example:

	`<activePackageSource>`
	`    <add key="All" value="(Aggregate source)" />`
	`</activePackageSource>`

`<solution>`	Holds settings related to solution-specific behavior. The `<solution>` element can contain `<add key="" value="">`, `<remove>`, or `<clear>` elements. This key works at the solution level and can be added only to the `NuGet.config` file present in the solution directory.
	Possible keys are as follows:
	• `disableSourceControlIntegration`: When the value is set to `true`, Visual Studio will not add the packages folder to source control.
`<apiKeys>`	Holds the list of API keys to connect with package sources. The `<apiKeys>` element can contain `<add key="" value="">`, `<remove>`, or `<clear>` elements.
	The key attribute should contain the full URL to the package source. Note this can be a local folder, a UNC path, or an HTTP(S) URL. The `value` attribute should contain the API key.
	Note that these values can be set by using the NuGet command line's sources command—for example, `nuget setApiKey <apikey> -Source http://feedurl`.

(continued)

Table D-1. (*continued*)

Element	Description
<packageSourceCredentials>	Holds credentials for connecting to package sources. The <packageSourceCredentials> element can contain one or more elements named after the feed name to which they apply.
	Each feed name element can contain <add key="" value=""> elements.
	Possible keys are as follows:
	• Username: The username to be used when connecting to the server.
	• Password: The encrypted password to be used when connecting to the server. This password should be encrypted by using the machine key.
	• ClearTextPassword: The clear text password to be used when connecting to the server. Note that this is not a recommended option to use, unless the password has to be shared across multiple machines.
	The Password and ClearTextPassword keys are mutually exclusive and cannot exist together.
	Note that these values can be set by using the NuGet command line's sources command, for example:
	nuget sources update -Name "Test feed" -Username xavier -Password secret123

For reference, the following sample configuration file holds all available settings and some sample values for them.

```xml
<?xml version="1.0" encoding="utf-8"?>
<configuration>
  <config>
    <!--
    Used to specify the default location to expand packages.
    See: NuGet.exe help install
    See: NuGet.exe help update
    -->
    <add key="repositorypath" value="C\External\Packages" />
    <!--
    Used to specify default source for the push command.
    See: NuGet.exe help push
    -->
    <add key="DefaultPushSource" value="http://MyRepo/ES/api/v2/package" />
    <!--
    Proxy settings
    -->
    <add key="http_proxy" value="host" />
    <add key="http_proxy.user" value="username" />
    <add key="http_proxy.password" value="encrypted_password" />
  </config>
  <!-- If specified, package restore is enabled -->
  <packageRestore>
    <add key="enabled" value="True" />
  </packageRestore>
```

```xml
<!--
Used to specify the default Sources for list, install and update.
See: NuGet.exe help list
See: NuGet.exe help install
See: NuGet.exe help update
-->
<packageSources>
  <add key="NuGet official package source" value="https://nuget.org/api/v2/" />
  <add key="MyRepo - ES" value="http://MyRepo/ES/nuget" />
</packageSources>
<!-- used to store credentials -->
<packageSourceCredentials />
<!-- Used to specify which one of the sources are active -->
<activePackageSource>
  <!-- this tells only one given source is active -->
  <add key="NuGet official package source" value="https://nuget.org/api/v2/" />
  <!-- -or- this tells that all of them are active -->
  <add key="All" value="(Aggregate source)" />
</activePackageSource>
<!-- Used to disable package sources  -->
<disabledPackageSources />
<!--
Used to specify default API key associated with sources.
See: NuGet.exe help setApiKey
See: NuGet.exe help push
See: NuGet.exe help mirror
-->
<apikeys>
  <add key="http://MyRepo/ES/api/v2/package" value="encrypted_api_key" />
</apikeys>
</configuration>
```

Index